❧ More Than a Contest Between Armies ❧

More Than a Contest Between Armies

Essays on the Civil War Era

EDITED BY JAMES MARTEN AND
A. KRISTEN FOSTER

The Kent State University Press
Kent, Ohio

© 2008 by The Kent State University Press, Kent, Ohio 44242

ALL RIGHTS RESERVED

Library of Congress Catalog Card Number 2007044975

ISBN 978-0-87338-912-9

Manufactured in the United States of America

Library of Congress Cataloging-in-Publication Data

More than a contest between armies : essays on the Civil War era /

edited by James Marten and A. Kristen Foster.

p.   cm.

Includes bibliographical references and index.

ISBN 978-0-87338-912-9 (hardcover : alk. paper) ∞

1. United States—History—Civil War, 1861–1865.

2. United States—History—1849–1877.

I. Marten, James Alan. II. Foster, A. Kristen.

E468.M58 2008

973.7—DC22   2007044975

British Library Cataloging-in-Publication data are available.

12 11 10 09 08   5 4 3 2 1

In memory of Frank L. Klement

Contents

Preface

GARY GALLAGHER, ONE OF THE authors in this anthology, has called the field of Civil War history a "big tent" with room for many interests and points of view. That inclusive approach to the historiography of the sectional conflict also characterizes this collection. Virtually all of its authors write both for academic and popular audiences. Whether they began publishing in the 1950s (as did Robert Johannsen) or in the 1990s (like William Blair, Lesley Gordon, and Joan Waugh), they are among those elite historians who are responsible for the continuing popularity of the Civil War era among both academics and the general public.

This glittering cohort comprises a Who's Who of Civil War–era historians. Nine were or are holders of endowed chairs. Together the authors have published dozens of books—many History Book of the Month Club selections—and have earned numerous awards, including the Allan Nevins Dissertation Prize (Blair), the Francis Parkman Prize (Johannsen), the Frank L. and Harriet C. Owsley Award from the Southern Historical Association (Ayers), the Douglas Southall Freeman Award (Gallagher and Rable), the Bancroft Prize (Blight), the Frederick Douglass Award (Blight), the Lincoln Prize (Ayers, Blight, Rable, and Simon), and the Pulitzer Prize (Neely).

These historians come together by way of Marquette University's Frank L. Klement Lectures: Alternative Views of the Sectional Conflict; a somewhat shorter version of each essay was originally delivered to students, faculty, Civil War Round Table enthusiasts, and other members of the Milwaukee community. The lecture series honors Frank L. Klement, a longtime professor of history at Marquette. Endowed by donations from more than three hundred of Klement's former students, colleagues, and admirers, the lectures examine unexplored aspects of the Civil War or reinterpret important themes of the sectional conflict.

Klement was, as he liked to say, "a country boy who grew up on the banks of the Embarrass River" in northeastern Wisconsin. Born in 1908, he taught school before entering the University of Wisconsin's graduate program in history, where he studied under the legendary William B. Hesseltine. Among his graduate school colleagues were Wisconsin natives T. Harry Williams and Kenneth Stampp as well as Richard Nelson Current—all of whom rose to great prominence studying the causes and results of the sectional conflict. Klement finished his Ph.D. in 1946 and taught briefly at Lake Forest College and at Eau Claire State Teachers College until he joined the history department at Marquette University in 1948. Over the next thirty-six years, Klement served as department chair and received the university's Award for Teaching Excellence. He also served as president of Phi Alpha Theta, the international History Honor Society for History (1973 to 1974), as President of the Lincoln Fellowship of Wisconsin, in many official capacities for the Civil War Round Table of Milwaukee (the nation's second-oldest round table), and on numerous editorial boards and national committees. Although Frank "retired" in 1975, he supervised graduate students and taught his popular Civil War course until the mid-1980s. He also continued to research and write, publishing *The Gettysburg Soldiers' Cemetery and Lincoln's Address* in 1993. Klement died a year later at the age of eighty-six.

Klement's choice to forsake the military history of the Civil War and to focus on home front issues was fairly unusual for his generation of historians, especially those who were active during the Civil War centennial from 1960 to 1965, which inspired a raft of books about the conflict's more sanguinary facets. (It should be noted that Klement served on the Wisconsin Civil War Centennial Commission and wrote a short book on Wisconsin's role in the Civil War.) But Frank always believed himself something of an outsider. As a devout Roman Catholic he never quite felt accepted by the overwhelmingly Protestant academic community of the 1930s and 1940s; even as that bias receded in the 1960s and 1970s, he still remained, at least in his own mind, rather on the fringes of the historiographical mainstream.

The title of this volume is borrowed from the first chapter of *The Copperheads in the Middle West* (1960) and reflects a belief that has grown over the last twenty years that Civil War historians should recognize that the conflict was "more than a contest between armies." Klement's focus on northern dissenters did just that. He authored over fifty articles and chapters in books and dozens of book reviews, but his best-known works are *The Copperheads in the Middle West*, *The Limits of Dissent: Clement L. Vallandigham and the Civil War* (1970), and *Dark Lanterns: Secret Political Societies, Conspiracies, and Treason Trials in the Civil War* (1984). In these works Klement placed northern dissenters in their economic and political contexts and debunked exaggerated notions of their treasonous designs. Along the way he criticized wartime Republicans—including, at times, Abraham Lincoln—for their politically inspired witch hunts, their propaganda campaigns against Democratic dissenters, and their violations of American standards of civil liberties.

Although the general outline of the "Klement Thesis" was gradually accepted by most historians—Mark E. Neely Jr., who delivered the first lecture of the series, acknowledged the importance of Klement's work in his Pulitzer Prize–winning *The Fate of Liberty*—Klement clearly relished his role as a revisionist and as a defender of civil liberties. In the introduction to his last major work, *Dark Lanterns: Secret Political Societies, Conspiracies, and Treason Trials in the Civil War*, he criticized "consensus history"—the school of thought that dominated the profession when he entered it in the late 1940s—for submitting to the nationalistic impulses that tended to "justify that which has happened." This point of view had led to the presentation of "majority views as the true views" and caused historians to "color . . . the roles of dissenters in black or gray because nationalism shapes the minds of men and guides the hands of historians." Too often, "the suppositions and apprehensions of the majority are presented as facts or as correct interpretations." In this way, "nationalism, it seems, blesses the marriage of myth and history."

Like Frank Klement, each of the historians represented in this collection has made an original contribution to our understanding of the sectional conflict. They may not wear their revisionist outlook on their sleeves in quite the same way as Klement—indeed, they may not even see themselves as revisionists at all—but they share his passion for exploring un- or under-examined events, people, and points of view. The essays they contributed to the lecture series and this volume, arranged more or less chronologically by the events they describe, engage emerging historiographies or approach old chestnuts with fresh insights. Several of the contributors explore the war's effects on race and gender, while the essay format allows others to explore the experiences of representative individuals as well as representative communities. A number of the topics come out of the growing field of memory studies, but a few tackle more traditional military topics, albeit from less traditional points of view.

Klement rather reluctantly agreed when a very junior colleague—and his successor at Marquette—asked permission to attach his name to the proposed lecture series. He finally relented, but he lived to see only a few of the lectures. Yet he would have been proud that this diverse and talented group of historians have shown that the "apprehensive and wearisome days" of the sectional conflict, as he once called them, can still provide plenty of grist for historians.

The dozen essays in this volume appear largely as they did in the originals published by the Marquette University Press. Some are the culmination of years of research, while others are the first steps toward larger projects. Although the editors have corrected a few typos that sneaked into the original publications, the lectures have not been revised by the authors. Some of the illustrations appeared in the originals, but most were selected specifically for this collection.

The editors would like to thank the authors for their cooperation and Marquette University Press for its permission to republish the essays. They also thank Joanna Hildebrand Craig and Mary Young at the Kent State University Press for their determined and terrific copyediting, and Kyle Bode for help with the index.

❧ EDWARD L. AYERS ❧

"Momentous Events in Small Places"

The Coming of the Civil War in Two American Communities

❧ Edward L. Ayers rode into Milwaukee in 1997 on the crest of the Internet revolution. After receiving his Ph.D. from Yale University and beginning his career at the University of Virginia in 1980, Ayers had rapidly earned a reputation for intellectual rigor, good humor, and graceful prose in two award-winning books: *Vengeance and Justice: Crime and Punishment in the Nineteenth-Century American South* (1984) and *The Promise of the New South: Life after Reconstruction* (1992). He pursued his interest in regionalism as a historical construct by helping to edit *All Over the Map: Rethinking American Regions* (1996).

Although he did not consider himself a Civil War historian, Ayers turned to the conflict to further explore the idea of regional identity. His plan to write a book about the everyday experiences of residents in a northern and a southern community developed into perhaps the most-used educational resource on the Internet, applauded by professional historians, social studies teachers, and Civil War buffs alike: the Valley of the Shadow Project. Founded in 1991, the project grew slowly with support from IBM and from the University of Virginia's Institute for Advanced Technology in the Humanities. With help from a team of enthusiastic graduate students, by 1996 the first phase (covering the years just before the war) was online and the project had won support from the National Endowment for the Humanities. Soon after, the Valley Project became the poster-child for the World Wide Web's potential to bring meaningful archival experiences into the lives of anyone with a computer and a modem.

In his Klement Lecture, Ayers blended a discussion of the opportunities and challenges posed by the digital revolution with a demonstration of how the intense examination of every single available source on two different communities could lead to some startling conclusions. Augusta County, Virginia, and Franklin County, Pennsylvania, he suggested, were more alike than different, despite their solidly Confederate and Union loyalties. Ayers developed these and other themes in *In the Presence of Mine Enemies: War in the Heart of America, 1859–1863* (2003).

For several years after his lecture, Ayers continued to serve as Hugh P. Kelly professor of history at the University of Virginia, where he later became dean of the College and Graduate School of Arts and Sciences. He is now president of the University of Richmond. Researchers continue to tweak the site—parts of which were published as a CD-ROM with a companion book—and it remains an inspiration to historians, teachers, and students seeking reliable and imaginative approaches to history on the Internet. ℘

ABRAHAM LINCOLN HAD A DIFFICULT time explaining the Civil War. In his remarkable Second Inaugural Address of March 1865, Lincoln tried to make sense of the conflict that had consumed him and the country over the past four years. No one wanted war and yet the war "came." Although "all dreaded it—all sought to avert it," the war arrived like an outside force, beyond the control of any person. Neither the North nor the South "expected for the war, the magnitude, or the duration, which it has already attained. Neither anticipated that the cause of the conflict might cease with, or even before, the conflict itself should cease. Each looked for an easier triumph, and a result less fundamental and astounding." Lincoln, killed only a few weeks after his brief speech, never had the opportunity to make more sense of the war. But Americans ever since have puzzled over the same sense of mystery, how it was that the war seemed both inevitable and surprising, easily explainable and yet somehow incomprehensible.[1]

It is easy to see why the Civil War is so perplexing. It grew out of an enormous democratic process involving millions of local decisions. The war came through hot elections, public debates, personal agonizing, and family arguments in communities scattered across a vast continent. It came through exulting enlistments and skulking resistance, through rousing speeches and editorials full of doubt. It came through elaborate interaction among families, neighborhoods, counties, states, and nation. It came through intention and through accident. It came through prominent events and through private soul-searching. To understand the coming of the Civil War, we need to understand the motivations and calculations that led millions into a war that shattered the lives of so many.

In order to gain a deeper sense of why the Civil War engulfed the United States, ironically, we may have to give up some of our sense of mastery, setting aside, at least temporarily, familiar generalizations and narrative devices. We might learn something essential by taking as our own the foreshortened knowledge of the people making decisions at the time. We might glimpse the mystery of the war's transformation and expansion by looking through the eyes of those navigating through the confusion. We might better understand familiar national events by seeing the many ways in which they were interpreted and reinterpreted by the people who had no choice but to act in response.

The idea of approaching large events through local study is, of course, hardly new. Historians, professional and otherwise, have written thousands of regimental histories, county histories, and town histories of the Civil War years. These studies make the coming of the war concrete and compelling. Inspired by such accounts, it seemed to me that two local portrayals could be even better than one, that exploring communities on both sides of the Mason-Dixon Line as they each confronted the events from the late fifties to the late sixties might make both sides more comprehensible. Even better, I thought, would be to present these dual histories in some way that allowed them to be compared at every level and virtually day by day. How to comprehend so much detail without being overwhelmed by it, however, was another question altogether.[2]

To make a long (and unfinished) story short, I decided that the new digital technologies emerging around us with so much fanfare and anxiety might be a way that the World Wide Web, CD-ROMs, and their successors might allow a history both capacious and subtle. To test the possibilities of the new media, I have worked with a group of dedicated people and good friends at the University of Virginia over the last few years to create a large digital archive devoted to understanding the Civil War years. We call this archive the Valley of the Shadow Project. Researchers painstakingly transcribed and indexed hundreds of pages of newspapers so those pages can be searched instantly for any individual or subject. They have entered tens of thousands of names from census records and have copied records of rich and poor, black and white alike. They have gathered wills, diaries, letters, and church records and created detailed maps of farms, hamlets, and towns.[3]

All these sources put the stubborn individuality of people on display and reveal the patterns of the past in beautiful complexity. The harder we look, the more complexity we see, the more circles within circles, the more individuals with their own faces and histories. The project welcomes visitors to its Web site and CD, inviting them to explore the evidence for themselves, to weigh and value and interrelate pieces of the past, to test their own understanding of why the Civil War came. The professional historian becomes a fellow explorer as well as a guide to the past.

The archive gains coherence from its "plot," as a northern county and a southern county that share many characteristics struggle with the decisions of the sectional crisis. The archive moves forward in time as well as across social space. Plots touch, connect, diverge. The war comes. Yet that plot shapes only a portion of the archive. Many of the stories in the Valley Project are about families, neighborhoods, and churches, about everyday life when people did not know a war loomed. Many of the questions raised about class, ethnicity, or gender, about economy, culture, and power, can stand on their own, independent of questions about the causation of the war. The archive is full of possibilities.

Merely because something is newly possible, of course, does not mean that it is worthwhile. Judging from press and television accounts, the new digital media promise to transform the classroom and the home into places of active democratic learning if those media do not drown us in pornography, cults, and terrorism first. It is far too early to know how the story of the new media will turn out; we are still in the crystal radio, nickelodeon, kinescope era of the technology. However, historians have the entire record of human experience and many unresolved questions to explore in new ways.[4]

It is obvious that no two places typified regions as vast and as varied as the American South and the American North. We might have chosen places far apart, say, pitting New England against the Deep South. There would have been nothing wrong with that (I hope someone will do such a study), and it would certainly fit the current understanding of the war more conveniently. Yet the fact is that much of the United States found itself arrayed along an uncertain border between the North and South in 1860. The states that supplied the critical votes (and the most troops and the most battlefields during the war) rested on that border. Those states faced the hardest decisions and those decisions largely determined the outcome of conflict between the North and South. By looking carefully at two places that went into the war only after great struggle—and then with great initial enthusiasm—we glimpse the experiences of a large portion of the American people.

The Valley Project follows Augusta County, Virginia, and Franklin County, Pennsylvania, resting about two hundred miles apart in the Great Valley of the Shenandoah and the Cumberland. The farmers who dominated both counties shared a common climate and raised the same crops. Both places turned around small towns—Staunton and Chambersburg—that served as the county seats, both of which in turn published two newspapers and anchored two political parties. Both counties contained rich and poor, black and white, immigrant and native. Both harbored many Protestant churches. Both divided among themselves on all the great questions of the day, right up through the election of 1860 and the firing on Fort Sumter. They both marched united into the war when it came, their men enlisting in enormous numbers at the first opportunity and dying for the next four years, its women sustaining the cause in every way open to them.

The individuality and personality of the people in Augusta and Franklin come through in every part of the archive. Distinct voices speak in their diaries and letters and newspapers. Yet there is a paradox: these two communities, so full of internal complexity and struggle, end up making the same decisions as thousands of other communities. Though we see the difference personality made—or class or marriage or neighborhood—when all the struggles were finished, the people of Augusta and Franklin subordinated their individuality into mass political decisions and died in numbers difficult for us to comprehend.

Augusta and Franklin typify many counties, in fact, by the speed with which they closed ranks in 1861. Despite the hard words they threw at one another, the citizens of these two places drew together at the crisis. Their deliberation transformed into determination almost overnight. The Virginia county of 21,000 white people, after voting heavily against secession early on, sent 6,000 men to war; the Pennsylvania county of 41,000, full of Democrats and southern sympathizers, sent over 10,000. Southern men who had denounced disunion for years died in the service of the Confederacy. Northern men who had defended slavery died in the service of the Union. The story of the coming of the Civil War is the transformation of indecision and the drift into resolve and death.

As the detail available in the Valley archive makes clear, far too much happened in Augusta and Franklin between 1859 and 1861 to convey in a single lecture, perhaps even in a book. What follows, therefore, is not a history of the coming of the war in Augusta and Franklin. Instead, what follows is a meditation on how this experiment might lead us to see the coming of the Civil War in a different way. It tries to see both the story and the medium at a distance, in perspective, with none of the individuals or individual stories the archive celebrates.

Let's talk first of the comparison between the North and the South. The view dominant since the 1970s looks something like this: the North nurtured a dynamic, entrepreneurial society while the slave South sustained a relatively static society that created wealth for a few. Free labor generated cities, immigration, class division, and a sense of moral superiority. Slave labor, by contrast, generated plantations, ethnic homogeneity, race division, and a sense of moral defensiveness. The society of the North bred reform organizations, possibilities for women, and an identification of economic growth with expanding freedom. The society of the South bred an antagonism to reform, narrow roles for women, and an identification of the growth of factories and cities with expanding tyranny. In this vision, the North and the South become steadily more distinct over time, their social and labor systems generating ideological differences that lead to political conflict that lead to war. This explanation ties everything together, interpreting the war as the clash of societies opposed top to bottom. Marxists, liberals, and conservatives all accept versions of this portrayal.[5]

The Augusta and Franklin archive shows both the strengths and weaknesses of this explanation. Reading the newspapers of the two places, it is often difficult to tell whether one is in the North or the South. The Democratic paper of Franklin County dripped with a contempt for African Americans displayed by neither of the newspapers in the slaveholding county. The papers of the Virginia county are filled with enthusiasm for railroads, business, and economic development of every sort, enthusiasm usually thought characteristic of Yankees. People in both places worried about the same social problems: delinquent youngsters, crime in the back alleys, flirtatious beaux, unscrupulous politicians, drinking, fires and floods, and moral decay brought on by prosperity. The papers reported the same international news and both viewed the American West with a mixture of admiration and anxiety. They argued among themselves and against their enemies in the same political language, and they both appealed to the same Protestant God for sustenance and vindication.

Yet Augusta, despite its proximity to the Mason-Dixon Line, despite its location outside the plantation districts of the South, despite its embrace of the modern life of the 1850s, was very much a slave society. Compared to Franklin and the North in general, this Virginia county had a low population density and relatively few towns. Slaves made up about a fifth of the county's population, a proportion typical of many counties in the slave states as a whole and a proportion of significant consequence. Virtually all of the wealthy and powerful white families of the county possessed slaves, often in large numbers.

Here, in a county that grew mainly grains and livestock, more than eight hundred white families owned slaves. Dozens of slaveholders owned ten or twenty people, and a few owned more than forty, placing them among the top few percent of slaveholders in the entire South. Just as important, more than six hundred slaveholders owned one or two slaves, showing the eagerness with which white people of average means bought into the institution even in nonplantation areas. Slaves worked in a wide array of jobs, stacking wheat and picking apples, building railroads and laboring in shops. An Augusta newspaper bragged that the number of slaves in the county had increased in the 1850s despite the relentless pull of the slave trade to the new lands of the Southwest.

The leaders of Augusta were determined to stay abreast of the North and to hold tightly to bondage at the same time. The men who claimed to speak for Augusta, like most white southerners, did not stress differences, and certainly not deficiencies, caused by slavery. Rather, they argued that slavery was essential to the continued growth of the county, the state, and the region. They spent little time defending the virtues of slavery but much time revealing what they saw as the hypocrisy of the North on matters of race.

Slavery existed in Augusta not because of any compelling need to produce a staple crop, and yet slavery was central to the economy and society of Augusta. The institution was not dying out there, but rather winding into the economic machinery of the New Age. Ideals of democracy, of Christianity, and of progress accommodated themselves to slavery, wrapped it in the language of the current day. Slavery was structurally central to Augusta, but the white people of the county remained largely silent on the institution in their newspapers as well as in their diaries and letters. Slavery shaped everything in the South, but white people learned to wall off slavery from much of their thinking and actions. They defended slavery at a remove, in sincere language about rights and the Constitution, translating it into elevated words and concerns they embraced all the more fervently for the words' refinement and elevation.

While Augusta remained resolutely quiet on slavery, Franklin was loud on slavery and all its implications. The southern border of Franklin County lay only five miles away from the northernmost border of Virginia, a narrow strip of Maryland intervening. Slaves escaped through and to Franklin using networks of black freedom fighters and white allies. Frederick Douglass visited the county in the late 1850s, attracting a large and largely black audience and some grudging respect from the white newspapers. (He also, unbeknownst to the papers, met with John Brown, who was living in Chambersburg under an assumed name and planning his attack on Harpers Ferry, but that is another story.) Antislavery opinion grew in Franklin County because people could see slavery firsthand.

Yet proslavery opinion flourished there as well, with anti-abolitionists sneering at black people and any whites who sympathized with them. The free blacks of Franklin were no better off than the free blacks of Augusta. The Pennsylvania African Americans, like their counterparts throughout the North, owned less property and were even more physically segregated than their southern counterparts, who were relegated to places such as the Toads Island slum of Chambersburg. Anything the free blacks of Franklin County had they created for themselves. Animosity among Franklin whites toward southern slaveholders did not bring sympathy for southern slaves; even less frequently did it bring sympathy and support for the black people among whom northern whites lived.

Franklin County, like most of the North, was devoted to farming. Fields dominated the landscape of the North just as they did the South. Economic differences alone created little animosity between the North and South, little direct competition over resources, labor, or markets. Contrary to many Americans' persistent belief today, the war did not come because an "industrial" North sought to extract tariffs and bounties from the South, or because a decrepit slave economy lashed out in its death throes against modernity. Slavery and free labor, when kept in distinct territories, actually complemented one another economically. The South's enormously profitable cotton plantations benefited everyone in the nation except the African

American people who worked on those plantations. Influential people on both sides said so repeatedly.[6]

Despite these well-known aspects of antebellum history, historians of the coming of the Civil War focus, naturally enough, on the inherent conflict between North and South. The North, we believe, embodied much of what we think of as "modern." It seems to be an individualistic society, politically democratic, geared to the market, and increasingly dependent upon technology. The South is often portrayed, in contrast, as wedded to the past, to organic and hierarchical ideals, to all manner of old-fashioned ways of doing things. The North seems to be the evolutionary branch that leads to an idealized America of today—free and prosperous and diverse—while the South is an evolutionary dead end. When the regions become adequately unified, it appears, when the boundaries are filled in, when southern nationalism reaches critical mass, the Civil War arrives. Each crisis from 1820 on seems to be a step in this process. When enough steps have been taken, the war comes. Modernity and resistance reach a breaking point.[7]

The Valley Project suggests, by contrast, that the Civil War might be seen instead as the clash of two modernizing societies. Augusta County, from an international perspective, contained much that appears modern ideologically, politically, culturally, and technologically. Like other white southerners, the white residents of Augusta identified themselves with the western world, its traditions and its bright future. They prided themselves on their schools and hospitals, their gas lights and waterworks. They saw slavery as a necessity of racial relations like that of other English-descended people living among people of dark skins, not as the basis for a contrary civilization. Modernity and progress were more flexible notions than we often acknowledge today, perhaps more flexible than we would like to acknowledge.[8]

Consider the role of print. Modern nations, we are beginning to see, took shape around the printed and disseminated word. Print permits people to cast their imaginations and loyalties beyond the boundaries of their localities, to identify with people they have never met, to see themselves in abstract causes. Societies built on print breed both a sense of interrelatedness and difference. People learn to imagine consequences of actions; people live in the future in the way they do not in an oral culture.[9]

Print shaped everything we associate with the coming of the Civil War. Although Bleeding Kansas was far removed from the East and John Brown's raid freed no slaves, these events gained critical significance because they were amplified and distorted by newspapers. The papers did not merely report the news but made the news, gave it shape and meaning. Without the papers, many events we now see as decisive would have passed without wide consequence. With the papers, however, events large and small stirred the American people every day. The press nurtured anticipation and grievance. Americans of the 1850s grew self-conscious, deeply aware of who they were and who others said they were. The Confederacy in particular was an alliance of strangers, of people marching off to war who had no common experience as a nation. The Confederacy existed through print before it existed through blood. The Civil War was brought on by extrapolation, people imaginatively constructing chains of action and reaction beyond the boundaries of their own time and space.[10]

Augusta and Franklin paid great attention to print. Every week two local newspapers came before the three thousand people of Staunton and two came before the five thousand people of Chambersburg. The papers (fortunately for the Valley Project) covered every small public occurrence in their counties, translating church meetings, pranks, minor disputes, and rumors into matters of public record and discussion. The papers, like the hundreds of other papers in each state, also printed news from all over the country. The newspapers traced the complex networks in which the people of Augusta and Franklin lived, webs of commerce, migration, the slave trade, churches, travel, and, especially, politics.

The political system gave the technology of print a reason to press forward so aggressively. It was highly mobilized political parties—another manifestation of modern societies—that created the competing newspapers in Augusta and Franklin, that generated most of their news, and that gave them their sense of identity. The papers did not merely reflect systemic social differences but, rather, refracted them, deflected them, amplified them. The newspapers reprinted insults from across town, across political boundaries, across the Mason-Dixon Line, telling their readers exactly what their enemies thought of them. Indeed, the newspapers exaggerated difference and created animosity where it would not have flourished otherwise.

The political system joined print in teaching Americans to think of themselves as connected to places beyond their communities. Long before an integrated national economy evolved, political parties welded American places together. The Democrats, Whigs, and Republicans gave Americans common cause with people who lived thousands of miles away while dividing them against their neighbors and relatives. The political system existed for such connections, for coordination and cooperation. The system created

policy to help feed the machinery, created controversy to attract the unde-
cided, created positions to reward the faithful. The system was the end as
well as the means.[11]

In both Augusta and Franklin, wealthy men and poorer men appeared in
both parties. Large slaveholders argued fervently both for secession and for
Union; northern capitalists argued strongly for both resistance and accommodation. Political identity did not merely reflect other, deeper identities
but in itself conveyed a man's sense of himself. Augusta huddled close to
the middle of the political road, voting for the Democrat Stephen Douglas
and the Constitutional Union candidate John Bell. Franklin split sharply,
the Republican Abraham Lincoln winning but the strong southern-rights
candidate John Breckinridge attracting thousands of votes. Proximity to the
border, in other words, bred compromise, concession, and defiance simultaneously and among the same population.[12]

By understanding the matrices of identity more fully, by seeing how
people were, at the same time, members of households, churches, parties,
lineages, neighborhoods, counties, and states, we can better see how they
acted as they did. Apparently irrational actions—such as the eager enlistment of nonslaveholders in the Confederacy or the willingness of northern
men to die for union with slaveholders—make more sense when we take
more networks of identity into account.

Seeing the matrices of action and identity also permits us to write a history more integrated by gender. Women played important, often central,
roles in all the institutions that gave shape to both northern and southern
society. Understanding the power and pervasiveness of print, for example,
lets us see how women could be influential members of the polity despite
their position on the sidelines of political rallies and in the balconies of legislative chambers. They read the papers as avidly as their husbands, fathers,
and sons, but in private. They could know as much about current events
as men, have opinions as fully informed and inflamed. Households thus
served as crucibles of decision making. Homages and toasts to the ladies as
the locus of real power were more than empty sexist gestures.[13]

Given the economic, ideological, geopolitical, and partisan identities
people had to balance in hundreds of communities such as Augusta and
Franklin, it is hardly surprising that people were confused then and now
about the causes of the war. When viewed week by week and through the
perspective of two fixed places, the war seems to arrive through sudden seis-
mic shocks rather than the slowly and inexorably gathering storm historians

often envision. One unexpected event after another—from John Brown's raid to failed compromises to the amount of supplies in Fort Sumter—jerked people from lines they expected to follow. The war came precisely because people kept expecting something to deflect the conflict into another channel, another course of human events. The entire process was full of potentialities that never materialized. The war descended on American communities as if from an outside force even though each of those communities was implicated in bringing on the crisis.

At the same time the political system extended people's vision and reach, it simplified the complexities of American life into a series of binary opposites. American political elections were winner take all; no parliamentary representation reflected the complexity of opinion. Men in power in 1860 repeatedly used the language of contests, struggles, fights, and victories. Party leaders, with much cheering and heckling from the sidelines, determined which candidates would confront one another. Voters had to choose one and only one. The forced simplicities of politics smothered the complexities of local life. State and national politics acted as filters of interest and identity, reducing complicated choices into simple ones. The narrow channeling of political opinion into a few candidacies constrained choice and silenced debate.[14]

The events of the late 1850s and early 1860s were accelerated and exaggerated by party and print. In distinctly modern ways, people anticipated the contingencies of events, made warnings and threats, imagined their responses, imagined the responses of others. People played out the game in their minds before they played it out with one another, entertaining and debating the possibilities they could imagine, extending the chain of action and reaction. This is one reason the Civil War seems to have "come," why it seems inadequately caused. People on both sides were playing out future scenarios even as they responded to immediate threats. When the political system broke down under its own weight, the rules of the game suddenly changed. Four candidates appeared in 1860 instead of two, explicitly sectional candidates instead of avowedly national ones. When the political system collapsed regional identity rushed in to fill the space.[15]

Secession and its response were discontinuous and unpredictable at every level. The several networks among which people lived pulled them in different directions. Slaveholding in the Upper South or Lower could lead to secession or to Unionism. Living in a northern city could breed identity with the Union or sympathy with white southerners with whom one did business. Strong antislavery feelings might lead to engagement in political parties or to estrangement from that system altogether. Church membership could foster identity with the denomination or a faction within it. Northern acquaintance with slavery might lead to sympathy for the slave or with the slaveholder. Everything was about alignment of system and circumstance.

Little was sheer accident; everything was connected to everything else. They were connected in patterned ways, as distinct systems with their own rules and dynamics. Economic motives, cultural motives, and political motives often clashed within the same community or even within the same person. Things were contingent—not in the sense of the word as "chance occurrence or accident," but rather in another of its meanings: "dependent for its existence on something else."[16]

We have seen how many characteristics Augusta and Franklin shared and the border lands stretching from Maryland to Illinois witnessed similar contestation and uncertainty. They were places where a wide range of possibilities were obvious to everyone deep into 1861. These places bred uncertainty within their borders and were themselves objects of uncertainty for the nation. The hybrid economic systems, the competing loyalties, the contentious politics all generated instability.[17]

The political system was by far the most contingent of the systems among which people lived. It was there that the decisions of one man could trump far broader and deeper structures. Due to politics, the options of 1859 narrowed for states, counties, and individuals until the spring of 1861, when they were reduced to bleak pairs: secede or not, fight or not. Some people embraced the starkness, glorying in the clarity, as some always will. Others accepted the stark decision with resignation. Some tried to avoid the decision but could not.

The coming, fighting, and aftermath of the Civil War should not be thought of as a single linear story. Rather, it was often discontinuous, with sharp breaks in the sets of choices and lack of choices it presented. The history of this era is often presented to us as the clashing of blocks, as large areas of textbook maps in collision. We might think instead of multiple, interlocking systems, sometimes congruent, sometimes in conflict. Some of the networks ran north and south, others operated only within regions, others stretched across the Atlantic. Some pushed the North and the South towards war while others pulled them away.[18]

War was not merely politics in a separate guise. The coming of the war and the war itself were driven by different imperatives, different calculations. The purposes of the war changed for both sides and then changed again at war's end. For those in the uniforms of enlisted men, sheer luck often superseded decision and choice. Those in officers' uniforms confronted choices whose results became known almost immediately and with consequences of life and death. For those on the home front, the usual uncertainties of life were compounded and accelerated by wartime.

If the Civil War was so complicated at every level, it would be difficult to comprehend and convey. For many people, that is reason enough to simplify the story. But perhaps the new technologies I've mentioned can offer us another way. Digital media allows us to see systems in suspension. It allows us to crystallize patterns in a historical source even as we maintain that source in its original form and entirety, to maintain particularity even as we draw generalizations. We can take the pieces apart and put them back together. We can shift from economic to ideological perspectives, from local to state to national, from public to private. The Valley Project is designed to let us trace as many connections as possible in as many directions and dimensions as possible.

The digital archive reveals the element of play, of guesswork and puzzle solving that underlies all historical research. More than this, the computer uses relentlessly linear and literal machinery to remind us that much of our connection to and understanding of the past is empathetic and intuitive. The computer reveals things we might not have seen otherwise, but it also reveals blank spaces and silences. It announces the limitations of our knowledge, the distance of the past. Its capacity lets us see that things we expected to connect did not necessarily do so, or at least not in the ways we expected. The connections among slavery, modernity, power, and regional identity, especially, turn out to be more oblique than we had anticipated.

The Valley Project makes exploring the records of the past easier while demonstrating how difficult it is to construct compelling historical narratives and analysis. It reminds us, though, that generalizations are models that leave out most of the evidence. It reminds us that narrative history cannot help but arrange messy things into neater story lines. Stories work by leaving out more than they tell, by dramatizing some contingencies while ignoring others. And yet we must tell stories.

It is not yet clear what the written history of Augusta and Franklin that grows out of our online archive will look like. Perhaps it will be a narrative like narratives based on conventional archives, for those have shown their power and usefulness for generations. Perhaps it will be more like a novel, floating detached from the evidence while permitting the archive to do the work of substantiation. Perhaps the written history will link itself even more tightly than footnotes permit, allowing readers to explore entire sources rather than mere references.

Many questions present themselves, including questions about the interpretive pressure created by the digital medium itself. The very nature of that medium emphasizes interrelation, complexity, and multiplicity. Does that suggest that the technology itself is imposing its characteristics on the way we see the past, pushing aside more obvious answers to our questions? Does the possibility of handling so much detail lead us to make a fetish of subtlety? Does the archive fragment and undermine what we need most—a connection to a coherent past? Or is the Valley of the Shadow Project like a microscope, showing us the complex structures we must understand if we are to understand the substance itself? Only time will tell, of course, and time brings surprises.

NOTES

Edward L. Ayers delivered his Klement Lecture in 1997.

1. Second Inaugural Address, Mar. 4, 1865, in *The Portable Abraham Lincoln*, ed. Andrew Delbanco (New York: Penguin, 1992), 320–21.

2. Recent examples include Stephen V. Ash, *When the Yankees Came: Conflict and Chaos in the Occupied South, 1861–1865* (Chapel Hill: Univ. of North Carolina Press, 1995); Wayne K. Durrill, *War of Another Kind: A Southern Community in the Great Rebellion* (New York: Oxford Univ. Press, 1990); Daniel E. Sutherland, *Seasons of War: The Ordeal of a Confederate Community, 1861–1865* (New York: Free Press, 1995); Warren Wilkinson, *Mother, May You Never See the Sights I Have Seen: The Fifty-seventh Massachusetts Veteran Volunteers in the Army of the Potomac, 1864–1865* (New York: Harper and Row, 1990); Kenneth W. Noe and Shannon H. Wilson, eds., *The Civil War in Appalachia: Collected Essays* (Knoxville: Univ. of Tennessee Press, 1997).

3. One form of the archive may be found online at http://valley.vcdh.virginia.edu. It was published by Norton in 2000 as *The Valley of the Shadow: Two Communities in the American Civil War–The Eve of War*. The CD-ROM version of the project, coauthored with Anne S. Rubin, contains much more material, especially images, maps, and sound, and is accompanied by a book. For a helpful overview of the current situation, see Michael O'Malley and Roy Rosenzweig, "Brave New World or Blind Alley? American History on the World Wide Web," *Journal of American History* 84 (June 1997): 132–55.

4. For a fascinating overview of the place of the new media in other narrative forms, see Janet H. Murray, *Hamlet on the Holodeck: The Future of Narrative in Cyberspace* (New York: Free Press, 1997).

5. For examples, see Eric Foner, "The Causes of the American Civil War: Recent Interpretations and New Directions," *Civil War History* 20 (Sept. 1974): 197–214; James M. McPherson, *Ordeal by Fire: The Civil War and Reconstruction* (New York: Knopf, 1982); Jeffrey Rogers Hummel, *Emancipating Slaves, Enslaving Free Men: A History of the American Civil War* (Chicago: Open Court, 1996).

6. The classic account of the reductionist "economic" perspective is Charles and Mary Beard, *The Rise of American Civilization* (New York: Macmillan, 1927). For the centrality of slavery to the American economy, the key book is Douglass C. North, *The Economic Growth of the United States, 1790–1860* (New York: Norton, 1966). A subtle and informed overview is Robert William Fogel, *Without Consent or Contract: The Rise and Fall of American Slavery* (New York: Norton, 1989).

7. Modernity is the basic organizing theme of McPherson's *Ordeal by Fire* and is invoked as a major reason for Union success in George Fredrickson, "Blue Over Gray: Sources of Success and Failure in the Civil War," *A Nation Divided: Problems and Issues of the Civil War and Reconstruction* (Minneapolis: Burgess, 1975). A recent book that offers "everything you need to know about America's greatest conflict but never learned" boils things down this way: "The America of the Union states was racing toward the twentieth century, with banks, booming factories, railroads, canals, and steamship lines. . . . The southern states of the Confederacy were, in many respects, standing still in time." Kenneth C. Davis, *Don't Know Much About the Civil War: Everything You Need to Know About America's Greatest Conflict but Never Learned* (New York: Morrow, 1996), 151–52.

8. Richard Graham, "Economics or Culture? The Development of the U.S. South and Brazil in the Days of Slavery," in Kees Gispen, ed., *What Made the South Different?* (Oxford: Univ. of Mississippi Press, 1990). For insightful portrayals of "modern" influences in the South, see J. Mills Thornton III, *Politics and Power in a Slave Society: Alabama, 1800–1860* (Baton Rouge: Louisiana State Univ. Press, 1978); Eugene D. Genovese, *The Slaveholders' Dilemma: Freedom and Progress in Southern Conservative Thought, 1820–1860* (Columbia: Univ. of South Carolina Press, 1992); and Kenneth W. Noe, *Southwest Virginia's Railroad: Modernization and the Sectional Crisis* (Urbana: Univ. of Illinois Press, 1994).

9. This is the argument of one of the most influential books to appear in recent years in the social sciences: Benedict Anderson, *Imagined Communities: Reflections on the Origin and Spread of Nationalism*, rev. ed. (London: Verso, 1991).

10. A stimulating and innovative account that emphasizes the modernity of the Confederacy is Drew Gilpin Faust, *The Creation of Confederate Nationalism: Ideology and Identity in the Civil War South* (Baton Rouge: Louisiana State Univ. Press, 1989). A useful Web site, headed by Professor Lloyd Benson of Furman University, that shows the possibilities of newspapers for understanding the coming of the Civil War can be found at http://history.furman.edu/~benson/docs/. On the projection of boundaries in time, see Peter S. Onuf, "Federalism, Republicanism, and the Origins of American Sectionalism," in Edward L. Ayers, Patricia Nelson Limerick, Stephen Nissenbaum, and Peter S. Onuf, eds., *All Over the Map: Rethinking American Regions* (Baltimore: Johns Hopkins Univ. Press, 1996).

11. Important books that emphasize the dynamics of the political system itself in bringing on the Civil War include Michael F. Holt, *The Political Crisis of the 1850s* (New York: Wiley, 1978); *Political Parties and American Political Development from the Age of Jackson to the Age of Lincoln* (Baton Rouge: Louisiana State Univ. Press, 1992); William E. Gienapp, *The Origins of the Republican Party, 1852–1856* (New York: Oxford Univ. Press, 1986); William W. Freehling, *The Road to Disunion: The Secessionists at Bay* (New York: Oxford Univ. Press, 1990); and *The Reintegration of American History: Slavery and the Civil War* (New York: Oxford Univ. Press, 1994).

12. The local bases of politics in Virginia have been brilliantly portrayed in Daniel W. Crofts, *Old Southampton: Politics and Society in a Virginia County, 1834–1869* (Charlottesville: Univ. Press of Virginia, 1992); the complexities of its state-level politics appear in William G. Shade, *Democratizing the Old Dominion: Virginia and the Second Party System, 1824–1861* (Charlottesville: Univ. Press of Virginia, 1996).

13. The high degree of engagement of women with political issues at the beginning of the war has been demonstrated in Drew Gilpin Faust, *Mothers of Invention: Women of the Slaveholding South in the American Civil War* (Chapel Hill: Univ. of North Carolina Press, 1996). Elizabeth Varon, in "'We Mean to Be Counted': White Women and Politics in Antebellum Virginia" (Ph.D. diss., Yale University, 1993), shows that the involvement of women did not begin with the secession crisis but had long been nourished (and resisted) in the party system.

14. On the dictates of the political system, see Peter H. Argersinger, *Structure, Process, and Party: Essays in American Political History* (Armonk, N.Y.: M. E. Sharpe, 1992).

15. See especially Holt, *Political Crisis of the 1850s.*

16. James McPherson stresses contingency, though with a somewhat different emphasis, in *The Battle Cry of Freedom: The Civil War Era* (New York: Oxford Univ. Press, 1988), 857–58.

17. On Maryland, for example, see Jean H. Baker, *The Politics of Continuity: Maryland Political Parties from 1858 to 1870* (Baltimore: Johns Hopkins Univ. Press, 1973); William J. Evitts, *A Matter of Allegiances: Maryland from 1850 to 1861* (Baltimore: Johns Hopkins Univ. Press, 1974); and Barbara Jeanne Fields, *Slavery and Freedom on the Middle Ground: Maryland During the Nineteenth Century* (New Haven: Yale Univ. Press, 1985).

18. For a fascinating account of the various networks in which the people of one Virginia city lived, see Gregg David Kimball, "Place and Perception: Richmond in Late Antebellum America" (Ph.D. diss., University of Virginia, 1997).

❧ David W. Blight ❧

Frederick Douglass and Abraham Lincoln

A Relationship in Language, Politics, and Memory

❧ Although he did not invent the field of the history of memory, David W. Blight is one of its most influential practitioners; that his 2001 Klement Lecture was the first of several presentations dealing all or in part with Civil War memory suggests the importance of this growing field. His most important book to date, *Race and Reunion: The Civil War in American Memory* (2001), explores the memory war that Americans waged after the fighting ended, when writers and politicians went to work casting and recasting the war in a variety of lights. White America achieved sectional reunion, Blight argues, through the segregation of memory itself. Despite the partisan origins of the war's memory, eventually northerners accepted, at least tacitly, the southern version of the causes and consequences of the war. For instance, white southern writers argued that southerners had not actually rebelled but had been invaded unjustly and that the North had imposed slavery on the South. The memory of black Americans, according to Blight, suggests a different interpretation—that "racial reconciliation, unlike sectional reconciliation, demanded a confrontation with the hostility rooted in rape, lynching, and racism." That his peers found the argument compelling as well as convincing is evident by the awards lavished on *Race and Reunion*, which included the Fred-

An 1881 chromolithograph depicting "Heroes of the Colored Race," including Blanche Kelso Bruce, Frederick Douglass, Hiram Rhoades Revels, Abraham Lincoln, James A. Garfield, Ulysses S. Grant, Joseph H. Rainey, John Brown, and Robert Smalls. Library of Congress Prints and Photographs Division.

erick Douglass Prize, the Lincoln Prize, three awards from the Organization of American Historians, and the Bancroft Prize.

Long before achieving fame in academia, Blight taught high school in his hometown of Flint, Michigan. After receiving his Ph.D. from the University of Wisconsin under the direction of Richard Sewell, Blight taught at Harvard University, North Central College in Naperville, Illinois, and, for thirteen years, at Amherst College. He became the Class of 1954 Professor of American History at Yale University in 2003, where he also succeeded David Brion Davis as director of Yale's Gilder-Lehrman Center for the Study of Slavery, Resistance, and Abolition, which seeks to bridge the gap between the academy and the public.

Blight's other books have also received critical acclaim. *Frederick Douglass's Civil War: Keeping Faith in Jubilee* (1986) established Blight as one of the foremost scholars of Frederick Douglass's life and career. Following on the heels of

Race and Reunion, Blight continued his work as a pioneer in the field of memory studies with *Beyond the Battlefield: Race, Memory, and the American Civil War* (2002), a collection of essays exploring the meanings within the causes, the war itself, and the consequences of the Civil War. Most recently, he edited *Passages to Freedom: The Underground Railroad in History and Memory* (2006), an anthology of essays examining the history and memory of the Underground Railroad.

Blight's Klement Lecture foreshadowed some of the themes of *Race and Reunion*, which was published in the same year that Blight delivered his lecture, by focusing partly on Douglass's role in the creation of the nearly mythic image of Lincoln as emancipator. 🖎

IN 1937 A FORMER SLAVE, Cornelius Garner, was interviewed at the age of ninety-one. Asked if he had fought in the Civil War, Garner replied to his black interviewer: "Did I fight in de war? Well if I hadn' you wouldn' be sittin' dere writin' today." He described the corner in his native Norfolk, Virginia, where slave auctions used to be conducted on New Year's Day. "Dat day, New Yeah's Day," said Garner, "should be kept by all de colored people. Dat is de day o' freedom. An' day ought to 'member Frederick Douglass too. Frederick Douglass tol' Abe Lincun, 'Give de black man guns an' let him fight.' Abe Lincun say, 'Ef I give him gun, when he come to battle, he run.' Frederick Douglass say, 'Try him an' you'll win de war.' Abe said, 'Alright, I try him.'"[1] Garner's story begins to guide us to the relationship between Abraham Lincoln and Frederick Douglass, in both history and memory.

In addressing the relationship between Abraham Lincoln and Frederick Douglass, we confront two towering personalities of American history—both, indeed, have become mythic figures in the deepest sense of that word, historical actors who, because of circumstances and as craftsmen of language, have transcended their own time, again and again, to serve various kinds of felt needs in our own time. Both have gone in and out of favor, of historical consciousness, serving as lodestars for current causes in one era, and then vilified or ignored in another.[2] Both have been asked to measure up to every kind of contemporary imperative. What would Lincoln do now? Where are the Lincolns in our time? Did Lincoln really want to free the slaves? Was his racism an impediment to real reform, or was he the master of timing and content in the American emancipation? What would Douglass do today? What would Douglass think of affirmative action? Would he support "reparations" for slavery? Did Douglass's integrationism make him a prophet of the late twentieth century's revolutions in race relations and civil rights? Or was he merely an American patriot, who fell out of touch with his own people, who enjoyed creating his own symbolic and heroic persona in autobiography after autobiography? To which Lincoln do people turn, or to which Douglass, when they feel the need for the power of transcendent, mythic leadership? In which places in their magnificent rhetoric do we find our own inspirations for what it means to be an American at the beginning of the twenty-first century? Where do we turn, especially, for guidance in our ongoing racial predicament? What did these two have in common, and how did they differ, during the crisis of the Civil War era? Did they make history together or at odds? How did the lives and ideas of the former slave who dreamed and wrote his way to freedom, and the poor farmer's son who dreamed and wrote his way to the presidency converge?

Comparative biography is risky business, but often irresistible. Both Lincoln and Douglass grew up in genuine poverty, albeit Douglass as human chattel and Lincoln amidst the desperation of poor farmers and a kind of wage slavery on the prairie frontier. Both received strokes of good fortune in their rise from obscurity, and both possessed great gifts of intellect, ambition, and a love of books and the music of words. In 1830, when Douglass was twelve years old, he discovered Caleb Bingham's *The Columbian Orator*, an elocution manual and a reader for schoolchildren consisting of prose, verse, plays, and especially political speeches from classical antiquity and the Enlightenment era. This "rich treasure" of a book, with its obvious antislavery tone, was crucial in the young slave's dreams of liberation, both physically and through language.[3] Just a year later, in his first winter in New Salem on the Illinois prairie (1831–32), the twenty-one-year-old Lincoln studied the same readings in *The Columbian Orator*—it was among the first books that Lincoln collected and cherished. They were destined to develop different temperaments: the former slave would become a radical abolitionist who would have to learn a begrudging pragmatism about the prospects of his people in slaveholding America; the self-taught lawyer-politician who would see the world in pragmatic, legal terms would have to learn to convert his instinctive gradualism about social change and his racial prejudices into the courage to use his power as president to free slaves in the midst of total war in order to save the nation he loved.

One of the most fascinating aspects of each man was his capacity for intellectual growth and change, how each could convert contradiction into hope. On February 12, 1959, in his famous speech eulogizing Lincoln at a joint session of Congress (on the occasion of the Lincoln Sesquicentennial), Carl Sandburg rhapsodized about Lincoln in interesting terms. "Not often in the story of mankind," said the poet, "does a man arrive on earth who is both steel and velvet, who is as hard as rock and soft as drifting fog, who holds in his heart and mind the paradox of terrible storm and peace unspeakable." Similarly, W. E. B. Du Bois, in 1922, reflected in unforgettable terms on Lincoln's capacity to grow. "I love him," wrote Du Bois, "not because he was perfect, but because he was not and yet triumphed. . . . The world is full of folk whose taste was educated in the gutter. The world is full of people born hating and despising their fellows. To these I love to say: See this man. He was one of you and yet became Abraham Lincoln." Like Sandburg, albeit in different tones, Du Bois was drawn to Lincoln's embodiment of paradox. "There was something left," he said of Lincoln, "so that at the crisis he was big enough to be inconsistent—cruel, merciful, peace-loving, a fighter, despising Negroes and letting them fight and vote, protecting slavery, and freeing slaves. He was a man—a big, inconsistent, brave man."⁴ How these two men of paradox found each other at that crisis is an important American story not yet fully told. In Douglass's case he didn't so much *embody* paradox as much as he *symbolized* it. His life stands across the nineteenth century as an emblem of the worst and the best in the American spirit. We ever return to Douglass's story because it has so much to teach us about that journey *from* slavery *to* freedom, a soul nearly lost and then found. By looking at Lincoln and the "other" Douglass, we can take a good measure of the transformations of Civil War America.

On March 4, 1865, Frederick Douglass attended President Abraham Lincoln's second inauguration. Standing in the crowd, Douglass heard Lincoln declare slavery the "cause" and emancipation the "result" of the Civil War. Over the crisp air he heard Lincoln's determination that to win the war "every drop of blood drawn with the lash shall be paid by another drawn with sword."⁵ Four years earlier, and many times in between, Douglass had dreamed of writing that speech for Lincoln. That the president himself wrote it in those tragic days of spring 1865 is a testament to the power of events, to Lincoln's own moral fiber, and to the political and rhetorical bond he shared with Douglass.

Douglass attended the inaugural reception that evening at the Executive Mansion. At first denied entrance by two policemen, Douglass was admitted only when the president himself was notified. Weary of a lifetime of such racial rejections, Douglass was immediately set at ease by Lincoln's cordial greeting: "Here comes my friend Douglass," said the president. Lincoln asked Douglass what he thought of the day's speech. Douglass demurred, urging the president to attend to his host of visitors. But Lincoln insisted, telling his black guest: "There is no man in the country whose opinion I value more than yours." "Mr. Lincoln," replied the former slave, "that was a sacred effort."[6] We can only guess at the thrill in Douglass's heart, knowing that the cause he had so long pleaded—a sanctioned war to destroy slavery and potentially to reinvent the American republic around the principle of racial equality—might now come to fruition. He could fairly entertain the belief that he and Lincoln, the slaves and the nation, were walking that night into a new history.

But nothing during the early months of Reconstruction came easily, especially in the wake of Lincoln's assassination at the dawn of peace. In her grief, and with the assistance of her personal aide, Elizabeth Keckley, Mary Todd Lincoln sent mementos to special people. Among the recipients of some of the president's canes were the black abolitionist, Henry Highland Garnet, and a White House servant, William Slade. But to Douglass Mrs. Lincoln sent the president's "favorite walking staff" (on display today at Cedar Hill, Douglass's home in Washington, D.C.). In his remarkable letter of reply, Douglass assured the First Lady that he would forever possess the cane as an "object of sacred interest," not only for himself but because of Mr. Lincoln's "humane interest in the welfare of my whole race."[7] In this expression of gratitude, Douglass evoked the enduring symbolic bond between the sixteenth president and African Americans, a relationship with a complicated and important history, the latest chapter of which is now represented by an ongoing scholarly and pedagogical debate over who and what really freed the slaves in the Civil War.

Douglass's relationship with Lincoln had not always been so warm. Indeed, Douglass's attitude toward Lincoln moved from cautious support in 1860 to outrage in 1861–62 and eventually to respect and admiration in 1863–65. At the outset of the war Douglass wanted precisely what Lincoln did not want: a "remorseless revolutionary struggle" that would make black freedom indispensable to saving the Union. In 1861–62, Douglass attacked the administration's policy of returning fugitive slaves to their owners. At one point he referred to Lincoln as "the most dangerous advocate of slave-hunting and slave-catching in the land." In September 1861, Douglass denounced Lincoln's revocation of Gen. John C. Frémont's unauthorized emancipation order in Missouri. In 1862–63 he was offended by the administration's plans for colonization of the freedpeople. Indeed, nothing disappointed Douglass as much as the president's August 1862 meeting with a black delegation at the White House, at which Lincoln told his guests that "we [the two races] should be separated" and that the only hope for equality rested in their emigration to a new land. Douglass reprinted Lincoln's remarks in his newspaper and penned his harshest criticism ever of the president, calling him an "itinerant colonization lecturer" and a "genuine representative of American prejudice and Negro hatred."[8]

But much changed in Douglass's estimate of Lincoln with the advent of the Emancipation Proclamation and the policy of recruiting black soldiers in 1863. As the war expanded in scale and purpose, Lincoln and Douglass began to move toward more of a shared ideological vision of its meaning. On August 10, 1863, Douglass visited Washington, D.C., for the first time and met with Lincoln for a frank discussion of discriminations practiced against black troops. Lincoln said he understood the anguish over unequal pay for black men, but considered it a "necessary concession" in order to achieve the larger aim of getting blacks into uniform. Although they did not agree on all issues, Douglass came away from this meeting impressed with Lincoln's forthrightness and respectful of the president's political skills. Douglass relished opportunities to tell of his first meeting with Lincoln. "I felt big there," he told a lecture audience, describing how secretaries admitted him to Lincoln's office ahead of a long line of office seekers. Disarmed, even awed, by Lincoln's directness, Douglass remembered that the president looked him in the eye and said: "Remember this . . . remember that Milliken's Bend, Port Hudson, and Fort Wagner are recent events; and . . . were necessary to prepare the way for this very proclamation of mine." (All were battles in which blacks had distinguished themselves.) For the first time, Douglass expressed a personal identification with Lincoln. The "rebirth" of the nation about which Lincoln spoke so famously at Gettysburg in November 1863 had long been Douglass's favorite metaphor as well. Lincoln had wished for a shorter war, one that had not necessitated the full conquest of the South—a "result," as he put it in the Second Inaugural, "less fundamental and astounding."[9] He would rather have left emancipation to the gradual work of history and statesmenship. But the reality of the war, of the wave of black freedom surging in front of and behind Union armies, made Lincoln the Emancipator in the timing and manner that was, at least in part, his own choice. Was Lincoln a reluctant or a willing emancipator? The best answer is both.

By the end of 1863, Lincoln and Douglass spoke from virtually the same script, one of them with the elegance and restraint of a statesman, and the other the fiery tones of a prophet. One spoke with an eye on legality and public opinion, the other as though he were the national evangelist. In his Annual Message of December 8, 1863, Lincoln declared that "the policy of emancipation . . . gave to the future a new aspect." The nation was engaged in a "new reckoning" in which it might become "the home of freedom disenthralled, regenerated, enlarged." Lincoln's language makes a striking comparison to a speech Douglass delivered many times across the North in the winter of 1863–64. In "The Mission of the War," Douglass declared that however long the "shadow of death" cast over the land, Americans should not forget the moral "grandeur" of the struggle. "It is the manifest destiny of this war," he announced, "to unify and reorganize the institutions of the country" and thereby give the scale of death its "sacred significance." "The mission of this war," Douglass concluded, "is National regeneration."[10] Together, Lincoln and Douglass had provided the subjunctive and declarative voices of the Second American Revolution—and by the last year of the war, they were nearly one and the same. Both had come to interpret the war as the nation's apocalyptic *regeneration*.

In the summer of 1864, with the war at a bloody stalemate in Virginia, Lincoln's reelection was in jeopardy and Douglass's support of him temporarily waned. He briefly considered supporting John C. Frémont's candidacy to unseat Lincoln in the Republican Party. However, in August Lincoln invited Douglass to the White House for their extraordinary second meeting. The president was under heavy pressure from all sides: Copperheads condemned him for pursuing an abolitionist war, while abolitionists sought to replace him with the more radical Frémont. Lincoln was worried that the war might end without complete victory and the end of slavery, so he sought Douglass's advice. Lincoln had drafted a letter, denying that he was standing in the way of peace and declaring that he could not sustain a war to destroy slavery if Congress did not will it. Douglass urged Lincoln not to publish the letter and ultimately, because of events and perhaps Douglass's advice, he never did.[11]

Even more importantly, Lincoln asked Douglass to lead a scheme reminiscent of John Brown and Harpers Ferry. Concerned that if he were not reelected and the Democrats pursued a negotiated, proslavery peace, Lincoln, according to Douglass, wanted "to get more of the slaves within our lines." Douglass went north and organized some twenty-five agents who were willing to work at the front. In a letter to Lincoln on August 29, 1864,

Douglass outlined his plan for a "band of scouts" channeling slaves north-ward. Douglass was not convinced that this plan was fully "practicable," but he was ready to serve. Because military fortunes had shifted dramatically with the fall of Atlanta, this government-sponsored underground railroad never materialized. But how remarkable this episode must have been to both Douglass and Lincoln as they realized they were working together now to accomplish the very "revolution" that had separated them ideologically in 1861. Garry Wills has argued that Lincoln performed a "verbal coup" that "revolutionized the revolution" at Gettysburg.[12] By 1864, that performance reflected a shared vision of the meaning of the war. Ideologically, Douglass had become Lincoln's alter ego, his stalking horse and minister of propa-ganda, the intellectual godfather of the Gettysburg Address and the Second Inaugural.

With time Douglass would contribute mightily to the creation of some of the Lincoln mythology. Douglass understood as well as anyone how neces-sary Lincoln's image was to sustaining the freedom and fledgling equality of his people forged in the war and early years of Reconstruction. He was fond of pointing (as Du Bois would later) to Lincoln's example in speaking of the educative nature of the war. "If he did not control events," Douglass said of Lincoln in a December 1865 speech, "he had the wisdom to be instructed by them. When he no longer could withstand the current, he swam with it." The idealist in Douglass saw this educative feature of the war as the bridge from wartime emancipation and black enlistment to peacetime racial democracy, but the realist in him knew that this final goal could only be reached through power politics, against a resurgent racism, an instinctive American constitu-tional conservatism, embittered war memories on both sides, and on behalf of a needy and largely illiterate population of ex-slaves. And, all of this would happen, of course, after Lincoln was gone. But Lincoln's symbol was extraor-dinarily useful to blacks, and no one understood this better than Douglass. Indeed, Douglass would demonstrate, and black communities would follow his lead through the decades, that for no other group was it more useful or important to "get right with Lincoln" than African Americans.[13]

Douglass spent much of his postwar life (he lived until 1895) trying to preserve an emancipationist-abolitionist memory of the Civil War. In a speech delivered in the wake of the assassination (probably in June 1865), Douglass said that "no class of people . . . have a better reason for lamenting the death of Abraham Lincoln, and for desiring to . . . perpetuate his mem-ory, than have the Colored people." Douglass complained that at some of the funeral parades blacks had been excluded from public mourning. In this emotional and transformative moment just after the war's end, the former slave paid a moving tribute to Lincoln. "What was Abraham Lincoln to the colored people, and they to him," he asked? "As compared to the long line of his predecessors, many of whom were merely the . . . servile instruments of the Slave Power, Abraham Lincoln, while unsurpassed in his devotion to the welfare of the white race, was in a sense hitherto without example, emphatically, the black man's President: the first to show any respect to their rights as men."

On any Lincoln monument, said Douglass, blacks demanded their part in expressing "love and gratitude."[14] What did Douglass mean here in 1865? Well, he meant what he said. But the context is crucial. In this post-assassination speech—before Reconstruction policies had taken shape, and in the national confrontation with martyrdom—Douglass was flushed with hope. In describing the results of the war, Douglass saw a whole new national inheritance. "Henceforth," he declared, "we have a new date, a new era for our great Republic. Henceforth, a new account is opened between the government and the people of the United States. Henceforth, this is to be a . . . common country of all for all." As he had so often done in the previous four years, Douglass saw the war in apocalyptic and rejuvenating terms, and he converted Lincoln's death into his own kind of ode to joy. "The storm cloud has burst," he announced, "and sent down its bolt, and has left the blue sky above, calm and bright as when the morning stars sang together for joy!" Douglass went on in this remarkable speech to proclaim the "inevitability" of the war and all its suffering as the necessary historical means by which a new American republic would be conceived. It was within this millennial conception of history that Douglass found Lincoln's appointed place. He honored the president as a real individual but also as a historical actor performing within the logic of history. Douglass employed the refrain "under his rule" to declare a litany of ways Lincoln expanded freedom and saved the Union. "Under his rule," shouted Douglass, blacks "saw millions of their brethren proclaimed free and invested with the right to defend their freedom. Under his rule, they saw the Confederate states—that boldest of all conspiracies against the just rights of human nature, broken to pieces." To Douglass, epochal events were "the great teachers of mankind."[15] Lincoln was thus an emancipator of black people, but so were the tides of history itself in which Lincoln had found himself swept along. Douglass understood that blacks would need Lincoln dearly if they were to hold on to the revolution of 1863. A martyred Lincoln would be even more trusted than the living one; dead, he could never disappoint the cause of black equality.

In no other speech did Douglass address Lincoln's place in Civil War and African American memory so poignantly as at the unveiling of the Freedmen's Memorial monument in Lincoln Park in Washington, D.C., in April 1876. The Freedmen's Memorial speech is too easily dismissed as merely eulogistic or particularly negative. Attended by President Grant, his cabinet, the Supreme Court justices, and many members of the House and Senate, the ceremony was as impressive as the bright spring day, which was declared a holiday by a joint session of Congress. After a reading of the Emancipation Proclamation and the unveiling of the statue (which Douglass later admitted that he did not like because "it showed the Negro on his knees"), Douglass took the podium as orator of the day. Here again, context is nearly all: in 1876, the centennial year, most of the ex-Confederate states were back under white Democratic control, the civil and political rights of blacks were in great jeopardy, and a new legacy of terror and violence hung over a decade of embittered Reconstruction. That apocalyptic ode to joy he had sung to the martyred Lincoln in 1865 hardly fit the scene of 1876.[16]

No black speaker had ever had an audience quite like this. The government itself was listening to the black orator instruct them on the meaning of Lincoln to African Americans. His address included strong doses of the rail-splitter Lincoln image, the "plebeian" who rose through honesty, common sense, and the hand of God to become the "great liberator." But Douglass spoke with blunt honesty for such a ceremonial occasion, and in words that have rung down through time and been put to many uses. "Abraham Lincoln was not . . . either our man or our model," declared Douglass. "In his interests . . . in his habits of thought, and in his prejudices, he was a white man." Douglass did not make everyone comfortable in the sentiment of a monument unveiling.

"He was preeminently the white man's president, entirely devoted to the welfare of white men." Douglass admitted that in the first year of the war, Lincoln would have sacrificed black freedom to save the Union. And in famous phrases, he spoke directly to his distinguished white audience: "You are the children of Abraham Lincoln. We are at best only his step-children; children by adoption, children by forces of circumstances and necessity."[17]

But it was Lincoln's growth to the moment of truth that most occupied Douglass in this remarkable address. He also understood that the occasion was a moment to forge national memory and practice civil religion. Through most of the speech, Douglass spoke to and for blacks (the monument had been commissioned and paid for almost entirely by blacks). But the monument was not only to Lincoln, but to emancipation. The occasion honored Lincoln, but Douglass equally stressed the events that transpired "under his rule and in due time." Most important, in contributing to the Lincoln myth and in commemorating emancipation, Douglass was staking a claim to nationhood and citizenship for blacks at this sensitive, even desperate moment of the spring of 1876. "We stand today at the national center," he announced, "to perform something like a national act." Douglass struck clear notes of civil religion as he described the "stately pillars and majestic dome of the Capitol" as "our church" and rejoiced that "for the first time in the history of our people, and in the history of the whole American people, we join in this high worship." Douglass was trying to make Lincoln mythic and therefore useful to the cause of black equality, but the primary significance of the Freedmen's Memorial speech lies in its concerted attempt to forge a place for blacks in national memory. "When now it shall be said that the colored man is soulless . . . ," Douglass concluded, "when the foul reproach of ingratitude is hurled at us, and it is attempted to scourge us beyond the range of human brotherhood, we may calmly point to the monument we have this day erected to the memory of Abraham Lincoln."[18] What Lincoln himself had called the "mystic chords of memory" as a source of devotion to the Union, Douglass now claimed as the rightful inheritance of blacks as well. He did so through language, the only secure means he possessed, and the one thing he had most in common with Lincoln.

Although Douglass served up his share of Lincoln legend over time, he never spoke publicly about the sixteenth president without a political purpose that served the cause of black freedom and civil rights. At age seventy-five, on February 13, 1893, at a Lincoln birthday celebration in Brooklyn, New York, before an audience of three hundred prominent Republicans, Douglass delivered a speech called "Abraham Lincoln: The Great Man of Our Century." With a "fine oil painting of the martyred President" hanging in the front of the dining hall, Douglass offered up a "reminiscence" of Lincoln designed to please his fellow Republicans. In this atmosphere of mystic hero worship, Douglass called Lincoln "godlike" and the greatest American who "ever stood or walked upon the continent." Douglass placed Lincoln in the line of classic heroes, those who had been tested by travail and led nations through their "darkest hours." "The time to see a great captain is not when the wind is fair and the sea is smooth," said Douglass, "and the man in the cross-trees . . . can safely sing out, 'all is well.'" Because he had taken the country through its worst storm, Lincoln was "such a captain" and a "hero worthy of your highest worship."[19]

This image of the savior Lincoln was a common theme in Lincoln oratory. But Douglass put it to his own ends. "I had the good fortune to know Abraham Lincoln personally and peculiarly," Douglass proclaimed. The "peculiar" part, of course, was as the black man welcomed at the White House without racist pretension. Douglass rehearsed his two official meetings with the president and even hinted that he had been "invited to tea" at the Soldiers' Home, the Lincoln family's summer retreat in Washington, on yet another occasion. This was Douglass's way of bringing attention to his own prominence and pride of place in history, but it was also a commentary on the racism so deep in human relationships all over American society. Douglass was fond of using Lincoln's ability to "make me at ease" as a metaphor for how race relations could be among equals in a society that might one day transcend its racial theories and habits. In this remembrance of Lincoln, Douglass further declared that he had never really witnessed the famed humorous side of Lincoln. He met only the sad and "earnest" visage. Almost anticipating Sandburg and other artists to follow, Douglass remembered Lincoln with a poet's sensibility: "The dimmed light in his eye, and the deep lines in his strong American face, told plainly the story of the heavy burden of care that weighed upon his spirit. I could as easily dance at a funeral as to jest in the presence of such a man." All this prepared his audience for a strong dose of martyrdom as the speech neared its conclusion. Douglass remembered walking in the mud of Pennsylvania Avenue behind Lincoln's carriage on the day of his second inauguration, a deep "foreboding" in his mind about plots to murder the president. And then, in a deft stroke, he acknowledged all the forms of criticism Lincoln withstood as a transition to quoting the most antislavery lines from the Second Inaugural ("If God wills that it [the war] continue until all the wealth piled by the bondman's two hundred and fifty years of toil shall be sunk, and until every drop of blood drawn by the lash shall be paid by another drawn by the sword . . . the judgements of the Lord are true and righteous altogether"). Such inspiration of spirit and language, Douglass claimed, he had never witnessed. "There seemed at the time to be in the man's soul," declared Douglass, "the united souls of all the Hebrew prophets."[20]

Douglass loved the opportunity to match Old Testament wits with his dead friend and symbol. As both friend and symbol, and eventual antislavery prophet, Lincoln had grown immeasurably with time in Douglass's own imagination, and in that of much of American society. Douglass never missed a chance to make Lincoln mythic and useful; he also relished moments to declare his genuine admiration for a man with whom he shared so much historically, ideologically, even spiritually. At the end of the 1893 speech, Douglass contended that Lincoln's assassination was the "natural outcome of a war for slavery." And this Lincoln the liberator was precisely the national memory Douglass used to remind his stalwart Republican audience that in their own day the United States government would exercise "no power . . . to protect the lives and liberties of American citizens in any one of our own southern states from barbarous, inhuman, and lawless violence."[21] Ever the embittered ironist, and even as an after-dinner speaker in the club of his friends, Douglass enlisted Lincoln in the fight against lynching.

During the final decade of Douglass's life, he lived well in a large house called Cedar Hill in Washington, D.C. As one entered the front door of Cedar Hill, in the public parlor to the right, immediately visible on the opposite wall, hung a portrait of Lincoln. It was the first symbolic object any visitor saw in a home filled with remembrances of the antislavery struggle and the Civil War era, and it still hangs there today. Douglass's Lincoln on the wall was more than an obligatory icon to impress guests. It was perhaps Douglass's statement that if Abraham Lincoln had not freed the slaves (which of course Douglass knew better than anyone was a complicated proposition), then the United States had not done so either. And if the nation had not forged emancipation out of civil war, then African Americans would have had no future in America. In Lincoln's image on the wall, Douglass could claim, the nation might continue to find a new narrative of its history and its destiny. On almost any occasion, Douglass could both honor and appropriate Lincoln. The Lincoln Douglass fashioned into his lifelong rhetorical, and even visual, companion was an endless storehouse of memory and a legacy to be used as a weapon against the forces of darkness.

When news of Lincoln's assassination reached Rochester, New York, on April 13, 1865, Douglass had just returned from a lecture tour and had witnessed great joy in several cities at the war's ending. He shared the shock of fellow northerners as a springtime of relief turned overnight into horror and mourning. A throng of Rochester citizens gathered at the city hall, as Douglass remembered, "not knowing what to do in the agony of the hour." Called upon to speak, Douglass described himself as "stunned and overwhelmed." "I had . . . made many speeches there [Rochester] which had . . . touched the hearts of my hearers," he recalled, "but never to this day was I brought into such close accord with them. We shared in common a terrible calamity, and this touch of nature made us more than countrymen, it made us Kin."[22]

Douglass would continue to write brilliantly and honestly about the necessity and the struggle of African Americans to sustain their sense of kinship with white Americans and with Abraham Lincoln. But history, with Douglass and Lincoln indispensably bound, had forged the possibility of such a national kinship—a brave dream we are still trying to achieve.

NOTES

David W. Blight delivered his Klement Lecture in 2001.

1. Cornelius Garner, interviewed May 18, 1937, in Charles L. Perdue Jr., Thomas E. Barden, and Robert K. Phillips, eds., *Weevils in the Wheat: Interviews with Virginia Ex-Slaves* (Bloomington: Indiana Univ. Press, 1976), 102–4.

2. On Lincoln and American memory, see Merrill D. Peterson, *Lincoln in American Memory* (New York: Oxford Univ. Press, 1994); and Barry Schwartz, *Abraham Lincoln and the Forge of National Memory* (Chicago: Univ. of Chicago Press, 2000). On Douglass and memory, see Waldo E. Martin Jr., "Images of Frederick Douglass in the Afro-American Mind: The Recent Black Freedom Struggle," in Eric J. Sundquist, ed., *Frederick Douglass: New Literary and Historical Essays* (Cambridge: Cambridge Univ. Press, 1990).

3. See Caleb Bingham, *The Columbian Orator*, bicentennial ed., David W. Blight, ed. (New York: New York Univ. Press, 1998), intro. For a comparative treatment of Douglass and Lincoln, see Christopher Breiseth, "Lincoln and Frederick Douglass: Another Debate," *Illinois State Historical Society Journal* 68 (1975): 9–26. For a recent and very critical approach to Lincoln's views on race and slavery, see Lerone Bennett Jr., *Forced Into Glory: Abraham Lincoln's White Dream* (Chicago: Johnson Publishing Co., 2000). For a more favorable approach to Lincoln's role as an emancipator and as commander in chief, see the essays in James M. McPherson, *Abraham Lincoln and the Second American Revolution* (New York: Oxford Univ. Press, 1991).

4. Carl Sandburg, quoted in Peterson, *Lincoln in American Memory*, 371; W. E. B. Du Bois, "Abraham Lincoln," *Crisis*, May 1922, and "Lincoln Again," *Crisis*, Sept. 1922, in *W. E. B. Du Bois: Writings* (New York: Library of America, 1986), 1196, 1198.

5. Roy P. Basler, ed., *The Collected Works of Abraham Lincoln*, vol. 8 (New Brunswick, N.J.: Rutgers Univ. Press, 1953), 332–33.

6. *The Life and Times of Frederick Douglass, Written by Himself* (1881; rpr. New York: Collier Books, 1962), 365–66.

7. See Benjamin Quarles, *Lincoln and the Negro* (New York: Oxford Univ. Press, 1962), 247–48; and Benjamin Quarles, *Frederick Douglass* (New York: Atheneum, 1968), 220. The letter is Frederick Douglass to Mrs. Abraham Lincoln, Rochester, N.Y., Aug. 17, 1865, Gilder Lehrman Collection, Pierpont Morgan Library, N.Y.

8. "The Inaugural Address," *Douglass Monthly*, Apr. 1861, in Philip S. Foner, *The Life and Writings of Frederick Douglass* (New York: International Publishers, 1952), 3:76; "Address on Colonization to a Deputation of Negroes," in Basler, ed., *Collected Works*, 5:370–75; "The President and

His Speeches," *Douglass Monthly* Sept. 1862, in Foner, *Life and Writings*, 3: 267–70. On Douglass and the colonization issue, see David W. Blight, *Frederick Douglass' Civil War: Keeping Faith in Jubilee* (Baton Rouge: Louisiana State Univ. Press, 1989), 122–47.

9. Douglass to George Luther Stearns, Aug. 12, 1863, Abraham Barker Papers, Historical Society of Pennsylvania, Philadelphia; Douglass, *Life and Times*, 346–50; Douglass, "Our Work Is Not Done," speech delivered at the annual meeting of the American Anti-Slavery Society, Philadelphia, Dec. 3–4, 1863, in Foner, ed., *Life and Writings*, 3:383; Lincoln, "Second Inaugural Address," in Basler, ed., *Collected Works*, 8:333.

10. Abraham Lincoln, "Annual Message to Congress," Dec. 8, 1863, in Basler, ed., *Collected Works*, 7:49–51, 53; Douglass, "The Mission of the War," delivered in late 1863 and throughout 1864, in Foner, ed., *Life and Writings*, 3:401.

11. See Blight, *Frederick Douglass' Civil War*, 183–84.

12. Douglass to Lincoln, August 29, 1864, in Foner, ed., *Life and Writings*, 3:405–6. The best record of this meeting is Douglass to Theodore Tilton, Oct. 15, 1864, in ibid., 422–24. Garry Wills, *Lincoln at Gettysburg: The Words That Remade America* (New York: Simon & Schuster, 1992), 38, 40.

13. Douglass, "Abraham Lincoln—A Speech," Dec., 1865, Frederick Douglass Papers, Library of Congress (LC), reel 14; David Donald, "Getting Right with Lincoln," in *Lincoln Reconsidered: Essays on the Civil War Era* (1947; rpr. New York: Vintage Books, 1956), 3–18.

14. Speech on Abraham Lincoln (on some pages titled "On Death of A. Lincoln"), probably June 1865, Washington, D.C., Douglass Papers, LC, reel 14.

15. Speech on Abraham Lincoln (on some pages titled "On Death of A. Lincoln"), probably June 1865, Washington, D.C., Douglass Papers, LC, reel 14.

16. See Blight, *Frederick Douglass' Civil War*, 227–28.

17. "Oration in Memory of Abraham Lincoln," delivered at the unveiling of the Freedmen's Memorial, Lincoln Park, Washington, D.C., Apr. 14, 1876, in Foner, ed., *Life and Writings*, 4:310–12.

18. Ibid., 314, 317–19.

19. "Abraham Lincoln: The Great Man of Our Century," address delivered in Brooklyn, N.Y., Feb. 13, 1893, in John W. Blassingame and John R. McKivigan, eds., *The Frederick Douglass Papers* (New Haven: Yale Univ. Press, 1992,) 5:535–37.

20. Ibid., 536, 538–43.

21. Ibid., 545.

22. Douglass, *Life and Times*, 371–72.

🦋 ROBERT W. JOHANNSEN 🦋

The "Wicked Rebellion" and the Republic

Henry Tuckerman's Civil War

🦋 For many years, Robert W. Johannsen filled the endowed chair named for one of the twentieth century's best-known historians of the Civil War era, James Garfield Randall, the author of, among many works, the classic textbook *The Civil War and Reconstruction*. As J. G. Randall Distinguished Professor of History at the University of Illinois at Urbana-Champaign, Johannsen had been a member of the University of Illinois Department of History for three-and-a-half decades when he delivered the third Klement Lecture in 1993. He was the last lecturer that Klement helped to choose, although Johannsen came to Milwaukee three months after Klement's death.

Best known for his work on Stephen A. Douglas—indeed, his legion of Ph.D. students called themselves the "Little Giants"—his interests lay in the intersection of slavery, western expansion, and politics. Among his books are *Stephen A. Douglas* (1973), which won the Francis Parkman Prize for literary merit from the Society of American Historians; *The Frontier, the Union, and Stephen A. Douglas* (1989); and *Lincoln, the South, and Slavery: The Political Dimension* (1991).

His masterful *To the Halls of the Montezumas: The Mexican War in the American Imagination* (1985) was less about the war itself than it was about the ideas and attitudes that Americans brought to bear on this, the United States' first "foreign" war. Notions of racial superiority, romantic images of exotic old Mexico, the almost juvenile patriotic fervor that the war inspired in the too many volunteers and the journalistic boosters of the conflict, the modern technology and all-too-familiar diseases that killed many more men than enemy bullets, all provide wider contexts for the Mexican-American war than those presented by any previous historian.

Johannsen's Klement Lecture focused, by necessity, on a much narrower subject, but he brought a similar intent—and his usual graceful prose—to examine the meaning of the sectional conflict to one American writer, Henry Tuckerman. In 1861 the Democratic intellectual published one of the first analyses of the causes of the Civil War, *The Rebellion: Its Latent Causes and True Significance*. Johannsen shows how this now practically unknown author's response to the outbreak of civil war in the summer of 1861 reflected many conservative Americans' reactions. Blaming the war on both the slave power and the abolitionists, Tuckerman nevertheless argued that the war would purify the Union and lead to a "Romantic salvation for the American spirit."

Johannsen retired in 2000 after nearly half a century as a professor at the universities of Kansas and Illinois. 🐚

I

WALT WHITMAN COULD NOT FORGET that moment on April 12, 1861. Walking down New York's Broadway around midnight toward the Brooklyn ferry and home, after attending a performance of Verdi's opera *A Masked Ball* at the Academy of Music on 14th Street, his thoughts were suddenly interrupted by the cries of newsboys as they came "tearing and yelling" up the street. Whitman bought a copy of the "extry *Herald*," crossed the street to the Metropolitan Hotel where the streetlamps were still blazing, and read aloud as a crowd gathered about him. According to a telegraphic dispatch received from Charleston, South Carolina, dated three o'clock that afternoon, Fort Sumter was under bombardment. A "terrible fight" was continuing at that very moment between the fort and the batteries that surrounded it. Declared the *Herald*: "Civil war has at last begun." The crowd listened "silently and intently," as Whitman read. When he had finished, they stood for a brief moment, then quietly dispersed.

The scene was repeated on almost every street and under almost every lamppost, in the hotels and in the barrooms. New York lawyer George Templeton Strong, returning home after a stormy committee meeting at Trinity Church, encountered the same newsboys. Suspecting a false report, he walked on before finally giving in to his curiosity. As he read the dispatch under a streetlamp, his skepticism mounted. He suspected the dispatch was just another example of Charleston's "taste for brag and lying." Besides, he could hardly believe that the "rebels" would be "so foolish and thoughtless as to take the initiative in civil war." Not until he read the next morning's papers was he convinced that Fort Sumter had been attacked.[1]

Telegraphic dispatches continued to arrive from Charleston all the next day. People gathered in front of the telegraph and newspaper offices to read the news as soon as it was received. Some refused to believe the reports and blamed the South Carolinians at the other end of the telegraph with trying to confuse them. Others felt the messages were deliberately exaggerated in order to arouse the other slave states against the government. Many of the reports were contradictory and inconsistent, some even false. At one point it was reported that the fort was ablaze, its magazines exploded and its walls crumbling; at another it was said that the garrison returned the fire, hurling hot shot into Charleston and burning the city. Finally, news was received that the exhausted garrison had ceased firing, the fort had surrendered, and the Confederate flag was raised over its battlements.

As lawyer Strong read of the surrender in the columns of a late edition of William Cullen Bryant's *Evening Post,* he confided to his diary, "So Civil War is inaugurated at last. God defend the Right."[2]

Like any private citizen, President Lincoln followed the reports as they appeared in the press. During the day, he met with commissioners sent by Virginia's secession convention to query the president as to his policy toward secession. Lincoln informed them in writing that he would pursue the course he had announced in his inaugural address, that he would "hold, occupy, and possess the property and places belonging to the government." If the news from Charleston were true, however, he would use all his power to repossess the government property, including Fort Sumter. He left no doubt in the minds of the commissioners that "actual war against the Government" had begun.

On April 15, the day following the evacuation of Fort Sumter, Lincoln publicly confirmed his determination to "repel force by force." In his first wartime proclamation, he called for 75,000 state militia troops to serve for ninety days, their first assignment to recapture the forts and other places that had been seized by the secessionists. Lincoln's announcement was the signal the border slave states were waiting for. With a haste that both surprised and disappointed Lincoln, Virginia seceded from the Union two days later. Arkansas, North Carolina, and Tennessee followed in the ensuing weeks.[3]

As the realization that Fort Sumter had surrendered sank into the national consciousness, stunned disbelief gave way to feelings of relief and revenge. What seemed at first to be a "national calamity" was soon viewed as an advantage to the Union cause. Less than two weeks before, Lincoln was being censured for his indecision and "fatal indifference" toward the secessionists; now it seemed clear that the fall of Fort Sumter had been anticipated by the administration. Those who had expressed dismay at the weak ambiguity of Lincoln's inaugural address and who had begun to think that the new president was unaware of the gravity of the crisis, now rejoiced that he apparently had had a plan all along. What James Russell Lowell had called Lincoln's "little Bopeep policy" toward the seceded states—"Let them alone, and they'll all come home Wagging their tails behind them"—was exploded by the "fiery tongues of the batteries in Charleston harbor." The loss of Sumter was not important militarily; its significance was in its impact on northern sentiment. "It was certainly a great piece of good-luck for the Government," wrote Lowell, "that they had a fort which it was so profitable to lose."[4]

Feelings of relief were mixed with an outburst of enthusiasm such as the nation had never before experienced. A "revolution in public sentiment," commented a Philadelphia paper, swept away all differences of opinion and "fired all hearts" with a common patriotic purpose. "I never before knew what a popular excitement can be," declared George Ticknor in Boston. In city after city, flags were unfurled on buildings, business activity was suspended, parades and rallies filled the streets. It was, in the words of one witness, a "carnival of patriotism."

On the day Maj. Robert Anderson and his beleaguered garrison left Fort Sumter—a Sunday—churches were filled to overflowing with people, forgetting "creeds and theological differences" in their anxiety for late news reports and analyses from the pulpit. Newspapers had never been in greater demand, prompting Oliver Wendell Holmes to observe that "only *bread and the newspaper* we must have, whatever else we do without."[5]

In New York, plans were immediately under way for a monster rally in Union Square that would exceed all other patriotic gatherings. On April 20, one week exactly after Sumter's surrender, business came to a standstill as crowds of people, estimated to be in excess of 100,000, filled the square and adjoining streets, gathered on rooftops, and stood in the windows of buildings. Cannon thundered and drums rolled, "gorgeously dressed" soldiers paraded, bands provided music, and flags were everywhere, flying from houses, hotels, bars, churches, and stores, from men's hats and women's bonnets. "The city," observed George Templeton Strong, "seems to have gone suddenly wild and crazy."

Scores of speakers delivered impassioned pleas for unity, patriotism, and sacrifice, while hurling abusive epithets against those in the South who spurned the constitution, resisted the government, and insulted the flag. Resolutions supporting Lincoln's coercive policy were passed by acclamation, followed by the singing of the *Star-Spangled Banner* over and over again. Shouts went up when flags that had flown over Fort Sumter, some showing the rents and tears of the bombardment, were unfurled. In midafternoon, a "tremendous excitement" passed through the crowd as Major Anderson himself appeared. The ovation lasted for twenty deafening minutes.

As the nation's greatest orator, Edward Everett, later commented, in words that have resonance in our own time, the thirteenth of April, the day of Sumter's surrender, was a "day forever to be held in inauspicious remembrance."[6]

That Americans would welcome a civil war with such an outburst of enthusiasm seemed little short of amazing. Had anyone predicted, wrote Lowell, that the "immediate prospect of Civil War would be hailed by the people of the Free States with a unanimous shout of enthusiasm, he would have been thought a madman." Yet there were still some who found a civil war to be disturbing, for it was incongruous with all that America stood for. "How little Americans of this generation," wrote one commentator, "supposed that they would ever hear the alarm of war." War was the instrument of oppressive regimes and had no place in a republic. On the contrary, republics were supposed to be dedicated to the peaceful resolution of conflict. That peaceful resolution had failed seemed to suggest some fatal flaw in republican government. What could be worse, some asked, than a civil war in America? The thought of Americans directing the implements of death against other Americans was abhorrent, shameful, and humiliating. There was no glory in a civil war. "Its noblest deeds are without honor, for they are won in fratricidal conflict, and their cost is fraternal blood."[7]

Most Americans, however, shrugged off such disturbing thoughts and instead embraced wholeheartedly a war spirit that only became more intense. All aspects of life took on a military cast. Soldiers marched through the streets and gathered at railway stations, children dressed like Zouaves played with toy muskets, bookshops displayed works on tactics and drill and placed portraits of military heroes in their windows. Theaters revived old battle melodramas and produced new ones; shops advertised camp stores and military equipage. "The people are soldiers," commented one observer. "The country is a camp." At the same time, a nervous restlessness seemed to pervade society. "Men cannot think," it was said, "or write, or attend to their ordinary business." There was only a single topic of conversation; all else— the interests and concerns of everyday life—seemed irrelevant. Young men hastened to volunteer, anticipating adventure and fearing that they might miss their chance to take part in the grand events that were about to occur. People walked the streets or gathered in public places, vying with one another in their demonstrations of patriotism. Some expressed their allegiance in less constructive ways, attacking the offices of newspapers that had supported peaceable secession, threatening the homes of suspected southern sympathizers, and forcing reluctant shopkeepers to display the flag. Philadelphia diarist Sidney George Fisher, who owned a Maryland plantation, viewed the excitement as a dangerous portent of mob rule and blamed it all on the Democrats.[8]

The war spirit boiled over on April 19, less than a week after Fort Sumter's surrender, when soldiers of the Sixth Massachusetts Regiment, the first to respond to Lincoln's call, were attacked in Baltimore as they moved through the city on their way to defend the national capital. Four of the soldiers were killed and seventeen were wounded; a dozen civilians lost their lives when the troops opened fire on the attackers. The North exploded in outrage as demands were made to bring to account the "traitors and murderers" who had led the attack. "How much longer is this to go on?" asked Horace Greeley's *New York Tribune*. George Templeton Strong thought it appropriate that the first blood of the war should be shed by Massachusetts men, on the anniversary of the Battle of Lexington in 1775. "This is a continuation of the war that Lexington opened," he observed, "a war of democracy against oligarchy."[9]

With the assault on the Massachusetts regiment, it appeared that the conflict would be longer and bloodier than had been supposed. The northern press called for an end to the administration's "half-measures" and launched a steady barrage of "malignant, bloodthirsty tirades" against the South and southerners. The "rebellious traitors" must be made to suffer; they must find poverty at their firesides, as one paper put it, and see privation in the eyes of their children. Their property should be confiscated and redistributed among the northern soldiers, those new pioneers who would be sent south to replace the "worn-out" race of southern aristocracy. A special vengeance was reserved for Baltimore: the city should be reduced to "cinders and ashes" and its inhabitants "either slaughtered, or scattered to the winds." One New York editor urged that the levees on the lower Mississippi River be breached at high water, thereby drowning the "traitors and rebels" as one would drown rats. Editors screamed for a war that would spread extermination and desolation from the Potomac to the Rio Grande.[10]

The war not only monopolized public discussion, it also had a chilling effect on literary production, paralyzing (according to one writer) all but military and periodical literature. "Our common mental food has become distasteful," said Holmes, "and what would have been intellectual luxuries at other times are now absolutely repulsive." What the nation now required was the discipline of the camp and the "manly energy" that would produce men of deeds rather than words. Bravery in battle, it was pointed out, was as inspiring as a "true poem." Nathaniel Hawthorne, resentful that the war had interrupted his "literary industry," despaired that "Romances" would never be in public demand again.[11]

Histories of past wars and battlefields enjoyed a new popularity, and publishers scurried to satisfy the demand. "A time of war," commented *Harper's Magazine*, "gives profound interest to all stories of war." None had more appeal than those that told of the American Revolution, with which the Civil War seemed somehow connected. People turned to the pages of Richard Hildreth, Washington Irving, George Bancroft, Benson Lossing, and John Marshall to refresh their faith in the republic's founding principles. "The best tonic for the time," suggested one writer, "is our own history." Ponder the events of 1776, individuals were advised, and discover the difference between "a wicked rebellion and a justifiable revolution."[12]

At the same time, the crisis awakened the romantic temperament that had slumbered ever since it had played so important a role in molding popular attitudes toward the Mexican War fifteen years before. In language reminiscent of the lofty eloquence of that earlier time, the Civil War was seen as a moral drama, fought for a noble cause, fulfilling a providential mission in the sweep of world history, offering honor and glory in abundance to its participants, spawning heroes, and demonstrating what James Fenimore

Cooper had described as the republic's "exulting manhood." The surrender of Fort Sumter, declared New York's *Knickerbocker Magazine*, aroused the "MANHOOD of the people." The nation's "heroic element" shrugged off its stupor and sprang into life to rescue northern society from the "luxury and effeminacy" in which it had been steeped. To the northern man was assigned the responsibility of defending "our national glory and greatness."

War called forth virtues that had been latent and corrupted during peacetime, virtues of valor, of honor, and of chivalry. The northern mechanics and farmers, exemplifying the chivalric qualities of generosity, magnanimity, and humanity, would be more than a match for the prideful and contemptuous southern cavaliers. The blood of nearly three centuries of heroes coursed through northern veins. "Up and arm!" exhorted *Vanity Fair*. "Do battle as of old in the holy cause. The world's last great struggle is before you—happy those who can die for it."[13]

Many in the North, however, wanted explanations more than exhortations. "Why are the American people to-day in bloody collision?" asked a Pennsylvania paper. The question, uppermost in the popular mind since the surrender of Fort Sumter, became more compelling as the conviction grew that the conflict was to be neither brief nor bloodless and as it became apparent that only a gigantic effort could reunite the sections. As one writer put it, "the thing is to be done on a great scale."[14]

In the early months of the war, editors, clergymen, public figures, essayists, and historians all scrambled to place their analyses of the conflict and its causes before the people. The result was an outpouring of pamphlets, published sermons, and serialized histories—a veritable Niagara of publication. Writers took stock of the republic's strength, its nature, and its mission, while emphasizing the responsibilities owed by the citizenry to its defense. War, it was said, encouraged—even demanded—introspection: "Men sound new depths of ability. . . . The cannonball shoots away veils; it opens eyes, and ears, and mouths."[15]

In Boston, Ralph Waldo Emerson was in the midst of a course of public lectures on "Life and Literature," when the attack on Fort Sumter seemed to render his meditations irrelevant. Interrupting his schedule, he turned his attention to the war, arousing his daughter's fears that by speaking of such a worldly matter in plain language he might lose his intellectual edge. ("It is really wonderful," remarked Hawthorne, "how all sorts of theoretical nonsense to which we New Englanders are addicted in peaceful times, vanish in the strong atmosphere which we now inhale.") The burst of public

enthusiasm following the fort's surrender surprised Emerson but also grati-
fied him. "How does Heaven help us when civilization is at a hard pinch?
Why," he said, "by a whirlwind of patriotism . . . magnetizing all discordant
masses under its terrific unity." Instincts were unleashed the people did not
know they had. To Emerson, it was a war of civilization against barbarism.
"Civilization," he insisted, "depends on morality," and morality meant an end
to slavery. "Why should not America be capable of a second stroke for the
well-being of the human race," he asked, "as eighty or ninety years ago she
was for the first?" The extension of the North's "higher state," carried by the
"brains and arms of good men," was inevitable and irresistible. Emerson
continued to make forays into the public discussion of the war's purposes,
melding the "noise of war" with "moral forces" in ways that surprised even
his friends. "Ah!" he remarked, "sometimes gunpowder smells good."[16]

Hawthorne was less confident and more ambivalent. Having years earlier
compared the volunteers who marched off to Mexico to medieval knights, he
reveled once again in the "heroic sentiment" that greeted Fort Sumter's surrender.
"I never imagined," he wrote, "what a happy state of mind a civil war produces,
and how it invigorates every man's whole being." The beating drums, the wav-
ing banners, the marching soldiers quickened his blood, and he regretted that
he was too old to shoulder a musket. Hawthorne approved of the war but yet
confessed that he had only a "very misty idea" of why it was being fought.[17]

George Bancroft, the period's most prominent and respected historian,
had just published the eighth volume of his magisterial history of the United
States, in which he finally reached the signing of the Declaration of Independence. He saw in the northern response to Fort Sumter an "uprising of
the irresistible spirit of the people" comparable to that of the colonists in
1776. It was, he wrote, the "sublimest spectacle" he had ever witnessed. The
rebellion proved the vitality of America's republican principles and demonstrated the truth of the ideals on which the nation was founded. "The North
is the *country*," he declared, charged with the responsibility to redeem the
"rights and the constitution of the country." John Lothrop Motley, whose
history of the *Rise of the Dutch Republic* still reminded Americans of their
own historic struggle for independence, rejected southern claims to the
right of revolution and argued that secession was nothing more than rebellion, treason, and plunder. The "noble and holy" mission of the North, he
strongly believed, was to extend civilization to the South. "There never was
a war more justifiable and more inevitable in history."[18]

Neither of the country's great romantic historians, however, applied his
talents to the history of the Civil War. That task was assumed by a swarm of

lesser luminaries who had already achieved reputation as writers of popular history, including individuals drawn from the ranks of the clergy, newspaper editors, literary critics, and even members of Congress. Their works, lavishly illustrated with heroic lithographs of valor and death in battle, were frequently issued in serial installments, thereby maintaining an up-to-date authenticity. Highly moralistic in tone, they uniformly placed the blame for the war upon southern institutions and ambitions, on slavery, and on the aggressions of the South's treasonable and conspirational leaders. They saw the conflict in the broadest perspective of world history. The war, wrote the popular John S. C. Abbott, "was but one . . . sublime act, in the drama of that great conflict" between aristocratic privilege and equal rights, that had for centuries "made our globe one vast battlefield."[19]

II

Most of the efforts to probe the meaning of the Civil War, its causes and its impact on the life of the republic, were embodied in the vast pamphlet literature that appeared almost before the guns at Charleston had cooled and extended throughout the entire war. An invaluable source for an investigation of what might be called the "spirit of the age" during the war years, the pamphlets have attracted relatively little scholarly attention and remain virtually untouched.

Among the earliest pamphlet publications was the effort of a forty-eight-year-old New York writer of independent means, Henry Theodore Tuckerman, who in the summer of 1861 published *The Rebellion: Its Latent Causes and True Significance*. Born in Boston to a successful and respected mercantile family, Tuckerman moved to New York where in 1845, he became a well-known figure in New York's literary circle, what Perry Miller has called the "Knickerbocker Set." A close friend of Washington Irving and William Cullen Bryant, and of such lesser lights as the poets Fitz-Greene Halleck and Charles Fenno Hoffman and the prominent critic and editor Evert Augustus Duyckinck, Tuckerman was a prolific and widely read writer of essays, poems, literary criticism and reviews, travel books, biographical studies, and commentaries on American art and artists.

In spite of his extraordinary production—over twenty books and uncounted reviews and essays in the popular periodicals of mid-nineteenth-century America—or maybe because of it, Tuckerman has suffered almost total neglect and is virtually unknown today. Edmund Wilson, in his study of Civil War literature, dismissed him as a "very active journalist" who also "wrote poetry, which was mediocre but which usually got into the anthologies." The author of the brief article in the *Dictionary of American Biography* concluded that Tuckerman passed for a "man of genius" in the "easy, romantic" atmosphere of the 1840s and 1850s. Man of genius or not, Tuckerman epitomized the romantic spirit of nineteenth-century America.[20]

Early in his life, ill health forced Tuckerman to give up his studies at Harvard for the warmer climes of Italy. It was the beginning of a lifelong love affair with the land and the people that later inspired a vigorous support of Italian independence and unification. His sojourns in Italy during the 1830s turned his mind to the pursuit of a literary career. Free of financial worries, unmarried, he embarked on an intense, systematic literary life; highly ordered, diligent, and very methodical. Literature for Tuckerman, it was said, became a business. Speaking of his broad interests and steady discipline, a friend commented, "Even ordinary talents, thus assiduously cultivated, secure extraordinary results." Quiet, modest, even-tempered, and "free from egotism," Tuckerman preferred the tranquility and seclusion of his chamber to the bustle of the city around him, leaving his work only occasionally to join his fellow literati in evenings of discussion and conviviality. Tuckerman complained about the "want of serenity" in American society and decried the "spirit of urgency" that seemed to grip his fellow Americans. "There is an efficacy in calmness," he declared. Edgar Allan Poe, whom Tuckerman utterly disliked, sarcastically labeled him "King of the Quietists."[21]

Tuckerman deplored the lack of independence and the "deference to hackneyed models" he saw in much of American literature, and he called out for a uniquely American expression that was worthy of the country's "novel elements": the beauty and grandeur of the landscape, the border life, and especially America's great political experiment. Too much of American literature, he lamented, lacked passion and was too "coldly elegant" to have popular effect. Of the writers of his time, he admired James Fenimore Cooper, who wrote on American subjects in an American spirit; and he respected Nathaniel Hawthorne for his imaginative scope and for his ability to invest commonplace subjects with moral significance.[22]

In words that echoed Cooper's social criticism, Tuckerman was troubled by what he called the "ultra tendencies" of American society: the subservience to public opinion, the restlessness of temper, the devotion to physical well-being, the absorption in the immediate, the calculating habits, and the reverence for wealth and "pecuniary ability," all of which stifled sensitivity and poetic feeling. His romantic faith in the innate wisdom and capacities of the individual did not always extend to a faith in the people collectively. He shared Alexis de Tocqueville's apprehensions for the influence of equality and democratic rule on civil society in the United States, and he lamented the cultural ignorance the times seemed to foster. "Trade and politics," he observed ruefully, "completely overshadow literature and art," while "invention exhausts itself upon machines and finance." Tuckerman shunned the real or practical world and sought his own world in the intuitions of the heart and the redemptive qualities of the imagination and feeling: "There is an intuitive wisdom above the lessons of the world," he insisted. "There are inward facts that outweigh seeming reality." Some of Tuckerman's contemporaries saw in his reflections a counterweight "to the false and chilling philosophy which sees nothing good but in material things which have a market value." Tuckerman's work, wrote one of the leading critics of the time, counteracted the "sordid and calculating spirit of the age."[23]

The guns of Charleston changed Tuckerman's life in ways he hardly anticipated. The real world suddenly broke into his ideal world, shattered his serenity, and forced him to come to terms with a crisis such as the nation had never before experienced. "The shock of actual bloodshed," one scholar has observed, "of death and atrocity, of civil insurrection in the Practical world against the highest principles of the Ideal, shook Tuckerman's complacent insularity to its very roots." The crisis called out for explanation, and Tuckerman was one of the earliest to answer the call. The result was the publication in the summer of 1861 of his analysis of the rebellion's "latent" causes. It was Tuckerman's first and only work to focus directly on a contemporary political problem.[24]

To Tuckerman, the firing on Fort Sumter was like the "shock of a bereavement," disrupting his sleep, producing tears, and rendering his daily occupations "flat, stale, and unprofitable." The unfamiliarity of war and the anomaly of treason in a republic that depended for its government upon "mutual confidence" added to his disbelief that such a thing could be happening to his country. No civil conflict in all of human history, he concluded, was so sharply defined by right and wrong. The very attack on Fort Sumter seemed an act of patricide against the country's founding fathers, for the fort bore the name of a southern general who had helped win America's independence.

The excitement of the northern response to the crisis quickly overtook Tuckerman's initial shock. The rapid succession of events following the fort's surrender, he asserted, made "history a vivid reality." "What spectacles has it been the lot of many of us to behold, what emotions to experience since the advent of spring!" All the "sensations and sentiments," he felt, pointed to a "new self-realization" among the people, an awakened sense of responsibility to the republic and a recognition of how "near and dear to the human heart" after all were the ties of American nationality. He thrilled at the sight of college graduates setting out for the battlefield, their military uniforms under their academic robes; and he found delight in the German war songs, the Hungarian battle cries, the Irish cheers, and the bugle calls of Garibaldi's invincibles, as New York's ethnic regiments left for the South, under America's banner of freedom.[25]

There was no doubt in Tuckerman's mind that the war was brought on by the "most wicked and wanton conspiracy" ever mounted against the life of a great nation. After having maintained a political ascendancy in the nation through the Democratic Party for decades, the southern slave aristocracy refused to recognize that the "inevitable expansion of free labor" had shifted political supremacy to northern and western elements. Beaten at the polls in a fair election, with no provocation but the election of a president of whom they disapproved, the slaveholders chose the path of treason and fratricidal war rather than acquiesce in rule by the majority, the very foundation of republican government. They "recklessly seek to destroy," he declared, "what they cannot honestly possess."

Tuckerman gave only fleeting attention to the political and constitutional questions that drove the crisis, perhaps because he felt uncomfortable and insecure in discussing issues raised in the political arena. For a person who had insulated himself from the real world, however, he exhibited a remarkable familiarity with the southern rhetoric of disunion. Secession, he simply asserted, was not authorized by state sovereignty. The sentiments of the Virginia resolutions of 1798 and of South Carolina's nullification ordinance three decades later, to which southern leaders appealed, had been rendered untenable by the national government's "emphatic authority." Beyond this simplistic conclusion he did not go. Instead, Tuckerman concentrated on those social and cultural characteristics of both North and South, what he called the "latent" causes, that explained the "moral complexion of the present crisis and strife."[26]

That Tuckerman should view the Civil War as the inevitable result of those "ultra tendencies" of society against which he had protested earlier was not surprising. Employing the familiar language of popular republicanism, touched by the sentiments of an equally popular romanticism, he concluded that the pervasive cause of the crisis was the "general neglect of civic duty" by the nation's citizenry. In a litany of decay and deterioration, he painted a grim picture of the atmosphere that prevailed in the United States. "Flattered into passivity by an overweening confidence in the stability of our institutions, . . . engrossed by private cares and enterprise, . . . deadened by material prosperity," Americans had "evaded the claims" of their country. Statesmanship was in steady decline, politics had become a trade and party contests merely a "vulgar scramble for emoluments." Patriotism was silenced by apathy and indifference. Irreverence was rampant, and public spirit was in decay. Lacking moral courage, blinded by ambition, the people had become easy prey to political adventurers, designing demagogues, and unprincipled renegades peddling fallacious theories.

Tuckerman reminded his fellow citizens that the superiority of democratic institutions depended upon moral and intellectual values rather than material considerations, and that it demanded of the people "honor and duty, high achievement, and holy sacrifice." This, to Tuckerman, was the stuff of heroism. To drive home his point, he alluded to the army and navy officers, the sworn defenders of the republic, who had yielded to the "juggling fiends of treason" and defected to the Confederacy. Deficient in manhood and insensible to the "sublime consciousness" of patriotic devotion, they lacked that "instinct of heroism" that was so important to the life of the republic.[27]

Tuckerman's censure of the American character—the taint of materialism and all its attendant abuses—was aimed at both sections, North as well as South. Clearly, however, he found the South more culpable. In the North, he pointed out, these tendencies were recognized as danger signals, whereas in the South, they were looked upon as positive aspects of social behavior. Underlying Tuckerman's argument was the assumption that northern civilization was innately superior to that of the South, and that therefore the social and cultural shortcomings of the South bore most of the responsibility for the coming of the Civil War.[28]

Most of Tuckerman's pamphlet was devoted to a discussion of those social and cultural characteristics that gave force to the decline of public spirit as a cause of the conflict. Among the most important was what he termed "provincialism," a narrowness of mind that inevitably produced a "dogmatic egotism." Broad views and ideas, he insisted, were the hallmarks of the liberal mind, leading to "dispassionate conviction" and "sound judgment." Such characteristics were not found in southern thinking. Isolation from the world and from the world's thought and experience, he declared, had fostered among southerners an exaggerated "pride of birth" and a "childish self-importance." They placed local loyalties above national allegiance, and their leaders (Tuckerman mentioned John C. Calhoun) spent their energy in "artful appeals" to ingenious theories of government and extravagant assertions of states' rights that only heightened their isolation. "This provincial instead of national spirit," argued Tuckerman, "this local instead of patriotic sentiment, which blinds with prejudice and dwarfs with passion the grand, beautiful and auspicious feeling of American citizenship, has been the moral basis of intrigue and seduction whereon ambitious southern politicians have worked." Invoking the authority of "philosophic observers" from Thomas Jefferson to John Stuart Mill, Tuckerman concluded that the southerners' "native arrogance of temper" resulted inevitably from their defense of human slavery, which in turn separated them from all the dictates and teachings of civilization, duty, and Christianity.[29]

It was as a "*caste*" rather than a people, Tuckerman suggested, that southerners raised the flag of insurrection, for it was in their character as slaveholders that they initiated the war. Unlike the people of the North, whose "industrious habits, disciplined minds, and social equality" had widened their horizons, softened their tempers, liberalized their attitudes, and bred self-control, southern society was dominated by a self-centered, narrow-minded, and overbearing class of wealthy individuals whose "unchastened and aggressive" temperaments allied them with lawless adventurers. The "dark and portentous" question of slavery, upon which southern society rested, shaped southern thought and determined the direction of southern action.[30]

Tuckerman found a striking contrast to southern disunion in the recent unification of Italy, where centuries of feudal wars, animosities, local jealousies, and rival interests had been overcome. He was frankly baffled, he said, that the United States, enjoying long years of union, unprecedented growth, freedom, and prosperity, should now fall victim to the same "obsolete provincial and feudal bigotry" that Italians had successfully put behind them. The explanation, he speculated, was again to be found in the nature of southern thought and character. National sentiment had not been a part of southern thinking as it had been in the North. National honor, pride, and affection apparently had no meaning to the "votaries" of states' rights. Furthermore, he felt that the secession crisis had exposed a state of southern society so "incongruous and demoralized" that a social revolution would surely have occurred if the crisis had not intervened. The planter aristocracy, enjoying years of prosperity and peace, had grown wealthier and more powerful, while the poverty of whites and negroes only deepened. Military adventure, turbulence, and bloodshed, moreover, had become virtually a way of life in the slaveholding South.

Literature and the arts, among the most important influences in strengthening national feeling, had found little fertile ground in the slaveholding South. Southern literary and artistic achievement lagged far behind that of the North. The memories and traditions of America's own revolutionary struggle, a strong and enduring prop to national feeling in the North, moreover, had languished in the South. "The written thought," mused Tuckerman, "when clothed with beauty and power, and inspired by genius, reflecting and embalming the traditions, the aspect, and the character of a people, and the trophies of art, which perpetuate historical and local fame, singularly endear the country of their origin." Influenced by an obsessive localism, isolated from the streams of world thought, and unmindful of the importance of literary and artistic expression, southerners had deprived themselves of the vital springs of national pride and feeling.[31]

One last point remained: the "vindictive hatred" expressed by the southern people for the North, which Tuckerman thought to be unaccountable, irrational, and wholly unjustified. What, he asked, were its causes? The answer, he believed, was found in the South's alienation from the rest of the country, for which northerners were just as responsible as southerners, maybe even more so. He identified three sources of alienation: "mendacious politicians, an irresponsible press, and malignant philanthropists," a triad of villainy.

The politicians, he charged, had placed every possible obstacle in the way of mutual understanding between North and South. "When the history of this rebellion shall be written," he predicted, "its most remarkable feature will be the number, enormity, and continuance of popular delusions, by means of which the leaders have kept up the strife and kept out the truth." Tuckerman only hoped that a day of reckoning would soon come when the deceptions and proscriptions perpetrated by the nation's politicians would "react fatally" upon their authors. Aiding and abetting the politicians was a newspaper press conducted by overzealous partisans who sought deliberately to widen the breach between the sections. With sharp words of his own, Tuckerman castigated the nation's newspapers (using the New York press as his example) for their "impudent defiance" and "reckless speculations," their lack of respect "for every sentiment dear to humanity," their mercenary motives, and their arrogance. By insisting that their deceptions represented popular opinion in the North, the papers further alienated the southern people and gave credibility to the false charges of the South's "political insurrectionists."[32]

Tuckerman was even more severe in his indictment of the "malignant philanthropists," by whom he meant the "small but unscrupulous class of men, who, in the ostensible promotion of an object which, in the abstract is right, advocate means practically wrong." He referred, of course, to the abolitionists.

To Tuckerman, the question of the abolition of slavery was largely one of means and ends. He shared the ultimate goal of an end to slavery but scornfully rejected the means offered by the militants. Borrowing the terminology of the phrenologist, Tuckerman described the zealots as those who "united combativeness and destructiveness to professed benevolence and [who] present the anomaly of ostensibly seeking the good of humanity while violating her primal instincts." Like their counterparts in the South, they too were "insurrectionists," reckless crusaders who would stop at nothing, not even the subversion of the republic, to achieve their ends. Intolerant, pertinacious, and impractical, they were unmindful of the feelings of others. By their incendiary speeches and writings, they aroused the South's instinct for self-preservation, tightening the bonds of servitude and enabling southern leaders to preach the "monstrous fiction" that their tactics were approved by a majority of northerners. Tuckerman hoped that southerners would realize that the militant abolitionists were without political power and prestige in the North and that "every rational lover of freedom" regarded them with horror.

Although he scarcely mentioned Abraham Lincoln, Tuckerman held a Lincolnian view of slavery and abolition. The northern people, he reminded the South, did not intend to intervene against slavery in the states where it existed; they wanted only to prevent its extension into the territories. The militant abolitionists, however, pursued that which was "abstractly right and true"—that is, the elimination of slavery throughout the United States—while they utterly disregarded the "existent circumstances" that stood in their way. Just such a dangerous combination, he warned, had resulted in the worst excesses of the French Revolution. The true abolitionists, on the contrary, were those who, like himself, counseled the eradication of slavery by practical and peaceful means, patiently awaiting what he called the growth of the nation to "moral maturity." Only through "sentiment and human sympathy" could the abolition of slavery be ultimately achieved. Tuckerman was arguing for a proper balance between the ideal and practical worlds, a theme, in fact, that runs through much of his response to the war. The true statesman, he once wrote, was the man who understood the "worth of abstract truth" while knowing intuitively how far it could be applied to human affairs. Tuckerman seemed to find that quality in Lincoln's movement toward emancipation, which he predicted would constitute a "new and advanced charter of American progress."[33]

III

In his speculations on the "latent" causes of the Civil War, those less discernible social and cultural characteristics that lay just beneath the surface, Tuckerman provided a bridge between the war and the romantic temperament that defined America in earlier years. He was not the only one to do so; indeed, there were other spokesmen more prominent than he who saw the coming of the war through the refractive lenses of American romanticism. If not unique, Tuckerman was among the most thoughtful of the early writers on the coming of the war, although one reviewer complained that he had kept the "true *casus belli*"—the slavery issue—a little too carefully out of sight, while indulging in the "rosy-colored hopes" characteristic of the "calm and conservative school."[34]

Tuckerman placed heavy responsibility for the conflict upon the slaveholding South, where the "peculiar institution" had taken such a heavy toll on both free and slave society, and where narrowness, arrogance, misunderstanding, and isolation had become distinguishing characteristics of the southern mind. At the same time, he did not absolve the North from a large share of the blame. Apathy and indifference toward the needs of the republic, and years of materialistic striving and personal gratification had produced its own provincialism, dulling sensitivity and weakening the country's ability to withstand the stresses and strains of sectional and partisan conflict. Patriotism, national feeling, public duty, and sacrifice were in decay. The moral decline was exacerbated by misguided and malevolent fanatics, both North and South, who drove a wedge deep into the heart of the republic.

The turning point came with unexpected suddenness in mid-April 1861. The attack on Fort Sumter jolted northerners out of their complacency, awakened the "dormant love of country," checked the decline of patriotic idealism, and restored hope to those who, like Tuckerman, had despaired of the republic's future. Heeding the appeal of their government (the "calm and conscientious tenor" of Lincoln's call for troops), thousands rose up to avenge the "wanton insults" against the national flag, putting aside their concern for self in favor of their nation's claims. Only the chastening experience of defeat could have so thoroughly aroused public sentiment. The surrender of the fort, the loss of the war's first martyrs struck down by a Baltimore mob as they marched to the defense of the capital, and the "sad and shameful . . . Sabbath struggle" at Manassas in July achieved what all earlier "pleadings and protests" had failed to achieve. "By no path but the valley of humiliation," wrote Tuckerman, "could the national will be guided to self-knowledge, the national rulers awakened to the vastness and the imminence of their duty, and the national heart be solemnized into the earnestness of self-sacrifice and intrepid purpose." The "Rebellion of the Slaveholders," testing the country's moral and physical resources, became the engine for moving the national character "in the right direction once again."[35]

Like some others who explored the causes, the nature, and the goals of the Civil War during its first days and weeks, Henry Tuckerman confidently believed that only good could come from the conflict. For years, he pointed out, discerning individuals had forecast "some convulsion" or calamity that would restore the republic to its "elemental purity." Tuckerman himself had predicted the inevitability of a national crisis, not the irrepressible conflict preached by politicians like Lincoln and William H. Seward, but rather a social upheaval that would reverse the self-centered and materialistically driven individualism that threatened to destroy the republic.

For Tuckerman, the attack on Fort Sumter was that crisis. When he wrote his treatise several months later, he felt the beneficial consequences of the war were already evident. The war had opened new "avenues of truth," purifying the national atmosphere of the "stagnant vapors" of corruption and subduing the "low throbbings of material care and selfish ambition." The people, he rejoiced, had been drawn together and taught mutual dependence. Whole communities became familiar with an "idea dearer than self." The "holy light of sacrifice" shone forth, distinguishing the patriot from the politician, the man from the coward, the heroic from the frivolous. "Youths," he observed, "suddenly have become men; women, angels of mercy, and pleasure-seekers responsible citizens." His rhetoric soared to new heights of romantic eloquence as he gave free rein to his imagination. The war now enabled Americans "to forswear private luxury and be loyal to public duty, to initiate frugal habits of life, to substitute . . . culture for gold-worship, comfort for ostentation, integrity for extravagance, principle for policy, contentment for ambition." Tuckerman envisioned nothing short of a radical change in the national character. His optimism was boundless.

The war also offered the opportunity to renew and purify the soul of the republic, as well as that of the people. The principle of emancipation, he felt, had already been established. There only remained the effort to purge public corruption, correct the nation's "charter" by amendments, nationalize the political parties, and reorganize the machinery of government. Tuckerman saw himself standing on the "brink of a great awakening." The possibilities were overwhelming. In short, the Civil War had become "the means to Romantic salvation for the American spirit."[36]

Tuckerman's euphoria was short-lived; he was bound to be disappointed. The harsh realities of a war that lasted much longer than anyone had expected, the fevered camps and blood-soaked battlefields, the political dissensions and partisan quarrels, the incompetence and even corruption in high places—soon overcame his optimism. The "holy light of sacrifice" seemed to dim in the face of a material prosperity that set new records for extravagance. It was questionable whether the republic's atmosphere was any more pure than it had been before. Although Tuckerman would continue to refer to the war as a "sacred object" and a "holy cause," his rhetoric no longer soared. He rejoiced at the resolution finally of the "vast and dark problem of slavery," and he could still insist that the war was "unparalleled in history for patriotic self-devotion and the lavish sacrifice of life and treasure." There were even echoes of his earlier belief that the war had converted "our self-indulgent young men" from luxury to self-denial, "made heroes," and "unmasked the selfish and treacherous," and undoubtedly there were examples to lend some credibility to his statements. The earlier enthusiasm, however, was lacking.[37]

Once he had left the serenity and solitude of his chamber, however, it was not easy for him to return. He continued to give much of his time and his literary energy to "patriotic service," although it is not clear how or in what capacity. He published a few war-related poems that more than anything revealed how disturbed he was with the war's toll in killed and wounded:

> For on the landscape's brightly pensive face,
>   War's angry shadows lie;
> His ruddy stains upon the woods we trace,
>   And in the crimson sky.

The work of the United States Sanitary Commission aroused his interest and support, partly perhaps, because it represented the kind of service and sacrifice he believed essential to the republic and partly because it was headed by his friend, New York's Unitarian minister Henry W. Bellows. In the spring of 1864, Tuckerman offered a special printing of a number of his fugitive (and clearly romantic) poems to the Commission's great New York Metropolitan Fair. Most of all, he spent the war years working on an ambitious study of European travel and travelers in the United States, a project he hoped would not only give him insight into the changing nature of the American character but also help him to place the impact of the Civil War in sharper perspective.[38]

Walt Whitman, looking back on the "four years of lurid, bleeding, murky, murderous war," despaired that the reality of the conflict could ever be conveyed in books. Who could "paint those years, with all their scenes?" Henry Tuckerman, however, looked to the future when historians, in "calm retrospect," should view the war's exciting incidents "in the chastened light of the past." Applying "new scientific methods of historical writing to the annals of our own country," they surely would be able to see the Civil War in the "sequence of memorable events . . . whereby it has pleased God to educate this nation, and induce moral results fraught with the highest duties and hopes of humanity." Perhaps there was hope for America yet.[39]

NOTES

Robert W. Johannsen delivered his Klement Lecture in 1994.

1. *Walt Whitman's Civil War*, comp. and ed. Walter Lowenfels (New York: Knopf, 1961), 21; Justin Kaplan, *Walt Whitman: A Life* (New York: Simon & Schuster, 1980), 261; *New York Herald*, Apr. 13, 1861 (morning ed.); *The Diary of George Templeton Strong*, 4 vols., ed. Allan Nevins and Milton Halsey Thomas (New York: Octagon Books, 1952), 3:118

2. *Diary of George Templeton Strong*, 3:119; *A Philadelphia Perspective: The Diary of Sidney George Fisher Covering the Years 1834–1871*, ed. Nicholas B. Wainright (Philadelphia Historical Society of Pennsylvania, 1967), 384; *Pittsburgh Post*, Apr. 15, 1861, in Howard C. Perkins, ed., *Northern Editorials on Secession*, 2 vols. (New York: D. Appleton–Century, 1942), 2:737.

3. Reply to a Committee from the Virginia Convention, Apr. 13, 1861, in Roy P. Basler *et al.*, eds., *The Collected Works of Abraham Lincoln*, 9 vols. (New Brunswick, N.J.: Rutgers Univ. Press, 1953), 4:329–31; Proclamation Calling Militia and Convening Congress, Apr. 15, 1861, ibid., 33–32; *Harper's New Monthly Magazine* 23 (June 1861): 121.

4. *New York Herald*, Apr. 11, 1861; *New York Times*, Apr. 3, 15, 1861; James Russell Lowell "The Pickens-and-Stealin's Rebellion," *Atlantic Monthly* 7 (June 1861): 757–63.

5. *Philadelphia Press*, Apr. 16, 1861, in Perkins, *Northern Editorials*, 2:742; Anna Ticknor, ed., *Life, Letters, and Journals of George Ticknor*, 2 vols. (Boston, 1876), 2:433; Orville J. Victor, ed., *Incidents and Anecdotes of the War: Together with Life Sketches of Eminent Leaders, and Narratives of the*

Most Memorable Battles for the Union (New York, 1862), iv; *New York Tribune*, Apr. 15, 1861; Oliver Wendell Holmes, "Bread and the Newspaper," *Atlantic Monthly* 8 (Sept. 1861): 346.

6. *Diary of George Templeton Strong*, 3:127–28; *New York Herald*, Apr. 21, 1861; *New York Times*, Apr. 21, 1861; Edward Everett, quoted in Paul Revere Frothingham, *Edward Everett, Orator and Statesman* (Boston: Houghton Mifflin, 1925), 417. The principal speeches delivered at New York's mass meeting are in Frank Moore, ed., *The Rebellion Record: A Diary of American Events, with Documents, Narratives, Illustrative Incidents, Poetry, Etc.*, vol. 1 (New York, 1862), 82–119.

7. Lowell, "The Pickens-and-Stealin's Rebellion," 757; *Harper's Magazine* 23 (July 1861): 266; *Albany Atlas and Argus*, Apr. 13, 1861, in Perkins, *Northern Editorials*, 2:692.

8. *Harper's* 23 (Aug. 1861): 411; *Philadelphia Perspective*, 385–86.

9. *New York Tribune*, Apr. 20, 1861; *Diary of George Templeton Strong*, 3:126.

10. *New York Tribune*, Apr. 20, 23, 1861; *Philadelphia Perspective*, 386; *New York Herald*, May 5, 1861; *New York Courier and Enquirer*, quoted in *Richmond Whig*, Apr. 30, 1861.

11. *Harper's* 23 (Aug. 1861): 414; Holmes, "Bread and the Newspaper," 346; Samuel Osgood, "The Pen and the Sword," *Harper's* 23 (Sept. 1861): 552–54; Hawthorne to William D. Ticknor, May 16, 1861, *Centenary Edition of the Works of Nathaniel Hawthorne*, vol. 18: *The Letters, 1857–1864* (Columbus: Ohio State Univ. Press, 1987), 379.

12. *Harper's* 23 (Oct. 1861): 704.

13. "A Few Words About the War," *Knickerbocker Magazine* 57 (June 1861): 651–52; *New York Herald*, Apr. 29, 1861; Samuel Osgood, "Valor," *Harper's* 23 (Aug. 1861): 407, 411; *Philadelphia North American*, May 6, 1861, in Perkins, *Northern Editorials*, 2:1074–75; *Vanity Fair* 3 (Apr. 27, 1861): 198.

14. *Wilkes-Barre Luzerne Union*, Apr. 17, 1861, in Perkins, *Northern Editorials*, 2:780–81; John Lothrop Motley to Wife and Daughters, June 14, 1861, *The Correspondence of John Lothrop Motley*, 2 vols., ed. George William Curtis (New York, 1889), 1:376.

15. *Harper's* 23 (Nov. 1861): 843–44. For the intellectual and literary responses to the Civil War, see Edmund Wilson, *Patriotic Gore: Studies in the Literature of the American Civil War* (New York: Oxford Univ. Press, 1962); George M. Fredrickson, *The Inner Civil War: Northern Intellectuals and the Crisis of the Union* (1965; repr. Urbana: Univ. of Illinois Press, 1993); Daniel Aaron, *The Unwritten War: American Writers and the Civil War* (New York: Knopf, 1973); and Stanton Garner, *The Civil War World of Herman Melville* (Lawrence: Univ. Press of Kansas, 1993).

16. Hawthorne to Henry A. Bright, Nov. 14, 1861, *Works of Nathaniel Hawthorne*, 18:422; Ralph L. Rusk, *The Life of Ralph Waldo Emerson* (New York: C. Scribner's Sons, 1949), 411; James Elliot Cabot, *The Memoir of Ralph Waldo Emerson*, 2 vols. (Boston, 1887), 2:599–601, 606–7, 784, 786–87; Ralph Waldo Emerson, "American Civilization," *Atlantic Monthly* 9 (Apr., 1862), 502–11.

17. Hawthorne to Horatio Bridge, May 26, 1861; Hawthorne to Francis Bennoch, [ca. July, 1861]; Hawthorne to Henry A. Bright, Nov. 14, 1861, all in *Works of Nathaniel Hawthorne*, 18:380–81, 387–88, 421.

18. George Bancroft to Dean Milman, Aug. 15, 1861, M. A. DeWolfe Howe, *The Life and Letters of George Bancroft*, 2 vols. (New York: Scribner's, 1908), 2:133, 138; John Lothrop Motley, *The Causes of the American Civil War: A Paper Contributed to the London Times* (New York, 1861); Motley to Wife and Daughters, June 14, 1861, *Correspondence of John Lothrop Motley*, 1:373, 376.

19. Thomas J. Pressly, *Americans Interpret Their Civil War* (Princeton, N. J.: Princeton Univ. Press, 1954), 12–15; John Steven Cabot Abbott, *The History of the Civil War in America: Comprising a Full and Impartial Account of the Origin and Progress of the Rebellion, of the Various Naval and Military Engagements, of the Heroic Deeds Performed by Armies and Individuals, and of Touching Scenes in the Field, the Camp, the Hospital, and the Cabin*, 2 vols. (New York, 1863), 1:1, 15.

20. Wilson, *Patriotic Gore*, 489; N[elson]. F. A[dkins].,"Tuckerman, Henry Theodore," *Diction-ary of American Biography*, 20 vols. (New York: Scribner's, 1936), 19:45. The only complete account of Tuckerman's life and writings, to which I am indebted, is an unpublished doctoral dissertation: Richard Grant Ellsworth, "Henry Theodore Tuckerman As Revealed in His Published Works" (University of Maryland, 1959).

21. Henry W. Bellows, *Address at the Funeral of Mr. Henry T. Tuckerman, at All Soul's Church, New York, December 21, 1871* (New York, 1872), 7–8, 10, 14; Tuckerman, "New England Philoso-phy," *The Optimist* (New York, 1850), 8, 12; Edgar Allan Poe, "Reviews of American Authors," in *Edgar Allan Poe: Essays and Reviews* (New York: Library of America, 1984), 871. For Tuckerman's fascination with Italy and his support of Italian independence, see his *The Italian Sketch Book, By an American* (Philadelphia, 1835); "Sardinia," *North American Review* 85 (Oct. 1857): 330–68; and "Guiseppe Garibaldi," ibid., 92 (Jan. 1861): 15–56.

22. Tuckerman, "Sketch of American Literature," in Thomas B. Shaw, *A Complete Manual of English Literature*, 1864 (New York, 1870), 477–78; Tuckerman, "James Fenimore Cooper," *North American Review* 89 (Oct. 1859): 303–7, 308–9; [Tuckerman], *Leaves From the Diary of a Dreamer, Found Among His Papers* (London, 1853), 153–54; Tuckerman, "American Literature," *North Ameri-can Review* 82 (Apr. 1856): 320, 346.

23. Tuckerman, "New England Philosophy," *The Optimist*, 3, 5–6, 14–15; Tuckerman, "American Society," *North American Review* 81 (July 1855): 26–50; [Tuckerman], *Leaves From the Diary*, 33, 44; Charles Knight, *Half-Hours with the Best Authors, with Short Biographical and Critical Notices*, 6 vols. (Philadelphia: Carey and Hart, 1848), 4:377; Rufus Wilmot Griswold, *The Prose Writers of America*, 2nd. ed. (Philadelphia: Carey and Hart, 1847), 43.

24. Ellsworth, "Henry Theodore Tuckerman," 110–11, 123. Tuckerman's pamphlet was published soon after the Union defeat at Bull Run, probably in late July 1861, by New York publisher James G. Gregory.

25. Tuckerman, *The Rebellion: Its Latent Causes and True Significance* (New York, 1861), 4–5, 45, 15.

26. Ibid., 17–20, 22, 37, 7, 18.

27. Ibid., 8–11.

28. Ibid., 20–22.

29. Ibid., 12–18.

30. Ibid., 18–25.

31. Ibid., 26–30.

32. Ibid., 30–32. For a more benign assessment of the cultural influence of newspapers, see Tuckerman's essay "Newspapers" in his collection of essays, *The Criterion; or the Test of Talk About Familiar Things* (New York, 1866), 252–91.

33. Tuckerman, *The Rebellion*, 32–35; Ellsworth, "Henry Theodore Tuckerman," 139n51; Tuck-erman, "Gouverneur Morris, the American Statesman," in Tuckerman, *Essays, Biographical and Critical; or, Studies of Character* (Boston, 1857), 421–22; Tuckerman, *America and Her Commenta-tors, with a Critical Sketch of Travel in the United States* (New York, 1864), 448–49.

34. *Knickerbocker Magazine* 58 (Dec. 1861): 537.

35. Tuckerman, *The Rebellion*, 45–46; Tuckerman, *America and Her Commentators*, 8, 44.

36. Tuckerman, *The Rebellion*, 46–48; Ellsworth, "Henry Theodore Tuckerman," 127–28.

37. Ellsworth, "Henry Theodore Tuckerman," 128; Tuckerman, *America and Her Commentators*, 450, 448; Tuckerman, "Note to Sketch of American Literature," in Thomas B. Shaw, *A Complete Manual of English Literature . . . With A Sketch of American Literature by Henry T. Tuckerman* (New York, 1870), 532.

38. Ellsworth, "Henry Theodore Tuckerman," 123; Tuckerman, "The Battle Summer," in *Lyrics of Loyalty*, arranged and edited by Frank Moore (New York, 1864), 109; Tuckerman, *A Sheaf of Verse Bound for the Fair* (New York, 1864).

39. *Walt Whitman's Civil War*, 271, 293; Tuckerman, "Virginia," *Continental Monthly* 4 (Dec. 1863), 690; Tuckerman, *America and Her Commentators*, 450. Tuckerman survived the Civil War by less than seven years. Declining health, including the almost total loss of his hearing, took its toll; he died in December 1871. Speaking of Tuckerman's contributions to "the fuller and riper culture of the country," Henry Bellows noted, "Hardly any one has been as attentive and careful an observer as he of the conditions of real progress in American art and letters and social refinements" (*Address at the Funeral of Mr. Henry T. Tuckerman*, 11).

❧ GEORGE RABLE ❧

News from Fredericksburg

*"Ill news hath wings, and with the wind
doth go, Comfort's a cripple, and comes ever slow."*
—Michael Drayton

❧ Like a man in a shooting gallery, George Rable has picked off one field of Civil War era historiography after another. And, according to reviewers, award committees, and book buyers, he has hit the bull's-eye every time. From Reconstruction violence to the lives of women on the Civil War home front, and from Confederate political philosophy to one of the major military campaigns of the war, Rable has cut a wide swath through the literature on the southern experience during the sectional conflict.

His first book, *But There Was No Peace: The Role of Violence in the Politics of Reconstruction* (1984), applied theories of counter revolution to the racial and political violence infesting the South after the war ended. His second, *Civil Wars: Women and the Crisis of Southern Nationalism* (1989), received the Jefferson Davis Award from the Museum of the Confederacy and the Julia Cherry Spruill Prize from the Southern Association of Women Historians. *The Confederate Republic: A Revolution against Politics* (1994), his next book, was a selection of the History Book Club.

Rable had just completed the manuscript for his next book, *Fredericksburg! Fredericksburg!*, when he delivered "News from Fredericksburg" in 2000. His lecture detailed the often speedy but usually unreliable news gathering and reporting of the Civil War, using the ill-considered Fredericksburg campaign as a case study. Moving beyond the familiar stories of preposterous rumors and mistaken casualty reports, Rable showed how the thirst for news—and the resulting sloppiness of the reporting—affected politics, home front morale, and even financial markets. Moreover, he suggests that the market for and the ready availability of news, however inaccurate, marked yet another way in which the Civil War helped usher Americans into the modern age by foreshadowing, in a sense, the embedded journalists of the early twenty-first century.

When *Fredericksburg! Fredericksburg!* appeared in 2001, it was immediately hailed as a model of the "new" campaign histories, which followed not only the movements of armies but also their effects on the political, social, economic, and moral facets of the Civil War. Among its many awards are the Lincoln Prize from the Lincoln and Soldiers Institute, the Distinguished Book Award in American History from the Society for Military History, and the Douglas Southall Freeman History Award from the Military Order of the Stars and Bars.

A recipient of a Ph.D. from Louisiana State University and longtime professor at Anderson University, Rable has held the Charles G. Summersell Chair in Southern History at the University of Alabama since 1998. His current project is on yet another field in Civil War history: religion. 〜

AMERICANS TODAY ARE INUNDATED with news available at any time on demand from a wide range of sources. Newspapers, magazines, twenty-four-hour news channels, and the Internet have made many of the standard clichés about an information age ring true. Shortly before the Civil War, the development of the telegraph and rapidly expanding newspaper circulation marked the beginning of a more modest but nevertheless significant revolution in communications. The war itself made the rapid and accurate transmission of information vital to government and citizens alike, though both Yankees and Rebels often suffered from the speedy arrival of unreliable news. This was never more true than after a major battle when politicians and families most wanted and needed the latest word.

Shortly after the fall elections in 1862, President Abraham Lincoln had replaced Gen. George B. McClellan as commander of the Army of the Potomac with Gen. Ambrose E. Burnside. The Federals had advanced quickly toward the Rappahannock River, but a series of delays had foiled Burnside's hope to steal a march on Robert E. Lee. As Federal troops began crossing the river on December 11 in preparation for a battle that would not begin until December 13, northerners and southerners alike nervously waited for word about this latest clash of arms.

Early in the morning of December 12, a lank, sad-looking man trod across the grass between the Executive Mansion and the War Department heading for one of his favorite haunts, the office of the United States Military Telegraph. There Abraham Lincoln often read aloud from Artemus Ward or some other humorist while waiting for the latest battlefield dispatches. Early news from Fredericksburg had been promising. On December 11, Sid Demming, chief Associated Press correspondent traveling with the Army of the Potomac, and J. G. Garland, a telegraph operator at Falmouth, had reported the shelling of the town, the successful crossing of the Rappahannock, and troops cheering Burnside. Their dispatches had gone directly to Anson Stager, superintendent of the military telegraph. Even a wire from Gen. Edwin V. Sumner to his wife—"Fredericksburg is ours. All well."—ended up in the pile of telegrams. Lincoln eagerly read the thin slips of paper hoping to learn of a Union triumph, but details remained sketchy. The Federal forces had secured a foothold, and there had been some skirmishing. So far so good.[1]

By the next morning, reports arrived of fighting on the Federal left. An early afternoon dispatch noted intense artillery and musket fire. "Cannot tell from this point who has the best of the fight," Garland added. Then at 2:50 P.M. a telegram from Stager brought the best news yet: word that "our forces have taken the first redoubt." An hour later, a wounded New York colonel was quoted as saying "we are getting the best of it." Yet the noise of the battle remained so intense that Stager could barely hear his instrument tapping out the messages, and he did report large numbers of wounded coming off the field. The *New York Times*, however, quoted Lincoln as saying, "The Rebellion is now virtually at an end." The president of course had made no such foolish statement, but hopes rose that Richmond would be in Union hands by New Year's.[2]

At 4:00 A.M. on December 14, Burnside wired the president that his troops held the "first ridge outside of the town" and "we hope to carry the crest today." But despite War Department rumors that the Army of the Potomac had "done well," Secretary of the Navy Gideon Welles remained skeptical. "There is something unsatisfactory or not entirely satisfactory in this intelligence." What little information was available seemed ominously vague. "They [War Department officials] fear to admit disastrous truths.

Adverse tidings are suppressed, with a deal of fuss and mystery, a shuffling over of papers and maps, and a far-reaching, vacant gaze at something undefined and indescribable." Then word started arriving of heavy casualties, and in official Washington, hopes for a Union victory began to fade. Tension mounted by the hour, especially because panicky friends of the administration jabbered about the fate of the Union hanging on this latest battle.[3]

Lincoln had sent one of his secretaries, John G. Nicolay, to visit Burnside. Before leaving Washington, Nicolay had told his wife that big things were afoot. Yet he doubted one great victory would break the rebellion's back and, reflecting his boss's fatalism, even suggested that "chance" played a large role in any war. He did not arrive at Falmouth until noon on December 14, and Lincoln impatiently telegraphed from Washington, "What news have you?" Nicolay witnessed looting in town and noted how vulnerable Burnside's men would be to enemy shelling, but what he conveyed to the president is unknown.[4]

That evening, reporter Henry Villard of the New York Tribune, who had slipped away from Falmouth hoping to scoop his rivals with news of the Fredericksburg disaster, called on Lincoln. The president impatiently pressed for details, and Villard finally blurted out the truth: this was the worst defeat ever suffered by the Army of the Potomac. Obviously stunned, Lincoln quietly remarked that perhaps the situation was not quite so bad as Villard had described.[5]

For once the usually talkative president did not tell one of his droll stories, but for several days afterward kept trying to come up with just the right anecdote to describe his plight. Subject to bouts of depression, Lincoln often used rustic and sometimes crude humor to shake off his own dark thoughts, but after Fredericksburg, his yarns seemed more pathetic than funny. Maybe he was like the boy with a fierce dog by the tail, unable to hang on but afraid to let go. Or like the old woman trying to sweep floodwaters from her cabin wondering whether her broom could outlast the storm. Many stuffy politicians, including cabinet members, could not appreciate such frontier tales and suspected that the president somehow misunderstood the gravity of the situation. Yet as Lincoln sadly explained to Congressman Isaac Arnold of Illinois, who had caught him reading Artemus Ward, "If I could not get momentary respite from the crushing burden I am constantly carrying, my heart would break."[6]

In this crisis, however, humor no longer helped much. Friends and visitors found Lincoln sadly subdued, not wallowing in self-pity, perhaps, but expressing a sense of despair bordering on powerlessness. Alarming reports coming in over the wires seemed to overwhelm him. Interrupting one congressman's litany of gloom, Lincoln cried out that more bad news would drive him "crazy." Nor would there be any respite from the information that flowed into the telegraph office, appeared in the newspapers, or escaped the lips of countless visitors. Inundated with reports, reliable and otherwise, Lincoln worried incessantly about the army and appeared terribly anxious. He mused about trading places with a soldier sleeping on the cold ground or even one killed in battle. In utter exasperation, he told a friend, "If there is a worse place than Hell, I am in it."[7]

Along with details about the battle came word of the casualties, the information of most importance to countless families. Wildy optimistic Confederates estimated Union losses at 20,000, and many Federals who witnessed the fighting on December 13 would have found such a figure quite believable. The New York Tribune reported a remarkably accurate 13,500 casualties on December 18, but some Republican editors, worried about sagging morale and eager to fend off political recrimination, published much lower numbers. Ironically, this fed skepticism among press-wary soldiers. It also played into the hands of Democrats who plausibly claimed the actual numbers were much higher and reflected the Lincoln administration's mismanagement of the war. Conservative editors could therefore use the widely bruited-about figure of 20,000 to badger Republicans while patriotically and safely praising the common soldiers' unparalleled valor.[8]

As for the Confederates, their triumph had in its own way been costly. Even a great victory carries many sorrows, one Richmond editor philosophized, and soon southern families suffered the pangs of scanning newspapers' casualty lists while praying to be spared the sight of that one sacred name among the dead or wounded or missing. In Milledgeville, it required three columns to record the losses from various Georgia regiments. Richmond and Charleston newspapers reported casualties almost immediately, but nothing appeared in many North Carolina or Georgia papers for another couple weeks. The Richmond Enquirer had the worst timing: three columns of casualties on Christmas Eve, two more on Christmas Day. In the Confederate capital, fragmentary reports dribbled out bad news to anxious family and friends, thus lengthening the agonizing suspense. Across the hinterlands of course, word came still more slowly.[9]

In the North, the news spread too quickly. An earlier attempt to have the Associated Press compile accurate casualty reports had foundered on the highly competitive nature of the newspaper trade. Reporters gathered lists from regimental muster rolls, but clearly the emphasis was on speed rather than accuracy. On Monday, December 15, as the Army of the Potomac prepared to recross the Rappahannock, the *New York Tribune*'s front page contained nothing but finely printed casualty lists and dispatches detailing a bloody battle at Fredericksburg, Virginia. Over the next several days, all the New York papers filled their columns with the names of the dead, wounded, and missing. Some editors shielded their readers a bit by placing this information on a back page, but people gathered at newspaper offices for updated lists. Within a week, the smaller papers were publishing casualty reports from their states; letters from particular regiments included more detailed information.[10]

Name after endless name in long printed columns drove home the costs of war. In Charleston, South Carolina, by December 20, the first meager battlefield reports appeared along with telegrams tersely announcing the fate of particular soldiers. Young Emma Holmes found that her diary had become "nothing but a record of death." In New York City, that same day, Elizabeth Freeman, though grateful for the safety of her son, commented about how word of heavy casualties at Fredericksburg had depressed everyone. From Lancaster, Wisconsin, Catherine Eaton advised her husband that only God's "restraining power" had saved his life. News of a great battle always cast families into pits of helpless anxiety. There was no way for any of them to be ready for the worst news if it came and their darkest fears were realized.[11]

After receiving the first accounts of a bloody battle in Virginia, a Michigan woman cried for three days before learning that her son had emerged unscathed. Many soldiers sent short notes to relieve the anxiety at home, but impatient families clamored for immediate news. Henry Wadsworth Longfellow fretted over his wounded nephew, a sergeant in the bloodied 20th Massachusetts. But he received no answer to a telegram sent to the Sanitary Commission and so wrote to a nurse in Washington and to Senator Charles Sumner begging for information. All too often, no word came, no name on a list, no account of a regiment's losses. Prayers and hopes became focused, selfish, and almost superstitious; a Maine volunteer perceptively remarked, "The peculiar feature of war is that each expects someone else to fall."[12]

As soldiers themselves recognized, rumors and false reports heightened fear at home. Men reported to have been badly wounded or killed might in fact have come through the battle without a scratch. A soldier would be listed as slightly wounded or rapidly improving on one day, and the next day he would be dead. In Madison Parish, Louisiana, Kate Stone learned that a Lieutenant Stone—not related to her family—had been killed at Fredericksburg. On Christmas morning, an elderly neighbor informed the family that the dead man was in fact Kate's brother. A hastily procured newspaper soon confirmed the earlier account. Despite their relief, the Christmas celebration was ruined. The family later learned that their boy had been slightly wounded after all.[13] For such families news of casualties eclipsed all other news of the battle.

In the North, however, reports of both the casualties and the fighting were equally depressing, as despair over one simply reinforced despair over the other. By December 15, with news of the clash along with the first of the wounded arriving, a deepening gloom spread over the capital as politicians and ordinary citizens began to digest and assess the latest word from the battlefield. Although Senator Zachariah Chandler of Michigan feared that the cursed Rebels might "skedaddle" before Burnside polished them off, he admitted that the fight so far had only produced casualties. Other politicians and generals sounded much more pessimistic. The word "defeat" began cropping up in correspondence and no doubt on street corners along with second-guessing over Burnside's tactics. News of the army's safe withdrawal across the Rappahannock hardly lifted anyone's spirits. This was worse than McClellan's retreat from the Virginia Peninsula during the summer of 1862, concluded the *Chicago Tribune*'s Washington correspondent. A Mexican diplomat overheard people in Washington saying that southern independence now seemed assured.[14]

To forestall the spread of defeatism, the War Department clumsily attempted to prevent newspaper correspondents from telegraphing details of the battle, especially information about the staggering losses. Yet the war had revolutionized the use of the telegraph in reporting and newspapers had roughly tripled the amount of space devoted to telegraphic dispatches. So maladroit attempts at official censorship were doomed to fail. Their only result was delay and confusion in transmitting casualty lists. Even Republicans complained that these efforts—presumably directed by Secretary of War Edwin Stanton (though some suspected Burnside)—only aroused public suspicion and made the defeat look worse.[15]

Away from Washington, the first accounts of the fighting had, as usual, been breathlessly optimistic. "All Glorious on the Rappahannock," "Terrific Bombardment Yesterday," "Fredericksburg in Ashes," blared the *Chicago Tri-*

bune on December 12. Across the North, Republican newspapers reported in much the same vein; a Rhode Island editor crowed that those who had despaired over earlier delays did not really know Burnside.[16] News that the Army of the Potomac had captured Fredericksburg produced more favorable reports the next day. The road to Richmond appeared open.[17] On the morning of December 14, prospects remained bright. The *New York Times* lauded Burnside for concentrating his forces to defeat the Rebels. But the day's telegraphic dispatches began hinting at a bloody defeat.[18]

By December 15, more details were slipping through the War Department censors, but Republican newspapers remained at least publicly cheerful. Expectations of still more fighting and predictions that the campaign could prove decisive persisted. Sanguine editors concluded that the Saturday engagement had tested enemy strength: now Burnside knew where to hit Lee's army. More ominously, a Boston editor—perhaps without meaning to—suddenly sounded cautious: "The news from our army at Fredericksburg contains nothing which should weaken hope or occasion despondency." The size of Lee's army (estimated by the *New York Tribune* at 130,000 troops) had been responsible for what a few papers were at least willing to call a "repulse," though some editors still found no reason for discouragement.[19]

The following day, several papers still carried outdated accounts of Gen. William B. Franklin's apparent success on the Federal left and the impending attack that would finish the job. Even word of Burnside's withdrawal from Fredericksburg hardly softened the bluff optimism. Rumors of an expedition under Gen. Nathaniel P. Banks sailing from New York to cooperate with the Army of the Potomac also made the rounds. It remained an article of faith that the Confederates were in trouble and the rebellion was tottering. Burnside would soon renew the fight with reinforcements from another direction. He would yet triumph over Lee, a "slow man," according to the *Philadelphia Inquirer.* Only the timid would despair, declared a Connecticut editor. Bluster, however, proved a thin disguise for desperation. "Don't treat the affair at Fredericksburg as a disaster," John W. Forney, a staunch Lincoln friend, frantically wired his managing editor in Philadelphia.[20]

Partisan demagogues, one Boston newspaper warned, could turn a temporary setback into an excuse for despair over the Union cause. But the demagogues hardly required assistance. Loud denials that the army was demoralized after withdrawing from Fredericksburg soon flooded the North. What had been lost aside from casualties, one prominent church publication asked, and then coldly added that the North had plenty more young men to send into the ranks. Lincoln himself reportedly endorsed this same cruel calculus, remarking that even if the Army of the Potomac kept suffering the same proportion of casualties but kept fighting Lee, the Confederates would soon be "wiped out to the last man." One of Lincoln's private secretaries later quoted the president as saying at this time, "No general yet found can face the arithmetic, but the end of the war will be at hand when he shall be discovered."[21] Yet such reasoning, even by Lincoln, could not paper over the defeat. One editor who actually used the word "disaster" still maintained that the "heart of the nation does not waver." The logic grew ever more strained. Advances and retreats occurred in any war, and indeed Burnside's withdrawal only proved his military prowess. Such a clever maneuver elicited comparisons to Napoleon and even the improbable assertion that Lee had been outfoxed. All the more reason then, several editors announced, to launch another drive toward Richmond. Efforts to pooh-pooh rumors that the Army of the Potomac would soon go into winter quarters signified more fear than hope. "Vigorous blows," declared the *Boston Evening Transcript*, could still defeat the Confederacy without conciliation or compromise.[22]

The brave front inevitably cracked. Given the high expectations for the campaign, recognition of the reality was a galling, often agonizing exercise. Another Union offensive had failed. Why had a decisive blow not been struck? This question haunted moderate Republicans. The editor of the bellwether *Springfield Republican* sharply questioned any "senseless palaver about strategy" to conceal the truth. The army had not, however, been destroyed or demoralized, and a distinction should be drawn between temporary "indignation and discouragement" and genuine "alarm" for the nation's future.[23]

Such mincing of words could hardly convince many Republicans much less buttress public morale. It became increasingly difficult to temper disappointment with hope. In a dispatch composed on the evening of December 13, *New York Times* correspondent William Swinton reported that whatever anyone chose to call it, Fredericksburg had been a "defeat" and "a black day in the calendar of the Republic." One Democratic editor observed that even if Burnside advanced again with reinforcements, he would occupy a less favorable position than McClellan had held in June. Given the inflated estimates of Rebel numbers (some 200,000 according to the *New York Herald* and other papers), Burnside's tactics seemed even more foolhardy. Newspaper maps—often far from accurate—nevertheless showed the strength of the Confederate positions and bolstered such popular perceptions. Shocking descriptions of a battlefield strewn with dead and wounded only added to the gloom. As more reports came in, despondency spread rapidly—especially in cities where anxious crowds gathered around newspaper office bulletin boards.[24]

By December 17, even some Republican newspapers were calling the Fredericksburg affair a "disaster." The *Albany Evening Journal*, edited by Secretary of State William H. Seward's ally Thurlow Weed, bemoaned the "butcheries in which the flower of our youth is sacrificed." Newspapers muted criticism of Burnside, but Democrats pointedly ridiculed Republican efforts to minimize the catastrophe and began hinting that the real responsibility rested in Washington.[25]

Even political sophisticates sounded downhearted and befuddled. In New York, George Templeton Strong had eagerly scanned the first newspaper bulletins describing the crossing of Federal forces on December 11 but was not sure whether to interpret the sketchy information as evidence of a setback. Word that "one redoubt" had been taken by the Federals led Elizabeth Blair Lee in Silver Spring, Maryland, to speculate that perhaps this time a Union army had "outwitted" the Rebels, "a great comfort after frequent blunders." Despite delays in receiving information, civilian opinion in the North likely mirrored Lincoln's emotional roller coaster—early hopes, growing doubts, and then bitter disappointment. Although wary observers had steeled themselves for another disaster, for a while they too accepted the common newspaper fiction that Burnside had only been testing the enemy defenses.[26]

Cringing at early reports of the carnage, Anna M. Ferris, a forty-seven-year-old Quaker, dreaded "another Sabbath profaned by scenes of horror and strife." War-weary northern civilians had to face the reality of a bloody repulse though some readily declared—with how much assurance is unclear—that the results could have been much worse. Hopes persisted that Burnside might renew the attack, but word of another defeat spread rapidly across the northern states. Had the tide now turned in the Rebels' favor? A few conservative Democrats and McClellan supporters actually crowed over the debacle—some reportedly smiling at the Republicans' discomfiture. Yet many citizens just appeared confused—unable to draw firm conclusions from fragmentary reports—and so went about their business. With the Christmas shopping season in full swing, people were spending money and enjoying amusements despite the tragedy along the Rappahannock. Newspapers not only allowed the home folks to vicariously participate in campaigns but also aroused deep anxieties and heightened the tensions of ordinary people waiting to hear about their friends and relatives. Thus word of the losses at Fredericksburg proved more disconcerting than informative. To politically sensitive observers, the situation appeared chaotic.[27]

Newspapers also helped people maintain ties between home and camp, but many civilians sought escape from the seemingly relentless news. The telegraph and photography brought the war home to people who might have preferred to avert their eyes and ears. False hopes, recurring alarms, cycles of exaltation and despair all frayed nerves. Depending on one's perspective, there was always too much war news or never enough. For their part, soldiers doubted that anyone at home really understood the realities of war, though some thought the Fredericksburg disaster might wake people up. Yet even as Burnside's boys inevitably wondered about how their families were reacting to the latest news, they also resented public impatience. A member of the 10th Pennsylvania Reserves wrote a scathing letter to his hometown newspaper sarcastically inquiring what the "on to Richmond, stay at home guards" thought about all the casualties. Men unwilling to shoulder even their fair burden of taxes kept screaming for generals to advance as if soldiers were mere machines that could be thrown into battle without considering the limits of human endurance or the terrible costs.[28]

Leading Republicans desperately searched for arguments to shore up public morale. A defeat and even a retreat did not justify murmuring and despair, several editors declared with perhaps more hope than faith. Correspondents dismissed reports of demoralization and claimed the army would quickly regain its fighting spirit. However, so long as disloyal Democratic newspapers spread alarmist news and cheered each Rebel victory, even patriots might waver.[29]

"The republican party is forever played out now the last Battle was its death knell," a disgusted New Yorker wrote to his bother in the army. Scathing editorials ridiculing Lincoln and lampooning official incompetence reflected growing confidence among administration opponents.[30] Although overblown claims that the nation was perishing likely fell on deaf ears, Democrats more convincingly pointed that the American people would not be patient forever. "The war is a failure!" one leading conservative newspaper screamed, and the country could no longer abide the administration's disastrous course. Even the moderate and temperate *Harper's Weekly* believed "matters are rapidly ripening for a military dictatorship."[31]

Administration critics charged that orders from Washington had produced the Fredericksburg debacle, an accusation that stung Republicans. The War Department had allegedly forced a reluctant Burnside to attack the Rebels' impregnable positions. Even a few Republicans acknowledged that Lincoln and Stanton had faltered, but Democrats insisted that direct orders from General-in-Chief Henry W. Halleck and the president had sent hundreds of poor soldiers to their deaths.[32]

On December 19, while perusing several newspapers, Burnside grew agitated over the acerbic editorials that blasted Lincoln, Halleck, and Stanton. "I'll put a stop to that," he abruptly announced. Despite protests from several staff officers, he refused to dodge responsibility, drafted a public letter, and quickly arranged to meet with Lincoln. When the general reached Washington about 10 P.M. the next evening, the president had already gone to bed but had not been able to sleep because of dyspepsia, and so hurriedly pulled on his trousers for a late-night meeting. Lincoln appeared depressed by criticism growing out of the Fredericksburg affair and so expressed much relief over the general's willingness to admit mistakes. The president warmly thanked Burnside for being the first person to ever lift any responsibility from his shoulders. Some time after midnight, Burnside returned to Willard's Hotel to put the finishing touches on his mea culpa. The next day he again conferred with Lincoln and also with Halleck and Stanton. Lincoln reassured the nervous general-in-chief that Burnside was his "real friend," but the impatient secretary of war sharply rebuked the general for not having his letter ready for publication. Even the affable Burnside bristled at this remark, though Lincoln cajoled Stanton into making a fulsome apology.[33]

Burnside addressed the letter to Halleck and backdated it to December 17 to avoid the appearance that someone in the administration had forced him to write it. After describing the army's movements, the battle, and the reasons for withdrawing from Fredericksburg, Burnside explained how he had decided on the Fredericksburg route against the advice of Lincoln, Halleck, and Stanton but that the administration "left the whole management in my hands, without giving me orders." He took complete responsibility for the defeat.[34]

Republican editors seemingly took the letter at face value. Burnside had displayed remarkable candor, and his plain honesty should have restored public confidence. Yet the general had no real political allies. Unlike McClellan or certain radical Republican generals, no partisan faction felt any great loyalty toward him, and so when Republicans praised his letter, they did so because it deflected criticism away from the Lincoln administration. Presidential secretary John Hay published an anonymous editorial in a leading Missouri newspaper lauding Burnside for taking responsibility and dismissing criticism of the government as unfounded. Hay criticized both conservative and radical generals but unstintingly praised Burnside while providing details on meetings with Lincoln that could only be known by an insider. Whether the statements reflected Lincoln's views is impossible to prove, but Hay clearly stated the administration's hope that political damage from the Fredericksburg disaster could somehow be contained. In modern parlance, he was trying to "spin" the story to the President's advantage. Mistakes had been made, Republicans admitted, but the question of responsibility remained up in the air. At least Burnside's frankness and sincerity offered a welcome change from the evasions and maneuverings of ambitious generals and conniving politicians.[35]

Leading Democrats would have none of it and detected political chicanery in a document whose timing and content proved so helpful to an administration desperate to defend itself. "Very Remarkable, Very Curious, Very Generous and Very Naïve Letter from General Burnside," ran the headline in the *New York Herald*. Burnside, a Pennsylvania editor complained, "has stepped forward to shield the blundering Halleck, the ambitious Secretary of War, and the imbecile President."[36]

Yet if Lincoln merited criticism for his course since Antietam, it was more for indecisiveness than interference. Despite the seemingly deft maneuvering during the cabinet crisis, the election defeats and now the terrible news from the Army of the Potomac left him both depressed and baffled. He had hardly lost his political touch but seemed less sure-footed. A case in point was his bizarre letter of congratulations to Burnside's battered army. Although the magnitude of the defeat was now painfully obvious, the president claimed that "the attempt was not an error, nor the failure other than an accident." After commending the troops for their skill and bravery, he congratulated them that the number of casualties had been "comparatively so small." Here again was Lincoln's sometimes odd sense of fatalism, this time combined with an incredible and misleading assessment of the battle's human costs.[37]

The president's letter boosted neither military nor public confidence. "Compared to what," the First Corps artillery chief exploded after reading the odd comment on the casualties. Only a few wishful thinkers either denied that Fredericksburg was a disaster or embraced Lincoln's fatalistic explanation.[38] Instead, the president's peculiar comments only offered more political ammunition to administration opponents. "As well attempt to hide the reeking graves of the soldiers under a coat of whitewash as varnish over the errors of the Generals and the blunders of the Cabinet," an Albany editor sniffed. The president wrote a "feeble letter," the *Boston Post* thundered, while "the bones may bleach, the wives and mothers weep, the soldiers murmur, the officers remonstrate, in vain; there is nobody to blame; a bloody sacrifice was not an error, but an accident."[39]

Perhaps official Washington was running out of excuses; rationalizations had simply been piled on top of each other. Two days after the battle, the *New York Tribune* had predicted that Burnside would soon force the Confederates into the "decisive struggle of the war." Despite the heavy casualties, reinforcements would allow him to strike the Rebels again. By December 19, Horace Greeley was claiming that Burnside had "outgeneraled" Lee in withdrawing his army from Fredericksburg and that the Army of the Potomac would have easily won any battle fought on equal ground. He even swallowed Lincoln's lame explanation for the battle's outcome, and a Christmas Day editorial declared that aside from the casualties little had been lost at Fredericksburg. The *New York Herald* waspishly commented: "At this Christmas time, when good fairies fill the air, we can hardly wonder at the sudden miracle which has shown us the Fredericksburg affair in its true light, and given us occasion for national joy instead of national sorrow."[40]

Confederate leaders must have been greatly relieved by news of the victory because like Lincoln, Jefferson Davis was feeling the political heat. Despite the losses at Antietam, the Confederate president had the utmost confidence in Lee's army, but the situation in the West was deteriorating. On December 10, Davis had left Richmond for Chattanooga to visit the faction-riven Army of Tennessee. During his stay with Braxton Bragg's troops at Murfreesboro, the president consulted with several generals about strategic and command problems. Back in Chattanooga on December 14, he received a War Department telegram about fighting at Fredericksburg. Anxious for news, he considered returning to Richmond immediately, but soon word arrived that Lee had handily beaten back the Yankee assaults. Varina Davis later passed along rumors that Burnside had made a fire-breathing speech to his generals right before the battle and that these same officers had later refused to renew the attacks.[41]

Burnside's crossing of the Rappahannock on December 11 had actually heartened folks in Richmond, where Lee's own confidence shaped official attitudes and spilled into the streets. Even with the rumble of artillery in the distance, people seemed most worried that the Yankees would avoid a decisive contest. Temporarily disquieting rumors that Lee was falling back made for anxious moments, though reports of spirited fighting and brave counterattacks buttressed hope. On Sunday morning, December 14, despite suspicions of renewed fighting, people went to church as usual and the capital appeared calm.[42]

With War Department permission, newspaper reporters had gone to Fredericksburg. Even with paper shortages and shrinking dailies placing war news at a premium, dispatches running a column and more began appearing a couple days after the battle, and soon the Richmond papers were crowing about how the outnumbered Army of Northern Virginia had easily repulsed the enemy. Most accounts adopted a dashing, fearless tone and were short on detail and long on praise for Confederate valor. No one bothered to mention temporary anxious moments on the Confederate right, though most readers cared little for tactical fine points anyway. What folks longed for was good news, but because of telegraph problems, reports of Lee's victory traveled slowly beyond Virginia.[43]

For many civilians, anxiety and prayers for deliverance quickly gave way to thanks for another victory—for which Lee, Jackson, and God Almighty received lavish praise. North Carolina plantation mistress Catherine Edmondston believed that Lee had allowed the Federals to cross the Rappahannock so he could "cut them off in detail." Word of casualties (including false reports of J. E. B. Stuart killed and A. P. Hill taken prisoner) naturally tempered the rejoicing. Like many northern civilians, southerners had learned not to credit vague accounts of great victories and so eagerly sought detailed confirmation. Eventually, reliable news of Lee's triumph erased doubts, but success brought its own improbable rumors. Had Burnside been killed? Was McClellan back in command? Was the Army of the Potomac in a state of mutiny? Civilians with access to northern newspapers or who devoured the excerpts in the Confederate press mulled over the confusing and contradictory accounts. They welcomed signs of their enemies' despair, including word that the Yankees no longer found Lincoln's jokes very funny.[44]

Still reeling from the news of Burnside's defeat, Lincoln faced a political firestorm in Washington. A Peace Democrat's call for the president's impeachment was easily dismissed, but Republican confidence in the administration, already shaky after the recent election losses, was eroding fast. Panic-stricken Ohio congressman William Parker Cutler decided that "God alone can take care of us." But even the Almighty recently seemed to favor Rebels and Democrats. Angry radicals began calling for a cabinet shake-up as soon as the first bad news from Fredericksburg reached the capital. Nervous moderates acknowledged the political fallout from the battle. "The President and cabinet stink awfully in the nostrils of the American people," one conservative New Englander groused.[45] A caucus of Republican senators convinced Seward to resign, but regaining his political footing, Lincoln managed to weather the storm and even keep his beleaguered secretary of state.

Unfortunately for the administration, no good news came from abroad either: the possibility of European intervention remained distinctly alive. Even though the British cabinet had recently rejected a French mediation proposal, American diplomats nervously awaited the latest war news. In London, a report that Burnside had taken Fredericksburg momentarily raised hopes, but by Christmas Day, news of the Army of the Potomac's defeat had dashed them and dampened holiday spirits. Henry Adams feared "another Antietam, only worse" and began "screwing [his] courage up to face the list of killed and wounded." His father, Minister Charles Francis Adams Sr., wrote in his diary about a "profitless war," predicted that Burnside was finished, and suspected that both sides had perhaps worn themselves out fighting.[46]

Extensive reporting and editorial comment by the conservative *Times* of London presented an especially gloomy picture of American affairs. "Another tremendous disaster has fallen on Federal arms," the *Times* commented on December 29. "So great has been the carnage, so complete and undeniable the defeat, that the North appears stunned by the blow." The Confederacy looked to be on the verge of winning independence. Even in England, the rumors swirled: McClellan would soon regain command; massive desertions might weaken Federal armies; Lincoln might well retreat on emancipation. Karl Marx raged over Union failures and even lent credence to the canard that Burnside had been forced into attacking Lee by the press—specifically the *New York Tribune*. Word of the cabinet crisis confirmed that despair had engulfed the northern states. A New York correspondent for the *London Times* described the soldiers' demoralization: "Slaughtered in vain at Fredericksburg with as much method as if they had been swine at Cincinnati, they ask one another why they should risk another such contest, without hope of achieving anything by it." Another reporter called December 13 a "memorable day to the historian of the Decline and Fall of the American Republic." The obvious conclusion hardly needed stating: it was now time to end the fighting.[47]

Similar reports of gloom and urgent requests for the latest information came from Brussels, Rome, and St. Petersburg. Northern diplomats acknowledged their fears but clung to their hopes.[48] As well they might. The news from Fredericksburg dealt another blow to the Union cause, though it hardly created a groundswell for European intervention. Proposals for mediation, though not entirely dead, had reached their political apogee and were steadily losing support, especially in Great Britain.

Ironically, given how closely the British had recently come to intervention, Confederates now doubted that the Europeans would ever act. Bitter disappointments, including the failure of the so-called "cotton famine" to force the politicians' hand, had greatly frustrated southern diplomats. Even news of the "glorious victory at Fredericksburg," propagandist Henry Hotze admitted, hardly affected the fainthearted British cabinet. According to an agent of North Carolina governor Zebulon Vance, the English government "is too well pleased to see both North & South exhausted to stop the strife." No loyal Confederate should expect anything from Europeans; only more Fredericksburgs would advance the southern cause. The Confederates appeared to be winning their independence on the battlefield, minister James Mason conceded, but neither Prime Minister Palmerston nor his opponents yet favored diplomatic recognition. Democratic victories in northern elections, heavy Federal losses at Fredericksburg, and the "derangement" of the Lincoln government had little influence on cautious British politicians.[49]

The same news and speculation that had spread from the battlefield across the North and to European capitals also rebounded back to the camps. Soldiers eagerly read newspapers for the "latest intelligence" from Washington. News of political commotion back home, including the cabinet crisis, and the latest diplomatic rumors also affected army morale. Soldiers dreaded change, especially the unknown, and signs of political disturbances made them uneasy. "The troubles at Washington," a Twelfth Corps general feared, "are casting a greater gloom over the country than the affairs of the army." Rumors circulated that Lincoln himself might soon be out and a military dictator appointed in his place.[50]

Confederates paid equally close attention to affairs in Washington, welcoming reports of division in the North and Yankees devouring their own. Snippets from the northern press made pleasant reading for Rebels settling into winter camps. Accounts of the cabinet crisis cheered Richmond and the rest of the South and became yet more evidence to show that the attempted subjugation of the southern people was bound to fail and that the war would soon be over. Speculations aside, one point was clear to most Confederates: Lee's victory at Fredericksburg had created a political crisis among their enemies.[51]

The New York gold market—that era's equivalent of the Dow—provided the most sensitive barometer of the battle's impact and the effect of the Washington political tremors. With news that Burnside had crossed the Rappahannock, gold prices had briefly fallen but by December 16 had crept up again as the first discouraging accounts from Fredericksburg reached New York. Greenbacks steadily lost value for the rest of December and the first two months of 1863 while gold prices rose from the low 130s to the high 150s. According to the newspapers, Fredericksburg had forced up gold prices because people assumed that the Treasury would likely print more greenbacks. And foreign investors, having lost faith in the Union's chances for survival, were also reportedly buying gold. Experts disagreed about whether the combination of Fredericksburg and the cabinet crisis had spooked the markets, but increasing gold prices reflected sagging public confidence in the administration. A Baltimore editor forthrightly blamed the government's timid military policies for speculation and gold hoarding. After Fredericksburg the value of government bonds dropped even more precipitously than the value of the greenbacks.[52]

Sophisticated Confederates followed the New York financial markets, and so rising gold prices buoyed southern hopes. One War Department official heard that Confederate bonds were selling briskly in New York. Regardless of wishful thinking about a northern economic collapse, the Confederacy suffered from much steeper inflation; consumer prices in the United States had increased only modestly. However, because workers' wages held steady throughout 1862, even small price hikes eroded incomes and pinched family budgets. As usual, perceptions mattered a great deal, especially given the absence of reliable statistical data for the national economy, and labor unrest in the cities grew. The macroeconomic picture, however dimly perceived, while not exactly stormy, did evince some dark clouds on the horizon.[53]

In the era of the telegraph, financial information was so quickly transmitted that much of the North was being integrated into a national market, a development that seemed remarkable in hindsight. At the time, however, military news mattered most to people. The first dispatches from a battlefield could be completely misleading, though fairly reliable reports about Fredericksburg had reached northern newspaper readers within a matter of days. Farmers, housewives, grocers, bankers, congressmen, and the president—

everybody—could read about the latest disaster for Union arms. The news traveled a bit slower in the Confederacy, but everyone there was just as eager for the latest word. Politicians and investors had precipitated the northern cabinet crisis and surge in gold prices on the basis of fragmentary reports from the battlefield. And fresh daily dispatches produced a glut of news that, whether trustworthy or not, fostered a sense of constant crisis, speeding up the pace and intensity of life at home and in camp.

Modern war, as Clausewitz observed, mobilized the resources of a whole people, and these included thoughts and emotions.[54] Energy and enthusiasm replaced deliberation; vigor substituted for reflection. Even the literary world got caught up in this whirl. Stunned by word of the carnage along the Rappahannock, Herman Melville hastily scrawled a few lines of verse "for the slain at Fredericksburg," though the evocation of "patriot ghosts" ascending had such a slapdash quality that he did not bother to publish them after the war in *Battle-Pieces*.[55] News, and even literature, was becoming disposable. But ephemeral and inaccurate information—false alarms about bloody engagements, Pollyannish accounts of real carnage, and, of course, incomplete and false reports of casualties, all kept Americans on edge as the expanding business of news carried them into a modern age where the world's problems would never be far away or easily ignored. The news from Fredericksburg thus became a harbinger of the nation's future even as it promised for the present nothing but the continuation of civil war, with its mounting anxieties and staggering costs.

NOTES

George Rable delivered his Klement Lecture in 2000.

1. David Horner Bates, *Lincoln in the Telegraph Office: Recollections of the United States Military Telegraph Corps during the Civil War* (New York: Century Co., 1907), 113; Earl Schenck Miers, *Lincoln Day by Day: A Chronology, 1809–1865*, 3 vols. (Dayton, Ohio: Morningside, 1991), 3:155. Sid Denning to Anson Stager, Dec. 11, 12, 1862; J. G. Garland to Stager, Dec. 11, 1862 (three dispatches); A. H. Caldwell to Stager, Dec. 12, 1862, O. H. Dorrance to Stager, Dec. 12, 1862; E. V. Sumner to Mrs. Sumner, Dec. 11, 1862, all in Abraham Lincoln Papers, Library of Congress (LC), Washington, D.C. The presence of these telegrams in the Lincoln papers strongly suggests that the president either read them at the War Department or they were later sent to the Executive Mansion. The Associated Press had a generally good relationship with the administration and became a quasi-official source of war news. Richard A. Schwarzlose, *The Newsbrokers*, 2 vols. (Evanston, Ill.: Northwestern Univ. Press, 1989), 1:242–54.

2. A. H. Caldwell to Anson Stager, Dec. 13, 1862 (three dispatches); Sid Denning to Stager, Dec. 13, 1862; J. G. Garland to Stager, Dec. 13, 1862 (two dispatches); Stager to Edwin M. Stanton, Dec. 13, 1862 (two dispatches), all in Lincoln Papers, LC; *New York Times*, Dec. 13, 1862. The reference to the "first reboubt" being taken likely referred to the false reports during the late afternoon that some Second Corps troops had gained a foothold on Marye's Heights.

3. *War of the Rebellion: A Compilation of the Official Records of the Union and Confederate Armies*, 128 vols. (Washington, D.C.: Government Printing Office, 1880–1901), ser. 1, vol. 21:65 (hereafter *OR*, with all references to this volume unless otherwise stated); Gideon Welles, *The Diary of Gideon Welles, Secretary of the Navy under Lincoln and Johnson*, ed. Howard K. Beale, 3 vols. (New York: W. W. Norton, 1960), 1:192; *Supplement to the Official Records of the Union and Confederate Armies*, 95 vols. (Wilmington, N.C.: Broadfoot, 1994–), pt. 1, vol. 3:671 (hereafter *OR: Supplement*); George Thornton Fleming, ed., *Life and Letters of Alexander Hays* (Pittsburgh, Pa.: Gilbert Adams Hays, 1919), 283; Gaillard Hunt, *Israel, Elihu, and Cadwallader Washburn: A Chapter in American Biography* (New York: Macmillan, 1925), 206; Willard L. King, *Lincoln's Manager: David Davis* (Cambridge, Mass.: Harvard Univ. Press, 1960), 206. The "first ridge" in Burnside's dispatch perhaps referred to the swale on the outskirts of town where so many Federals had taken shelter.

4. John G. Nicolay to Therena Nicolay, Dec. 11, 17, 1862, Nicolay Papers, LC; Abraham Lincoln, *The Collected Works of Abraham Lincoln*, ed. Roy P. Basler, 9 vols. (New Brunswick, N.J.: Rutgers Univ. Press, 1954), 5:552, 6:2.

5. Henry Villard, *Memoirs of Henry Villard, Journalist and Financier, 1835–1900*, 2 vols. (Boston: Houghton Mifflin, 1904), 1:384–91. By his own account, Villard became something of a social lion in Washington, recounting what he had seen of the battle and his dramatic journey to the capital (*Memoirs*, 2:3).

6. King, *Lincoln's Manager*, 207; Carl Sandburg, *Abraham Lincoln: The War Years*, 4 vols. (New York: Harcourt, Brace, 1939), 1:630–31; Adam Gurowski, *Diary*, 3 vols. (New York: Burt Franklin, 1968), 2:29; Francis Fisher Browne, *The Every-day Life of Abraham Lincoln* (Minneapolis: Northwestern, 1887), 573–74.

7. Herman Haupt to his wife, Dec. 18, 1862, Haupt Letterbook, Lewis M. Haupt Papers, LC; Orville Hickman Browning, *The Diary of Orville Hickman Browning*, ed. Theodore Calvin Pease and James G. Randall, 2 vols. (Springfield: Illinois State Historical Library, 1925–32), 1:596; John Gibbon, *Personal Recollections of the Civil War* (New York: G. P. Putnam's Sons, 1928), 106; Francis Becknell Carpenter, *The Inner Life of Abraham Lincoln: Six Months at the White House* (New York: Hurd and Houghton, 1870), 177; Allan Nevins, *The War for the Union*, 4 vols. (New York: Charles Scribner's Sons, 1959–71), 2:352; Mary A. Livermore, *My Story of the War: A Woman's Narrative of Four Years Personal Experience* . . . (Hartford, Conn.: A. D. Worthington, 1890), 561. Sight of the Fredericksburg wounded may have further depressed the president. Both Lincoln and his wife visited hospitals shortly after the battle. William McCarter, *My Life in the Irish Brigade: The Civil War Memoirs of Private William McCarter, 116th Pennsylvania Infantry*, ed. Kevin E. O'Brien (Campbell, Calif.: Savas Publishing, 1996), 217; Erasmus C. Gilbreath *Reminiscences*, p. 55, Indiana State Library.

8. *New York Tribune*, Dec. 18, 23, 1862; *Chicago Daily Tribune*, Dec. 18, 1862; Noah Brooks, *Mr. Lincoln's Washington: Selections from the Writings of Noah Brooks: Civil War Correspondent*, ed. P. J. Staudenraus (South Brunswick, N.J.: Thomas Yoseloff, 1967), 51; Emerson F. Merrill to his parents, Dec. 21, 1862, Merrill Papers, Fredericksburg and Spotsylvania National Military Park (hereafter FSNMP); *Harrisburg (Pa.) Patriot and Union*, Dec. 20, 1862; *Albany (N.Y.) Atlas and Argus*, Jan. 9, 1863.

9. *Richmond Daily Enquirer,* Dec. 15, 16, 24, 25, 1862; *Milledgeville (Ga.) Southern Recorder,* Jan. 6, 1863; *Richmond Daily Examiner,* Dec. 16, 1862; *Charleston Mercury,* Dec. 17, 23, 1862; *Augusta (Ga.) Daily Chronicle and Sentinel,* Jan. 1, 1863; *Wilmington (N.C.) Daily Journal,* Jan. 9, 1863; *Weekly Raleigh (N.C.) Register,* Dec. 31, 1862; *Raleigh (N.C.) Weekly Standard,* Dec. 31, 1862, Jan. 7, 1863; *Richmond Daily Dispatch,* Dec. 15, 1862.

10. J. Cutler Andrews, *The North Reports the Civil War* (Pittsburgh: Univ. of Pittsburgh Press, 1955), 74; *New York Tribune,* Dec. 15, 16, 20, 1862; *New York Times,* Dec. 15, 16, 18, 1862; *Philadelphia Inquirer,* Dec. 15, 17, 1862; *Baltimore American and Commercial Advertiser,* Dec. 23, 1862; Charles Royster, *The Destructive War: William Tecumseh Sherman, Stonewall Jackson, and the Americans* (New York: Alfred A. Knopf, 1991), 240; *Boston Evening Transcript,* Dec. 15, 1862; *New York Herald,* Dec. 16, 1862; *Hartford (Conn.) Daily Courant,* Dec. 19, 23, 1862; *Flemington (N.J.) Hunterdon Gazette,* Dec. 24, 1862; *Rochester (N.Y.) Daily Democrat and American,* Dec. 23, 1862; *Carlisle (Pa.) Herald,* Dec. 26, 1862. As early as Dec. 12, the *New York Herald* had published a list of casualties from the 50th New York Engineers that had been involved in the bridge building on Dec. 11 (*New York Herald,* Dec. 12, 1862).

11. Cornelia Peake McDonald, *A Woman's Civil War: A Diary, with Reminiscences of the War, from March 1862,* ed. Minrose C. Gwin (Madison: Univ. of Wisconsin Press, 1992), 100; Emma Holmes, *The Diary of Miss Emma Holmes,* ed. John F. Marszalek (Baton Rouge: Louisiana State Univ. Press, 1979), 218; William Thompson Lusk, *War Letters of William Thompson Lusk* (New York: privately printed, 1911), 252–53; Catherine Eaton to Samuel W. Eaton, Dec. 15, 1862, Edward Dwight Eaton Papers, State Historical Society of Wisconsin (SHSW); Anzolette E. Pendleton to William Nelson Pendleton, Dec. 18, 1862, Pendleton Papers, Southern Historical Collection, Univ. of North Carolina (hereafter SHC); L. Minor Blackford, *Mine Eyes Have Seen the Glory: The Story of a Virginia Lady, Mary Berkeley Minor Blackford, 1802–1896* (Cambridge, Mass.: Harvard Univ. Press, 1954), 207.

12. Orson Blair Curtis, *History of the Twenty-fourth Michigan of the Iron Brigade, Known as the Detroit and Wayne County Regiment* (Detroit: Winn and Hammond, 1891), 107; Wesley Brainerd, *Bridge Building in Wartime: Colonel Wesley Brainerd's Memoir of the 50th New York Volunteer Engineers,* ed. Ed Malles (Knoxville: Univ. of Tennessee Press, 1997), 309; Susan Leigh Blackford, *Letters from Lee's Army; or, Memoirs of Life in and out of the Army in Virginia during the War between the States* (New York: Charles Scribner's Sons, 1947), 149–50; Samuel V. Dean to his wife, Dec. 22, 1862, Dean Letters, FSNMP; Henry Wadsworth Longfellow, *The Letters of Henry Wadsworth Longfellow,* ed. Andrew Hillen, 4 vols. (Cambridge, Mass.: Harvard Univ. Press, 1967–82), 4:304; Robert Wentworth to his daughter, Dec. 25, 1862, Edwin O. Wentworth Papers, LC; Edwin R. Gearhart, *Reminiscences of the Civil War* (Stroudsburg, Pa.: Daily Record Press, 1901), 32; John Haley, *The Rebel Yell and the Yankee Hurrah: The Civil War Journal of a Maine Volunteer,* ed. Ruth L. Silliker (Camden, Maine: Down East Books, 1985), 60.

13. Henry Livermore Abbott, *Fallen Leaves: The Civil War Letters of Major Henry Livermore Abbott,* ed. Robert Garth Scott (Kent, Ohio: Kent State Univ. Press, 1991), 160; George Wilson Welsh and Philip Rudsil Welsh, "Civil War Letters from Two Brothers," *Yale Review* 18 (Sept. 1928): 161; Curtis, *History of the Twenty-fourth Michigan,* 82; Patrick R. Guiney, *Commanding Boston's Irish Ninth: The Civil War Letters of Colonel Patrick R. Guiney, Ninth Massachusetts Volunteer Infantry,* ed. Christian G. Samito (New York: Fordham Univ. Press, 1998), 155; Kate Stone, *Brokenburn: The Journal of Kate Stone, 1861–1868,* ed. John Q. Anderson (Baton Rouge: Louisiana State Univ. Press, 1955), 164–65.

14. Margaret Leech, *Reveille in Washington, 1860–1865* (New York: Harper and Brothers, 1941), 222; Fleming, ed., *Hays,* 284; Zachariah Chandler to his wife, Dec. 15, 1862, Chandler Papers, LC; *OR: Supplement,* pt. 1, vol. 3:672–73. Ethan Allan Hitchcock to "Dear Mrs. Mann," Dec. 15, 1862,

Hitchcock Papers, LC; Browning, *Diary*, 1:596; Welles, *Diary*, 1:193; Joseph Logsdon, *Horace White, Nineteenth Century Liberal* (Westport, Conn.: Greenwood, 1971), 92; Matias Romero, *A Mexican View of America in the 1860s: A Foreign Diplomat Describes the Civil War and Reconstruction*, ed. Thomas Schoonover (Rutherford, N.J.: Fairleigh Dickinson Univ. Press, 1991), 138.

15. Andrews, *North Reports the Civil War*, 333–34; L. A. Gobright, *Recollections of Men and Things at Washington* (Philadelphia: Claxton, Remsen, and Haffelfinger, 1869), 318; Robert Luther Thompson, *Wiring a Continent: The History of the Telegraph Industry in the United States, 1832–1866* (Princeton, N.J.: Princeton Univ. Press, 1947), 373; Fletcher Pratt, *Stanton: Lincoln's Secretary of War* (New York: W. W. Norton, 1953), 262–63; *Rochester (N.Y.) Daily Democrat and American*, Dec. 18, 1862.

16. *Chicago Daily Tribune*, Dec. 12, 1862; *New York Times*, Dec. 12, 1862; *New York Tribune*, Dec. 12, 1862; *Albany (N.Y.) Atlas and Argus*, Dec. 12, 1862; *Philadelphia Inquirer*, Dec. 12, 1862; *Providence (R.I.) Daily Journal*, Dec. 12, 1862.

17. *Chicago Daily Tribune*, Dec. 13, 1862; *Philadelphia Public Ledger*, Dec. 13, 1862; *Albany Atlas and Argus*, Dec. 13, 1862.

18. Andrews, *North Reports the Civil War*, 330; *New York Herald*, Dec. 14, 1862; *New York Times*, Dec. 14, 1862; Leech, *Reveille in Washington*, 221.

19. *Newark (N.J.) Daily Advertiser*, Dec. 15, 1862; *Philadelphia Public Ledger*, Dec. 15, 1862; *New York Times*, Dec. 15, 1862; *Boston Evening Transcript*, Dec. 15, 1862; Thomas H. O'Connor, *Civil War Boston: Home Front and Battlefield* (Boston: Northeastern Univ. Press, 1997), 121; *Springfield (Mass.) Daily Republican*, Dec. 15, 1862; *Philadelphia Inquirer*, Dec. 15, 1862; *New York Tribune*, Dec. 15, 1862; *Boston Daily Advertiser*, Dec. 15, 1862. One Boston editor even grimly observed that "the price of blood must be paid" (*Boston Post*, Dec. 15, 1862).

20. *Baltimore American and Commercial Advertiser*, Dec. 16, 1862; *Albany (N.Y.) Evening Journal*, Dec. 16, 1862; *Philadelphia Public Ledger*, Dec. 16, 1862; *Providence Daily Journal*, Dec. 16, 1862; *New York Times*, Dec. 16, 1862; *Newark Daily Advertiser*, Dec. 16, 1862; *Philadelphia Inquirer*, Dec. 16, 17, 1862; *Washington Daily National Intelligencer*, Dec. 16, 1862; *Hartford Daily Courant*, Dec. 16, 17, 1862; Andrews, *North Reports the Civil War*, 335. Banks was in fact sailing for New Orleans to assume command in the Department of the Gulf.

21. William O. Stoddard, *Inside the White House in War Times: Memoirs and Reports of Lincoln's Secretary*, ed. Michael Burlingame (Lincoln: Univ. of Nebraska Press, 2000), 101.

22. *Rochester Daily Democrat and American*, Dec. 17, 19, 20, 1862; *Philadelphia Inquirer*, Dec. 17–20, 22, 1862; "The Repulse at Fredericksburg," *Independent* 14 (Dec. 18, 1862): 4; *Easton (Pa.) Free Press*, Dec. 18, 1862; *New York Times*, Dec. 18–19, 1862, Jan. 7, 1863; *Kokomo (Ind.) Howard Tribune*, Dec. 18, 1862; *Albany Evening Journal*, Dec. 17, 1862; *Boston Evening Transcript*, Dec. 17, 22, 1862. Even a Rochester Democratic editor hedged his bets, claimed to be still hopeful, but for good measure wished that Burnside would not have to face, à la McClellan, political interference from Washington (*Rochester [N.Y.] Daily Union and Advertiser*, Dec. 15, 1862).

23. *New York Tribune*, Dec. 16, 1862; *Poughkeepsie (N.Y.) Daily Eagle*, Dec. 20, 1862; *Springfield Daily Republican*, Dec. 17, 18, 1862. (The candor of some accounts in Republican newspapers apparently infuriated Burnside. Andrews, *North Reports the Civil War*, 331–32, 334–35.)

24. *New York Times*, Dec. 17, 18, 1862; *Indianapolis Daily Journal*, Dec. 15, 1862; *Albany (N.Y.) Atlas and Argus*, Dec. 15–16, 1862; Andrews, *North Reports the Civil War*, 335; *Richmond Daily Dispatch*, Dec. 22, 1862; David Bosse, *Civil War Newspaper Maps: A Historical Atlas* (Baltimore: Johns Hopkins Univ. Press, 1993), 113; *New York Herald*, Dec. 17, 21, 1862. Swinton's Dec. 13 dispatch did not appear in print until Dec. 17.

25. *New York Times*, Dec. 17, 1862; *New York Herald*, Dec. 17, 1862; *Albany Evening Journal*, Dec. 18, 1862; *Rochester Daily Union and Advertiser*, Dec. 17, 1862; *Boston Post*, Dec. 17, 1862. A leading Catholic

weekly carried somber headlines: "Great Disaster in the Army of the Potomac. Terrible Slaughter of the Best Blood of the Country" (*Boston Pilot*, Dec. 27, 1862).

26. George Templeton Strong, *The Diary of George Templeton Strong*, ed. Allan Nevins and Milton Halsey Thomas, 4 vols. (New York: Macmillan, 1952), 3:276–78; Elizabeth Blair Lee, *Wartime Washington: The Civil War Letters of Elizabeth Blair Lee*, ed. Virginia Jeans Lass (Urbana: Univ. of Illinois Press, 1991), 214–15. A disaster such as Fredericksburg of course created a great demand for news, but many citizens had already grown skeptical of press accounts, and in such an atmosphere, rumors helped people make some sense of a seemingly dangerous, chaotic situation. Tamotsu Shibutani, *Improvised News: A Sociological Study of Rumor* (Indianapolis: Bobbs-Merrill, 1966), 31–46, 57–59, 163–64.

27. Harold B. Hancock, ed., "The Civil War Diaries of Anna M. Ferris," *Delaware History* 9 (Apr. 1961): 242; Maria Bryant to John Emory Bryant, Dec. 14, 1862, Bryant Papers, William R. Perkins Library, Duke University, Durham, N.C.; Strong, *Diary of George Templeton Strong*, 3:279; Benjamin F. Butler, *Private and Official Correspondence of Gen. Benjamin F. Butler during the Period of the Civil War*, ed. Jessie Ames Marshall, 5 vols. (privately printed, 1917), 2:539; Sidney George Fisher, *A Philadelphia Perspective: The Diary of Sidney George Fisher Covering the Years 1834–1871*, ed. Nicholas B. Wainwright (Philadelphia: Historical Society of Pennsylvania, 1967), 444; Royster, *Destructive War*, 237–39; 246–47; Maria Lydig Daly, *Diary of a Union Lady, 1861–1865*, ed. Harold Earl Hammond (New York: Funk and Wagnals, 1962), 208–9. During a period of what one sociologist has termed "sustained collective tension," civilians (and soldiers) exchanged rumors in an effort to comprehend a chaotic situation. Rumors can flourish in the absence of "news" but also when there is a surfeit of "news," especially unreliable "news." By the same token, the passage of rumors between battlefield and home front reinforced (and sometimes upset) prevailing ideas about the war's course. Shibutani, *Improvised News*, 46–49, 64–65; Gordon W. Allport and Leo Postman, *The Psychology of Rumor* (New York: Henry Holt, 1947), 1.

28. Royster, *Destructive War*, 241; J. Matthew Gallman, *The North Fights the Civil War: The Home Front* (Chicago: Ivan R. Dee, 1994), 77–80; Max L. Heyman Jr., ed., "The Gay Letters: A Civil War Correspondence," *Journal of the West* 9 (July 1970): 389–90; "George Breck's Civil War Letters from the 'Reynolds Battery,'" in Blake McKelvey, ed., *Rochester in the Civil War* (Rochester: Rochester Historical Society, 1944), 113–14; *Indiana (Pa.) Weekly Democrat*, Dec. 25, 1862.

29. OR, 860; *Providence Daily Journal*, Dec. 19, 1862; *Chicago Daily Tribune*, Dec. 17, 27, 1862; Albert Richardson, *The Secret Service: The Field, The Dungeon, and the Escape* (Hartford, Conn.: American Publishing, 1865), 309–10; *New York Tribune*, Dec. 24, 1862; *Hartford Daily Courant*, Dec. 23, 1862; *Albany Evening Journal*, Dec. 22, 1862; *Easton (Pa.) Northampton County Journal*, Dec. 24, 1862; Lounger, "What We Are," *Harper's Weekly* 6 (Dec. 27, 1862): 818; *Portsmouth (N.H.) Daily Morning Chronicle*, Dec. 24, 1862; *New York Tribune*, Dec. 18, 1862, Jan. 8, 1863.

30. William Harris to George Hopper, Dec. 26, 1862, George Hopper Papers, United States Army Military History Institute, Carlisle Barracks, Pa. (hereafter USAMHI); *Cannelton (Ind.) Reporter*, Dec. 26, 1862; *Albany (N.Y.) Atlas and Argus*, Dec. 19, 1862.

31. *Baltimore American and Commercial Advertiser*, Dec. 17, 1862; *Albany Atlas and Argus*, Dec. 17, 18, 1862; "The Reverse at Fredericksburg," *Harper's Weekly* 6 (Dec. 27, 1862): 818.

32. *Portland (Maine) Eastern Argus*, Dec. 16–18, 1862; *Albany Atlas and Argus*, Dec. 15, 17, 1862; *Harrisburg Patriot and Union*, Dec. 18, 1862; *Indianapolis Daily State Sentinel*, Dec. 17, 1862; *New York Herald*, Dec. 16, 1862; *Philadelphia Public Ledger*, Dec. 17, 1862; *Boston Post*, Dec. 18, 1862; *Rochester Daily Union and Advertiser*, Dec. 18, 1862; *Springfield Daily Republican*, Dec. 20, 1862; "The Civil War: A Week of Grave Events," *The Albion* 40 (Dec. 20, 1862): 606–7.

33. Henry W. Raymond, ed., "Extracts from the Journal of Henry J. Raymond," *Scribner's Monthly* 19 (Jan., Mar. 1880): 424; *New York Times*, Jan. 27, 1863; Ambrose E. Burnside to Lincoln, Dec.

19, 20, 1862, Lincoln Papers, LC; Lincoln, *Collected Works*, 6:10; Daniel Reed Larned to his sister, Dec. 23, 1862, Larned Papers, LC; W. Lloyd Aspinwell to Ambrose E. Burnside, Dec. 23, 1862, box 3, entry 159, Burnside Papers, Record Group 94, National Archives, Washington, D.C. Burnside could also read harsh criticism of his own conduct in the press. "It can hardly be in human nature for men to show more valor, or generals to manifest less judgment, than were perceptible on our side that day," a Cincinnati newspaper correspondent remarked. Frank Moore, ed., *The Rebellion Record: A Diary of American Events*, 11 vols. (New York: Putnam and Van Nostrand, 1861–68), 5:100; *Chicago Daily Tribune*, Dec. 22, 1862. For the most part, Republican editors stuck by Burnside, praising his courage, his masterly withdrawal from Fredericksburg, and his determination to keep the campaign going. Vice President Hannibal Hamlin saw no reason to dump a general for "one mistake." *Chicago Daily Tribune*, Dec. 19, 1862; *Cahors (N.Y.) Cataract*, Dec. 20, 1862; *Watertown (N.Y.) Daily News and Reformer*, Dec. 17, 1862; *Providence Daily Journal*, Dec. 17–18, 1862; H. Draper Hunt, *Hannibal Hamlin of Maine: Lincoln's First Vice President* (Syracuse, N.Y.: Syracuse Univ. Press, 1969), 166.

34. *OR*, 66–67; There are drafts of Burnside's letter dated Dec. 19 in both the Lincoln and Stanton Papers with the notation that it was to be sent to the Associated Press. In his official report on Fredericksburg, Burnside denied that his letter had been written at Lincoln or Stanton's behest. Burnside to Halleck, Dec. 19, 1862, Lincoln Papers, LC; Burnside to Halleck, Dec. 19, 1862, Edwin M. Stanton Papers, LC. *OR*, 95.

35. *Boston Evening Transcript*, Dec. 23, 1862; *Rochester Daily Democrat and American*, Dec. 23, 1862; *Philadelphia Inquirer*, Dec. 23, 1862; *Providence Daily Journal*, Dec. 23, 1862; John Hay, *Lincoln's Journalist: John Hay's Anonymous Writings for the Press, 1860–1864*, ed. Michael Burlingame (Carbondale: Southern Illinois Univ. Press, 1998), 324–27; *Cincinnati Daily Gazette*, Dec. 23, 1862; *Springfield Daily Republican*, Dec. 23, 1862; *New York Times*, Dec. 23–24, 30, 1862; *Albany Evening Journal*, Dec. 23, 1862; *New York Tribune*, Dec. 23, 1862; Charles Whittemore and Ruth Whittemore, "'Despotism of Traitors': The Rebellious South Through New York Eyes," ed. Walter Rundell Jr., *New York History* 45 (Oct. 1964), 349; Strong, *Diary of George Templeton Strong*, 3:282; Salmon P. Chase, *The Salmon P. Chase Papers*, 4 vols. (Kent, Ohio: Kent State Univ. Press, 1993–): 3:345; D. Robinson to William H. Seward, Dec. 23, 1862, Seward Papers, University of Rochester, Rochester, N.Y.; J. Van Buren to Ambrose E. Burnside, Dec. 23, 1862, box 3, entry 159, Burnside Papers, National Archives.

36. *Rochester Daily Union and Advertiser*, Dec. 23, 1862; *Philadelphia Public Ledger*, Dec. 25, 1862; *Harrisburg Patriot and Union*, Dec. 23, 1862; *Yonkers (N.Y.) Examiner*, Dec. 25, 1862; *New York Herald*, Dec. 23, 26, 1862.

37. Lincoln, *Collected Works*, 6:13. Lincoln scholars, including such notables as James G. Randall, David Donald, Stephen Oates, and Phillip Palludan, do not even mention the document. The president's private secretaries, Nicolay and Hay, along with Carl Sandburg and Benjamin Thomas, quoted from it but left off the statement about the casualties. John G. Nicolay and John Hay, *Abraham Lincoln: A History*, 10 vols. (New York: Century Co., 1890), 6:211; Sandburg, *Lincoln: The War Years*, 1:632; Benjamin P. Thomas, *Abraham Lincoln: A Biography* (New York: Alfred A. Knopf, 1952), 350.

38. *OR*, 68; Charles Shields Wainwright, *A Diary of Battle: The Personal Journals of Colonel Charles S. Wainwright, 1861–1865*, ed. Allan Nevins (New York: Harcourt, Brace and World, 1962), 149–50; Walt Whitman, *Walt Whitman's Civil War*, ed. Walter Lowenfels (New York: Alfred A. Knopf, 1961), 38–39; "The Cabinet Imbroglio," *Harper's Weekly* 7 (Jan. 3, 1863): 2.

39. *Harrisburg Patriot and Union*, Dec. 27, 1862; *Albany Atlas and Argus*, Dec. 25, 1862; *Boston Post*, Jan. 1, 1863. A Confederate editor also ridiculed Lincoln's effort to somehow turn a defeat into a victory (*Lynchburg Daily Virginian*, Jan. 4, 1863).

40. *New York Tribune*, Dec. 15–17, 19, 24–25, 1862; *New York Herald*, Dec. 25, 1862.

41. William C. Davis, *Jefferson Davis: The Man and His Hour* (New York: Harper Collins, 1991), 482–84; *OR*, 1062–63; Jefferson Davis, *The Papers of Jefferson Davis*, ed. Lynda Lasswell Crist and Mary Seaton Dix, 9 vols. (Baton Rouge: Louisiana State Univ. Press, 1971–), 8:549, 552–53.

42. J. B. Jones, *A Rebel War Clerk's Diary at the Confederate States Capital*, 2 vols. (Philadelphia: J. B. Lippincott, 1866), 1:210–13; Edmund Ruffin, *The Diary of Edmund Ruffin*, ed. William K. Scarborough, 3 vols. (Baton Rouge: Louisiana State Univ. Press, 1972–89), 2:509; Robert Garlick Hill Kean, *Inside the Confederate Government: The Diary of Robert Garlick Hill Kean*, ed. Edward Younger (New York: Oxford Univ. Press, 1957), 33.

43. Andrews, *South Reports the Civil War*, 223–31; W. C. Corsan, *Two Months in the Confederate States: An Englishman's Travels Through the South* (Baton Rouge: Louisiana State Univ. Press, 1996), 82–83; *Augusta Daily Chronicle and Sentinel*, Dec. 13, 1862; *Richmond Daily Dispatch*, Dec. 15, 1862; *Richmond Daily Whig*, Dec. 15, 1862; *Richmond Daily Enquirer*, Dec. 15–17, 1862; *Columbus (Ga.) Daily Enquirer*, Dec. 16, 1862.

44. Judith Brockenbrough McGuire, *Diary of a Southern Refugee During the War* (New York: E. J. Hale, 1867), 174–75; J. Michael Welton, ed., *"My Heart Is So Rebellious": The Caldwell Letters, 1861–1865* (Warrenton, Va.: Fauquier National Bank, n.d.), 162–63; Dec. 14, 1862, Fannie Page Hume Diary, LC; McDonald, *A Woman's Civil War*, 99; Anne S. Frobel, *The Civil War Diary of Anne S. Frobel of Wilton Hill, Virginia*, ed. Mary H. Lancaster and Dallas M. Lancaster (Florence, Ala.: Birmingham Printing and Publishing, 1986), 142, 144–45; Lucy Rebecca Buck, *Shadows of My Heart: The Civil War Diary of Lucy Rebecca Buck*, ed. Elizabeth R. Baer (Athens: Univ. of Georgia Press, 1997), 164; Robert Patrick, *Reluctant Rebel: The Secret Diary of Robert Patrick, 1861–1865*, ed. F. Jay Taylor (Baton Rouge: Louisiana State Univ. Press, 1959), 67–68; Catherine Ann Devereux Edmondston, *"Journal of a Secesh Lady": The Diary of Catherine Ann Devereux Edmondston*, ed. Beth G. Crabtree and James W. Patton (Raleigh, N.C.: Division of Archives, 1979), 315–22.

45. Frank L. Klement, *The Copperheads in the Middle West* (Chicago: Univ. of Chicago Press, 1960), 39; Allan G. Bogue, "William Parker Cutler's Congressional Diary of 1862–63," *Civil War History* 33 (Dec. 1987): 319–20; Nevins, *War for the Union*, 2:351–52; John Jay to Charles Sumner, Dec. 18, 1862, George F. Williams to Sumner, Dec. 19, 1862, and several other letters, Dec. 1862 passim, Sumner Papers, Harvard University, Cambridge, Mass.; Moses H. Grinnell to William H. Seward, Dec. 17, 1862; C. Becker Jr. to Seward, Dec. 23, 1862; Jonathan Longfellow to Seward, Dec. 25, 1862, in Seward Papers, Univ. of Rochester.

46. Benjamin Moran, *The Journal of Benjamin Moran, 1857–1865*, 2 vols. (Chicago: Univ. of Chicago Press, 1949), 2:1098, 1100–1101; Charles Francis Adams, *A Cycle of Adams Letters, 1861–1865*, ed. Worthington Chauncey Ford, 2 vols. (Boston: Houghton Mifflin, 1920), 1:221–22; Dec. 27–29, 1862, Charles Francis Adams Diary, Adams Family Papers, Massachusetts Historical Society, Boston, Mass.

47. *The Times* (London), Dec. 26, 29, 30, 1862, Jan. 2, 3, 5, 9, 13, 14, 1863; Karl Marx and Frederick Engels, *The Civil War in the U.S.*, 3d Ed. (New York: International Publishers, 1961), 263–64; *London Illustrated News* 42 (Jan. 10, 1863): 38–39.

48. Henry Shelton Sanford to William H. Seward, Dec. 30, 1862; and Richard M. Blatchford to Seward, Jan. 2, 1863, Seward Papers, Univ. of Rochester; Bayard Taylor to Simon Cameron, Jan. 3, 1863, Cameron Papers, LC. Conversely, news of the European reaction to Fredericksburg added to the despair in the American press. *New York Herald*, Jan. 15, 1863.

49. *Official Records of the Union and Confederate Navies in the War of the Rebellion*, 31 vols. (Washington: Government Printing Office, 1894–1922), ser. 2, vol. 3:629–33, 653–54, 662–63; Zebulon Baird Vance, *The Papers of Zebulon Baird Vance*, ed. Frontis W. Johnston and Joe A. Mobley, 2 vols. (Raleigh, N.C.: Division of Archives and History, 1963–1995), 2:18.

50. Dec. 22, 1862, Robert Taggart Diary, Jay Luvaas Collection, USAMHI; Robert McAllister, *The Civil War Letters of General Robert McAllister*, ed. James I. Robertson Jr. (New Brunswick, N.J.: Rutgers Univ. Press, 1965), 244; John White Geary, *A Politician Goes to War: The Civil War Letters of John White Geary*, ed. William Alan Blair (University Park.: Pennsylvania State Univ. Press, 1995), 72–73; Stephen Minor Weld, *War Diary and Letters of Stephen Minor Weld, 1861–1876* (Cambridge, Mass.: Riverside Press, 1911), 154–56.

51. Edmondston, *"Journal of a Secesh Lady,"* 321–22; McDonald, *A Woman's Civil War*, 108–9; *Charleston Mercury*, Dec. 31, 1862; *Richmond Daily Enquirer*, Dec. 27, 1862; Kean, *Inside the Confederate Government*, 35; Richard Henry Watkins to Mary Watkins, Dec. 28–29, 1862, Watkins Papers, Virginia Historical Society, Richmond, Va.; Buck, *Shadows of My Heart*, 168; Ruffin, *Diary of Edmund Ruffin*, 2:518–19; *Charleston Daily Courier*, Dec. 24, 1862; *Richmond Daily Dispatch*, Dec. 24, 1862; Thomas Claybrook Elder to Anna Fitzhugh Elder, Dec. 27, 1862, Elder Papers, Virginia Historical Society; S. G. Pryor, *A Post of Honor: The Pryor Letters, 1861–1863* (Fort Valley, Ga.: Garret Publications, 1989), 302–3; W. T. Kinzer to his mother and sister, Dec. 25, 1862, Kinzer Letters, West Virginia University, Morgantown. A North Carolina colonel struck a rare note of pessimism, suggesting that the reinstatement of Seward dimmed prospects for peace. Bryan Grimes to William Grimes, Dec. 26, 1862, Grimes Family Papers, SHC.

52. *New York Times*, Dec. 13, 16, 1862; *New York Herald*, Dec. 16–18, 1862; *New York Tribune*, Dec. 16, 1862; "The Price of Gold," *Banker's Magazine and Statistical Register* 12 (Jan. 1863): 560; "Notes on the Money Market," ibid., 573; "The Price of Gold," ibid., 647; Wesley Clair Mitchell, *A History of the Greenbacks* (Chicago: Univ. of Chicago Press, 1903), 196, 211, 423–24; *Baltimore American and Commercial Advertiser*, Jan. 21, 1863; Richard Roll, "Interest Rates and Price Expectations During the Civil War," *Journal of Economic History* 32 (June 1972): 478–79. Military news often arrived at the so-called "Gold Room" in New York from War Department dispatches before it reached the newspapers, and the major gold traders had other sources of confidential information. Gold prices also fluctuated during this period in response to the fate of congressional legislation making greenbacks legal tender. It is also difficult to measure the effects of Fredericksburg as compared to other war news—mostly bad—on the New York financial markets. For differing interpretations of how price fluctuations related to war news, see Wesley C. Mitchell, "The Value of the 'Greenbacks' During the Civil War," *Journal of Political Economy* 6 (Mar. 1898): 144–45, 155; Mitchell, *History of the Greenbacks*, 216; Timothy W. Guinnane, Harvey S. Rosen, and Kristen L. Willard, "Messages from 'The Den of Wild Beasts': Greenback Prices Commentary on the Union's Prospects," *Civil War History* 41 (Dec. 1995): 313–28; George T. McCandless Jr., "Money, Expectations, and the U.S. Civil War," *American Economic Review* 86 (June 1996): 661–71. The Jan. rise in gold prices likely also reflected the passage of a bill in Congress increasing the volume of greenbacks. Kristen L. Willard, Timothy W. Guinnane, and Harvey S. Rosen, "Turning Points in the Civil War: Views from the Greenback Market," *American Economic Review* 96 (Sept. 1996): 1013. Gold prices were calculated according to the number of paper dollars it would take to buy 100 gold dollars. So if the price was 130, it would take 130 paper dollars to purchase 100 gold dollars—the higher the price of gold the weaker both the dollar and public confidence.

53. James Longstreet, *From Manassas to Appomattox, Memoirs of the Civil War in America*, ed. James I. Robertson Jr. (Bloomington: Indiana Univ. Press, 1960), 317; *Charleston Daily Courier*, Dec. 27, 1862; Jones, *Rebel War Clerk's Diary*, 1:222; United States Bureau of the Census, *Historical Statistics of the United States*, 2 vols. (Washington, D.C.: Government Printing Office, 1975), 1:165, 201, 212, 214, 2:1104, 1118; Mitchell, *History of the Greenbacks*, 101–5, 248; Ralph Andreano, ed., *The Economic Impact of the American Civil War* (Cambridge, Mass.: Schenkman, 1962), 178–79, 181. Whether wages lagged significantly behind price increases has been subject to considerable debate. For useful summaries and data, see Phillip Shaw Paludan, *"A People's Contest": The Union*

and the Civil War, 1861–1865 (New York: Harper and Brothers, 1988), 113, 182–83; J. Matthew Gall-man, *Mastering Wartime: A Social History of Philadelphia during the Civil War* (Cambridge, Eng.: Cambridge Univ. Press, 1990), 225–26, 271–72.

54. Carl Von Clausewitz, *On War*, ed. and trans. Michael Howard and Peter Paret (Princeton, N.J.: Princeton Univ. Press, 1984), 592.

55. Herman Melville, *Collected Poems of Herman Melville*, ed. Howard P. Vincent (Chicago: Packard and Co., 1947), 404; Stanton Garner, *The Civil War World of Herman Melville* (Lawrence: Univ. Press of Kansas, 1993), 207–8, 215–16. Literary scholar Stanton Garner has argued that Melville's "Inscription for the Slain at Fredericksburg" was the only one of his war poems actually written during the war.

❦ John Y. Simon ❧

Grant and Halleck

Contrasts in Command

❦ For most of his adult life and virtually all of his professional life, John Y. Simon has been associated with the Ulysses S. Grant Association, where he has been executive director and managing editor since 1962. The association's main purpose—and Simon's professional passion—is the publication of the papers of the Union's savior and eighteenth president of the United States (the twenty-eighth volume, which brings the series up to the autumn of 1878, appeared in 2005).

Simon is, of course, one of the leading experts in the world on all things related to Ulysses S. Grant—particularly his military record, his family (Simon edited the best-known version of Julia Dent Grant's memoirs), and the era and places in which he lived. Among other things, Simon teaches courses on Illinois history at Southern Illinois University, where the association is headquartered. In addition, as managing editor of one of the last great presidential publishing projects, he has also served in many posts for the Association for Documentary Editing, including president. His work on the Grant Papers earned a special Lincoln Prize in 2004. "It is inconceivable," the jury noted, "that any historian would write on the Civil War without having these volumes at hand. The papers have influenced the writing of the history of this era, providing scholars and popular writers with access to essential documents. Simon has been an ambassador to the academic and public world, demonstrating the quality of Civil War scholarship, while remaining vitally responsible for the quality of this outstanding editorial work."

Irony is one of the favorite tools of historians with a literary bent, and Simon, whose perceptive talks and personal congeniality have made him one of the most popular speakers on the Civil War era to academic and popular audiences alike, employs it to great effect in "Grant and Halleck: Contrasts in Command." He argues that command opportunities in the Civil War brought out the best in Ulysses S. Grant, who was widely considered to be a failure in the Old Army, and the worst in Henry W. Halleck, one of the prewar army's golden boys. On one hand, Simon shows how Grant's aggressive and innovative military qualities—and the fact that he had nothing to lose—led the unassuming and unknown officer to become commander-in-chief of Union forces and savior of the Union. On the other hand, limited by his ego, mired in tradition, and far more interested in protecting his reputation than in winning the war, the hapless Halleck's cautious, narrow-minded generalship eventually made him "irrelevant" to the Union war effort.

Simon and his staff are presently editing the twenty-ninth and thirtieth volumes of the Grant Papers, which will take them up to the general's death. 🖎

IN THE SUMMER OF 1854, TWO captains resigned on consecutive days: Ulysses S. Grant as of July 31, Henry W. Halleck as of August 1. Halleck had made the shrewder move: for years bureaucrats questioned whether Grant deserved pay for the entire month of July. Each regiment had ten captains but only two majors, the next higher rank. Promotion to major represented a bottleneck in the promotional process. On the day he resigned, the mail had finally brought Grant his commission as captain, although the appointment was backdated to August 5, 1853. Grant had attained the rank of captain at age thirty-one. Halleck had also attained the rank of captain in the summer of 1853, but he was seven years older than Grant. Both knew that many years would elapse before further promotion.[1] Military service made so few demands and paid so poorly that many officers, especially on the Pacific Coast, had already launched new careers. Halleck had joined a law firm in 1850; Grant had attempted several business ventures, all disappointing.

Before the Civil War, the army lacked any retirement provisions except for disability. Peacetime officers often aged at low rank waiting for their seniors to die. An officer might serve for forty years without attaining rank higher than captain.[2] An 1836 projection of current promotion intervals indicated that the average West Point graduate would achieve the rank of colonel at age 79.[3] Not far from that mark, Col. John De Barth Walbach had commanded the Fourth Artillery for fifteen years before he died in 1857, nearly ninety-one years old.[4]

Following the Mexican War, many younger and more ambitious or restless officers tired of waiting for promotion. Some resigned to pursue opportunities in industry or commerce. They had received an engineering education at West Point, which Andrew Jackson had called the best school in the world.[5] Others resigned to escape the stagnation of life at dreary frontier forts, punctuated only by sudden transfers that disrupted family life. Grant and Halleck resigned for vastly different reasons.

After leaving the army, Halleck continued his lucrative practice as a lawyer in San Francisco, while Grant joined his wife and two children on a hardscrabble farm in St. Louis County, Missouri. In the seven years before the Civil War, Halleck achieved wealth and respect, while Grant failed at farming, proved unsuccessful as a St. Louis businessman, and moved to Galena, Illinois, to work in his father's leather-goods store. Like other officers of the old army, Halleck heard rumors that Grant had been forced to resign because of intemperance. When the Civil War began, Grant spent two months seeking an opportunity to serve his country at suitable rank and had nearly abandoned hope before he was suddenly and unexpectedly commissioned colonel of a regiment of Illinois volunteers. After the first hostile shot of the war, however, top federal commanders looked expectantly toward Halleck.

Halleck had begun life in 1815, the eldest of thirteen children born to an unprosperous upstate New York farm family. While still young, he ran away from rural drudgery to his grandfather, who took him in, gave him an academy education, sent him to Union College for one year, and secured him an appointment to the U.S. Military Academy. At West Point he flourished, ranking fourth in his class of fifty-seven in his first year, third of thirty-two survivors in his final year. During that last year he also taught chemistry as an assistant professor, and he remained at the academy one year after graduation to teach engineering. Assigned to headquarters of the Engineer Corps in Washington, he prepared a well-received report on the military uses of asphalt, then was sent to the fortifications of New York Harbor. After a tour of inspection in Europe, Halleck published an essay on coast defense, which earned him an invitation to lecture at the Lowell Institute of Boston. These lectures grew into the book *Elements of Military Art and Science*, published in 1846 and reprinted, revised, and enlarged, in 1861.[6]

Sent to California at the outbreak of the Mexican War, Halleck spent seven months on a tedious voyage around the tip of South America translating from the French Henri Jomini's life of Napoleon, eventually published in four hefty volumes in 1864.[7] The military governor of California appointed the young lieutenant as secretary of state. As such, he mastered and translated complex Spanish land laws, initiated the movement for statehood, and was the principal author of the state constitution.[8]

After his resignation from the army, now a prosperous partner in the leading law firm in San Francisco, Halleck, Peachy and Billings, and drawing on his expertise in Spanish land codes, he declined a professorship at the Lawrence Scientific School of Harvard. In 1850 he was elected president of the New Almaden mercury mine, the largest in the country, and in 1855 became president of the Pacific and Atlantic Railroad, a pretentious name for a line that ran only between San Francisco and San José. He declined an appointment to the state supreme court and rejected overtures to run for U.S. senator. He also prepared a lengthy study on international law, published in 1861. Like Grant, Halleck married the sister of his West Point roommate. Schuyler Hamilton's sister Elizabeth was a member of the aristocratic Schuyler family of New York and a descendant of Alexander Hamilton.[9]

Little wonder, then, that Washington officials turned to Halleck for military leadership. He left San Francisco on October 10, 1861, with a commission as major general enthusiastically recommended by seventy-five-year-old Winfield Scott, who expected Halleck to take up the responsibility of general-in-chief.[10] Before Halleck arrived in Washington, however, Scott had been forced into retirement by Gen. George B. McClellan, who blamed his own mistakes on the old hero and succeeded him as general-in-chief.

Renowned as a military scholar, Halleck had never commanded troops in the field and possessed no inclination to do so. Cast in the role of administrator, Halleck looked the part, with a pudgy physique, double chin and flabby cheeks, and a disconcerting habit of staring at people with wide-open owlish eyes. McClellan immediately ordered Halleck to the Western Department, with headquarters in St. Louis, to restore order to a command appallingly mishandled for one hundred days by Gen. John C. Frémont. Halleck arrived in St. Louis on November 19 determined to root out corruption and reinstate sound military procedure. In the southeast corner of his imperial domain, at Cairo at the tip of Illinois, Brig. Gen. Ulysses S. Grant commanded the District of Southeast Missouri, extending from Cape Girardeau, Missouri, to Paducah and Smithland, Kentucky, strategic points at the mouths of the Tennessee and Cumberland rivers that Grant had seized in September.

Aggressive, unmilitary, and unproven, Grant was not the general Halleck would have chosen for any crucial command. Raised in rural Ohio, the son of enterprising businessman Jesse Grant, young Grant had attended two nearby academies, then told his father that he wanted more education. Learning privately that the son of a neighbor had flunked out of West Point, Jesse moved quickly to place his own son in the vacancy before the news leaked out and attracted better-qualified applicants. Among those not informed was seventeen-year-old Ulysses, kept in the dark until the appointment was made. Paternal authority forced Ulysses to attend West Point.

For someone who disliked military education, Grant did well enough, graduating twenty-first among thirty-nine class members and demonstrating skill in mathematics as well as horsemanship. After his graduation in 1843, Grant hoped to return to West Point as an assistant professor of mathematics; if that failed, he wanted to teach elsewhere. Before Grant could take steps toward his goal, the army sent him to remote posts in Louisiana and Texas, preparatory to war with Mexico. During that war, Grant once again did well enough, participating in all but one of Zachary Taylor's battles in northern Mexico, then accompanying Scott's campaign from Vera Cruz to Mexico City, winning promotion to first lieutenant and brevet captain. By the time he returned from Mexico in 1848, he had dropped his study of mathematics and had sufficient rank for comfort in the peacetime army. He then married Julia Dent, whom he had courted through four years of separation.

Their time together lasted four years, producing one child and another pregnancy, before his regiment was ordered to the Pacific Coast in 1852. Grant left Julia behind. He feared to take his wife and child across the deadly Panamanian Isthmus, a fever-ridden jungle that ultimately claimed the lives of many who did accompany the regiment, especially women and children. Since he had not brought his family to the Pacific Coast when the government furnished transportation, he had to find means to pay their way. Army pay was inadequate to meet inflated western prices, but all Grant's attempts to earn extra money turned out poorly. After a year at Fort Vancouver, Grant was transferred to Fort Humboldt in California. There he found magnificent scenery but no business prospects and a small, isolated garrison commanded by a martinet with whom he had already quarreled. Malaria and loneliness also plagued Grant before he resigned to start over as a farmer. Including West Point, Grant had spent fifteen years in the army and had no wish ever to return to military life.

The guns of Sumter changed Grant's mind but not the opinions of those who gossiped that he had drunk himself out of the army. During his search for command, Grant had visited McClellan's headquarters in Cincinnati, where he waited two days to see the general before realizing that his cause was hopeless. His appointment as colonel came from Governor Richard Yates of Illinois; his appointment as brigadier general came through U.S. representative Elihu B. Washburne of Illinois, a Galena neighbor of Grant and an old friend of President Abraham Lincoln. Grant's friends from his years in the old army included neither McClellan nor Halleck.

Grant commanded at Cairo when Confederates rashly violated Kentucky's self-proclaimed neutrality by occupying strategic points along the Mississippi River, foolishly ignoring the vital Tennessee and Cumberland rivers. Grant telegraphed to General Frémont in St. Louis for permission to occupy Paducah and received authorization to do so in Hungarian, which nobody at headquarters could translate.[11] Before the matter was clarified, Grant had seized Paducah, believing incorrectly that he had advanced without orders and that he had barely forestalled a Confederate occupation.

In the interval between Frémont's removal from command on November 5 and the announcement that Halleck would replace him on November 9, Grant fought his first Civil War battle at Belmont, Missouri, on November 7, 1861. In his tangled explanations following the battle, Grant cited vague instructions from headquarters, information received from a spy, and the pressure of circumstance; yet the overriding factor appeared to be Grant's wish to strike the enemy. Grant's successful attack on a Confederate camp opposite Columbus, Kentucky, was followed by a successful counterattack that drove the Union forces back to their transports in disorder. The two armies suffered nearly equal casualties and neither gained any real advantage. Fought while McClellan idled on the banks of the Potomac, Belmont brought Grant acclaim as an aggressive commander, a reputation that might not commend him to Halleck.

Grant remained idle at Cairo while Halleck turned his attention to eliminating fraud in his department and countering the rebel threat to Missouri. A firm believer in concentration of force, Halleck had little sympathy for offensive operations in Kentucky or Tennessee before Missouri was secure. During the period of Kentucky's neutrality, Confederates had built Fort Henry on the Tennessee River and Fort Donelson on the Cumberland River in Tennessee close to the Kentucky border. Fort Henry was especially vulnerable because of its location on low ground subject to wintertime flooding. Recognizing their error, Confederates had already begun to construct Fort Heiman nearby on higher ground. Both Grant and Capt. Andrew H. Foote, commanding the gunboat fleet, recognized the advantage of attacking Fort Henry. On January 6 Grant went to St. Louis to ask Halleck for permission to attack, received "little cordiality," and returned rebuffed and "crestfallen."[12] Later that month, backed by Foote, Grant telegraphed to Halleck renewing the request. Alarmed by reports that Confederates had sent reinforcements to Tennessee and reassured by the limited nature of Grant's expedition, Halleck reluctantly consented.

Fort Henry fell even more easily than Grant anticipated, surrendering to gunboat attack before most of Grant's forces arrived to block the escape of nearly the entire garrison to Fort Donelson on the Cumberland a dozen miles away. Announcing the surrender on February 6, Grant added to his message to Halleck: "I shall take and destroy Fort Donelson on the 8th."[13] Delaying because of muddy roads and allowing time for Foote's gunboats to ascend the Cumberland, Grant did not move on Donelson until February 12, giving Halleck ample time to respond. "General Halleck did not approve or disapprove of my going to Fort Donelson," marveled Grant. "He said nothing whatever to me on the subject."[14] In messages to McClellan and to Gen. Don Carlos Buell, whose cooperation he implored, Halleck displayed full awareness of the Donelson expedition. At the same time, he had no intention of accepting responsibility if his aggressive subordinate failed.

Characteristically cautious, Halleck prepared better for failure than for dazzling success. Grant advanced his army on two parallel roads to Donelson without fear that his inept opponents would leave their fortifications to attack. Then he surrounded the more numerous rebel army. When Confederates launched a successful breakthrough attack on February 15, Grant immediately counterattacked and the next day compelled the demoralized Confederates to accept "unconditional and immediate surrender."[15] Grant won the first major Union victory of the war, bagged some 15,000 prisoners, cracked the Confederate defense line in Kentucky, and forced the evacuation of Nashville.

Halleck joined in the public jubilation in St. Louis but was reluctant to accept Donelson as Grant's victory. Even before Donelson fell, Halleck requested the appointment of Ethan Allen Hitchcock as major general to command Grant's forces.[16] Born in 1798, Hitchcock was an elderly and respected officer better known for scholarship on mystical subjects than for military prowess. Upon his appointment, Hitchcock responded with horror to the prospect of field command and served throughout the war at a Washington desk negotiating prisoner exchanges. After Donelson fell, Halleck asked McClellan to promote Buell, Grant, and John Pope to major generals and "give me command in the West. I ask this in return for Forts Henry and Donelson."[17] Halleck promised great results if given command of Buell's department. As for promotions, Halleck also urged one for Grant's subordinate, Charles F. Smith, who "by his coolness and bravery at Fort Donelson when the battle was against us, turned the tide and carried the enemy's outworks."[18]

Of all these post-Donelson demands, the promotion of Grant was the first honored in Washington and perhaps the least gratifying to Halleck. Among officers in his department, Smith held Halleck's greatest respect. An officer since graduating from West Point in 1825, Smith had served with distinction in Mexico and held the rank of lieutenant colonel when the Civil War began. Smith had been commandant at West Point when Grant entered, and Grant found it awkward to command an officer he had so admired. Halleck prepared to end that awkward situation.

On March 3, 1862, Halleck telegraphed to McClellan:

> I have had no communication with General Grant for more than a week. He left his command without my authority and went to Nashville. His army seems to be as much demoralized by the victory of Fort Donelson as was that of the Potomac by the defeat of Bull Run. It is hard to censure a successful general immediately after a victory, but I think he richly deserves it. I can get no returns, no reports, no information of any kind from him. Satisfied with his victory, he sits down and enjoys it without any regard to the future. I am worn-out and tired with this neglect and inefficiency. C. F. Smith is almost the only officer equal to the emergency.[19]

McClellan responded: "The future success of our cause demands that proceedings such as Grant's should at once be checked. Generals must observe discipline as well as private soldiers. Do not hesitate to arrest him at once if the good of the service requires it, and place C. F. Smith in command. You are at liberty to regard this as a positive order if it will smooth your way."[20]

Halleck then pushed his case. "A rumor has just reached me that since the taking of Fort Donelson General Grant has resumed his former bad habits. If so, it will account for his neglect of my often-repeated orders. I do not deem it advisable to arrest him at present, but have placed General Smith in command of the expedition up the Tennessee. I think Smith will restore order and discipline."[21] Finally, Halleck communicated directly with Grant. "You will place Major Genl C. F. Smith in command of expedition, & remain yourself at Fort Henry. Why do you not obey my orders to report strength & positions of your command?"[22]

Grant wrote in response that he was "not aware of ever having disobeyed any order from Head Quarters, certainly never intended such a thing."[23] Halleck answered that he had repeatedly asked Grant for information about his strength and had received no answer, which "certainly indicated a great want of order & system in your command, the blame of which was partially thrown on me, and perhaps justly, as it is the duty of every commander to compel those under him to obey orders & enforce discipline. Dont let such neglect occur again, for it is equally discreditable to you & to me. I really felt ashamed to telegraph back to Washington time & again that I was unable to give the strength of your command."[24] Halleck lied directly to Grant about these nonexistent telegrams to Washington, just as he lied when he telegraphed to Grant that his "going to Nashville without authority" had provoked such serious complaint in Washington "that I was advised to arrest you on your return."[25] Of course only Halleck had complained to Washington. In the belief that "I must have enemies between you and myself," Grant asked to be relieved.[26] Halleck responded that there was no "enemy between me & you," but that McClellan was "out of all patience" awaiting information concerning Grant's strength and position.[27] Grant again asked to be relieved.[28] On March 13 Grant received a copy of an anonymous letter complaining of looting after Donelson, forwarded by Halleck on March 6 with a warning that "Unless these things are immediately corrected, I am directed to relieve you from the command."[29] For the third time, Grant asked to be relieved.[30] Halleck responded that he knew "no good reason" to relieve Grant. Authorities in Washington asked merely "that you enforce discipline & punish the disorderly." "Instead of relieving you," wrote Halleck, "I wish you . . . to assume the immediate command & lead it on to new victories."[31] Answering a final letter from Halleck concerning charges of impropriety, Grant wrote: "I most fully appreciate your justness Gen. in the part you have taken . . ."[32]

So Halleck concluded his first quarrel with Grant by assuming credit for protecting him from detractors in Washington. On the day before Halleck receded, Smith injured his leg while jumping into a boat. At first the injury seemed only a temporary incapacitation, but Smith died of its consequences on April 25. Years later, Gen. William T. Sherman wrote: "Had C. F. Smith lived, Grant would have disappeared to history after Donelson."[33] Sherman's comment in a private letter leaked to the press stirred angry debate, and Sherman quickly recanted to avoid offending Grant's family and friends. Only Halleck, then dead, could have confirmed Sherman's intuition and never would have responded honestly.

Something about Grant brought out the worst in Halleck. Did he resent Grant's success, his age, his lack of prior military accomplishment—perhaps all three? Did he foresee that eventually Grant might become his superior? Did this consummate military administrator, believing that victories were won at the desk rather than in the field, resent those honored for battlefield achievements?

Restored to command of the Tennessee River expedition, Grant assembled his army at Pittsburg Landing, Tennessee, awaiting the arrival of reinforcements from Buell's Army of the Ohio for a combined overland campaign against the Confederate railroad center at Corinth, Mississippi. While still waiting, Grant's troops received an unexpected attack at Shiloh Church and were sent reeling back to the Tennessee River. Reinforced by the vanguard of Buell's forces, Grant counterattacked on a second day of battle that more than recaptured ground lost during the first day and hurled the rebel army back to Corinth with losses equal to those of the Union. At Shiloh Grant displayed his characteristic indomitability and resilience at their peak, but he received merciless criticism for his unpreparedness and the appalling loss of life.

Halleck decided to lead a model campaign against Corinth, uniting the armies of Grant and Buell with the Army of the Mississippi under John Pope, fresh from victories at New Madrid and Island No. 10. Arriving at Pittsburg Landing on April 13, he plunged into disciplining and reorganizing the armies, work that he loved. At first, Grant welcomed Halleck: "I am truly glad of it. I hope the papers will let me alone in future."[34] Much criticism, thought Grant, "originates in jealousy. This is very far from applying, however, I think, to our Chief, Halleck, who I look upon as one of the greatest men of the age."[35] In his reorganization, Halleck gave Grant the position of second in command, which Grant found "anomylous" and differing little from arrest.[36] He believed that Halleck would do him no injustice but might have orders to remove him from command. He asked, therefore, that he be restored to command or relieved of duty. In his response, Halleck feigned surprise that Grant found any cause for complaint: "You certainly will not suspect me of any intention to injure your feelings or reputation, or to do you any injustice. . . . For the last three months I have done every thing in my power to ward off the attacks which were made upon you. If you believe me your friend, you will not require explanation; if not, explanation on my part would be of little avail."[37] Somehow this satisfied Grant during what seemed an endless advance on Corinth, as the army crawled forward, halting each day to erect elaborate fortifications. With an army of 120,000 opposing a force of 47,000, Halleck advanced twenty miles in three weeks. When Halleck reached the city, the hopelessly outnumbered garrison, weakened by disease, had evacuated. "Put Halleck in the command of twenty thousand men," remarked Senator Benjamin F. Wade, "and he will not scare three setting geese from their nests."[38] Halleck's single venture in field command had proved a fiasco, which he followed by fortifying Corinth on an unnecessarily elaborate scale. Although this massive army could have moved anywhere in the Confederacy with impunity, Halleck preferred to entrench when successful. He sent Buell eastward to pursue the enemy with orders to repair the railroad as he advanced, a policy that prevented Buell from reaching the foe and did little good for the railroad, torn up by guerrillas as fast as it was repaired.[39] Frustrated and depressed, Grant may have considered leaving the army before Halleck eventually gave him an independent command at Memphis. Halleck soon left for Washington to serve as general-in-chief, fulfilling Scott's plan of the previous year. He left with Grant's good wishes. "He is a man of gigantic intellect and well studied in the profession of arms. He and I have had several little spats but I like and respect him nevertheless."[40] Halleck believed that not a single western general was "fit for a great command" and offered his former place to his chief quartermaster, Col. Robert Allen.[41]

Halleck filled a technical vacancy created when Lincoln removed McClellan as general-in-chief on March 11, 1862, on the eve of the Peninsula campaign. Lincoln, who had held the reins himself in the interim, wanted Halleck to share responsibility but not necessarily power. Ever since the conclusion of the Seven Days' battles, McClellan had kept the Army of the Potomac inert at Harrison's Landing, freeing Confederates to threaten northern Virginia. Pope commanded forces gathered at Washington for defense, grown numerous enough to advance southward. Halleck took command of all the armies on July 23 at a moment of tremendous opportunity: if Pope pushed southward while McClellan renewed his campaign toward Richmond, Robert E. Lee might have been crushed. Halleck instinctively made the worst possible decision. The armies must concentrate for the defense of the capital before undertaking offensive operations. He began to withdraw McClellan's army from the Peninsula to join Pope; when McClellan's army was depleted and before Pope's could be consolidated, Lee struck at Second Manassas. After Corinth fell, Halleck had dispersed a mighty army, placing it, as Grant put it, "where it would do the least good."[42] During that same summer, Halleck threw away another strategic opportunity in the East. Although Pope was the commander at Second Bull Run, Halleck's insistence that McClellan move his forces from the James River to Washington and McClellan's dilatory compliance gave Lee a remarkable military opportunity.

McClellan and Halleck deserved each other. Halleck wrote to McClellan that he had not wanted to leave the West, that he held the position of general-in-chief "contrary to my own wishes," and that the "country demands of us that we act together and with cordiality."[43] "I would have advised your appointment," McClellan answered, offering his "full and cordial support" and denying any "jealousy in my heart."[44] Privately, McClellan thought Halleck's appointment a "pretext" to "supersede" him.[45] McClellan had received "a slap in the face" from Lincoln, and McClellan found it "grating to have to serve under the orders of a man I know by experience to be my inferior."[46]

Even before being called to Washington, Halleck considered McClellan "selfish" yet feared being drawn into the quarrel between him and Secretary of War Edwin M. Stanton. After his first visit to McClellan, Halleck judged him "a most excellent and valuable man, but he does not understand strategy and should never plan a campaign." His friends "have excited his jealousy," so that he eventually would "pitch into me." "I cannot get General McClellan to do what I wish," he moaned, yet resisted pressure from Lincoln and his cabinet to remove McClellan from command.[47]

Petty personal maneuverings cost the Union dearly at the battle of Second Bull Run. Nonetheless, Halleck believed that he had "saved the capital from the terrible crisis brought upon us by the stupidity of others."[48] According to McClellan, Halleck begged him "to help him out of the scrape & take command," and McClellan "mad as a March hare . . . had a pretty plain talk with him & Abe."[49] Resuming command, McClellan led the army to the battle of Antietam, afterward taking "some little pride in having with a beaten and demoralized army defeated Lee so utterly, & saved the North so completely."[50] As his reward, McClellan expected the removal of both Stanton and Halleck, the latter "an incompetent fool" and "the most stupid idiot I ever heard of."[51] Within a few weeks, McClellan himself was relieved of command for ignoring repeated pleas from Lincoln and Halleck to advance.

In the case of both Grant and McClellan, Halleck exhibited managerial capacity without corresponding skill in personal relations. Brusque and insensitive with subordinates, Halleck was obsequious toward Lincoln and Stanton. Halleck may have been appointed general-in-chief to manage McClellan, but he remained in office after McClellan's fall. Lincoln continued to make the major decisions as he had when the office was vacant. Sometimes he used Halleck to implement such decisions or to take responsibility for such unpleasant acts as removing commanders. Those who expected professional military wisdom from Halleck were repeatedly disappointed. Halleck acted as the agent of his superiors, Lincoln and Stanton. Secretary of the Navy Gideon Welles called Halleck "a national misfortune" who had "done nothing but scold and smoke and scratch his elbows."[52] Secretary of the Treasury Salmon P. Chase thought that Halleck was "good for nothing, and everybody knew it but the President."[53] On the contrary, Lincoln, who may have been the first to recognize Halleck's faults, used him to accomplish indirectly what the president wanted done without assuming responsibility.

While declining to dispute the president, Halleck was not averse to circumventing executive policy, something he did to further Grant's Vicksburg campaign. In September 1862, Grant's ambitious subordinate John A. McClernand persuaded Lincoln to authorize a special campaign to open the Mississippi River using troops recruited among midwestern Democrats. Grant did not rank among Halleck's favorites but was preferable to an ambitious politician like McClernand. During late 1862 and early 1863, Halleck did everything possible (without showing his hand) to thwart McClernand's efforts to displace Grant. Halleck forwarded to Memphis troops recruited by McClernand and encouraged Grant to use them, as he did in Sherman's ill-fated December 1862 assault on Vicksburg. When McClernand arrived to claim his command, Halleck supported Grant in placing McClernand in a subordinate position as corps commander. Near the conclusion of the Vicksburg campaign, with Halleck's full support, Grant finally removed his troublesome subordinate. Halleck also played a supporting role in thwarting Lincoln's plan to unite Grant's Vicksburg forces with those of Gen. Nathaniel P. Banks, another uniformed politician, campaigning before Port Hudson. When Vicksburg fell, Halleck awarded Grant his highest praise by comparing the Vicksburg campaign to that of Napoleon before Ulm.[54]

In early 1864, Congress authorized the appointment of a lieutenant general. Although congressmen clearly intended this rank for Grant, who had added to his Vicksburg laurels the defeat of Confederate forces at Chattanooga, Lincoln retained the option of selecting another officer. By nominating the current general-in-chief, Lincoln could have circumvented the intent of Congress without altering the command structure of the army. Lincoln hesitated, however, until assured that Grant would present no political threat to the president's reelection. When Lincoln appointed Grant lieutenant general, Halleck immediately resigned as general-in-chief. Grant had already indicated that he had "great confidence in and friendship for" Halleck.[55] In an ingenious move, Lincoln and Grant arranged to have Halleck appointed chief of staff. Since Grant already had a chief of staff, his adjutant John A. Rawlins, some at headquarters perceived Halleck's appointment "under the direction of the Secretary of War and the lieutenant-general commanding" as a device to thwart Grant, a suspicion soon allayed by Halleck's complete subordination.[56] Halleck was a "first-rate clerk" who had "shrunk from responsibility wherever it was possible," said Lincoln, who told Grant to "take the responsibility and act."[57]

Grant himself established headquarters with the Army of the Potomac without displacing its commander, George G. Meade. By leaving Halleck in Washington and Meade with his army, Grant took command with minimum upheaval. He also freed himself of the burdens of desk duty in Washington, constant communication with civilian authority, and potential political pressure. Halleck, too, had been reluctant to leave the West for the pressures of Washington but had found no way to avoid the assignment.

Halleck initially performed well in supplying Grant's massive overland campaign with men and supplies, conveying Grant's orders to other commanders and buffering the resistance that accompanied Grant's efforts to replace political generals with professional soldiers. Halleck might have achieved a fine reputation as a military manager had not Lee sent Jubal A. Early down the Shenandoah Valley to menace Washington in the summer of 1864.

With Grant pinned down with the Army of the Potomac at Petersburg, Halleck had responsibility for meeting the threat of a Confederate army. Reluctant to consolidate the network of divided commands encircling the District of Columbia, Halleck vacillated while Early's troops neared the capital. The battle of Monocacy on July 9, although a defeat for Gen. Lew Wallace, delayed Early long enough for Grant's Sixth Corps, under Horatio Wright, to secure the capital. With Early still threatening vital northern cities, Lincoln conferred with Grant at Fort Monroe. Halleck did not attend this major strategic conference. As a result, Philip H. Sheridan received orders to take command of all forces near Washington and "to put himself south of the enemy and follow him to the death."[58] Soon afterward, Grant recommended that Halleck take command of the Department of the Pacific.[59]

In August 1864, Grant reappraised the command structure that he had established before the opening of the spring campaign. General-in-Chief Grant had intended to leave Meade in command of the Army of the Potomac while former General-in-Chief Halleck administered the distant armies of the Union from an administrative center in Washington. Meade had disappointed Grant by failing to coordinate the overwhelming numbers of his army to inflict maximum damage on Lee; Halleck had failed to exercise power effectively in Washington by evading responsibility for command changes and neglecting to provide a concerted defense against Early's raid against the capital. Grant sent Sheridan to take overall command of the forces opposing Early, disappointing Meade who hoped to escape Grant's shadow by exercising independent command. Grant had come to understand that Halleck would never leave his office or support bold movements against the enemy. For the remainder of the war, however, Grant retained both Halleck and Meade in their assignments while effectively holding the reins himself. Gradually generals in the field realized that Grant himself was their commander, Halleck and Meade mere intermediaries. Grant's aggressive and relentless plans must be followed. In March, Lincoln, Grant, Sherman, and Adm. David D. Porter met at City Point to discuss the final campaigns of the Civil War. Nobody expected Halleck to attend; his absence was unremarked at the time and since.

In the final days of the war, Grant made explicit his seizure of command. Meade was a forgotten man when Grant took direct control of the Appomattox campaign. Even while leading his forces against Lee, Grant remained in direct communication with Sherman. Lincoln's death, shortly after Lee's surrender, completed the process of Halleck's reassignment. Lee's surrender brought Grant back to Washington; Lincoln's death gave unprecedented power to Stanton, who detested Halleck and assigned him to command at Richmond, as much to remove him from the capital as to award him an administrative position.

While currying favor with Stanton, Halleck committed his final blunder of the Civil War, one that cost him dearly for the remainder of his life. When Sherman stumbled in providing terms of capitulation to Confederate general Joseph E. Johnston, terms that exceeded the latitude that Lincoln provided to Grant and shocked a North already reeling from Lincoln's assassination, Halleck ignored a long friendship with Sherman to echo Stanton's denunciations of Sherman's conduct. As usual, Halleck was far more concerned about pleasing his superiors than about protecting his friends. Grant went to North Carolina to solve the problems of the surrender and managed tactfully to maintain Sherman's respect and friendship, something that Halleck lost forever. Sherman's unwillingness to make peace with Halleck made easier Grant's decision to revive the plan to transfer Halleck to the Pacific Coast.

In the meantime, Halleck had plunged into his Richmond command with customary administrative energy. He labored to revive the local economy, closed churches that omitted prayer for the president of the United States, and forbade issuing marriage licenses to those unwilling to take an oath of allegiance to the United States to thwart "the propagation of legitimate rebels."[60] Scholarly instincts combined with a hope of implicating the Confederate government in the Lincoln assassination drove Halleck's assiduous effort to gather and preserve Confederate archives.

Ironically, Halleck the archivist suffered at the hands of another Union officer with a historical bent. Adam Badeau, Grant's wartime military secretary, began a postwar career as Grant's biographer. Late in 1866 he pursued Halleck's telegraphic correspondence with McClellan in the early months of 1862, telegrams that Halleck had never dreamed might ultimately fall into Grant's hands, especially after Grant had become his superior officer. At first offended by any implication that he had carried off important army headquarters records, McClellan warmed when he realized that Badeau sought evidence of Halleck's duplicity. Badeau had the damning evidence by the end of 1866. Badeau published Halleck's telegrams, "obtained by me after long research and repeated efforts," before the 1868 presidential election.[61] No word of explanation or protest came from the Pacific Coast; Halleck had no defense.

After the Civil War, Halleck seemed defeated, even dejected, as he bore insults without response. During an 1866 Fourth of July oration, Gen. Lew Wallace sneered that Halleck, "the only one of all our generals who never saw a battle," eventually found his reward as "chief of an unnamed staff."[62] Halleck's early death in 1872, days before his fifty-seventh birthday, thwarted his participation in the battle of Civil War memoirs. Yet there is no evidence that he had even attempted any justification of his wartime role. Lincoln's death had robbed him of his strongest Washington supporter and his effort to substitute Stanton's approval had cost Halleck the goodwill of his best friend among senior commanders. Of those who published postwar memoirs, Sherman came closest to defending Halleck.

When writing his *Memoirs* in 1885, Grant clearly had not forgiven Halleck for his conduct after the fall of Fort Donelson. Halleck had believed that Smith was better qualified for command than Grant, who was "rather inclined" to agree.[63] Grant, however, was still aggrieved by Halleck's telegrams to Washington and his pretense of sustaining Grant against unnamed detractors. Grant's son, Frederick Dent Grant, even more resentful, published "Halleck's Injustice to Grant," an article that reprinted the deceitful correspondence virtually without comment.[64] Halleck found a defender in Gen. James B. Fry, once chief of staff to General Buell and later head of the provost marshal bureau. Fry argued that the matter rested upon misunderstandings, that Halleck had no intention of giving Smith higher rank than Grant, and that Grant had yet to win the trust of his superiors. Grant had written that "Halleck reported to Washington . . . that my army was more demoralized by victory than the army at Bull Run had been by defeat."[65] Fry responded that "Halleck did not say that Grant's army was *more* demoralized—in fact, he did not say that it was demoralized at all. He said, 'it *seems* to be *as much* demoralized by the victory of Fort Donelson as was that of the Potomac by the defeat of Bull Run.'"[66] Fry accomplished little on behalf of his fellow bureaucrat through such ill-advised quibbling.

"After almost four decades it appears to be still the fashion to abuse General Halleck," James Grant Wilson noted in 1905. Halleck's "shortcomings have been grossly exaggerated," asserted Wilson, who turned for support to the opinion of George W. Cullum, Halleck's staff officer who later married Halleck's widow. Wilson trusted the *Official Records* to vindicate "the patriotic and scholarly soldier who sacrificed his life in the earnest, loyal and unselfish efforts to maintain and uphold the integrity of the National Government."[67]

In 1959, the posthumous fifth volume of *Lincoln Finds a General* by Kenneth P. Williams included an appendix calling for a favorable reappraisal of Halleck. Williams noted such positive points as both Grant's and Sherman's wartime admiration of Halleck, exceptions to Halleck's habitual caution, and even rare examples of his humor. Lincoln was not "always easy to deal with," wrote Williams, who concluded with a call for a "competent study of Halleck," which "should be undertaken only by a soldier with important command experience, or at least with staff closeness to command."[68]

Although not the commander that Williams had solicited, Halleck found a biographer in 1962 when Stephen E. Ambrose published the first—and only—full-length biography. Ambrose attempted to evaluate Halleck's strengths and weaknesses, describing him as frequently "petty, vindictive, and unforgiving" in personal relationships, yet "always competent, intelligent, well-organized, and sometimes brilliant" as an administrator.[69] His knowledge of the art of war so inhibited his capacity to adapt to change that he never achieved greatness as a general. His major contribution, Ambrose argued, came through a relentless insistence on military professionalism throughout the army, especially in command. West Pointers led the North to victory after political generals had been shelved. Halleck so detested political interference in military matters that he resented even what Lincoln did to keep the war going. "I am utterly sick of this political Hell," Halleck had moaned to Grant.[70]

In explaining *How the North Won*, Herman Hattaway and Archer Jones presented a strong case for a reappraisal of Halleck. Resolutely favoring military professionalism, they praised Halleck as both prophet and practitioner. Earlier writers had often commended Lincoln's instinctive strategic grasp; Hattaway and Jones instead emphasized what Halleck taught Lincoln about logistics and military protocol. Ultimately they portrayed a consummate military administrator, neither warrior nor commander.[71]

Both Halleck's strengths and weaknesses influenced his relationship with Grant. In the final year of the Civil War, Halleck's capacity to conduct correspondence with clarity and dispatch, to juggle administrative details, and to coordinate military bureaucracy benefited Grant. His brief field experience in 1862 taught him to make the wisest use of his talents by remaining behind a desk and to appreciate those, like Grant, better able to command troops and to fight battles.

Like Jefferson Davis, another product of the old army, Halleck insisted unnecessarily on proclaiming himself in the right. An overblown sense of his own achievements made him reluctant to advance the careers of officers younger or, in his opinion, less accomplished. His unmatched knowledge of the history and practice of warfare gave him a distaste for innovation. A petty personality drove his gigantic talent. Grant's unassuming ways, quiet self-confidence, and unmilitary bearing brought out the worst in Halleck. He early prepared the ground for his ultimate downfall by repeating (or inventing) rumors that Grant was drinking. Grant forgave Halleck for distrusting the generalship of the victor of Fort Donelson and Shiloh, but slander was less pardonable.

In November 1861, Halleck was the ideal choice to clean up the mess Frémont had made in Missouri. By August 1864, Grant had concluded that Halleck was superfluous, a verdict strengthened at the close of the war. Unaware that Halleck had betrayed him after Donelson, Grant knew that Halleck had behaved disloyally to Sherman after Johnston's surrender. Professional soldiers whose careers Halleck had furthered preferred not to share their triumph with him. The need for his administrative expertise had ended.

The old army had shaped both Grant and Halleck. At the outbreak of war, older officers assessing prewar service looked to Halleck for leadership and considered Grant a questionable choice for command. Halleck had successfully mastered military history and technique but, unlike Grant, did not rise above the traditional to meet new challenges of war. Grant had acquired practical experience as quartermaster, commissary, adjutant, and company commander but, unlike Halleck, had no fondness for the culture of the old army. Grant's ambivalent attitude toward the military led to creative solutions of strategic problems. "The laws of successful war in one generation would insure defeat in another," Grant once remarked.[72] By war's end, each had found an appropriate role: Grant as victorious commander, Halleck as military housekeeper.

NOTES

John Y. Simon delivered his Klement Lecture in 1996.

1. William B. Skelton, *An American Profession of Arms: The Army Officer Corps, 1784–1861* (Lawrence: Univ. Press of Kansas, 1992), 201–2; Milton H. Shutes, "Henry Wager Halleck: Lincoln's Chief of Staff," *California Historical Society Quarterly* 16 (1937): 198; Lloyd Lewis, *Captain Sam Grant* (Boston: Little, Brown, 1950), 311–12, 316–19.

2. Skelton, *American Profession*, 198.

3. Ibid., 193; Edward M. Coffman, *The Old Army: A Portrait of the American Army in Peacetime, 1784–1898* (New York: Oxford Univ. Press, 1986), 49.

4. Skelton, *American Profession*, 215.

5. Stephen E. Ambrose, *Duty, Honor, Country: A History of West Point* (Baltimore: Johns Hopkins Univ. Press, 1966), 108.

6. James Grant Wilson, "General Halleck—A Memoir," *Journal of the Military Service Institution of the United States* 36 (1905): 537–41; Stephen E. Ambrose, *Halleck: Lincoln's Chief of Staff* (Baton Rouge: Louisiana State Univ. Press, 1962), 5–7.

7. George W. Cullum, *Biographical Register of the Officers and Graduates of the U.S. Military Academy . . .* , 3d ed. (Boston: Houghton, Mifflin, 1891), 1:735.

8. Shutes, "Halleck," 196–99; Ambrose, *Halleck*, 7–8.

9. Shutes, "Halleck," 198–200.

10. Ibid., 200–201; Winfield Scott to Simon Cameron, Oct. 4, 1861, *The War of the Rebellion: A Compilation of the Official Records of the Union and Confederate Armies*, 128 vols. (Washington, D.C.: Government Printing Office, 1880–1901), ser. 1, vol. 51, 1:491–93 (hereafter *OR*); T. Harry Williams, *Lincoln and His Generals* (New York: Alfred A. Knopf, 1952), 43.

11. John Y. Simon, ed., *The Papers of Ulysses S. Grant* (Carbondale: Southern Illinois Univ. Press, 1967–), 2:191–92.

12. Ulysses S. Grant, *Personal Memoirs of U. S. Grant* (New York: Charles L. Webster, 1885–86), 1:287.

13. Grant to Capt. John C. Kelton, Feb. 6, 1862, Simon, ed., *Grant Papers*, 4:157, 158.

14. Grant, *Memoirs*, 1:296.

15. Grant to Simon B. Buckner, Feb. 16, 1862, Simon, ed., *Grant Papers*, 4:218.

16. Halleck to George B. McClellan, Feb. 8, 1862, *OR*, 7:594, 595; Simon, ed., *Grant Papers*, 4:196–97.

17. Halleck to McClellan, Feb. 17, 1862, *OR*, 7:628.

18. Halleck to McClellan, Feb. 19, 1862, ibid., 637.

19. Halleck to McClellan, Mar. 3, 1862, ibid., 679–80.

20. McClellan to Halleck, Mar. 3, 1862, ibid., 680.

21. Halleck to McClellan, Mar. 4, 1862, ibid., 682.

22. Halleck to Grant, Mar. 4, 1862, Simon, ed., *Grant Papers*, 4:319.

23. Grant to Halleck, Mar. 5, 1862, *OR*, 7:318.

24. Halleck to Grant, Mar. 9, 1862, ibid., 319.

25. Halleck to Grant, Mar. 6, 1862, ibid., 331.

26. Grant to Halleck, Mar. 7, 1862, ibid.

27. Halleck to Grant, Mar. 8, 1862, ibid., 335.

28. Grant to Halleck, Mar. 9, 1862, ibid., 334.

29. Halleck to Grant, Mar. 6, 1862, ibid., 354.

30. Grant to Halleck, Mar. 13, 1862, ibid., 353.

31. Halleck to Grant, Mar. 13, 1862, ibid., 354–55.

32. Grant to Halleck, Mar. 24, 1862, ibid., 415.

33. Sherman to Robert N. Scott, Sept. 6, 1885, in Sherman, "An Unspoken Address to the Loyal Legion," *North American Review* 142 (1886): 302–3.

34. Grant to Julia Dent Grant, Apr. 25, 1862, Simon, ed., *Grant Papers*, 5:72.

35. Grant to Julia Dent Grant, Apr. 30, 1862, ibid., 102.

36. Grant to Halleck, May 11, 1862, ibid., 114.

37. Halleck to Grant, May 12, 1862, ibid., 115.

38. T. Harry Williams, *Lincoln and the Radicals* (Madison: Univ. of Wisconsin Press, 1941), 151.

39. Grant, *Memoirs*, 1:381–84.

40. Grant to Elihu B. Washburne, July 22, 1862, Simon, ed., *Grant Papers*, 5:226.

41. Halleck to Mrs. Halleck, Aug. 13, 1862, Wilson, "Halleck," 557; Adam Badeau, *Military History of Ulysses S. Grant* (New York: D. Appleton, 1868–81), 1:108; Sherman to Robert N. Scott, Aug. 30, 1885, Sherman, "Unspoken Address," 301.

42. Grant, *Memoirs*, 1:579.

43. Halleck to McClellan, July 30, 1862, *OR*, vol. 11, pt. 3:343.

44. McClellan to Halleck, Aug. 1, 1862, ibid., 345.

45. McClellan to Mary Ellen McClellan, July 18, 1862, Stephen W. Sears, ed., *The Civil War Papers of George B. McClellan: Selected Correspondence, 1860–1865* (New York: Ticknor & Fields, 1989), 364.

46. McClellan to Mary Ellen McClellan, July 20, 1862, and McClellan to Samuel L. M. Barlow, July 23, 1862, ibid., 368, 369.

47. Halleck to Mrs. Halleck, July 5, 28, Aug. 9, 1862, Wilson, "Halleck," 556–57.

48. Halleck to Mrs. Halleck, Sept. 5, 1862, ibid., 558.

49. McClellan to Mary Ellen McClellan, Sept. 2, 1862, Sears, ed., *McClellan Papers*, 428.

50. McClellan to Mary Ellen McClellan, Sept. 20, 1862, ibid., 473.

51. McClellan to Mary Ellen McClellan, Sept. 20, Oct. 2, 1862, ibid., 473, 488.

52. July 15, 1863, Howard K. Beale, ed., *Diary of Gideon Welles: Secretary of the Navy Under Lincoln and Johnson* (New York: W. W. Norton, 1960), 1:373.

53. Sept. 29, 1863, ibid., 1:448.

54. Halleck to Grant, Aug. 1, 1863, Simon, ed., *Grant Papers*, 8:523.

55. Rawlins to Elihu B. Washburne, Jan. 20, 1864, James Harrison Wilson, *The Life of John A. Rawlins* (New York: Neale, 1916), 387.

56. *OR*, 33:669; Badeau, *Military History*, 2:18.

57. Mar. 24, Apr. 28, 1864, Tyler Dennett, ed., *Lincoln and the Civil War in the Diaries and Letters of John Hay* (New York: Dodd, Mead, 1939), 167, 176; Grant, *Memoirs*, 2:122.

58. Grant to Halleck, Aug. 1, 1864, Simon, ed., *Grant Papers*, 11:358.

59. Grant to Stanton, Aug. 15, 1864, ibid., 422.

60. Ambrose, *Halleck*, 203.

61. Badeau, *Military History*, 1:65; Grant to McClellan, Dec. 10, 1866, Simon, ed., *Grant Papers*, 16:409–13; Grant, *Memoirs*, 1:326–28; George B. McClellan, *McClellan's Own Story* (New York: Charles L. Webster, 1887), 217–21.

62. July 4, 1866, "Return of the Flags," in Thomas B. Reed, ed., *Modern Eloquence* (New York: American Law Book, 1903), 9:1125.

63. Grant, *Memoirs*, 1:328.

64. F. D. Grant, "Halleck's Injustice to Grant," *North American Review* 141 (1885): 513–22.

65. Grant, *Memoirs*, 1:327.

66. James B. Fry, "Halleck and Grant—Misunderstandings," *Military Miscellanies* (New York: Brentano's, 1889), 334.

67. Wilson, "Halleck," 344.

68. Kenneth P. Williams, *Lincoln Finds a General* (New York: Macmillan, 1949–59), 5:271–82.

69. Ambrose, *Halleck*, 207.

70. Halleck to Grant, July 11, 1863, Simon, ed., *Grant Papers*, 9:99.

71. Herman Hattaway and Archer Jones, *How the North Won: A Military History of the Civil War* (Urbana: Univ. of Illinois Press, 1983).

72. John Russell Young, *Around the World with General Grant* (New York: American News Co., 1879), 2:625.

"Public Women" and the Confederacy

❦ Catherine Clinton has ably and confidently taken on controversial topics in the field of southern women's history in particular and in the larger field of Civil War history in general. Indeed, in the best sense of the word, she has even *made* some topics controversial. She teaches, lectures, and writes—for adults as well as for children—all the while asking her readers to consider Civil War history from fresh perspectives. She has largely succeeded. Her greatest influence has been in women's history. Her books, *The Plantation Mistress: Women's World in the Old South* (1982) and *The Other Civil War: American Women in the Nineteenth Century* (1999), have played an important role in the revival over the last twenty years of work on southern women. One scholar called *The Other Civil War* a "signpost in the development of women's history." Both books have demanded that romantic and unrealistic visions of white southern women give way to more historically accurate assessments.

Clinton's diverse scholarly interests mirror her diverse educational background. She received her A.B. in Sociology and Afro-American studies from Harvard University, her M.A. in American studies from the University of Sussex, England, and her Ph.D. in history at Princeton University. Since then, she has taught at Harvard

RICHMOND LADIES GOING TO RECEIVE GOVERNMENT RATIONS.—Sketched by A. R. Waud.—[See the First Page.]
"Don't you think that Yankee must feel like shrinking into his boots before such high-toned Southern ladies as we?"

Harper's Weekly depicting defiant women in occupied Richmond in June 1865. Library of Congress Prints and Photographs Division.

University, Union College, Brandeis University, and Wesleyan University and has also held endowed professorships at the University of Richmond and the Citadel.

Although she made her name in women's history, Clinton has authored, coauthored, edited, or coedited nearly thirty books on topics ranging from loyalty on the Civil War home front to women's poetry to African American soldiers. *Taking off the White Gloves: Southern Women and Women Historians* (1998), which she edited with Michele Gillespie, is a unique look at both the history of women in the South and the unique approaches of historians who are women. Her interest in African American history has also guided her choice of projects: *Harriet Tubman: The Road to Freedom* (2004) was named one of the best nonfiction books for 2004 by both the *Christian Science Monitor* and the *Chicago Tribune*. She is also the author of a number of books for children, including an encyclopedia and a textbook on the Civil War, as well as *Hold the Flag High* (2006), which tells the story of William Carney (the first African American to be awarded the Congressional Medal of Honor) and his regiment, the 54th Massachusetts.

Clinton's Klement Lecture brought together a number of her interests and skills. By examining the real and rhetorical relationships between southern women on the home front and the many prostitutes in the Confederate capital of Richmond, she arrives at typically provocative conclusions about public roles for women and questions about female virtue. 〰

I DID NOT TOUR CIVIL WAR battlefields as a child. I did not have rows of soldiers on my bedroom shelf or the names of regiments and battles dancing in my head before I went to bed at night. Indeed, when I walked into Jim McPherson's graduate seminar in the fall of 1975, I had no idea what "Little Round Top" was—and certainly no plans to become a Civil War historian.[1]

But over the past twenty-five years, the field of Civil War studies has been expanding and has transformed itself. American social historians have tried to move us away from the dialectics of "winning or losing," away from focus strictly on Civil War battle tactics. Documentary historians such as Ken Burns have insisted that we provide human faces for this momentous event, to connect lives and individuals to the great sweep of history the Civil War represented. And even now scholarship by political and revisionist military historians takes into account the "will" of the people and the significance of civilian mobilization, more of a "hearts and minds" school of history than the "guns and butter" of previous investigators.

Simultaneously, Civil War history has been dramatically shaped by the questions posed and issues explored by historians working in fields in which I have labored—in women's history, in African American history, and, finally, in southern history. The war's many layers of meanings have grown exponentially in the past quarter-century—as has the literature, with a conservative tally of 60,000 volumes on this watershed event, and more titles churned out every year.

With all this writing, you might well think one or more of these thousands of books would have covered every single subject on the war. But it was my distinct displeasure to discover, as I did in 1988 following the 125th anniversary celebration of the Battle of Gettysburg, that there were only a handful of references to the topic of prostitution during the Civil War. This grand celebration at Gettysburg included a reenactment with thousands upon thousands of buffs, fans, costumed participants, and media in attendance. I found myself besieged by women, several seeking authentic information on brothels and bawdyhouses and on public women, as prostitutes were called in the nineteenth century.

Dipping into library catalogs to try to find information about Civil War prostitutes, I came up virtually empty. I was able to find some statistical information on venereal diseases, and some astute observations in the work of Bell Wiley and Mary Elizabeth Massey; but other than these limited findings, it was a very disappointing search.[2] But because I had pestered scholars seeking information, my colleagues at the *Encyclopedia of the Confederacy*, who drafted me for the board of advisors, dragooned me into writing a brief article on prostitution for inclusion in our 1993 volumes. Too much of my essay was concerned with the lack of information, the problems of censorship, and the need for future work.[3]

But I confronted this issue afresh in the fall of 1995 when I was involved in radio interviews about my then-most-recent book, *Tara Revisited: Women, War, and the Plantation Legend* (1995). Not once, but twice—in different New England venues—callers phoned in to ask me about the topic of "Southern women as prostitutes." They indicated they had heard that because of the war, most of the white women in the South became prostitutes.

It apparently remains a folkloric notion that starvation drove masses of white southern women into selling their bodies. Allegedly some did so to survive the ravages of war and some to feed their children, and, incredibly, some allegedly were motivated to infect Union troops with disease. Notions of Confederate women's tumble "from pedestal to brothel," and/or dosing soldiers with VD as if it were some kind of weapon, fascinated me. Usually these legends are built upon some grain of truth, but I could not really find any historical or literary foundation for rumors of mass conversions. Certainly there might have been hundreds of women forced to sell sex to survive, but not the thousands these callers had suggested.

I wondered if there wasn't some sort of time-warp element in all of this disinformation. Perhaps callers were influenced by the idea that the "Southern lady" might not be so much of a lady after all—which had been somewhat of a cultural bombshell during civil rights agitation. This significant demystification is represented by a generation of novels, plays, and films, such as *To Kill a Mockingbird*, which features a courtroom drama where the defense of white womanhood is put on trial by Harper Lee's hero, Atticus Finch. Perhaps the revised and sullied reputation of southern white womanhood was being projected backward a hundred years or so—and this "temptress" image was being embellished and exaggerated into legions of southern prostitutes.

Again, even if this preposterous turn of events were the case, where would evidence be found? On the topic of sexual licentiousness of any kind, we know that scholars have encountered deliberate obfuscation. Bell Wiley complained about families censoring soldiers' letters and veterans avoiding the subject during his investigation of the topic.[4] Even the ladylike Mary Elizabeth Massey would have included some hint of the issue if she had found it—after all, it was she who introduced me to "the Floating Whorehouse," to which I shall return later. But I determined to look beyond the borders of sexology, above and beyond the "commerce of sex" and "wages of sin" schools, to satisfy my growing curiosity about the Civil War experience.

On the question of language,[5] I asked a few historians innocently at a conference what they thought of my looking into the careers of nineteenth-century public women. Most enthusiastically endorsed the topic. When I tipped my hand and asked what they thought it meant to be a "public woman" in the nineteenth century, most confessed they assumed it meant women moving into the public sphere. Only one or two were aware that the term "public woman" had a totally different connotation during the nineteenth century, which made it all the more challenging with my research interests.[6]

Why should the feminine counterpart to master—"mistress"—come to mean corruption and degradation, rather than a term of empowerment and approbation? Why should a "public woman" be embraced and scorned while a "man of the public" was embraced and exalted? The topsy-turvy quality of shifts in language and the hangover of Victoriana intrigued me.

Surely this was a good time to be exploring these kinds of questions in conjunction with the Civil War. Recent work by Elizabeth Leonard and Ella Forbes has examined what kind of women, white and black, were found in army camps.[7] More frank assessments of southern interracial sexual relations during the nineteenth century have emerged in the past few years with work by Martha Hodes, Edward Ball, and Henry Wiencek.[8] Other compelling research has been ongoing concerning the role of Confederate women during wartime—the role of women at the level of "state-building," both their symbolic and real roles.[9]

The southern family was seen as the anchor of Confederate civilization. Even privilege could not insulate planter families from the ravages of war.

Wealthy as well as struggling farm families were uprooted from their lands when Yankees invaded. Dislocation, discomfort, and despair roamed the roads with refugees, who felt their worlds turned upside down.[10]

Mothers and wives were expected to hold families together, especially while patriarchs and male heirs marched off to conquer the enemy. Even the most genteel of gentlewomen was forced by the pressures of patriotism to mobilize for her nation. Most undertook patriotic activity, and, as war went on, necessity drove many into paid employment to keep families afloat. Judith McGuire of Alexandria was from one of the first families of Virginia but a refugee in 1861. While Jefferson Davis and his family were comfortably ensconced in the former home of her kinsman (the Brokenbrough mansion had been designated as the White House of the Confederacy), McGuire was forced to wander the streets of Richmond, begging for shelter for herself and her children. McGuire had status and connections denied to many of her southern sisters and finally found refuge. But for many hundreds and eventually thousands of women, survival was not so simply assured. Doubtless, many females without resources or alternatives were reduced to selling their bodies.

At the same time, poverty was a constant throughout the century. Hard times could not be the main factor creating the boom in prostitution from 1861 to 1865. Rather, it was the mobilization of rival national armies that was the greatest causal factor. And thus the Civil War was the primary cause of the largest increase in the sex trade in the nineteenth century, perhaps the single greatest spurt of growth in the nation's history. The dramatic leap in the number of American prostitutes—this exponential expansion of the sex trade—was a mounting concern during wartime. Yet civilian moral reformers were forced to delay any preventive or punitive campaigns until a military resolution to the war was concluded.[11]

But before tackling prostitution during the war, perhaps we need to understand its dimensions before 1861. We know there were brothels throughout the United States, in bustling port cities as well as rural hamlets. We know that large numbers of women who sold sex were affiliated with "houses," but larger numbers operated independently as "streetwalkers," although their lack of affiliation makes them difficult to calculate. However, whatever these combined numbers, they were overshadowed by those who participated in "casual prostitution." Evidence indicates that poor and/or wage-earning women frequently sold sexual favors to acquaintances. Most viewed this as a minor exchange. These women never thought of themselves as "prostitutes," who were considered professionals.[12] "Public women" was a term reserved for those women who supported themselves solely through supplying multiple partners with sex for money.

Evidence indicates that hundreds of nineteenth-century women were involved in private contractual arrangements with individual men. These women might provide sexual favors in exchange for upkeep—and were therefore known as "kept women."[13] But for the purposes of this investigation, discussion will be limited to those women who supported themselves through the sex trade—in brothels or on the street. We know there were brothels and even "blue" guides for major cities (describing and ranking establishments) along the eastern seaboard.[14] New Orleans had its own guide, which produced several editions in the late nineteenth and early twentieth centuries.

Work on prostitution before the Civil War is extremely thin, and data is sparse. The bulk of material is drawn from criminal court records, which offer little insight into the daily lives of prostitutes, their thoughts and opinions.[15] Thus, our limited evidence on prostitution comes mainly from the records of a legal system which criminalized their activity and extracted few, if any, opinions from these public women themselves.[16]

Much of our information comes exclusively from one major urban center that had the largest number of prostitutes in antebellum America and might well be called "the Prostitution Capital of the United States": New York City. (Only New Orleans could perhaps usurp this claim, because New Orleans had a larger *percentage* of its female population involved in the sex trade, although its *numbers* were considerably smaller than the more densely populated Manhattan.)

What we know about prostitutes in antebellum Manhattan has been drawn mainly from a single valuable source, William W. Sanger's *The History of Prostitution* (1858). Dr. Sanger was the chief resident physician at Blackwell's Island Hospital in New York City in 1855 when he began his investigation of venereal diseases among the poor. His study was based on more than 2,000 questionnaires, and Sanger also conducted research at each Manhattan police precinct, making his the most sophisticated, scientific, and comprehensive survey of its day.[17]

Moral reformers in the 1830s claimed there were 10,000 prostitutes in the city—an outlandish and exaggerated claim. The chief of police of New York estimated there were 2,500 prostitutes, and by 1856 the official police estimate was 5,000—one prostitute for every forty-seven adult females. (These police statistics mainly came from arrest records, however, and did not reflect multiple charges, or those who evaded the law.) Between 1830 and 1860 the population of New York City quadrupled and sexual commerce perhaps grew at an even more rapid rate—alarming reformers and police alike.

Sanger discovered from his investigations that over 60 percent of New York prostitutes were foreign born—certainly disproportionate to their numbers in the population. (And of these foreign born, Irish women were overrepresented.) Half the prostitutes Sanger interviewed were mothers; 75 percent of the widows were mothers, and 30 percent of the never-married women were mothers. Nearly half the children born to prostitutes were born before these women began to accept money for sex. Forty-nine percent of the women were domestics prior to becoming prostitutes, and 21 percent were in the sewing trades.

Contrary to popular literary themes, most prostitutes were not seduced and abandoned by a man, leading them to a life of sin. (Roughly 10 percent claimed this motive/excuse in Sanger's survey.) Most poor women, with limited opportunities, found prostitution a lucrative alternative to the hardscrabble lives they were living, especially those mothers who lost male heads of household to desertion or death. When Walt Whitman's brother died in Brooklyn in 1862, his sister-in-law was five months pregnant. She turned to prostitution to support herself.[18]

At midcentury, a New York City woman with two children required approximately $135 a year for food, clothing, and shelter. The average earnings of a prostitute were $10 per week, nearly five times what a servant or seamstress might earn. Further, a prostitute might see her trade as a means of upward mobility. Indeed, 40 percent of women property owners in New York City in the decade before the Civil War were brothel owners. Urban mythology declared that there were no old prostitutes, and indeed it was a young woman's, or even a girl's, profession.[19] George Ellington in his exposé *The Women of New York* (1869) declared that 99 out of 100 prostitutes perished young, contributing "to the many unhallowed graves."[20]

Dr. Sanger suggested the career span of a New York City prostitute was four years. Further, he opined, "one fourth of the total number of abandoned women in the city die every year."[21] Despite these declarations, evidence suggests that not all sex workers ended up derelict on the streets they once strolled or dead in paupers' graves.

Most prostitutes were in the business because they had no economic alternatives.[22] When they found an alternate means of support, they might retire; a healthy percentage left the sex trade to become wives, even of clients. So there might not have been many old prostitutes at work, but there were many retired ones who led long lives.

New York City prostitutes were not confined to any single geographic area but could be found dispersed throughout the city. However, there were high concentrations of brothels, especially from the 1860s onward. During the Civil War, the vice districts moved northward from Washington Square to Union Square (the "Rialto") and West 25th Street, near the Tenderloin district. Along West 25th Street, seven infamous brothels lined the road and became known as "the Seven Sisters."

In the 1860s there were nearly 600 houses of prostitution in New York.[23] Ironically, the handful of homes for wayward women established as refuges for women on the streets were relatively empty. In 1866 the Magdalen Asylum had only eleven inmates, and the American Female Guardian Society's Home of the Friendless housed eighty-nine women—this in a city with a population of 6,000 prostitutes and half a million people.

Investments in New York brothels skyrocketed during the war years. A landlord might command a rent of anywhere between $500 to $9,000 per house, with the average rent of a brothel in the 1860s approximately $1,000. Individual sex workers paid their weekly room and board—plus a portion of their earnings known as "bed money." A successful Manhattan brothel might take in $25,000 a year, during a period when the average male worker earned $250 to $600. Certainly there was a high rate of commercial profit—which is why so many prostitutes felt fines were negligible (a sin tax) and madams paid bribes (substantially more, but worth it). Sex workers were determined to keep cash rolling in despite occasional tangles with the law.

Police did try to crack down on women who worked with male partners in "panel houses." Prostitutes' accomplices, who popped out from behind a "panel" in the prostitute's room once the intended victim had disrobed, robbed male clients. But most men who got rolled this way were too embarrassed to report incidents to the police. This con game thrived during midcentury.

This era also saw the rise of concert saloons where "waiter girls" might take customers to an upstairs room for a quick exchange of sex for money. In 1862 New York tried to halt this expansion by passing a law to close concert saloons.[24] But vice still flourished. By 1866 there were nearly 6,000 arrests in New York annually for prostitution. A Methodist Bishop announced the city was overrun with nearly 12,000 prostitutes.[25] Despite New York's preeminence, the reputations of wartime Washington and Richmond as dens of iniquity escalated from 1861 onward. When the war broke out, certainly the focus was on the raising and assembling of armies, which naturally drew near the two capitals of the warring Union and the Confederacy.

In 1864 there were 450 brothels in Washington[26] and more than seventy-five brothels in nearby Alexandria, Virginia.[27] A newspaper estimated there were 5,000 public women in the District and another 2,500 in Alexandria and Georgetown, bringing the total to 7,500 by the war's third year. In 1864 the provost marshal of D.C. drew up a list of District brothels, offering not only the names and addresses of establishments, but the number of "inmates" and a ranking: "1," "2," "3," or "low." (The provost marshal's report did not include some of the picturesque names assigned these houses: "the Ironclad," "the Blue Goose," and the "Haystack," run by a Mrs. Hay.) The smallest house contained two prostitutes, with the largest establishment listing eighteen. But the provost claimed there were only eighty-five bawdy houses.[28] This was a far cry from what the popular press reported.

Richmond was a small city of 38,000 (less than one-fourth the population of New Orleans) when the war began. The town was overrun with soldiers, adventurers, gamblers, and con men within months of Davis's arrival at the new Confederate capital. After years of war, the city was drastically transformed. The mayor complained in August 1864 about his crumbling domain: "Never was a place more changed than Richmond. Go on the Capital Square any afternoon, and you may see these women promenading up and down the shady walks jostling respectable ladies into the gutters."[29] So brothel residents were not content to keep to their bordellos but paraded in daylight, defying dictates of propriety and respectability.

Nightlife in Richmond centered on an area only four blocks from Capital Square, where the Ballard and Exchange hotels reigned on Franklin Street. Infamous madams set up shop above gambling and grog shops along Locust Alley. One of them, a woman named Clara, kept a diary describing her customers.[30] She recalled demanding only Union money from one of her regular clients, a Confederate general. She sarcastically commented, "Wonder what old sourface would say if he knew one of his plate-lickers had so much Yankee money."[31] She then goes on to describe, "Rednose Mayo [the Mayor] had some of his bully police break in 7 houses around the corner last night. I sent $50 in metal this morning. Let them come *here!*"[32] Clara, like most madams, found legal interference annoying but considered police bribes and court fines a small price to pay for conducting her profitable business.

Prostitution, which had been a minor nuisance to the Virginia capital before the war, became a major headache to its "respectable" inhabitants, especially society women. The population multiplied fourfold in a matter of a few years, and vice was rampant and notorious. The flash and boldness of public women offended the ladies of quality who flocked to Richmond seeking more power for their husbands and a rise in their own social status. Some fashionably bedecked public women were even accompanied by uniformed officers, which offended the wives of cabinet members and other ladies of Richmond.

Further, as the war dragged on, prostitutes maintained their access to hard cash (metal vs. paper money) and a flow of European goods through their connections with smugglers. The latest fashions denied to the wives of generals and government officials might be found on the "strumpets" or "harlots" who had overrun Capital Square. Envy as well as anger fueled respectable women's campaigns against public women.

Certainly the mobilization of large armies, the movement of regiments, and the construction of tent cities created "camp followers" and other nicknames for prostitutes on the move. (We know that the term "hooker" to indicate a "loose woman" predated the Civil War; but we also know the term "Hooker's Divisions," which refers to specific districts in Washington where houses of prostitution flourished, was a reference to Union general Joseph Hooker and his proclivity for contact with prostitutes.) Large numbers of women seeking clients settled near the military headquarters of each warring nation.

But when we start to look at this question of prostitution and its dimensions during the Civil War, we are really much more dependent on military records than civilian courts. Most civilians viewed prostitution as a negligible crime even before the war, but among law enforcement officials North and South, prosecutorial zeal appears to have hibernated during the war. As a result, much more is available by examining military records—especially the comparatively ample Union documents.

We have no idea what the moral imperatives were, but we do know prostitution was *not* an equal opportunity issue for soldiers North and South. Both Confederate and Union soldiers had contact with prostitutes, but because Union soldiers were better paid and offered more frequent and easy access to cities, soldiers in blue were more likely to frequent prostitutes than soldiers in gray. Yet because of prolonged embattlement within the

Confederacy—months and even years of occupation—the numbers would suggest as well that the majority of Civil War prostitutes were drawn from the South. Thus the irony remains that sex for sale was most often across enemy lines.

Both Confederate and Union sources claimed that the South was being flooded with Yankee women of bad character. But registers of local prostitutes operating out of cities in the upper South indicate the women were drawn, in the main, from the South. The demand for prostitutes seemed to have been met by a local supply, not any massive import of migrant or immigrant women.

Certainly both sides engaged in the game of demonizing the enemy. It was not unusual for a nation to brand enemy women as "wanton" or "loose," therefore any acts of defilement were excused by the women's own base morals. However, the American Civil War is characterized by a low level of violence against women, especially sex crimes, compared to other civil conflicts. (At the same time, racial dynamics came into play during this volatile epoch, and African American women suffered most from both smear campaigns and actual assaults.)[33]

Members of both armies commented on the way in which the advent of war transformed moral behavior for both men and women. A recruit confessed, "The more we see the more we are convinced that this war is the most damnable curse that ever was brung upon the human family."[34]

Private Orville Bumpass with the Rebel army in northern Alabama wrote with considerable scorn of his environs: "The state of the morals is quite as low as the soil, almost all the women are given to whoredom & the ugliest, shallowfaced, shaggy headed, bare footed dirty wretches you ever saw."[35] (And I must comment this is perhaps the harshest statement I have ever read by a Confederate soldier about southern white women—so conditions must have been appalling to make him drop all pretense of chivalry.)

Another son of the South with the 4th South Carolina wrote to his wife in disgust about prostitutes visiting the camp, blaming his fellow soldiers: "You would think there was not a married man in the regiment but me."[36] Fraternization was at full tilt: "The lower class (both blacks & white in the South) seem to be totally ignorant of the meaning of the word 'Virtue' & both officers & men appear to have cast off all the restraints of home & indulge their passions to the fullest extent."[37]

A member of the 8th Indiana Cavalry stationed in Savannah complained that husbands in his unit had "undue communication with negro wenches down here."[38] Savannah, like New Orleans, sported an exotic vice district, featuring interracial sexual connections.[39] Brothels dotted the area along Factor's Walk. Bay Street and the bluff were equally disreputable, described as "thronged by sailors, slaves and rowdies of all grades and color." A racially mixed atmosphere reigned in the Yamacraw district, which was outside the city wards (and the city watch) until 1854. This area boasted four "houses of ill fame," where clients might choose black or white women.[40]

War, especially federal occupation, brought about drastic changes in Savannah. A grand jury complained in 1864 about "the intrusion into the more public and respectable streets of the city, of houses of ill fame."[41] This encroachment continued despite both civil and military attempts to curb spreading corruption. A Union comrade explained that while his company was stationed in Savannah, "I'm on duty every other day; but the reasons of it is because there are so many hore houses in town which must have a Sentinel at each door for to keep them Straight."[42] Another one of Sherman's men confessed, "You can not imagine the temptations that beset a soldier on every hand."[43]

A Union officer in Tennessee described how lewd women lured two Union pickets from their post.[44] The soldiers were later shot for the crime of desertion. The officer went on to complain that "female virtue if it ever existed in this Country seems now almost a perfect wreck. Prostitutes are thickly crowded through mountain & valley, in hamlet & city." He does lay the blame on the wantonness of southern women but is willing to admit "that the influence of the armies has largely contributed to this state of things, as soldiers do not seem to feel the same restraints away from home, which at home regulated their intercourse with the gentler sex."[45]

A Union soldier described the army as "a graveyard for morals."[46] One Connecticut soldier stationed in Virginia near Portsmouth and Norfolk recalled that the towns were nicknamed "Sodom and Gomorrow on account of the wicketness." But he also confessed that a lot of the public women he encountered were from his own home state.[47] In April of 1863 boatloads of "women of ill fame" docked in Memphis, and many believed "the importation of lewd women from the North is at high tide."[48]

One observer of camp life under Confederate general Albert Sidney Johnston commented:

> It is really curious to observe how well and how strictly the three classes of women in camp keep aloof from each other. The wives and daughters of Colonels, Captains and other officers constitute the first class. The rough cooks and washers who have their husbands along . . . form the second class. The

third and last class is happily the smallest; here and there a female of elegant appearance and unexceptional manners, truly wife-like in their tented-seclusion, but lacking that great and only voucher of respectability for females in camp—the marriage tie.[49]

Having public women in camp, no matter how small their numbers, could and did influence bawdy behavior. In March of 1863, when officers' wives were safely tucked away at home, Confederate soldiers near Fredericksburg staged an all-male review, which witnesses reported included one completely nude male. There were several civilians in the audience, including females. An observer sniffed that although they were wearing dresses, there was "not much of the Lady" about the women in this audience.[50] A Confederate soldier discouraged his wife from a visit to camp, confiding, "Don't never come here as long as you can ceep away for you will smell hell here."[51] Another Virginia soldier asked his wife not to visit for fear she would be identified as a prostitute because he knew "this country is filled up with Prostitutes who pass as soldiers wives."[52]

Camps located near towns, and especially ports, proved most vulnerable to invasion by prostitutes. Petersburg was a booming center for the sex trade. Soldiers would sneak into town to avail themselves of prostitutes' services, or women might set up shop a few hundred yards outside camp.[53] By 1864 City Point had become a notorious crossroads in Virginia.[54] A soldier from the 14th Indiana wrote to his wife about nearby Alexandria, Virginia: "It is said that one house of every ten is a bawdy house—it is a perfect Sodom. The result will be that in a week or two, there will be an increase of sickness in camp."[55]

And now we get to the crux of the matter—that men who frequented prostitutes might have to pay a steep price. Moral decay was not the primary concern of military leaders; rather, they hated to see their ranks decimated by disease. Few soldiers *died* of venereal diseases during wartime, although it has been suggested secondary stages of tertiary syphilis was the leading cause of death in veterans' hospitals late in the nineteenth century. Primarily, during wartime, officers saw prostitutes as a health hazard to their men.

At the same time, soldiers—many of them young men away from home for the first time and perhaps never to return—were willing to take their chances in a brothel before they faced the odds on a battlefield. It's not that Civil War soldiers were indifferent to venereal disease, but they were not as concerned about the possibility of infection as their commanders were.

Confederate leaders witnessed with alarm the growing numbers of men struck down by sexually transmitted diseases. In December 1862, an article in the *Richmond Examiner* entreated: "If the Mayor of Richmond lacks any incentive to . . . breaking up the resorts of ill-fame in the city, let him visit the military hospitals, where sick and disabled soldiers are received for treatment . . . wrecked upon the treacherous shoals of vice and passion."[56] And even in the Richmond hospitals disabled soldiers weren't safe, as in 1862 when one enterprising madam opened a brothel directly across the street from a hospital run by the YMCA. Females hawking their wares appeared in windows in various states of undress to try to entice patients from their beds. The manager of the hospital remonstrated that this activity was interfering with soldiers' speedy recoveries.[57]

Despite these lighthearted stories appearing in local papers or jokes about "Pox" and "Clap" in soldiers' letters, venereal diseases were no laughing matter.[58] Modern scholarship demonstrates that three out of five Civil War soldiers died of diseases unrelated to any battle wounds.[59] So Civil War medicine was a vital issue for armies hoping to keep their ranks stocked with able bodies.

Five million Union soldiers reported to sick bay during the war: 1,100,000 cases of acute diarrhea led to 27,000 deaths, 238,000 cases of dysentery led to 4,000 deaths, and 49,000 cases of malaria led to another 4,000 deaths. By comparison, the reported 73,000 cases of syphilis led to only 123 deaths and the nearly 31,000 cases of gonorrhea led to just six deaths.[60] Sexually transmitted diseases did not cause significant fatalities, but they did cause significant absences from the ranks. Evidence suggests that among white troops, eighty-two per thousand soldiers per year reported venereal diseases. Statistics cannot tell us the whole story, but roughly one in every eleven Yankee soldiers suffered the effects of venereal disease sometime during the war years.

Medical science offered no effective preventive medicine during the Civil War era. Although rubber had been vulcanized as early as the 1840s, it was not until the Philadelphia Exposition in 1876 that the rubber condom was introduced.[61] Before that, young men employed condoms made of lamb guts—known as "sheepskins." Prostitutes might have offered sheepskins to clients, which could prevent pregnancy, but were ineffective against the spread of disease.

Nevertheless, Civil War doctors were adept at diagnosing and curing sexually transmitted diseases. However, one surgeon with the 11th Illinois

Cavalry carped, "It was impossible to cure gonorrhea while the patients were exposed to the rain and had to sleep on the damp ground and live on a salt and stimulating ration."[62] Another surgeon with the 115th Pennsylvania near Alexandria, Virginia, described his gonorrhea cure: "injecting a solution of chlorate of potach, one drachm in eight ounces, every hour for twelve successive hours, and then gradually ceasing its use during the next two or three days by prolonging the interval between each injection."[63] This was an intensive course of treatment. Syphilis also proved entirely curable, as a surgeon with the 17th Massachusetts described his remedy: "Cauterization of the chancre in the first instance, followed by the continuous application of black wash."[64] These treatments were at times painful and always time-consuming. They kept the soldier incapacitated for days—as long as a fortnight—from the time the disease was diagnosed and treated until the return to duty.

Complications could be severe and painful. For example, the Union army reported over 2,500 cases of stricture of the urethra (resulting in eight deaths and nearly 250 discharges). Almost all of these stricture cases were attributed to the effects of syphilis. One medical report described the horrors of this condition and treatment. Pvt. P. Slater with the 7th U.S. Colored Troops was admitted to the hospital:

> with cold sweats and hiccoughs; there was a tumor in the hypogaster, and the penis was swollen and of a purplish color, and there was phymosis, with incipient gangrene of the prepuce and glans. A director was introduced and the prepuce freely incised. A catheter passed into the urethra encountered a false passage, made by previous attempts at catheterization. This being avoided, the catheter was forced through the stricture, free bleeding taking place, and a large quantity of ammonical urine was drawn off. The penis was enveloped in compresses wet with zinc lotion, and subsequently with dilute nitric acid lotion and charcoal poultices; a generous diet was ordered, with anodynes. For a few days the patient was semi-delirious and almost collapsed, his urine dribbling away involuntarily. Some time after admission, an abscess formed in the groin and opened spontaneously, leaving a large sloughing sore from which the man insisted, urine was discharged. Another abscess formed in the perineum, from which urine unmistakably issued, yet still it passed in a small stream by the natural channel. Gangrene attacked one foot. A line of demarcation formed above the ankle, and the superficial parts above sloughed. He now contracted discrete variola. In April he was improving, the inguinal sores

being healed and the ulcerated surface on the foot being nearly well. He lost by sloughing two inches of the penis. His urine passes mainly by the natural channel, but there is a fistulous opening from the urethra at the seat of stricture, and the patient has iritis. He will probably have to undergo urethrotomy for his stricture at some future time.

Unfortunately, Slater died of smallpox two weeks after his transfer to a convalescent hospital.[65]

Slater was one of the black victims of this venereal scourge. Among African American troops there were thirty-three cases of syphilis per thousand soldiers per year and forty-three cases of gonorrhea, making the rate of disease slightly lower (seventy-six vs. eighty-two) for the black soldier as compared with white.[66]

The Medical and Surgical History of the War of the Rebellion suggests that "venereal diseases were associated with intemperance in the conditions which favored their causation." This would seem to explain some of the obfuscation Bell Wiley mentioned when any subject touching on sexuality arises. But the section on venereal diseases observes further: "Hence they were more frequent at the beginning and the close of the war than during its progress, and among troops stationed in the vicinity of cities than among those on active service."[67] There is more evidence to suggest that period was not as important as proximity. The Army of the Potomac sustained twice the rate of venereal disease from November 1864 to April 1865 than that suffered by Sherman's troops during their advance through Georgia and the Carolinas during the same period.

During the Atlanta campaign, Confederate commanders were concerned by the stampede of prostitutes into the area. An officer wrote to the post commander in Dalton, Georgia, that "complaints are daily made to me of the number of lewd women in this town."[68] The problem became so extreme that Gen. Albert Sidney Johnston took extraordinary measures. He ordered his men to "sweep" the town. Any woman who could not document her respectability would be expelled. Females who returned would be confined to the military guardhouse and given a diet of bread and water.[69]

General Johnston did not pioneer this extreme measure of banishment. Individual prostitutes were frequently expelled from army camps. One Mississippi commander in 1862 proclaimed that all "company laundresses who do not actually wash for the men must be discharged."[70] Further, there were incidents involving women disguised as soldiers.[71] But large-scale deportation attempts were relatively rare, and during the Civil War they originated with federal officers. Union commanders initiated these Draconian measures in alarm over growing numbers of public women in the occupied South.

Nashville had been a thriving rivertown before the Civil War. The 1860 census listed 198 white prostitutes and nine mulatto prostitutes. A little less than half of these women were illiterate and more than half were born in Tennessee. Most bawdy houses did not just support sex trade workers, but the largest brothel in prewar Nashville housed seventeen prostitutes, eight children, and three adult men. The vice district in Nashville was concentrated in a neighborhood known as Smokey Row, a riverfront area two blocks wide and four blocks long.[72]

Following the federal occupation of Nashville in February 1862, prostitutes flocked to the city as the surrounding countryside was teeming with 30,000 federal troops. In the winter of 1862–63 one Union officer described how 1,500 prostitutes were summarily driven out of town: rounded up and forced to take a train to Louisville. By the summer of 1863, the problem had grown worse. In June of 1863, Gen. R. S. Granger, in command at Nashville, was "daily and almost hourly beset" by the commanders and surgeons of the regiments. These officers wanted to be rid of "diseased prostitutes."[73]

So the military once again devised a plan for mass deportation. On July 6 the provost marshal, Lt. Col. George Spalding, issued an order requiring the public women of Nashville to abandon the town. On July 8 he requisitioned a steamboat, the *Idahoe*, demanding that her captain, John Newcomb, transport the women to Louisville. Spalding failed to provide Newcomb with any guards or the provisions he requested. With only a crew of three, Newcomb was reluctant to proceed but was required by law to comply. As he sailed away with his cargo of prostitutes, the Nashville *Dispatch* bestowed its blessing: "Wayward sisters, go in peace."

When the *Idahoe* tried to buy food along the way, Newcomb encountered inflated prices and open ridicule. Many of the women fell sick, and conditions on board were deplorable. Approaching Louisville five days later, the women were prevented from debarking by military guards, and the ship was ordered to proceed to Cincinnati (where the ill-fated steamer had been first launched in pristine condition only three months before). Some women were able to make it to dry land, as a handful were rescued through the intercession of friends by writs of habeus corpus at Newport, Kentucky. The majority remained on shipboard, in limbo.

At Cincinnati on July 17, their luck was no better as the authorities denied the boat safe harbor in Ohio, and the ship was forced to weigh anchor across the river from the docks. Newcomb and his increasingly rowdy passengers remained there for nearly two weeks. Finally, orders came from Washington for Newcomb to return with his cargo to Nashville. When the *Idahoe* landed back in Tennessee, the women were angry and bedraggled, and the boat completely trashed. The entire enterprise was declared a disaster.

Newcomb demanded that Spalding reimburse him for the food and medicine purchased for the over one hundred women for nearly a month. He also sought financial compensation for the permanent damages the *Idahoe* sustained: "I told them it would forever ruin her reputation as a passenger boat if they were put on her, (It has done so—she is now since known as the Floating Whorehouse)."[74] After two years of petitions and a trip to Washington, Newton finally received over $5,000 worth of compensation for loss and damages.

Lt. Col. Spalding immediately devised another plan of attack. He wanted to register the town's prostitutes and require medical inspections. There was no precedent for this within the United States. The practice had been employed previously in Europe and licensed prostitution was still in force in France. In 1810 Paris police had devised a special squad, which became known as "police des moeurs." This morals squad forced prostitutes to register with a central bureau and to pass monthly inspection with a police doctor—paying three francs for the privilege of a clean bill of health. Those women unlucky enough to contract venereal diseases were locked up in a prison hospital, confined to the dreaded St. Lazare. This system was enforced from the teens onward.[75] Also, there was a move afoot in England in the 1860s to prevent prostitutes from spreading diseases in naval ports and garrison towns, which resulted in the Contagious Diseases Act, passed by parliament in June 1864.[76] However, Lt. Col. Spalding was the first American to institute medical inspection of prostitutes within the United States, which he specified was a war measure. After the *Idahoe* debacle, Union command wanted to regain mastery, before the situation spiraled even further out of control. The provost marshal issued a stern set of regulations:

1st That a license be issued to each prostitute, a record of which shall be kept at this office, together with the number and street of her residence.

2nd That one skillful surgeon be appointed as a Board of Examination whose duty it shall be to examine personally every week, each licensed prostitute, giving certificate soundness to those who are healthy and ordering those into hospital those who are in the slightest degree diseased.

3rd That a building suitable for a hospital for the invalids be taken for that purpose, and that a weekly tax of fifty cents be levied on each prostitute for the purpose of defraying the expense of said hospital.

4th That all public women found plying their vocation without license and certificate be at once arrested and incarcerated in the workhouse for a period of not less than thirty days.[77]

This last provision was especially important because it warned public women that they could no longer pay off negligible fines to evade the law. Lack of compliance meant they would be put out of circulation for a minimum of a month. Licenses and certificates were required by August 20.

As Spalding established his program, the hospital admitted its first group of diseased prostitutes. Twelve women were confined to hospital the first month. However, two months later, twenty-eight new cases were received. By January 1864 "the whole number examined, licensed and registered was 300, of whom 60 were diseased."[78] Army inspectors noted that the women who had originally been "filthy" and "coarse," over time exhibited "marked improvement," as "cleanliness and propriety was instilled."[79]

By August 1864, a year after Spalding issued his first directive, "456 white cyprians had been registered." The army believed the increase in the number of public women could be attributed to the fact that a "better class of prostitutes had been drawn to Nashville from northern cities by the comparative protection from venereal disease which its license system afforded."[80] Federal officials decided to expand the system to include "colored prostitutes" and registered fifty black women shortly thereafter. Nashville authorities declared their experiment a great success. By February 1864, Hospital No. 15 had been converted into a facility for soldiers' venereal cases only. Surgeons saw nearly one thousand cases over the following five months, but only thirteen of the men had been infected in Nashville.[81]

Women reported to No. 11, the "Female Venereal Hospital." In January 1865 the doctor in charge, William Chambers, offered a "sanitary report":

+ 207 women treated
+ 40 gonorrhea (10 days-average length of stay)
+ 137 primary syphilis (11 days-average length of stay)
+ secondary cases (38 days-average length of stay)

Once these women were cured, they were returned to duty.

At the beginning of the occupation, surgeons offered treatment on average to ten to twenty officers per month. After registration and inspection, this number dropped to one case per month. Perhaps officers were careful to request documentation. A federal official claimed that prostitutes might "gladly exhibit to their visitors the 'certificate' when it is asked for, a demand, I am informed, not unfrequently made."[82] In spite of the system's success, Spalding had underestimated the medical costs of treating licensed prostitutes. The inspection fee of fifty cents was raised to one dollar—but proved difficult for many women to manage and some simply "declined" to pay for certification."[83]

Despite this financial handicap, medical officers praised the Nashville system. Dr. Fletcher, head of the Female Venereal Hospital, commented in August 1864: "It is not to be supposed that a system hastily devised, established for the first time on this continent, and certain to encounter all the obstacles that vicious interests or pious ignorance could put forth, should be other than imperfect." However, he went on to argue,

> We have here no Parisian "Bureau des Moeurs" with its vigilant police, its careful scrutiny of the mode of conduct of houses of prostitution, and its general care of the public welfare both morally and in its sanitary consideration. This much, however, is to be claimed, that after the attempt to reduce disease by the forcible expulsion of the prostitutes had, as it always has, utterly failed, the more philosophic plan of recognizing and controlling an ineradicable evil has met with undoubted success.[84]

Fletcher perhaps exaggerated when he claimed that prostitutes went from opponents of the system to its advocate.[85]

In the summer of 1864, Lt. Col. Thomas Harris, the provost marshal of Memphis, aware of the "undoubted success" of Nashville colleagues, sent L. L. Coxe, an agent of the U.S. Sanitary Commission, on a fact-finding trip to Nashville. Coxe reported back to Harris and urged him to institute similar programs. A federal officer from Ohio claimed that Memphis could "boast of being one of the first places of female prostitution on the continent."[86] The bordellos along Beale Street were notorious. One satisfied Union soldier reported that black prostitutes "felt lovingly toward us because they thought we were bringing them freedom and they would not charge us a cent."[87]

Union brass moved quickly, once Harris drew up a plan: two military officers would be assigned to the task of weekly examinations and admissions to hospital. On September 30, Harris sent out a document labeled "private circular," which had the strange injunction: "This circular is intended for the information of the women only, and must not be shown or given to men."[88] The memorandum offered very specific intentions: "All women of the town, in the city of Memphis and vicinity, whether living in boarding houses, singly or as kept mistresses, are notified that they must hereafter be registered and take out weekly certificates."

"Kept mistresses" who were supported by men of "good character" were exempt from inspection, although they were required to pay the weekly fees to cover hospitalizations. Harris provided very particular directions on the place for women to go for medical examination ("a private office" on the "second story over a confectionary shop"). Women could also receive medical certification in their own homes, but they would have to pay one dollar extra for house calls: $3.50 instead of the usual $2.50 a week fee. All registered women were required to call in person and pay $10 for their license. Funds from fees would cover hospitalization for infected women. Females with certificates were guaranteed free care in wards with "all the privacy and comfort of a home, and nursed by an experienced matron and female nurses."[89]

Harris also wanted public women aware of regulations that would be strictly enforced: "'Street walking,' soliciting, stopping or talking with men on the streets; buggy or horseback riding for pleasure through the city in daylight, wearing a showy, flash or immodest dress in public; any language or conduct in public which attracts attention; visiting the public squares, the New Memphis theater, or other resort of LADIES, are prohibited and forbidden."[90] He ended by warning, "Any woman of the town, public or private, found in the city or vicinity after the 10th day of October, 1864, without her certificate of registry and medical exemption certificate will be arrested by the police and punished."[91]

By February 1865 the new provisional mayor of Memphis, Channing Richards, described Harris's accomplishments: "one hundred and thirty four public women have been registered, of whom one hundred and ten are now in the city, to wit: 14 housekeepers, 4 kept mistresses and 92 boarders."[92] Richards reported with even more delight that cash collected from the women greatly exceeded expenses. The excess profit of over $3,800 was passed on to the city's hospital fund.[93] Over the course of five months, only forty-four public women had been admitted to hospital, with ten still recovering from their diseases.

The new mayor concluded that "I shall certainly regret the abandonment of the system for the result of my own observation has been decidedly favorable to it . . . while it does not encourage vice it prevents to a considerable extent its worst consequences."[94]

By February 1865, the Union army decided to withdraw from the business of licensing prostitutes. Far from seeing this system as progressive, high-ranking officials were increasingly uncomfortable with this regulatory role. After one year of registrations and inspections, officers in Nashville described their program in detail, documenting its success and its results. They forwarded their report to Washington with a request that systems of licensing prostitutes be adopted extensively. The Nashville surgeons who advocated this reform emphasized that their recommendations were vital to public health. Further, it was a military necessity to keep soldiers disease-free to serve in the fighting ranks. No official response was made, no action taken, except, within a few months, these registries were dismantled. The experiment had been a great success, but its results would not yield imitators until parts of Nevada implemented registration of prostitutes in the twentieth century.[95]

While all of this tells us about public health issues surrounding prostitution within the occupied Confederacy, what about the larger role of women, the public platform, and prostitution within the wartime South?[96]

I will conclude by providing three sketches of important incidents, moments in time, when issues surrounding public women are crucial to our appreciation of the dynamics at stake within the Civil War South. These are examples of when prostitution, by way of accusation or rumor, reared its head to create intrigue, scandal, and, above all, an issue for scholars to debate.[97] The first, most notorious, and most explicit case deals with Union commander Benjamin Butler's infamous General Order No. 28, issued on May 5, 1862:[98]

> As the officers and soldiers of the United States have been subject to repeated insults from the women (calling themselves ladies) of New Orleans, in return for the most scrupulous non-interference and courtesy on our part, it is ordered that hereafter when any female shall, by word, gesture or movement insult or show contempt for any officer or soldier of the United States, she shall be regarded and held liable to be treated as a woman of the town plying her avocation.[99]

Gen. Benjamin Butler had been no friend of emancipation when the war broke out. But he had become increasingly hostile to slaveowners as the war progressed. By the time of the capture of New Orleans in April 1862, Butler had zero tolerance for the levels of disrespect heaped upon the federal government and its representatives by secessionists.

When Butler, the Union general in charge of occupation, arrived in New Orleans, he met with resistance in every quarter. Butler especially resented the way in which ladies in New Orleans would withdraw from pews in church should a Union man choose to sit nearby, would depart from streetcars should a Yankee board, would gather up their skirts and desert the sidewalk rather than to pass close by a federal soldier. This constant charade was annoying but did not draw any fire until an incident when a white southern woman spat into the faces of two officers.[100] Butler was outraged and feared that his men would not be able to resist retaliation without some appropriate measure in place. He decided to take matters into his own hands with his "Order Number 28." With Butler's explicit approval, women who exhibited insulting behavior in public would be treated as public women: arrested, booked, put in jail overnight, and subject to a fine in front of a magistrate the following morning.

Butler's men certainly appreciated the promise of a new regime, but southern whites howled foul. New Orleaneans became hysterical. The mayor of New Orleans responded immediately, complaining about Butler's license for his men to "commit outrages" upon "defenseless women." A local white girl, Clara Solomon, confided to her diary that she would like to see Butler tied up in ropes by the women of her city, or better yet, fried in a frying pan.[101] General Butler's southern nickname became "Beast Butler." The prostitutes of New Orleans paid their own tribute by pasting his portrait on the interior of their chamber pots.[102]

Butler was not just reviled in Louisiana but throughout the Confederacy. Mary Chesnut, wife of a former South Carolina senator and a member of Jefferson Davis's inner circle, was infuriated by Butler's audacity. She believed that the general should have instead been restraining his "brutal soldiery" and feared for her countrywomen at the mercy of this "hideous cross-eyed beast."[103] Southern newspapers heaped invective, and editors reprinted a poem about Butler that used the first letter of his name to begin each line:

Brutal and vulgar, coward and knave,
Famed for no action, noble or brave,

Beastly by instinct, a drinkard and sot
Ugly and venomous, on mankind a blot,
Thief, liar and scoundrel in highest degree,
Let yankeedom boast of such heroes as thee,
Every women and child shall for ages to come.
Remember thee monster, thou vilest of scum.[104]

Complaints were not limited to Confederates. Even Lincoln's secretary of state, William Seward, was unhappy with the wording of the order. He confided that he regretted, "in the haste of composition, a phraseology which could be mistaken or perverted could be used."[105] Seward, like many others sympathetic to Butler's aims, objected to the ambiguity of the order's language. Couldn't this lead to soldiers "having their way" with insulting women, rather than just arresting them?

Seward wasn't the only one concerned about this. But he was dead wrong to imagine Butler's "haste of composition," as the order was discussed and dissected before it was sent to the printer. A member of Butler's own staff, a Major Strong, raised objections to Butler's language, wondering if "some of the troops may misunderstand." He was concerned what might happen if even one man "should act upon it in the wrong way."[106] General Butler was resolute and wanted to move forward with the order as it was: "We are conquerors in a conquered city; we have respected every right, tried every means of conciliation, complied with every reasonable desire; and yet cannot walk the streets without being outraged and spit upon by green girls. I do not fear the troops; but if aggression must be, let it not be all against us."[107] And, to Butler's credit, incidents of insult were precipitously reduced. A northern journalist crowed, "The morals and manners of no class of women in the world were ever so rapidly improved as have been those of the Secession women of New Orleans under the stern but *admirable regime* of General Butler."[108]

There were very few arrests. Charges ranged from women displaying Confederate flags (usually replicas on their person) to threatening the life of a soldier. But most were arrested, found guilty, fined lightly, and released. Butler even sent some of the confiscated hand-sewn flags to Massachusetts schoolchildren as souvenirs.[109]

There was only a single arrest that caused widespread publicity. Eugenia Phillips, the wife of a former Alabama congressman, had already been charged with espionage in 1861 and detained in Washington.[110] She was finally set free and settled in New Orleans. But she defied Butler's orders and was insolent during an interview after her arrest on June 30, 1862. Phillips was sent into exile, confined to a railroad car on Ship Island, and spent ten weeks as a martyr to her cause, scribbling a diary and sending letters filled with the horrors of her incarceration and treatment. After two and a half months, Phillips was released and escaped New Orleans and Butler's reach. Despite her celebrity, few women wished to follow her example, which suited Butler.

The Union general had taken a gamble with his Order Number 28. Butler felt if he had merely issued a directive that Confederate women cease and desist their campaigns against Union soldiers, it might have simply fueled stronger defiance. After the fall of New Orleans, patriotic ladies were disgusted by what they felt was males' too ready accommodation to the occupation. Julia LeGrand described how "the women only do not seem afraid. They were all in favor of resistance."[111] And their resistance took an increasingly public and disruptive direction.[112]

As a result, Butler took direct aim—below the belt. By accusing southern ladies of being no ladies at all, he was trying to beat them at their own game.[113] He suggested that their behavior dishonored southern civility. They were stepping outside the boundaries of ladyhood, which made them liable to the consequences of their acts—as were public women.

Butler could not expect Confederate women to switch allegiance, but he could and did insist that they keep their views private—which was, after all, their designated sphere. Most had vented their fury in letters, in diaries, in parlors, and even in prayer—oh, to be rid of the "wicked Yankees." But when New Orleans women unleashed these feelings in the streets, Butler let it be known they would be given no better treatment than other "women of the streets," which shocked them into submission.

This image of southern "women in the streets" leads us into the next important incident where the issues of women's place and public women intersected dramatically, in the Confederate capital in April 1863. By this time,

The very streets of Richmond became a kind of complex stage onto which the players were thrust without scripts. Women did not know exactly the outcome or what roles they might play. Unescorted females were always subject to danger on city streets.... What was new was the way in which the public space was being taken over by "public women" or "women of the streets," and ladies were being crowded back into their homes, to knit and roll bandages—to prove their ladyhood through confinement and self-sacrifice.[114]

But the battle over the streets became even more articulated when respectable women began to question if even they would be apprehended when walking in the evenings without escort. The mayor proclaimed that he thought it unwise for any "sort of lady" to be out after 12 o'clock at night, and further warned that the watchman could "tell whether their appearance involved circumstances of a suspicious nature." So appearances were extremely important and would determine a woman's fate were she to find herself alone and apprehended on the street.

Again, Richmond had become overcrowded—poverty and vice plagued the city by the early spring of 1863. A horrible accident on March 13 engulfed the city with grief. The Confederates States Laboratory was where poor women and young girls worked grueling shifts for low pay, filling cartridges with gunpowder. When it blew up, leaving nearly fifty workers dead and twenty more injured in the fiery explosion, a pall fell over the town. The mayor raised money to help the victims' families; over half of those buried were under sixteen—"most little indigent girls."

It was during this period of mourning that the city suffered a ten-inch snowfall on March 20. Crops were threatened and farmers couldn't get their goods to market. Serious food shortages were beginning to panic the citizens of Richmond. Less than a fortnight later, a group of women from a working-class neighborhood called Oregon Hill, southwest of the city, decided to organize a meeting to discuss what was to be done about the high price of food. The women met in a church the evening of April 1 to formulate a plan. They decided to go in person to confront Virginia governor Lechter to demand that they offered food from government warehouses and at government prices, and to threaten to storm the storehouses if their demands were not met.

By eight A.M. the next morning (Easter Thursday, April 2), a large group of women showed up at the capital to offer their petition. Another contingent had gone directly to the governor's mansion to make their plea. The governor addressed the women assembled on the capital steps and warned them that although he understood their concerns, any attempts to "liberate" goods would be met with police action. Word of his refusal spread like wildfire. The largest mob, restless and resentful, moved into the mercantile area near Twelfth and Cary. By nine o'clock, looting and violence broke out. Merchants had locked their stores, but women wielding axes and knives broke in and cleaned out groceries, clothing, and other goods. Police using fire hoses could not stop the plundering women.

Mayor Mayo arrived to "read the riot act." When Governor Lechter appeared to ask them to disperse, he took out his watch and promised arrests would be made within five minutes. This cleared his immediate area, but, by now, there were several gangs of angry women scattered throughout the city in search of food and vengeance, with more females joining in with each passing hour. Even President Davis ventured out of the White House of the Confederacy to try to calm the masses; reports are mixed as to what the results of his negotiations were.[115]

But by nightfall, peace had been restored. Yet throughout all the next day and into the Easter weekend, women, some carrying children, wandered the streets to beg for food. The YMCA opened its doors and distributed supplies, as did, finally, the government—in the form of bags of rice. The so-called "Richmond Bread Riot" was over in a matter of hours, but its impact would last for days and longer.[116]

The city of Richmond, the capital of the Confederacy, reeled from this disturbance. The secretary of war forbade reports of the incident in the press and prohibited telegraphers from transmitting messages that even hinted at events. The Richmond papers circumvented this directive by covering the court cases of those women arrested for their roles in the disturbance, as over forty women (and twenty-five men) were jailed on April 2. Most of the women were given light sentences, but what is more interesting is the way in which both the city council and the local press decided to portray this event.

The Richmond city council took the position that looters had broken into jewelry stores and millinery shops—there was no truth to the matter that they were just poor women seeking bread. Loyal Confederate newspapers offered counterattacks to the story that Richmond was on the brink of starvation—a Richmond roiled in disaster. Journalists found scapegoats. The *Examiner* complained that any commotion was all the doing of Yankees and foreigners—the "outside agitator" school. Richmond papers scrupulously covered the trials of women charged with crimes. The reporter from the *Examiner* offered sly comments on the dress, appearance, and legal counsel of the women defendants. At best, the reader could not imagine that these women were the starving indigents painted by those sympathetic to their cause. At worse, the reader would assume these women were familiar with courtroom procedure because several of those caught up in these disturbances were public women.

And within this context, we find that Confederate authorities in Richmond in 1863 may have been as guilty of smear campaigns against women as "Beast" Butler was in New Orleans the year before. In order to salvage the political situation, white southern men had to turn against these women who had taken to the streets—to demonize them as if they were "women of the streets." The only significant public protest involving women in Richmond had taken place during the previous fall when more than 300 prostitutes mobbed the coroner's office following the brutal murder of one of their own at Alice Hardgrove's brothel on Fifteenth Street. This public disorder was much less of a riot and more of a rally.

Perhaps a few months later the women of the Richmond Bread Riot seemed to echo this earlier incident. Regardless, the civil and military authorities in Richmond struggled to minimize any fallout. They wanted the women who had participated in this riot to be remembered not for their courage, but to be diminished by a smear campaign to undermine their actions and their cause. These Richmond women, like the women of New Orleans before them, were threatened with the dishonorable label "public women" if they dared to disturb the public domain.

My final incident is much murkier, less clearly about public women, and more about rumor mongering—which is, after all, how my scholarly sojourn on prostitution and the Civil War originally began. Three or four times during lectures and travels over the past few years, I have been approached by interested parties sharing with me an incident that took place in Georgia during Sherman's March. The first time I was told the story, I was informed Sherman accused large numbers of women in a small Georgia town of being prostitutes and then shipped them northward. I could find no such incident. Indeed, it was a Confederate general, Albert Sidney Johnston, who in Dalton, Georgia, had ordered the evacuation of prostitutes.

Next it was described to me that Sherman rounded up women mill workers in Roswell, Georgia, and shipped them north so they couldn't make Confederate uniforms. They were treated like cattle, then abruptly abandoned—so the story goes. As a result, they had no alternatives but to become prostitutes, to service Yankee soldiers. These folktales were of keen interest to me—but only recently has some of the mystery cleared up concerning nineteenth-century Roswell.[117]

When federal troops arrived in Roswell in July 1864, the mill owner flew the French flag over his cotton factories, claiming his property was neutral, not subject to search and seizure. Union officers found "CSA" sewn into cloth being manufactured at these mills and demanded the evacuation of all workers—mainly women and children—on July 6. The mill employees tried to resist but were forced out.

After all salvageable cloth was cleared out, the mills were burnt to the ground. A Union private described the scene: "It did seem at first blush to be a wanton act, to fire those polished machines which filled the building from basement to the top story, after they came to a stand still, but all is fair, it has been stated, in love and war."[118] On July 7 Sherman instructed his men to arrest all workers and "let them foot it, under guard, to Marietta, whence I will send them by cars to the North." Well aware of what the response would be, he added, "the poor women will make a howl."[119] Sherman nevertheless insisted on deportation.

This was an incredibly harsh action. More than half the mill-working force of 800 melted away, while the Union troops camped in Roswell behaved so badly—"foolishly drunk" and "making love to the women"—that their commander had to move his troops out of city limits.

When the roughly 400 mill workers arrived in Marietta, the Union medical corps tried to draft Roswell women to take in laundry or nurse sick soldiers for pay. They were confined in an old seminary building at the former Georgia Military Institute. An Indiana soldier on guard duty complained, "Some of them are tough and it's a hard job to keep them straight and to keep men away from them. General Sherman says he would rather try to guard the whole Confederate Army, and I guess he is right about it."[120]

So here is when the tale begins to cloud. At first Sherman is clearly removing mill workers from factories, but by the time the workers arrive in Marietta, the image shifts: a forced march of hundreds of young women, kept under lock and key, appearing tough and increasingly troublesome because men (presumably soldiers) are trying to make contact with them. A correspondent for the New York Tribune created a highly sympathetic portrait of these Roswell captives: "Four hundred weeping and terrified Ellens, Susans, and Maggies transported, in the springless and seatless Army wagons, away from their lovers and brothers and the sunny south, and all for the offense of weaving tent-cloth and spinning stocking yarn!"[121]

The news had spread about the torching of the factory town, about the innocent women caught up in the drama of war. Roswell captured the popular imagination. The women's fates were causing concern North and South—especially as the imaginations of Union captors might run wild, such as the Illinois soldier who "just wish they would issue them [the women] to us soldiers."[122]

Sherman ordered the detainees transported by rail to Kentucky, and on July 21 the first group arrived. These Georgia refugees, most unfortunately, were transshipped to Louisville via Nashville. Only a year before, recall, large shipments of public women from Nashville to Louisville had caused a furor; perhaps this incident dredged up memories of previous Union roundups and deportations.

By August even articles in the northern press were calling it Sherman's "War against the Women." A New York journalist questioned why "drive four hundred penniless girls hundreds of miles away from their homes and friends to seek livelihoods amid a strange and hostile people?"[123]

Even when the Union tried to assist these women, to secure jobs for them, their efforts backfired. After these females were advertised as potential servants, a newspaper article fumed that while emancipated slaves were "rioting and luxuriating" in Union camps, white women and children were being "sold into bondage."[124]

Descriptions of the living conditions in Louisville for these Roswell mill workers confirmed Union indifference to these enemy civilians. One memoir of a survivor described how two sisters, sixteen and twelve, were confined in a "cavernous stench-filled building" and had to work to save their ailing father.[125]

By August, several solicitations had appeared in the Louisville paper; the ladies of Louisville sought donated supplies for these Roswell refugees. Reports also described an outbreak of typhoid in September. That same month Dr. Mary Walker, a commissioned contract surgeon with the Union army, was put in charge of the women confined to the prison hospital. But, by January, this too had backfired.

Women prisoners rioted over their female warden, leveling serious charges. Walker challenged the Roswell women's complaints about poor food and bad treatment. She claimed her unpopularity stemmed from the fact that she would not allow familiarity between the guards and prisoners.[126] The Louisville commandant failed to support Dr. Walker, and by March her request for transfer was honored. But certainly Walker's letter indicates that because she was unwilling to turn a blind eye to the corruption of these women, she was unsuitable. The Roswell women were driven out of Georgia and perhaps too many were steered toward harm's way, thrust into the clutches of Union soldiers. In April 1865 the last of the Roswell refugees were released from federal custody and allowed to go home.

NOTES

Catherine Clinton delivered her Klement Lecture in 1999.

1. I wish to acknowledge the Charles Warren Center at Harvard University under the direction of Laurel Ulrich for its assistance. And most especially, the Gilder-Lehrman Center at Yale University for its continuing support of my scholarly research. To those at the University of Virginia who sat through my presentation of ideas at the very earliest stages of this project, my gratitude. I also wish to thank several colleagues who offered advice or shared their research: Emily Epstein, Joseph Glatthar, Timothy Lockley, Mason Robertson, and Judith Schafer. Finally, my deepest appreciation goes to Michele Gillespie, whose input is always invaluable.

2. A recent electronic survey of fifteen history journals published between 1900–95, with millions of pages, yielded no matches to the keyword search for "Prostitution" and "Civil War."

3. I am happy to report a significant contribution has been made with Thomas Lowry's *The Story the Soldiers Wouldn't Tell: Sex in the Civil War* (Mechanicsburg, Pa.: Stackpole Books, 1994), which is a useful compendium.

4. Although Wiley did find some colorful references, such as the soldier who writes about "horizontal refreshments" then refines himself by adding, "in Plainer words Riding a Dutch gal." Bell Wiley, *The Life of Billy Yank* (Indianapolis: Bobbs Merrill, 1951), 258.

5. I would like to confess that I will not be using euphemisms such as "Cryprians," "ladies of the night," or "nymphs de pave" unless these expressions are found in quotes. And I have confined much of the crude language I did find in soldier's letters to the footnotes.

6. And, after all, as a scholar whose first book on plantation mistresses was mistakenly cataloged by the Library of Congress under "sex customs" (something to which Winthrop Jordan alerted me), why wouldn't this be a logical detour?

7. See Elizabeth Leonard, *All the Daring of a Soldier* (New York: W. W. Norton, 1999); and Ella Forbes, *African American Women during the Civil War* (New York: Garland Press, 1998).

8. Martha Hodes, *White Women, Black Men* (New Haven, Conn.: Yale Univ. Press, 1997); Edward Ball, *Slaves in the Family* (New York: Farrar, Straus & Giroux, 1998); and Henry Wiencek, *The Hairstons: An American Family in Black and White* (New York: St. Martin's, 1999).

9. See Amy Murrell, "'Of Necessity and Public Benefit': Southern Families and Their Appeals for Protection," in Catherine Clinton, ed., *Southern Families at War: Loyalty and Conflict in the Civil War South* (New York: Oxford Univ. Press, 2000); Anne Sarah Rubin, "Redefining the South: Confederates, Southerners, and Americans, 1863–1868" (Ph.D. diss., Univ. of Virginia, 1999); and Drew Gilpin Faust, *Mothers of Invention* (Chapel Hill: Univ. of North Carolina Press, 1996).

10. See Clinton, *Southern Families at War.*

11. For postwar reform, see David J. Pivar, *The Purity Crusade: Sexual Morality and Social Control, 1868–1900* (Westport, Conn.: Greenwood Press, 1973); and Joel Best, *Controlling Vice: Regulating Brothel Prostitution in St. Paul, 1865–1883* (Columbus: Ohio State Univ. Press, 1998).

12. See Christine Stansell, *City of Women: Sex and Class in New York, 1780–1860* (New York: Knopf, 1986).

13. For a fascinating look at these lives North and South, see Patricia Cline Cohen, *The Murder of Helen Jewett: The Life and Death of a Prostitute in Nineteenth Century New York* (New York: Knopf, 1998); and Dell Upton, ed., *Madaline: Love and Survival in Antebellum New Orleans* (Athens: Univ. of Georgia Press, 1996).

14. See, for example, Free Loveyer, *Directory to the Seraglios in New York, Philadelphia, and All the Principal Cities in the Union* (New York, 1859).

15. Welcome exceptions to this are Marilyn Wood Hill, *Their Sisters' Keepers: Prostitution in New York City, 1830–1870* (Berkeley: Univ. of California Press, 1993); Timothy J. Gilfoyle, *City of Eros: New York City, Prostitution, and the Commercialization of Sex, 1790–1920* (New York: Norton, 1992).

16. For penetrating analysis of the legal system and public attitudes toward prostitution, see Cohen, *Murder of Helen Jewett*; and Judith Kelleher Schafer's paper delivered to the Louisiana Historical Society Conference in March 1999, "The Murder of a 'Lewd and Abandoned Woman': *State of Louisiana v. Abraham Parker*." See also Carol Leonard, *Prostitution and Changing Social Norms in America* (Syracuse, N.Y.: Syracuse Univ. Press, 1979).

17. Although his conclusions were based on extensive interviews, he did not investigate street-walkers or child prostitutes. Willian W. Sanger, *The History of Prostitution: Its Extent, Causes, and Effects Throughout the World* (New York: Harper & Bros., 1858).

18. George Hutchinson, "Whitman, Family, and Civil War," paper presented at the "Society and Conflict: From the Age of Revolutions to the 'American Century'" conference, University of Genoa, June 1999.

19. Comparisons of antebellum prostitution in New York and in comparable European capitals indicate that American prostitutes were several years older on average than their continental counterparts. See Barbara Meil Hobson, *Uneasy Virtue: The Politics of Prostitution and the American Reform Tradition* (New York: Basic Books, 1987), 86. Also, Sanger's evidence indicates that most prostitutes were mothers.

20. Quoted in Gilfoyle, *City of Eros*, 156. The complete title of Ellington's book was *The Women of New York; or, The Under-World of the Great City* (New York: New York Book Co., 1869).

21. Gilfoyle, *City of Eros*, 156.

22. Ibid.

23. Ibid., 163.

24. Wiley, *Life of Billy Yank*, 257.

25. Again, it would seem that only New Orleans garnered a similarly sinful reputation for vice. We have very little work on the Civil War era, but I hope Judith Schafer's work will pioneer a path. The dimensions of the sex trade in New Orleans have been well documented for the later period: Bergen Brooke, *Storyville: A Hidden Mirror* (Wakefield, R.I.: Asphodel Press, 1994); Al Rose, *Storyville: New Orleans* (Tuscaloosa: Univ. of Alabama Press, 1974); and especially Ruth Rosen *The Lost Sisterhood: Prostitution in America, 1900–1918* (Baltimore: Johns Hopkins Univ. Press, 1982).

26. Wiley, *Life of Billy Yank*, 257.

27. E. Susan Barber, "'Sisters of the Capital': White Women in Richmond, Virginia, 1860–1880" (Ph.D. diss., Univ. of Maryland, 1997), 166.

28. Lowry, *Story the Soldiers Wouldn't Tell*, 73–75.

29. Bell Wiley, *The Life of Johnny Reb* (Indianapolis: Bobbs Merrill, 1943), 54.

30. Lowry refers to this woman as "Clara A.," but she might have been Clara Coleman, a prominent madam. See Catherine Clinton, "Reading Between the Lines: Newspapers and Women in Confederate Richmond," *Atlanta History* 42, 1–2 (Spring–Summer 1998): 21.

31. Lowry, *Story the Soldiers Wouldn't Tell*, 157. "Old sourface" is most likely President Jefferson Davis.

32. Ibid. Clara may have gotten some of her cash by selling the army surplus blankets brought to her by some of her high-ranking customers.

33. Most of this falls under the category of nonconsensual, noncommercial sex and is therefore beyond the scope of this essay.

34. Joseph T. Glatthar, *The March to the Sea and Beyond: Sherman's Troops in the Savannah and Carolinas Campaigns* (New York: New York Univ. Press, 1985), 93.

35. Wiley, *Life of Johnny Reb*, 54.

36. Lowry, *Story the Soldiers Wouldn't Tell*, 32–33.

37. Glatthar, *March to the Sea and Beyond*, 93.

38. Ibid., 94.

39. Lowry cites instances where white soldiers talk lasciviously about interracial sex (*Story the Soldiers Wouldn't Tell*, 28, 34–36).

40. Timothy J. Lockley, "Crossing the Race Divide: Interracial Sex in Antebellum Savannah," *Slavery and Abolition* 18, 3 (Dec. 1997): 168.

41. Ibid., 169.

42. Wiley, *Life of Billy Yank*, 259.

43. Glatthar, *March to the Sea and Beyond*, 96.

44. We have no information as to whether these two women were Confederate sympathizers or spies or simply women plying their trade.

45. Wiley, *Life of Johnny Reb*, 55.

46. Wiley, *Life of Billy Yank*, 247.

47. Ibid., 258.

48. Lowry, *Story the Soldiers Wouldn't Tell*, 84.

49. Wiley, *Life of Johnny Reb*, 52.

50. Ibid.

51. Ibid., 58.

52. John T. Thornton to [wife], Oct. 1, 1861, John T. Thornton Papers, University of Virginia, Charlottesville. I want to thank Joseph Glatthar for providing me with this citation and sharing his work on the Army of the Potomac.

53. Ibid., 53. Also an officer spied one of his men in the woods with a black prostitute. When the man returned to camp and the officer asked where he had been, the soldier told his commanding officer that he had developed a cold and was in the woods "looking for Sassafras Root." The officer had the soldier charged with "Hunting for Sassafras Root," and after his punishment, the story circulated and the soldier was given the nickname Sassafras. Lowry, *Story the Soldiers Wouldn't Tell*, 34.

54. Frank Lyman wrote to his friend Royal Cook, "We cannot get any thing here but fucking and that is plenty" (Lowry, *Story the Soldiers Wouldn't Tell*, 31).

55. Ibid., 32.

56. Wiley, *Life of Johnny Reb*, 57.

57. Ibid., 54.

58. See J. M Jordan to his wife in Wiley, *Life of Johnny Reb*, 51.

59. By war's end, of the 259,000 dead Confederate soldiers, 94,000 were attributed to deaths in battle and battle-related wounds, while 164,000 were caused by disease. Comparable Union numbers were 359,000 dead: 110,000 deaths in battle, 224,000 from disease (the remaining 25,000 were chalked up to suicides and accidents among federal troops). Stewart Brooks, *Civil War Medicine* (Springfield, Ill.: Charles Thomas Publishers, 1966), 127.

60. Ibid.

61. Lowry, *Story the Soldiers Wouldn't Tell*, 94.

62. Charles Smart, ed., *Medical and Surgical History of the War of the Rebellion*, pt. 3, vol. 1, 3d Medical Volume (Washington, D.C.: Government Printing Office, 1888), 891.

63. Ibid., 891–92.

64. Ibid., 892.

65. Ibid., 386.

66. There could be a number of reasons for this discrepancy: 1) perhaps black soldiers underreported the disease; 2) we know black troops had fewer surgeons available; or, 3) perhaps black soldiers had fewer assignations with prostitutes by choice, by economic status, or because of segregated facilities. There could have been any number of scenarios.

67. Smart, *Medical and Surgical History of the War*, 891. This is echoed by Wiley in *Life of Johnny Reb*, 55–56.

68. Wiley, *Life of Johnny Reb*, 53.

69. Ibid.

70. Ibid., 52. The next year Confederate army regulations required that all four company laundresses had to furnish evidence of their good character to secure employment. Ibid., 358.

71. Mary Elizabeth Massey, *Bonnet Brigades: American Women and the Civil War* (New York: Knopf, 1966), 84–85.

72. Lowry, *Story the Soldiers Wouldn't Tell*, 77.

73. Ibid., 78.

74. See Massey, *Bonnet Brigades*, 76–78; and Lowry, *Story the Soldiers Wouldn't Tell*, chap. 8.

75. Nickie Roberts, *Whores in History: Prostitution in Western Society* (New York: HarperCollins, 1992), 202. By the 1820s, the police prohibited public women from certain areas, such as Luxembourg Gardens, Place Vendome, and along the Champs-Elysées. By 1830 prostitutes were forbidden to parade on any streets, and in 1833 they were barred from standing in doorways. Prostitutes were confined to "maisons closes," regulated brothels with registered women; customers were required to offer madams a name for their records. See also Richard Symanski, *The Immoral Landscape: Female Prostitution in Western Societies* (Toronto: Butterworths, 1981); and Vern Bullough and Bonnie Bullough, *Prostitution: An Illustrated Society History* (New York: Crown, 1978).

76. The Contagious Diseases Act provided for compulsory hospitalization of any women suspected of being a prostitute with a venereal disease. If the disease was confirmed, she could be locked up for three months. In 1866, the bill was renewed and allowed magistrates to institute fortnightly inspections of women. Detention was extended to six months and religious instruction of women in hospital lockup was provided. In 1868 reformers hoped to expand the acts, to extend the campaign to London. A successful female reform movement led to the repeal of the acts in 1886. See Mary Spongberg, *Feminizing Venereal Disease: The Body of the Prostitute in Nineteenth-Century Medical Discourse* (New York: New York Univ. Press, 1997), 63–65. See also Judith Walkowitz, *Prostitution and Victorian Society: Women, Class, and the State* (New York: Cambridge Univ. Press, 1982).

77. Smart, *Medical and Surgical History of the War*, 894.

78. Ibid.

79. Ibid.

80. Ibid.

81. Ibid.

82. Ibid.

83. Ibid.

84. Ibid.

85. Ibid. And here is a juncture where I wish we could have the testimony of prostitutes themselves rather than always filtering public women's responses through the official records— documents created, collected, and preserved almost exclusively by men.

86. Wiley, *Life of Billy Yank*, 260.

87. Lowry, *Story the Soldiers Wouldn't Tell*, 84.

88. Smart, *Medical and Surgical History of the War*, 895.

89. Ibid.

90. Ibid.

91. Ibid.

92. Ibid., 896.

93. Only counties with populations of less than 250,000 were allowed to have legalized prostitution, which created ranch brothels.

94. Smart, *Medical and Surgical History of the War*, 896.

95. There was a brief attempt at police "reglementation" (as it was called) in St. Louis in 1870,

which was also short-lived. See Thomas Mackey, *Red Lights Out: A Legal History of Prostitution, Disorderly Houses, and Vice Districts, 1870–1917* (New York: Garland, 1987), chap. 5.

96. See Catherine Clinton, *The Plantation Mistress: Woman's World in the Old South* (New York: Pantheon, 1982), 93.

97. Again, a vivid memory of my graduate years in my first American social history seminar, where the professor in charge challenged those women who wanted to include a unit on the history of prostitution. He ridiculed our request by asking if we would include the topic under "women" or "labor" or "the professions." His withering indifference to the topic led to its omission.

98. For interesting insights, please consult Mary Ryan, *Women in Public: Between Banners and Ballots* (Baltimore: Johns Hopkins Univ. Press, 1990); and George Rable, "'Missing in Action': Women of the Confederacy," in Catherine Clinton and Nina Silber, eds., *Divided Houses: Gender and the Civil War* (New York: Oxford Univ. Press, 1992).

99. James Parton, *General Butler in New Orleans: History of the Administration of the Department of the Gulf in the Year 1862* (Boston: Houghton Mifflin, 1868), 327. When you go into the National Museum of History in Washington, D.C., this document, along with the Ordinance of Secession and the Gettysburg Address, is one of the few available for purchase in a facsimile edition—and the only one which deals with women explicitly.

100. There were other aggravating circumstances as well, such as women dumping "slops" and on one occasion the contents of a chamber pot from a balcony onto Union soldiers below. See Rable, "'Missing in Action,'" 140.

101. Ibid., 141.

102. Ibid.

103. Massey, *Bonnet Brigades*, 229.

104. Richard M. McMurray, "The Confederate Newspaper Press and the Civil War," *Atlanta History* 42, 1–2 (Spring–Summer 1998): 69.

105. Parton, *General Butler in New Orleans*, 326.

106. Ibid., 327.

107. Ibid., 328.

108. Massey, *Bonnet Brigades*, 229–30. Despite his success, Butler was relieved of his command in New Orleans in Dec. 1862.

109. Rable, "'Missing in Action,'" 141.

110. See Massey, *Bonnet Brigades*, 90–91.

111. Rable, "'Missing in Action,'" 138.

112. Ibid., 141.

113. New Orleans diarists confirmed that true southern women would treat Union soldiers with disdain and not resort to the vulgar rudeness of the lower classes (Massey, *Bonnet Brigades*, 229).

114. Clinton, "Reading Between the Lines," 23. All subsequent quotes dealing with Richmond are taken from this article, 28–32.

115. See Clinton, "Reading Between the Lines," 31.

116. Ironically, there is almost no mention of this incident in the "Letters Received" file in the Papers of President Jefferson Davis (Rice University, Houston, Tex.), nor does his correspondence treat the matter to any large extent.

117. See the primary reference material provided in Michael D. Hitt, *Charged with Treason: Ordeal of 400 Mill Workers during Military Operations in Roswell, Georgia, 1864–65* (Monroe, New York: Library Research Associates, 1992).

118. Ibid., p. 18. Indeed, many of the workers had hoped the Union would simply take over the factory and keep the mills running so they might maintain their livelihood. Ibid., 120.

119. Ibid., 22.

120. Ibid., 61.

121. Ibid., 89.

122. Ibid., 74.

123. Ibid., 104.

124. Ibid., 125.

125. Ibid., 111. Prisoners could secure freedom by settling in nearby Indiana; but without any means of support, most elected to remain in Louisville until they could go home to Georgia.

126. She also claimed that the Roswell women were angry that she had replaced the four male cooks with women. And she complained that these stubborn southern women wanted men to hold the doors open for them and to let them sing Rebel songs with impunity—indulgences she was unwilling to grant.

✒ LESLEY J. GORDON ✒

"I Never Was a Coward"

Questions of Bravery in a Civil War Regiment

✒ Lesley J. Gordon, associate professor of history at the University of Akron, has spent her career carefully and cheerfully navigating the rough confluence of academic history and popular military history. When she appeared on "Civil War Talk Radio"—a show broadcasting on the Internet-based World Talk Radio network—in the spring of 2005 to discuss her work on General George Pickett, her interviewer raised the following questions: Why don't academic historians take Civil War military history seriously? And why do many Civil War buffs fail to take female writers seriously?

Gordon has answered these questions in part through the quality of her work. Her first book, *General George E. Pickett in Life and Legend*, applies the contemporary methods of social history to explore in new ways the life of one of the most romanticized Confederate generals and his third wife, LaSalle Corbett Pickett. This book proved to be not only a unique look at the military career of General Pickett but also an innovative approach to understanding how historical actors shape and often control the memory of events and people. For instance, after Pickett's death LaSalle hit the lecture circuit, playing up her role as a southern belle and her husband as the embodiment of southern masculinity, thus shaping the ways that the Lost Cause and the Old South would be remembered.

Gordon's fascination with the Civil War began as a young girl growing up in New England. She loved vacationing with her parents at Civil War battlefields and, when the time came to tour potential colleges, her list included schools near these important historical sites. In the end, Gordon attended the College of William and Mary, surrounded by sites related to countless Civil War campaigns. She completed her M.A. and her Ph.D. at the University of Georgia under the direction of Emory Thomas. Since that time, in addition to her work on Pickett, she has coauthored *"This Terrible War": The Civil War and Its Aftermath* (2003; rev. ed. 2007) with Daniel Sutherland and Michael Fellman and coedited *Intimate Strategies of the Civil War: Military Commanders and Their Wives* (2001) with Carol K. Bleser. She has also written about the Battle of Gettysburg, Ulysses S. Grant's relationships in the military, violence in the Confederacy, and military wives, demonstrating her ability to move deftly between—and ability to combine—traditional military history and social history. Even more than most historians in the field, she is particularly generous in the time she gives to speaking at Civil War Roundtables.

Gordon's Klement Lecture was drawn from her ongoing research on the 16th Connecticut and historical memory. In illuminating the personal and public processes of defining bravery and cowardice, she once again shows how military history, one of the most plowed over fields in Civil War studies, can still be refreshed with new perspectives.

HISTORIANS HAVE DEVOTED considerable time and energy to studying, and in many ways celebrating, the common soldier of the Civil War. Dating from Bell Irvin Wiley's pioneering works on "Johnny Reb" and "Billy Yank" to James McPherson's award-winning *For Cause and Comrades*, most historians conclude that the majority of men who served North and South were dutiful, honorable, and brave. Some did acknowledge the coward, the deserter, or the skulker. But, as James I. Robertson affirmed, "For every man lacking in fortitude, the record is clear that 100 or more rose to the heights of heroism in the Civil War."[1]

However, not all Civil War soldiers consistently "rose to the heights of heroism." Not all veterans had valiant stories to tell. A concern repeatedly on these soldiers' minds, cowardice was never a static term. Its meaning, and men's reactions to it, shifted and changed with the altering tides of war. By examining this very fluid discourse of cowardice, we can gain a deeper sense of soldiers' expectations, identity, and motivation. Through counterpoint, we can better understand conceptions of bravery, too. And contemplating cowardice helps to reveal a good deal about Americans' memory of the war. In veteran memoirs and later histories of the war, considerations of cowardly behavior became obfuscated, and only the hero remained.

This essay probes the broad concept of Civil War cowardice within the specific context of a single northern regiment. The wartime record of the 16th Connecticut Infantry Regiment includes accusations, confessions, and observations of cowardice in battle, in camp, at home, and in prison. My research relies primarily on soldiers' wartime letters and diaries and local newspapers. Letters and diaries, of course, provide valuable insight into regimental attitudes throughout the conflict. Newspapers included soldiers' correspondence, but they also provide a fascinating sense of the interplay between home front and battlefront. These sources display a vigorous dialogue on cowardice among soldiers and civilians.

Although Civil War soldiers wrote and spoke of "cowards," they frequently applied other words such as "skedaddle," "skulk," and "shirk" to describe cowardly behavior. Initially, "cowardice" meant showing fear in battle.[2] However, as the conflict grew bloodier, more destructive, and vast, basic definitions of cowardice expanded and changed. A coward could be someone who refused to serve voluntarily in the military and thus never actually set foot on a battlefield. Deserting the ranks was also cowardly even if combat was not imminent. Motive mattered too. What *caused* a soldier to flee battle or desert often determined whether his conduct was actually deemed cowardly by his comrades.[3]

Rank, ethnicity, and race counted as well when it came to defining Civil War cowardice. Acting the coward was much less acceptable for officers than it was for the men in the ranks. But if expectations were high for officers, they could be very low for some types of soldiers. White, native-born northern volunteers expected black, immigrant, and drafted troops to be less courageous, despite clear examples to the contrary. And at least before any shots were fired, federals believed that they were more courageous than their southern foe.[4]

To a group of Connecticut men in the summer of 1862, however, words like "hero" and "coward" were simple and uncontested. Infused with martial fervor, patriotism, and a thirst for adventure, enlistees in the 16th Connecticut Infantry Regiment were determined to claim the mantle of the hero.

By the summer of 1862, the war was well into its second year and an end did not seem imminent. George B. McClellan's disappointing Peninsula campaign convinced President Abraham Lincoln that he needed more men to fight the determined Confederates, many more men than anyone originally imagined. On July 1, 1862, he issued a call for 300,000 volunteers. Two days later Connecticut's governor William Buckingham added his own exhortation leading to the creation of the 16th Regiment Connecticut Volunteers.[5]

From the start, expectations were high for the regiment. Drawing solely from Hartford County, the unit reflected the region's economic prosperity. Volunteers were farmers and machinists, artisans, and teachers. Muster rolls list some of the state's best-known and oldest family names, in addition to a spattering of recent immigrants. A number of the men were single and young, many just eighteen and nineteen years old. Husbands and fathers also joined in high numbers.[6]

Members of the 16th Connecticut, like all northern soldiers, went to war for a variety of reasons. Some felt strongly that the Union had to be preserved; a few were abolitionists and sought an immediate end to slavery. Many were devout Christians who saw a religious purpose in the war. There was also social pressure to enlist, as well as a belief that the war would be an exciting adventure. Sometimes idealistic motivations mixed with practical ones; certainly the promise of bounties and steady pay was attractive to many. These men believed, as did most Americans early in the war, that courage and cowardice were issues of character, not context. And few were truly prepared for the transition from free citizen to soldier.[7]

During those first days of its existence, the 16th Connecticut seemed little more than a gang of rowdy, excited males on a holiday lark. Visitors mingled freely with volunteers at their Hartford base at "Camp Williams," bringing food, clothing, and other items to ensure the comforts of home. Crowds lined the parade ground to cheer militia officers leading the weaponless and civilian-dressed men through crude drills. It was hot and dusty, but the mood was festive—at least until the arrival of their newly appointed commander, Col. Francis Beach, on August 15.[8]

Colonel Beach was appalled by the ragtag appearance and disorganized behavior of his unit, and he immediately demanded improvements. He issued polish to brighten brass and blacken shoes. Uniforms and equipment soon arrived, although guns were conspicuously absent. Beach also instituted strict restrictions on travel and visitations. When he ordered a review and inspection of the regiment, he blasted the troops for their shortcomings, vowing that such sloppy soldiering would not be tolerated under his command. Openly frustrated with his raw volunteers, he often laced his orders with unbridled profanity. Although only twenty-seven years old, Beach was already a seasoned soldier. He had graduated from the United States Military Academy in 1857, served on the Utah frontier, and taught at West Point. When the war began, Beach was an officer in the 4th United States Artillery. As aide de camp to Brig. Gen. Philip St. George Cooke, he accompanied the Army of the Potomac through the Peninsula campaign. As a professional soldier, Beach understood the importance of training and discipline. It was imperative that Beach have time and opportunity to train his raw troops so that when combat came, they would be ready. A disciple of the "rules of war," Beach fervently believed that repetitive drill would help his soldiers keep their fear in check and not panic when thrust into the shocking pandemonium of combat. It was an attempt to impose order on the chaos of war, but it was a belief by which nineteenth-century professional soldiers like Beach swore.[9]

Col. Beach's arrival to camp underscored the tension between green troops' expectations for battle and that of experienced officers. The men chafed at military discipline, convinced that it had nothing to do with preparing them for battle but was instead a conspiracy to deprive them of their rights and spoil their fun. Eighteen-year-old George Robbins recalled, "Each day brought some restraint on our freedom."[10] Some felt depressed and dispirited; no longer could they easily slip away from camp to visit friends and family. Bernard Blakeslee recalled these early days in camp as a "shock to most of the men" and a "complete revolution in their method of life."[11] A few so bitterly resented the "unfeeling" Beach and his rules and restrictions that they threatened to "fill his back full of bead" the first chance they got.[12]

Beach's frantic efforts to prepare his men for battle only lasted two weeks. On August 24, 1862, the 16th Regiment Connecticut Volunteers was formally mustered into three years of service for the United States, and five days later it left for Washington, D.C. As the men marched to the city wharf, cheering crowds lined the streets and Governor Buckingham fell in step in front of the regiment. The unit boarded two steamers and traveled down the Connecticut River, greeted by people lining the riverside. A soldier remembered: "Hartford County had given to this regiment a large portion of its very best citizens. Expectations ran high as to its regimental career, and frequent 'God Bless you's' mingled with goodbyes."[13] Newspapers agreed. The *Hartford Daily Courant* proclaimed, "A better regiment of men never left the State than the 16th Conn," and the *Evening Press* declared, "The Sixteenth carries off many brave Hartford boys, and we hope to hear a good account of the regiment."[14]

As Beach's "brave Hartford boys" rushed to the front, civilians at home worried that the cowards remained behind. Convinced that some able-bodied men were avoiding enlistment to pursue their private business, or worse, to await larger more lucrative bounties, civilians wrote angry letters to the local newspapers admonishing all to serve. Even in the avowedly Democratic *Hartford Daily Times*, articles appeared throughout the summer imploring volunteers to support Lincoln and fight the rebels or face a national draft.[15] The town of Windsor Locks raised their bounty to $200, but also passed a resolution: "To make a record of those who had skedaddled, hoping to avoid the anticipated draft, so that their children and children's children may see who left the country in its greatest time of need."[16] A few weeks after the 16th Connecticut left for the front, a letter to the editor signed "Not A Skedaddler" similarly demanded that the "names of all those, who have in any shape tried to avoid the draft be published in the Hartford papers." Doing this, the letter argued, would not only "confer a favor on those who may survive the calamities which [have] befallen our once happy and prosperous country," but this sort of public record of those evading military service would "do justice to the offspring of those noble heroes who have" willingly enlisted.[17]

Volunteers in the 16th Connecticut were about to test this theory and discover if, in fact, simply and willingly serving ensured their heroism. The next three weeks proved a harsh introduction to the realities of war. The 16th Connecticut endured exhausting marches, insufficient food, and little rest. A few weeks after leaving Connecticut, one soldier wrote home, "You in Hartford have no idea what war is, or of the life of a soldier."[18] Beach attempted to continue drill and discipline, but this only stirred more resentment. Guns, tents, and blankets finally reached the regiment, but at least one private realized that having the accoutrements of war was simply not enough. "We have our guns now [and] rubber blankets and everything necessary to go into battle," Pvt. Jacob Bauer wrote his wife Emily on September 5, "but we are not drilled enough with the guns to do any mischief." He observed "a kind of despondency and fear of being led into battle before we are fit which can not be overcome."[19]

By dusk on September 16, the Connecticut unit had marched into a line of battle just outside Sharpsburg, Maryland. The Battle of Antietam commenced the next day. Throughout the morning, the unit sat in reserve, listening nervously to the sound of shot and shell not far in the distance. At noon sick call, a considerable number of the men reported sudden illness, alleging that they were too unwell for battle. A member of the regiment scoffed at these "brave skulks" who had been, he claimed, the loudest braggerts until actual battle loomed. William Relyea later contended that this sick call rid the 16th Connecticut of "regimental rubbish," freeing it "from everything that would or could tarnish our good name."[20] Would just facing the enemy ensure bravery? The 16th Connecticut would soon find out.

Late in the afternoon of September 17, the regiment moved forward. Crossing Antietam Creek about a mile below Burnside's Bridge, the soldiers pressed on into a cornfield, with the air thick with shot and shell. Officers screamed, and men lost their way. The 16th was caught in a cross fire from its own troops and that of the enemy. A few later recalled firing only one round, and others alleged an actual charge was made. Some recalled hearing orders to "fall back"; but it is unclear whether there was ever any official call to retreat. Either way, the 16th Connecticut could not bear the enfilade fire: the regiment broke and fled in wild panic. Caught up in the swarm of panicked soldiers, Beach stubbornly fought to regain control. He desperately tried to rally a small remnant of the 16th Connecticut with parts of another Connecticut unit and redraw a battle line. But most of the 16th Connecticut were dead, wounded, or gone from the field. Dropping from mental and physical exhaustion, stragglers slept the night of September 17 under fences, on rocks, and in thickets. Wounded remained on the field all night and into the next day, moaning and crying for water.[21]

Less than one-third of the regiment answered morning roll call on September 18. Throughout the day some 200 men stumbled into camp, groggy, disoriented, and fatigued. Over the next two weeks, one soldier recalled, only a few hundred could be mustered for service. Days after the battle, straggling continued to be a serious problem. On September 23, Leland O. Barlow wrote his sister that there remained "roughs" in the regiment who would "skedaddle if they had a chance." Barlow counted sixty guards "around our little camp" treating everyone as a potential deserter. The once-proud regiment of "brave Hartford boys" was shattered and shaken.[22]

In the days and weeks that followed, members of the 16th Connecticut groped to explain what had happened. Had they failed the test of combat? Were they cowards?

Their commander refused, at least publicly, to admit his regiment's failed performance. Col. Frank Beach's official report from Antietam is brief and empty of details. He described his men enduring enemy artillery fire all day, "until about 5 o'clock when we were brought against the extreme right of the rebel infantry." He made no mention of his exasperated efforts to rally his regiment or of the panicked retreat. Beach simply stated: "I transmit the casualties. They [*sic*] were probably about twenty taken prisoner." The only indication Beach gave that there had been any problems was his admission that "the missing are constantly coming in and it is impossible to give a correct list of them."[23]

Hartford newspapers were markedly free of negative accounts, refusing to impugn anyone of cowardice. The *Hartford Daily Courant* had repeatedly reported that the 16th Connecticut was in fine condition and high spirits during the days leading up to the battle. On September 18, just before news of Antietam reached Connecticut, the paper described the regiment as withstanding the march to the front "bravely, very few giving out." Acknowledging Beach's serious doubts about the regiment's preparedness, the paper reported that "they were thoroughly drilled, and now the Colonel feels safe in taking them into battle." "Connecticut troops always have fought well," the *Courant* assured readers, "and we have no fears of the brave Sixteenth."[24] Five days after the battle, when word of the bloody day began to reach home, the *Daily Courant* announced that readers should be proud of all Connecticut soldiers: "The universal testimony is that they fought desperately and bravely, the new troops as well as the old. Although terribly cut up, there was no flinching."[25]

The *Evening Press* mixed praise of the 16th with that of the 14th Connecticut, proclaiming that both regiments "without drill or previous discipline, fresh from their peaceful pursuits, also went in [to battle] without fear or flinching." The paper's editors admitted that there may have been "a little unavoidable disorganization under the terrible fire and lack of drill, but there was not a symptom of panic. The Sixteenth was for a long time forced to stand and take it without leave to reply, and they did stand like heroes." The paper concluded, "If any new troops behaved more handsomely than the Fourteenth and Sixteenth Connecticut, we have yet to learn it."[26] The Democratic *Harford Daily Times* reported that the "valiant 16th" "performed the part of heroes in the great battle of Antietam."[27]

Few letters from Connecticut soldiers published in these local newspapers questioned their glowing assessments. Acknowledging the regiment's high losses, one member maintained: "There was no faltering or flinching, but simple confusion." Adj. John H. Burnham proudly reported, "The Sixteenth sustained unbroken ranks under the most destructive fire for an hour, when they fell back, having suffered severely."[28] Lt. Henry Beach, whose letter to his father appeared in the *Hartford Daily Times* on September 23, recounted that the 16th Connecticut was "badly used" and that his company in particular suffered "the worst of any company in the regiment." Still, Lieutenant Beach affirmed, "General Burnside says the 16th fought better than any regiment in the field—but they are mostly gone now." The editors added their own endorsement to Beach's words: "The regiment behaved nobly. It was in the thickest of the fight and though never drilled, and scarcely one month in existence as a regiment, the officers and men alike fought like veterans and won high honors and lavish praises from the old officers."[29]

A few days later, a more sober account of the battle appeared in the same paper authored by eighteen-year-old Cpl. Samuel B. Mettler. Recounting the horrific fight in the cornfield, Mettler wrote, "The slaughter was great on both sides of that encounter, and our retreat was made in great confusion." Grazed by a bullet as he ran, Mettler recalled, "The men were so scared, they fled in all directions." The *Times* published this surprisingly candid letter without comment.[30]

Private, unpublished letters home supported Mettler's account, conceding the regiment's poor performance and confessing cowardice with striking honesty. Private Martin V. Culver in Company A wrote his brother matter-of-factly on September 21, 1862, that the 16th Connecticut "had one hard battle, a very hard one," and that "some have skedaddled."[31] Twenty-nine-year-old William Relyea wrote his family that he did not consider running until he looked around and "saw only dead men." At that moment he confessed: "I very quickly decided it was no place for me."[32] Relyea tried to find some humor in his admission: "It is over now," Relyea wrote, "and we laugh at our fears, that is human, so am I."[33] William Drake was just as blunt when he told his cousin, "there was some pretty tall running in the 16th and I guess that I made myself scarce rather fast."[34] Young George Robbins was slightly hurt and fell out of formation, losing track of the regiment in all the confusion. He did not run, he assured his sister, "until the rest did," hiding in the woods until rejoining the 16th the next morning.[35] Elizur D. Beldon's diary described the fight in the cornfield as a "scene of terror, every man for himself." Beldon was slightly wounded during the frenzied retreat and fell into a "small gutter" with several other men. "There I lay," he confided, "not daring to stir until dark when the firing ceased."[36] Pvt. John B. Cuzner of Company B wrote his fiancée, Ellen, on September 21 that there were members of the regiment who "did not frighten," but he was not one of them. "As for myself," he confessed, "I am a big coward." He claimed that he only "ran when they gave the order to retreat" and then hid behind a stone wall. The regiment, Cuzner wrote, was "cut off most shockingly" after having "few drills and no experience."[37] German-born Jacob Bauer wrote his wife Emily three days after the battle that he was surprised he had survived. Reflecting on that "dreadful hour" in the cornfield, Bauer recalled forgetting everything, even his wife and his own safety. Instead his "only thought and word was forward, forward, forward, which I could think of and sing out." But after he fired one shot, he ran with the rest of the regiment in "Bull Run Fashion."[38]

Eighteen-year-old Pvt. Robert H. Kellogg, one of the most articulate and thoughtful men in the ranks, wrote his father a long missive three days after Antietam. In great detail Kellogg recounted the 16th Connecticut's movements on the field and their panicked retreat. Even though he described his comrades "breaking and retreating" and admitted to feeling a "sort of quailing," and himself fleeing the field to hide behind a fence, Kellogg refused to call anyone a coward. "We were murdered," he charged, reasoning that a green regiment such as the 16th should not have been left "unsupported in a cornfield in the immediate vicinity of a cunning foe—and as it were, left to take care of itself." Kellogg told his father that he fervently prayed to God throughout the day for "peace of soul." "God gave me courage & strength," the pious young soldier assured his father, "to bear up through the fearful scenes of that terrible day." It was the rebels, Kellogg believed, who "skedaddled early Friday morning" off the field, fearing another confrontation with the Federals.[39]

Adj. John H. Burnham also reflected on cowardice in a lengthy letter he wrote his mother a few weeks after the battle. Burnham had publicly praised his regiment's performance in the newspapers, but he was more frank in his letter home. Trying to describe his "personal feelings in the fight," Burnham admitted, "I could sit down and talk to you and tell you all about it easily but I find it more difficult to write how I felt." He remembered little leading up to the attack as he busily issued orders and prepared the men for battle. He had no time to think of personal danger until he spotted the enemy on his left forming with calm intrepidity, methodically planting a battery in close range to the regiment. At that moment, Burnham wrote, "I am frank to confess that although I had no idea of running away—I trembled. You may call the feeling fear or anything you choose for I don't deny that I trembled and wished we were well out of it." He was afraid, but he did not act on it: "I tried to do my duty and am satisfied." Nonetheless, the experience left the young officer with deeply mixed feelings. On one hand, he "should not be sorry to see the war ended tomorrow without firing another shot"; on the other hand, he admitted, "I am a little eager to see one more battle.

Not from any reckless desire for the excitement but I have a little practical knowledge now and I should be more at home next time and perhaps do better. I should be considerable cooler I have no doubt." He assured his mother that he hoped to survive the war, but there was something he wanted much more. "I hope as I always have," Burnham explained, "that I may have the courage to do my duty well, not recklessly but with simple bravery and fidelity, so that if I fall you may have the consolation of knowing that I not only lose my life in a good cause but did it like a man." He added one final observation on this subject. "I wish to say particularly this romance about men being shot in the back is all a humbug. A mounted officer is as likely to be hit in the back, and more likely to be hit in the side than in the front and don't ever do any injustice to think ill of him."[40]

These letters reveal not just surprising admissions of fear. They also show Civil War soldiers grappling with the concepts of bravery and cowardice. After the trauma of battle, defining heroes and cowards did not seem so easy. In the coming weeks and months, men in the 16th Connecticut would continue to think hard about these subjects.

After Antietam, the morale of the unit plummeted. Lincoln, exasperated by McClellan's boastings and failures, replaced him with Ambrose Burnside, the 9th Corps's beloved commander. As Burnside planned for a renewed offensive, the regiment approached Fredericksburg. The weather turned cold and snowy, and the 16th Connecticut lacked shelter, tents, or adequate blankets. Illness ran rampant.[41] Desertion seemed a viable option, although the humiliation of such an act remained strong. Martin Culver wrote his brother on November 16, 1862, that if he could get home "any way" he would do it "if i get a chance without deserting."[42] In early December, letters appeared in the *Hartford Daily Times* attesting that the unit had done nothing since arriving at Fredericksburg except "drill and *starve*." Recounting how the 16th rushed to the front without being "properly organized and equipped, and when almost to a man they were ignorant of the use of a musket," one letter noted that the men arrived at the battle exhausted and hungry with their knapsacks left behind. However, at Antietam they fought "side by side with old veterans, these 1,000 brave boys (so Antietam tells) did their full share toward turning the tide of battle and winning a reputation that every Connecticut boy may be well proud of." Claiming that the "brave Connecticut soldiers" were terribly neglected, these letters urged citizens at home to pressure Governor Buckingham "or somebody else [to] send suitable agents at once to look after and provide" for the "brave Yankee boys from old Connecticut, who are now suffering on the banks of the Rappahannock."[43]

The Battle of Fredericksburg did little to improve the mood of the regiment or silence complaints. The contest between the hapless Burnside and aggressive Lee was a stunning Union defeat. The 16th Connecticut regiment remained in reserve throughout the day of battle. Positioned about a mile from the fighting, the regiment could only look at and listen to the successive and futile charges upon the Confederate position.

By the end of December, the gloom hung thick over the camp of the 16th Connecticut. After witnessing two grisly battles and peace nowhere in sight, soldiers began to believe that violence would solve nothing. "When you read about the 'Soldiers being in good spirits and eager for a fight,'" Cpl. Leland Barlow warned his father, "you may know that it is a lie. What has our fighting amounted to lately? This war will never be closed by fighting."[44] A few days later, Barlow wrote his sister in a similar vein: "The boys are getting sick of the war. I have heard lots of soldiers say they would never go into another fight." He quickly added that it was not the 16th Connecticut that made such claims, although he predicted that such low morale even among his own comrades "might increase the number of sick ones in ours some."[45] Harrison Woodford from Company I already discerned the grim mood among his comrades. "It is hard work to get the men into a fight," he wrote home on Christmas Day. "There is a great lack of patriotism in the army," he observed, "and I must say for myself that I cannot see from the present aspect of things what all this loss of life is fore. We may fight forever and then another way will have to be devised to settle it."[46] Private Martin Culver agreed. Referring to the Battle of Fredericksburg as "nothing but a slaughter," he too judged that "the troops dont fight as they did a[w]hile ago for they begin to see this war is a humbug and they are cared for so poorly that they dont care[;] they all want to get home." Culver told his brother unashamedly that he was done with soldiering: "If we go into winter quarters and have anothers summers campane they wont have me to go with them." If Culver could "play sick enough," he would "get away" if there was not "a pretty good sign of peace."[47]

Yet, despite these clear signs of demoralization, the shame of cowardice remained, especially when it involved another regiment. Corporal Barlow scornfully described "a comical sight" in the nearby camp of the 4th Rhode Island soon after the Battle of Fredericksburg: "They have got two crotches set in the ground with a pole put across them about eight or ten feet high; with three men riding on it with boards on their backs; on one it says, 'I skulked,' in another it says 'So did I' and the third it says 'I did too.' It is punishment for skedaddling from the fight the other day."[48]

Newly promoted Lt. Col. John H. Burnham was very self-conscious about the consequences and necessary punishment of cowardly behavior. As acting commander of the regiment—Beach was absent on sick leave—Burnham did not want his family to think that he was unfair to the men. He admitted that there were "always shirks, sneaks and some ugliness to deal with," but he warned that, if his family heard stories of his punishing such men unfairly, not to believe that he was "getting hard-hearted." "I intend to treat every man well," Burnham wrote, "and see that he gets everything possible for his comfort and in return I intend that every man shall do his duty and his whole duty." Burnham seemed to accept that "shirks and sneaks" would always be present in camp and in battle, but that he also had to work hard to ensure that all of his men behaved dutifully.[49] The specter of cowardice was constant.

By mid-January 1863, the regiment settled into more comfortable winter quarters near Fredericksburg, and the mood in camp improved considerably. Still, Martin Culver, the same private who was looking to "play sick" so that he could go home, wrote his brother that he was done with soldiering—"i have seen enough of war and so have all the rest of the soldiers." The regiment had not been paid since leaving Hartford in August, and this was getting to be a pressing issue. Culver wrote, "i think the reason they don't pay us off is they kno that half of the soldiers will run away."[50]

As spring approached, the 16th Connecticut focused on a different kind of cowardly behavior: political dissent. Connecticut was nearing its gubernatorial election, and the two candidates represented two sides to the war: Republican William A. Buckingham, who vowed to support Lincoln and the war, and Democrat Thomas Seymour, who challenged the war's human and monetary cost. Soldiers in the 16th Connecticut were acutely aware of this election. The pages of the Hartford newspapers were filled with pronouncements of the various troops' positions, but several members of the 16th sent letters to the papers expressing their positions. The pro-Democrat *Times* published accounts attesting to soldiers' demoralization and discontent with the war; the pro-Republican *Daily Courant* and *Evening Press*, on the other hand, countered with reports affirming soldiers' unwavering support of Lincoln and the war. The 16th Connecticut appeared to represent both sides.

A "Patriotic Appeal," published in the *Daily Courant* on March 21, 1863, for example, included the signatures of Lt. Col. John H. Burnham and eighteen other unnamed commissioned officers in the unit, in addition to seventy-seven officers from the 8th, 11th, 17th, and 21st Connecticut. "We learn," the appeal stated, "with sorrow, that in our noble State of Connecticut, within whose borders so many homes have been made desolate by traitors' hands, an effort has been made to sow the seeds of dissension in the North, and to excite the people to acts of hostility against the federal Government." As men in uniform they felt a "soldier's regard for our foes on the James and the Rappahannock on account of their skill and courage; but towards the enemies of the Republic on the Thames, the Connecticut and the Housatonic, we can have no other feelings than those of the most unmitigated scorn and contempt." These men clearly distinguished between legitimate enemy combatants who fought valiantly with "shot and shell," and dissident civilians, whom they deemed as disgraceful traitors. Implied again in these words was a distinction between a brave enemy and cowardly citizenry.[51]

Indeed, a few days after this appeal appeared in the *Courant*, N. M. Bowen wrote the paper attesting to the loyalty of Pvt. Charles F. Bowen, of Company H, 16th Connecticut. Private Bowen, the letter stated, "is particularly anxious that a few of the croakers at the North be sent down and compelled to 'shoulder arms,' and participate in the struggles which good and loyal men are maintaining, (at the hazard of life and limb) for the love they bear to their country." Bowen predicted that if such Democrats were forced to serve, he and his fellow veterans would "see some of the tallest skedaddling they had ever witnessed."[52]

While this public discussion over worthy and unworthy soldiers—in effect, who were the cowards and who were the heroes—played out in the Hartford papers, men in the ranks continued to reveal their own feelings on the subject in private letters and diaries. Martin Culver, who had previously disclosed his deep disillusionment with soldiering soon after Antietam, had not changed his mind. On April 22, 1863, he wrote from Suffolk to his brother that he was very ill, feverish and vomiting, and content to stay away from active duty indefinitely. He declared, "i am agoing to play deadbeat a[w]hile and see how they will like it for i have done other boyes duty long enough."[53]

By April 1863, the 16th Connecticut was no longer part of the Army of the Potomac. Transferred to the Virginia peninsula in early February, the regiment manned the defenses of Suffolk as part of George W. Getty's Third

Division. That spring, Lee dispatched James Longstreet's corps to lay siege to the town and to gather necessary provisions for his hungry army. The siege of Suffolk would prove a failed endeavor for the Confederates, but for the 16th Connecticut it would offer a renewed opportunity for battle. Just the anticipation of combat cheered the men. Sergeant Robert Kellogg described the 16th in April 1863 as "greatly improved and now looked upon as a 'crack' regiment." The men felt properly fed, armed, and trained. "Suffolk is very strong fortified," Kellogg reported to his father, "and our troops are eager and willing to fight."[54]

The 16th Connecticut did fight again at Suffolk but it was nothing like Antietam. As Confederates tried to break the Union stronghold, the unit participated in several armed clashes with the enemy. These encounters (skirmishes really, with relatively low casualties) nonetheless tested the regiment's abilities. And this time, the men performed well.

The first incident occurred on April 24, 1863. Sergeant Kellogg recalled how the regiment, acting as skirmishers, encountered the advancing rebels, who were "pretty thick and saucy, but we followed them up closely and peppered them so that they had to retreat to their rifle pits." The regiment continued "to make a stand," giving a cheer and charging forward. This, Kellogg described, "produced panic among them [the Confederates] and they fled like sheep, leaving many things behind them in their haste, including several of their men, whom we took prisoners." Kellogg admitted, "It was an exciting sort of fight, but it was not a battle really."[55] Casualties were low, one man killed and seven wounded, but spirits were high and apparently there were no stragglers. Lt. Bernard F. Blakeslee later remembered, "This was a very successful skirmish and gave the men great confidence in themselves."[56]

On Sunday, May 3, the 16th Connecticut again went into action, this time along the Providence Church Road. The unit quickly found itself charging across a "broad, plowed field," flanked by woods filled with rebel soldiers. The fighting was hot, and the 16th was "within a few rods of the rebels." Kellogg recalled: "We held this exposed situation until our ammunition was exhausted and were then relieved by some of the 15th C.V. and part of our reserve." Later that night the regiment returned to camp "all tired out but feeling that we had done our duty well."[57] The regiment's loss was again slight: two killed and eight men wounded. One of those killed was nineteen-year-old Henry W. Barber. Regimental historian Blakeslee would later claim that "Young Barber's last words were 'Tell Mother that I never was a coward.'"[58]

Indeed, the men of the 16th Connecticut could proudly claim that, at least at Suffolk, none were cowards. Existing accounts from these two engagements report no straggling, although after the battle William H. Relyea remembered Capt. Henry Beach from Company I being "placed under arrest and we saw him going through camp, doing no duty at all, and soon after he resigned and went home, thus severing his connection with the regiment."[59] The regiment had faced the enemy really for the first time since their panic at Antietam. But the question remained: Would their affirming experience at Suffolk end discussion of cowards for the 16th Connecticut?[60]

Over the next year, the 16th Connecticut essentially conducted garrison duty. Moved first from Suffolk to Portsmouth, Virginia, and then to Plymouth, North Carolina, the unit manned coastal defenses, made periodic raids, and lived rather well for soldiers at war. The regiment found itself even further removed from active campaigning. In Portsmouth, men built winter cabins, a church, and a hospital. Military discipline was lax and there were poker games, theatrical productions, and plentiful liquor, food, and clothing available. Mail was steady and visitors from home a constant. Life for the 16th Connecticut was about as comfortable it could be.[61]

Despite their pleasant quarters, relaxed discipline, and frequent civilian visitors, men of the 16th Connecticut began to fret. They filled their letters and diaries with complaints about bad food, unfair officers, continual sickness, and depravity. They felt like "nomads" set adrift from the rest of the Union Army and active campaigning. The work they did—building and manning breastworks, and raiding nearby towns—was hardly the kind of perilous military service that brought accolades and honors.[62]

During their many weeks in Portsmouth, tensions between officers and men spilled into the hometown newspapers. It began in early September 1863 when Pvt. Horace B. Steele of Company F sent a letter to the editors of the *Daily Times* angrily accusing regimental officers, in particular Lieutenant Colonel Burnham, of abuse. Steele claimed, "In this regiment men have been ordered to the guard house for some trivial offence and abused most shamefully." He described a recent incident where a man was made to "carry a log that weighed from 50 to 60 pounds on his back, when the thermometer marked 102 in the shade." He then bitterly recounted his recent attempt at obtaining a furlough, something Steele considered himself "entitled to by the regulations of this army." One of his children was seriously ill, and Steele desperately wanted to be home with his wife and sick child. Steele's request, however, was turned down by Lieutenant Colonel

Burnham. He closed his letter by asserting that the committee appointed by the governor to investigate the regiment's condition had been "feasted by the officers and not allowed to go into the privates' tents for fear they will tell the truth and expose the practices on the privates."[63]

Lieutenant Colonel Burnham responded a few weeks later with his own letter to the paper, clearly rattled by Steele's decision to air such grievances publicly. "The publication by an officer or soldier of such a letter as that of Steele's," Burnham stated, "even if its statements were true, would be one of the grossest violations of military discipline, and the falsity of this one certainly aggravates the offense." He vowed not to punish Steele but instead offered to send him before a court-martial where he could properly air his grievances and "where he cannot fail to be treated with strict impartiality." It turned out that the "trivial offense" committed by Pvt. Patrick O'Brien from Company H was going AWOL from camp and being spotted "drunk in Portsmouth" days after his one-day pass expired, "thereby rendering himself liable to a charge for desertion." The regimental surgeon attested that O'Brien's exhaustion was not due to the punishment but to sunstroke intensified by his days of "dissipation."[64]

An anonymous private from the 16th was quick to disagree, sending another angry letter to the paper in early October accusing Burnham of making up facts out "of whole cloth." "We have been most shamefully abused by our commissioned staff," reaffirmed the unnamed soldier, "pretty much since we left Hartford, being kept upon half rations, &tc, &tc, while other regiments close by us have had enough and to spare." Sick men too, this man asserted, were also suffering: "For I have known men to lie in their tents for days and then died from the neglect, because the doctor did not pay them proper attention." When commissioners came to investigate the regiment's conditions, Lieutenant Colonel Burnham wined and dined them, "telling them such stories as he pleased, and they not going around to see how the privates lived!" Why did officers and doctors treat the 16th Connecticut so shabbily? These two soldiers insisted that it was incompetence, selfishness, and fear: Lieutenant Colonel Burnham "was afraid to have things exposed, and to have it known how such a gentleman as he professes to be, treats his fellow beings."[65]

There are several revealing aspects to this brief but heated flurry of accusations. As an officer, Lieutenant Colonel Burnham clearly viewed his treatment of the offender wholly warranted to ensure, as he had told his mother in January 1863, that men like O'Brien "do his duty and his whole duty." Burnham could have actually meted out a more serious punishment than simply carrying a log. Private Steele, desperately seeking a furlough himself so he could be home with his family, could only sympathize. He and his comrade viewed O'Brien's behavior—previously and usually viewed as cowardly and dishonorable—as inconsequential, even understandable, and his punishment entirely unjustifiable. They resented Burnham's demand for discipline and proper behavior. The "coward" in this case was not their fellow soldier, but their lieutenant colonel, who abused his power and position.[66]

By the time the 16th Connecticut garrisoned Plymouth, North Carolina, concerns about cowardice centered on both the battlefront and home front. It was January 1864, and general war-weariness had settled in among northern citizens and soldiers. The draft had been in effect for a year with mixed results. The regiment's strength, reduced considerably by the losses at Antietam, sickness, and desertion, was low, so conscripts began to fill the gaps. But those who had joined in 1862 resented the new arrivals. They continued to believe that many able-bodied men avoided the draft by paying misfits and crooks to serve in their place. Leland Barlow wrote to his sister in April: "If we could see things go on as they should, you would not hear of so many desertions, but it is enough to discourage a soldier to see so much rascality out here, and it is not very encouraging to see the North, good Union men, to contrive every way to keep out of it themselves, and send out such poor, miserable, good-for-nothing fellows to do the fighting." Few conscripts, Barlow insisted, "will ever do anything, some are natural farm fools, some with one hand gone, some blind in one eye, and old men that will hardly hold together." Others Barlow regarded as criminal: "If a man commits any crime except murder, it pardons him, to go into the army." Barlow, like many jaded federal soldiers, wondered out loud how the North could win the war with "so much corruption and wickedness in the country."[67]

Others were equally disillusioned and ready to come home. One day in late March 1864, Pvt. George N. Champlin recorded in his diary that although the regiment was in "good spirits," he noted, "We had roll call several times this afternoon to keep the men from going straggling."[68] Austin Thompson explained to his fiancée Electra that he considered straggling himself, only he dreaded the public shame: "But if I can stand it through to the end," he added, "I had much rather do it, than go home with a name that some of the boys have."[69] The pressure from home was also strong. When one private's family urged him to be safe, he responded angrily, "Your advice in begging me to keep out of danger sounds harsh coming from a friend of his country." Private Leander Chapin wrote his brother, "I know how you feel and highly appreciate your motive but I beg of you not to write in such a way. It is productive of no good, rather harm. Shall I not do my duty wherever I am called to go? It is much safer to go right along even though the enemy's balls are dealing death on all sides than it is to seek a better place. Experience proves this. Let me die a hero rather than live a coward."[70]

Dying a hero still meant performing well in combat, and questions lingered about the battle-worthiness of the 16th. John H. Burnham, the regiment's beleaguered lieutenant colonel, defended the regiment's reputation in letters to his mother. The same man accused in the press of being abusive and unfair had actually been offered promotion to colonelcy of the 11th Connecticut. Burnham declined, judging the 11th "miserable rabble" that "cannot be trusted near the enemy." Burnham preferred to stay with the 16th, of whom he declared, "A better set of boys were never got together in any regiment."[71] Later, in March when the regiment clashed with Confederates near New Bern, Burnham assured his mother that the 16th "have done nobly," but complained that there were "cursed cowards who are sneaking to the rear [and] are spreading all sorts of hobgoblin stories about our being cut to pieces and that."[72]

On April 20, 1864, everything changed for the 16th Connecticut. This unit that had so ignobly panicked at Antietam, successfully skirmished in Suffolk, but languished in garrison duty for a year was about to face the second greatest test of its wartime career. On April 17 Confederates attacked Plymouth, an important anchor to the Federal occupation of the North Carolina coastline. The 16th Connecticut, stationed just outside of town with several other regiments, doggedly fought back, but they found themselves assailed by sea and by land. Lieutenant Colonel Burnham sensed raw fear beginning to take hold of the regiment, so in desperation, he ordered the band to play patriotic songs. This temporarily soothed their jittery nerves. "Brave hearts became braver," a soldier later recalled, "and if the patriotism of any waxed cold, and the courage of any faltered, they here grew warmer and stronger until the pride of country had touched the will, and an indomitable principle had been kindled that virtually declared the man a hero until death." But before long, a Confederate battery took aim at the musicians, and shells began to explode over their heads. The band members dropped their instruments and ran.[73]

Surrounded and heavily outnumbered, Federal commander Henry Wessels had little choice. On the morning of April 20, he surrendered the entire garrison at Plymouth. "The 'rebs' took us all," wrote Samuel Grosvenor in his diary on April 20, and, indeed, nearly the whole 16th Connecticut Volunteer Infantry Regiment was captured except for one company and a scattering of men on detached service.[74]

None of the existing letters or dairies from the 16th Connecticut express any shame or embarrassment over the surrender. Robert Kellogg maintained that giving up was done "with no willing grace, yet it could not but be attended with the consciousness that we had tried the virtue of resistance to the utmost."[75] Oliver Gates similarly explained, "We could not do much against such odds so we were obliged to surrender."[76]

Newspapers contained scanty reports of the fight at Plymouth but nonetheless sought to soothe any doubts about the regiment's gallantry. On April 26 the *Hartford Evening Press* reported rumors of the capture, attesting, "The 16th was there and bravely stood their position; the state may justly be proud of them." "In fact," the paper added, "the Connecticut regiments are all much thought of here and there is no such thing as run attached to their names."[77]

Men hastily wrote letters home, assuring loved ones that they were safe and predicting a quick exchange. Kellogg sent his father a short note and told him not to worry. "The rebs treat us very kindly and as a whole [are a] fine set of men & good soldiers," Kellogg confessed. "I can but laugh at the ridiculous plight we are in."[78]

It was a ridiculous plight, but nothing to laugh over. The regiment was bound for the notorious Andersonville prison, where they would remain for the next six months. Of the estimated 400 members of the 16th who entered the prison in early May 1864, nearly one-third would die there. Hunger, exposure, and terrible illness wreaked havoc on them, as it did with all of Andersonville's inmates. More would perish in South Carolina pens when anxious Confederates evacuated the Georgia prison in late 1864. Even those who lived to gain their freedom never recovered their health, and they spent the postwar years physically and emotionally scarred.[79]

During those many months in prison, members of the 16th Connecticut faced new questions of bravery and cowardice. Stripped of their guns and any real ability to fight the enemy, their only weapon was mental and physical toughness. Being brave now meant "waiting in quiet patience," as rumors of exchange swirled and men starved and died.[80] Succumbing to disease and hunger in the squalid prison seemed much less dignified than dying in battle. "I had rather," Ira Forbes wrote in his diary, "see men shot down while fighting for their country than see them dying in this manner."[81] Abject cowardice now meant taking an oath of allegiance to the Confederacy to gain parole and release from the stockade.

At first, most soldiers from the 16th Connecticut refused parole. They found refuge and strength in each other, keeping special tabs on how other members fared.[82] When a band of ruthless raiders from within the prison targeted new arrivals, the 16th stayed safe. Sergeant Major Kellogg recalled: "We as a regiment presented a united front, and were therefore too strong for them." Kellogg admitted, "It required no little vigilance and sacrifice to adapt ourselves to all these circumstances of our prison life."[83]

Prisoners too clung to their faith in God and country, and memories of home, to help them persevere. On July 4, 1864, Cpl. Charles Lee mused: "This is the anniversary of our national independence and instead of celebrating it in Connecticut as I have done every year of my life except last year, I am a prisoner of war shut up in this nasty bull-pen with no immediate prospect of getting out. Yet I am perfectly willing to suffer it all, if it does anything towards saving the union."[84] Oliver Gates marked the anniversary of his enlistment in his prison diary, acknowledging that he never believed he would be away from his wife and young daughter for so long. "But," he reflected, "my Country needed my services and thus far [I] have tried to do a Soldier's Duty faithfully and in an active service of two years we have necessarily seen more or less hardship but nothing can compare with this imprisonment[.] No human suffering can exceed what we witness here." He noted, "When I came in here three months ago I was a strong healthy man and could endure almost anything as I thought but now I am but the wreck of my former self almost a Cripple."[85] This truly seemed to be the greatest test of their lives.

As the terrible ordeal continued, however, some did the unthinkable and swore their allegiance to the enemy so they could get out. Augustus Moesner volunteered as a clerk so that he could obtain extra rations. Hiram Buckingham accepted a parole to become a hospital steward and Andrew Spring a cook.[86] Their actions brought scorn from their comrades. Kellogg judged such parolees "foolish," and George N. Champlin declared, "They have disgraced themselves." "I will die in prison," he affirmed, "before I will aid the Rebels one iota."[87] When Oliver Gates learned of his comrades' behavior he was equally disgusted. But later he too took the oath to save himself. He later reflected how "terrible we looked upon them [those who accepted paroles] then as the next thing to traitor but afterward we were glad to accept the same condition ourselves and we have learned to be more Charitable to others while we are ignorant of the nature under which they act."[88] It is unclear just how many members of the unit accepted paroles.

Meanwhile the remains of the regiment, a mere skeleton of its former self, continued as the 16th Connecticut stationed at Roanoke Island. The core of the unit was Company H, which left Plymouth in the midst of the fight to ferry civilians away from the forts and thus escaped capture. Draftees made up the rest of the weakened unit, only worsening the regiment's already bad reputation. Even Lieutenant Colonel Burnham, who had stubbornly defended the unit from rumors of cowardice, realized their dire straights. Rejoining the regiment after his own imprisonment, Burnham was shocked by what he saw. "The regiment is not only demoralized," he wrote his mother in January 1865, "but has been taken from the front and scattered about a company in a place on detached duty." "They were taken from the front," he explained, "because they deserted so freely to the enemy." And it was not merely a question of poor discipline or mismanagement, something that could probably be fixed. It was, Burnham concluded, because "the material composing the regiment is evidently of the worst character." After more than two years stubbornly and publicly defending the 16th, even Burnham recognized their "evil reputation." He admitted his own unwillingness to lead a regiment "that cannot be trusted in [the] face of the enemy."[89]

Those final months of war seemed an eternity for the beaten and battered 16th Connecticut. Survivors released from Confederate prisons were given a short furlough but had to return to service after thirty days. Few had any stomach for remaining in the army at all. Sgt. Jacob Bauer felt depressed after having to return to the regiment so soon, finding army life tedious, discipline nonexistent, and many of his comrades prone to excessive drinking. He, like many others, counted the days until his three-year enlistment was up or the war ended, whichever came sooner.[90] The month-long furlough to Connecticut only made their homesickness worse. "I never since I enlisted longed so much for next August," Cuzner wrote, "as I have since I came home. When my time is out I shall not be thinking well, I have to report at such and such a time but will go and come when I please."[91] When the fighting ceased in April, the 16th Connecticut still awaited orders to go home.

Finally, the unit was mustered out in June 1865. A mere 130 men marched the streets of Hartford on the official day of mustering-out before a shocked and saddened crowd of onlookers. A city official addressed the regiment's "thinned ranks," citing its "torn colors" as "convincing proof of your deeds of bravery." Lieutenant Colonel Burnham also spoke, giving a final emotional farewell. Certainly, he would make no mention of cowards, nor would he spin tales of heroism. Instead, he honestly assessed the regiment's war record: "Although a less amount of glory in the field has fallen on our lot than to some others, no regiment from the State has been subjected to so much suffering." At that moment in June, nearly three full years after the regiment's creation, Burnham felt only pride: "Whenever in the future I am asked of what in all my life I am proudest, I shall always answer 'that I belonged to the 16th Connecticut in the Union army.'"[92]

Burnham's words were prophetic for nearly all of the regiment's veterans, indeed for most Civil War veterans. Pride would replace any lingering disillusionment, bitterness, or war weariness. Eventually, all talk of cowards abated, and, instead, a celebration of heroes remained. By the turn of the century, few northern or southern veterans, publicly or privately, spoke of anything but brave, loyal warriors. When survivors from the 16th Connecticut met to dedicate monuments at Antietam and Andersonville, they too dwelled only on heroic sacrifice. On October 11, 1894, the Reverend Charles Dixon described the 16th Connecticut as entirely full of "noble men whose hearts glowed and burned with patriotic fire."[93]

The 16th Connecticut also led efforts to build a state monument at Andersonville, honoring all prisoners who died during the war. Three of the four commissioners chosen by the state to design the memorial were from the 16th Connecticut, and they consulted with many fellow members. Seeking the appropriate image, the commission explained that they wanted "a figure which should represent a very young man, in Civil War uniform to the smallest details, and whose expressions should be that of courage and heroism that are developed in suffering,—strong, modest[,] hopeful." They wanted to portray "a typical soldier-boy of the northern people, and his bearing that of one who has learned poise by endurance." He would be "the ideal young soldier, as he stood for all that is noble and loyal and enduring when he offered himself and his life, if need be for our loved country."[94] Bela Lyon Pratt, a student of Augustus Saint-Gaudens, was named the sculptor, and the man chosen as a model for "Andersonville Boy" was allegedly the 16th Connecticut's former sergeant major Robert Kellogg. The bronze figure, completed in 1907, depicts a young, beardless private stripped of his gun and equipment, standing with his left foot forward and his kepi in one hand by his side. More civilian than soldier, only his uniform marks him as a warrior. The *Boston*

Transcript characterized the statue as "a simple figure of a private infantry soldier, disarmed and helpless, standing with a sober foreknowledge of the very probable fate before him." He seemed "a mere boy, a typical New England lad" fresh from school and the New England town in which he resided. The paper described him as "manly and modest, he is one of the kind who take things as they come, without bravado and without posing. But there is something in the genuineness, the simplicity, the rugged naturalness of the boy's bearing which makes it seem safe to predict that he will be constant and faithful to the end."[95] A modern observer has noted that the statue has "little that identifies his terrible ordeal as a prisoner at Andersonville."[96]

At the monument's dedication in October 1907, an aging Robert Kellogg stood beside the likeness of his younger self and briefly addressed a crowd of fellow comrades, family, and state officials. Remembering how daunting the prison experience was in "testing the courage of the bravest," he stressed that "Connecticut boys," especially his fellow comrades from the 16th Connecticut, "stood for order and restraint." Referring to offers for parole, he stated: "Solicitations to enter the military service or civil employment of the Southern Confederacy were turned aside with scorn by them, though acceptance meant instant release from the fate that now so clearly stared them in the face." Prisoners died "not in the heat and excitement of the battle," but "in the loneliness of a multitude, with a comrade only by their side, within an enemy's lines and under a hostile flag." "One by one," he recalled, "our brave boys gave up the fight and passed away." "Andersonville," he concluded, "becomes an object lesson in patriotism," where Americans could visit "to learn again and again the lessons of heroic sacrifice made by those who so quietly sleep in these long rows of graves."[97]

Kellogg's words, and the statue itself, conveyed renewed affirmations of the regiment's courage, but they also represent a subtle shift away from the traditional dichotomy of hero vs. coward. His emphasis, some forty years after the war, was on self-control, patriotism, and quiet dignity, traits needed to withstand extended imprisonment but not necessarily violent combat.

Other postwar records grew silent about the regiment's failures and disappointments. Newspapers, published histories, public speeches, and private letters repeatedly labeled them "noble," "gallant," "brave," and the "Fighting 16th Regiment of Volunteers."[98] With time, all the many versions of and reactions to cowardice—in battle, camp, and prison, among privates and officers, soldiers, and civilians—vanished.

This essay has focused on a single northern regiment's Civil War experiences and its grapplings with bravery and cowardice. Certainly, the analysis presented here is not meant to end discussion or suggest any broad generalizations about the topic. Instead, this essay is merely a starting point to reassess accepted assumptions about Civil War soldiers. Yes, there were some who remained "loyal, true and brave," never questioning their initial ideology to fight and fight well. But then there were others, like the men studied here, who from the shock, monotony, and sufferings of war, behaved poorly, even disgracefully. These stories too deserve a place in our history of the war.

NOTES

Lesley J. Gordon delivered her Klement Lecture in 2005.

1. James I. Robertson, *Soldiers Blue and Gray* (Columbia: Univ. of South Carolina Press, 1988), 222; see also Bell Irvin Wiley, *The Life of Johnny Reb: The Common Soldier of the Confederacy* (Indianapolis: Bobbs-Merrill, 1943); Bell Irvin Wiley, *The Life of Billy Yank: The Common Soldier of the Union* (Indianapolis: Bobbs-Merrill, 1952); and James M. McPherson, *For Cause and Comrades: Why Men Fought in the Civil War* (New York: Oxford Univ. Press, 1997). Earl Hess, in his *Union Soldiers in Battle: Enduring the Ordeal of Combat* (Lawrence: Univ. Press of Kansas, 1997), and Steven Woodworth, in his edited *The Loyal True and Brave: America's Civil War Soldiers* (Wilmington, Del.: SR Books, 2002), concur with Robertson, Wiley, and McPherson that the majority of Civil War soldiers behaved honorably and courageously. The exception is Gerald Linderman, whose fascinating but controversial *Embattled Courage* sees both concepts of courage and cowardice as fluid and changing. He also recognizes that postwar America purified the war of "any reference to war's fear and futility; community ritual celebrated all wounds as evidence of courage and enshrined all deaths as efficacious deaths." Gerald Linderman, *Embattled Courage: The Experience of Combat in the American Civil War* (New York: Free Press, 1987), 284. Nonetheless, since Linderman based his conclusions exclusively on printed postwar memoirs, the accuracy of his arguments is suspect. My research here focuses on wartime sources, both public and private, although some postwar accounts are consulted. There have been important works on desertion, especially related to the South, but the topic of soldier cowardice has not received comparable treatment. The definitive study of desertion remains Ella Lonn, *Desertion During the Civil War* (1928; repr. Lincoln: Univ. of Nebraska Press, 1998). See also Brian Holden Reid and John White, "'A Mob of Stragglers and Cowards': Desertion from the Union and Confederate Armies, 1861–1865," *Journal of Strategic Studies* 8 (1985): 64–77.

2. James Robertson cites phrases such as "showing the white feather," having "cannon fever" or "chicken heart disease" to mean acting the coward, although in my research I have not found any of these phrases used. Interestingly, Robertson provides no sources for these allegedly contemporary phrases. See Robertson, *Soldiers Blue and Gray*, 216–17. The opposite of cowardice was courage, and, as Gerald Linderman has explained, courage to Civil War soldiers meant self-control, maturity, manliness, and even piety. Thus, the lack of it implied weakness, immaturity, and godlessness. It is important to note that there seemed to be a dramatic difference between being afraid,

even admitting to it, and acting on it. Linderman disagrees and argues that merely feeling fear "was to be a coward, Civil War soldiers thought." See Linderman, *Embattled Courage*, 18, also 8, 10, 23, 25, 64. Margaret Creighton has most recently argued that the definition of courage needs to be expanded beyond armed "physical daring" to include women's nurturing self-sacrifice and African Americans' steady perseverance during the crisis. See Margaret Creighton, *The Colors of Courage: Gettysburg's Forgotten History: Immigrants, Women, and African Americans in the Civil War's Defining Battle* (New York: Basic Books, 2005), x.

3. Reid and White, "'A Mob of Stragglers and Cowards,'" 64–65.

4. Robertson, *Soldiers Blue and Gray*, 128; also Creighton, *Colors of Courage*, viii–ix. Draftees drew special scorn from the early volunteers who looked down on them as "bounty-jumpers, cowards and the refuse of the cities." See Linderman, *Embattled Courage*, 2.

5. The State of Connecticut had a quota of 7,155 men to fill, and by the end of August 1862 the state surpassed that number. See W. A. Croffutt and John M. Morris, *Military and Civil History of Connecticut During the War of 1861–1865* (New York: Ledyard Bill, 1869), 223–29. The 16th Connecticut was one of two Hartford County regiments; the 14th Connecticut was the other unit formed at the same time, and it enjoyed a much more storied war experience.

6. Croffutt and Morris, *Military and Civil History of Connecticut*, 227–29, 276; Bernard Blakeslee, *History of the Sixteenth Connecticut Volunteers* (Hartford: Case, Lockwood & Brainard Co., 1875), 5; *Catalogue of the 14th, 15th, 16th, 17th, 18th, 19th, 20th and 21st Regiments and the Second Light Battery Connecticut Volunteers; and the 22d, 23d, 24th, 25th, 26th, 27th and 28th Regiments Connecticut Volunteers for Nine Months, Compiled from Records in the Adjutant-Generals Office 1862* (Hartford: Press of Case, Lockwood and Co., 1862), 47–67; "Muster and Descriptive Rolls, 16th Regiment Connecticut Volunteers," Records of the Military Department, Connecticut Adjutant General's Office, RG 13, Connecticut State Library, Hartford (hereafter CSL).

7. McPherson's *For Cause and Comrades* contends that ideology and patriotism strongly induced the first two years of volunteer enlistment and kept men in the ranks through the entire conflict.

8. This description of Fort Williams is based on a variety of soldiers' firsthand accounts, including Blakeslee, *History of the Sixteenth Connecticut Volunteers*, 5; George Robbins, "Recollections," George Robbins Papers, Connecticut Historical Society, Hartford (hereafter CHS); William H. Relyea, "History of the 16th Connecticut Volunteer Infantry," 3–4, William H. Relyea Papers, CHS; Robert H. Kellogg to father, Aug. 19, 1862, Robert H. Kellogg Papers, CHS; and Charles Gilbert Lee Diary, Aug. 20–23, 1862, CHS. See also Croffutt and Morris, *Military and Civil History of Connecticut*, 229.

9. John Keegan discusses this belief that professional officers have in the "rules of war" and the necessity of drill in *The Face of Battle* (New York: Viking Press, 1976): 18–20. For biographical details on Col. Beach, see Relyea, "History of the 16th Connecticut," 3; *Hartford Courant* Aug. 9, 15, 1862; John C. Kinney, "The Memorial History of Hartford," in J. Hammond Trumbull, ed., *The Memorial History of Hartford County Connecticut, 1633–1884*, 2 vols. (Boston: Edward L. Osgood, 1886), 2:1n98; "Francis Beach," in Military and Biographical Data on Officers and Men of the Regiment, box 7, folder "Officers," RG 69:23, George Q. Whitney Collection, CSL; and Rev. W. H. Gilbert, *Sermon Delivered in Granby, Conn., Jan. 4, 1863, at the Funeral of Roswell Morgan Allen, Private in Co. E., 16th Reg't. C. V. Who Died at the Hospital Near Washington, Sunday, Dec. 28, 1862* (Hartford: Charles Montague, 1863), 12.

10. Robbins, "Recollections."

11. Blakeslee, *History of the Sixteenth Connecticut Volunteers*, 5.

12. "Unfeeling," from Gilbert, *Sermon*, 12; "fill his back full of bead," from Relyea, "History of the 16th Connecticut," 4. Another soldier confirmed this angry sentiment against Beach in a letter

written just three days before Antietam when he too stated, "Many of the men swear they will shoot him [Beach] if he ever goes into action with us." See J. Edward Shipman to "Friend Hubbard," Sept. 14, 1862, Lewis Leigh Collection, United States Military History Institute, Carlisle, Pa. (hereafter USMHI); see also Croffutt and Morris, *Military and Civil History of Connecticut*, 228–29, 265; and Blakeslee, *History of the Sixteenth Connecticut Volunteers*, 6.

13. William H. Relyea, *16th Connecticut Volunteer Infantry: Sergeant William H. Relyea*, John Michael Priest, ed. (Shippensburg, Pa.: Burd Street Press, 2002), 7.

14. *Hartford Daily Courant*, Sept. 12, 1862; *Hartford Evening Press*, Aug. 29, 1862. See also Croffutt and Morris, *Military and Civil History of Connecticut*, 229; and Blakeslee, *History of the Sixteenth Connecticut Volunteers*, 6.

15. See, for example, the *Hartford Daily Times*, July 23, 24, 1862.

16. Ibid., Aug. 14, 1862.

17. Ibid., Sept. 13, 1862.

18. Letter published in the *Hartford Daily Courant*, Sept. 12, 1862.

19. Jacob Bauer to Emily Bauer, Sept. 5, 1862, typescript copy of original, "16th Regiment Connecticut Volunteers," file folder, Antietam National Battlefield, Sharpsburg, Md. (hereafter ANB).

20. Relyea, *16th Connecticut Volunteer Infantry*, 24.

21. Description of Antietam based on John Niven, *Connecticut for the Union: The Role of the State in the Civil War* (New Haven: Yale Univ. Press, 1965), 222–23; Blakeslee, *History of the Sixteenth Connecticut Volunteers*, 16–17; Blakeslee, "The Sixteenth Connecticut at Antietam," 19; Robbins, "Recollections"; and Relyea, "History of the 16th Connecticut," 27. A more extended discussion of the 16th at Antietam is Lesley J. Gordon, "'All Who Went Into That Battle Were Heroes': Remembering the 16th Regiment Connecticut Volunteers at Antietam," in Gary Gallagher, ed., *The Antietam Campaign* (Chapel Hill: Univ. of North Carolina Press, 1999), 169–91.

22. Leland O. Barlow to his sister, Sept., 23, 1862, Leland O. Barlow Papers, CSL. Oct. regimental returns listed twenty-eight men as deserters—most leaving the day of battle, three disappearing before Sept. 17, and seven deserting after Antietam. See Monthly Returns, 16th Regiment Connecticut Volunteers, Oct. 1862," Records of the Military Department, Connecticut Adjutant General's Office, CSL, RG 13; also Blakeslee, *History of the 16th Connecticut*, 17–19. Total casualties for the 16th Connecticut at Antietam were over 25 percent. Out of an estimated 940 soldiers engaged, the 16th Connecticut lost 43 killed, 164 wounded, 20 captured, and 19 deserted. Casualty numbers do vary from source to source. These numbers are abstracted from *Adjutant-General Record of Service of Connecticut Men in the Army and Navy of the United States During the War of the Rebellion* (Hartford: Press of the Case, Lockwood & Brainard Co., 1889), 619–39. The regiment's monument erected at Antietam in 1894 lists 779 engaged, 43 killed, and 161 wounded.

23. Francis Beach to J. D. Williams, Sept. 19, 1862, copy of original, ANB.

24. *Hartford Daily Courant* Sept. 18, 1862.

25. Ibid., Sept. 23, 1862.

26. *Hartford Evening Press*, Sept. 27, 1862.

27. *Hartford Daily Times*, Sept. 23, 1862.

28. *Hartford Daily Courant*, Sept. 22, 1862.

29. *Hartford Daily Times*, Sept. 23, 1862.

30. Ibid., Sept. 27, 1862.

31. Martin VanBuren Culver to Brother, Sept. 21, 1862, Martin VanBuren Culver Letters, 1862–1865. Transcribed letters in possession of author.

32. Wartime letter qtd. in Relyea, "History of the 16th Connecticut," 43–44.

33. William H. Relyea to wife, Sept. 26, 1862, William H. Relyea Letterbook, CHS.

34. William H. Drake to Timothy Loomis, Sept. 29, 1862, Civil War Letters Collection, CHS.

35. George Robbins to sister, Sept. 23, 1862, George Robbins Letters, CHS.

36. Elizur D. Beldon Diary, Sept. 19, 1862, CHS.

37. John B. Cuzner to Ellen, Sept. 21, 1862, typescript copy of original, ANB.

38. Jacob Bauer to Emily Bauer, Sept. 20, 1862, ANB. A few weeks later Bauer reassessed his view of the rout. If he survived the war, he wrote to his wife, he would return to Antietam and show her where "the heros rest side by side." The 16th had its share of cowards, Bauer wrote, but he was not one of them. Cowards were the ones who cursed the most, he maintained, "and they were the ones who stayed back in the hour of trial." See Jacob Bauer to Emily Bauer, Oct. 2, 1862, ANB. For a more extended discussion of how the regiment's initial impressions of Antietam changed, see Gordon, "'All Who Went Into That Battle Were Heroes.'"

39. Robert H. Kellogg to Father, Sept. 20, 1862, Robert H. Kellogg Papers, CHS. Kellogg retained this impression one month after Antietam when he wrote his father that Lee and his army had retreated in "complete disorder from Maryland" and "skedaddled over the river." See Robert H. Kellogg to Father, Oct. 17, 1862, Robert H. Kellogg Papers, CHS.

40. John H. Burnham to Sarah B. Burnham, Oct. 4, 1862, John H. Burnham Papers, CSL.

41. *Hartford Daily Times*, Nov. 20, 1862.

42. Martin VanBuren Culver to Brother, Nov. 16, 1862, Martin VanBuren Culver Letters, 1862–65.

43. *Hartford Daily Times*, Dec. 8, 9, 1862.

44. Leland O. Barlow to father, Dec. 24, 1862, Leland O. Barlow Papers, CSL.

45. Leland O. Barlow to Jane Barlow, Dec. 29, 1862, Leland O. Barlow Papers, CSL.

46. Harrison Woodford to "My Dear Friends at Home," Dec. 25, 1862, Letters of Harrison Woodford. Transcribed letter possession of author.

47. Martin VanBuren Culver to "Brother Jon," Dec. 31, 1862, Martin VanBuren Culver Letters, 1862–65.

48. Leland O. Barlow to Jane Barlow, Dec. 29, 1862, Leland O. Barlow Papers, CSL.

49. John H. Burnham to Sarah and Lottie Burnham, Jan. 12, 1863, John H. Burnham Papers, CSL.

50. Martin VanBuren Culver to Brother, January 19, 1863, Martin VanBuren Culver Letters, 1862–65.

51. *Hartford Daily Courant*, Mar. 21, 1863.

52. Ibid., Mar. 27, 1863.

53. Martin VanBuren Culver to Brother, Apr. 22, 1863, Martin VanBuren Culver Letters, 1862–65.

54. Robert H. Kellogg to Father, Apr. 18, 1863, Robert H. Kellogg Papers, CHS.

55. Ibid., Apr. 25, 1863.

56. Blakeslee, *History of the Sixteenth Connecticut Volunteers*, 36, 107. See also Steven A. Cormier, *The Siege of Suffolk: The Forgotten Campaign, April 11–May 4, 1863* (Lynchburg, Va.: H. E. Howard, 1989), 230–33.

57. Robert H. Kellogg to Father, May 6, 1863, Robert H. Kellogg Letters, CHS.

58. Blakeslee, *History of the Sixteenth Connecticut Volunteers*, 37, also 34, 107.

59. Relyea, *16th Connecticut Volunteer Infantry*, 84. Beach resigned on May 18, 1863. See *Adjutant-General Record of Service*, 635.

60. If desertion can be classified as cowardly, especially desertions just before or after battle, regimental records indicate very low desertion at this time, too. Seven men deserted the unit between Feb. 11 and Apr. 17, 1863, but only two deserted between May 1 and July 7, 1863. In mid-June

the regiment moved to Portsmouth, where it remained for several months. From early July until mid-September, there was another wave of deserters, six recorded in the adjutant general's records. Numbers abstracted from *Adjutant-General Record of Service*, 619–39.

61. This description of the regiment's camp at Portsmouth is drawn from a variety of firsthand accounts, including Leander Chapin to mother, Nov. 25, 1863, CHS; Austin D. Thompson to Electra Churchill, Nov. 30, Dec. 6, 19, 1863, CHS; and Joseph Barnum Diary, Jan. 6, 1864, CHS. See also Robert H. Kellogg, *Life and Death in Rebel Prisons: Giving a Complete History of the Inhuman and Barbarous Treatment of Our Brave Soldiers by Rebel Authorities, Inflicting Terrible Suffering and Frightful Mortality, Principally at Andersonville, Ga, and Florence, S.C. Describing Plans of Escape, Arrival of Prisoners, with Numerous and Varied Incidents and Anecdotes of Prison Life* (Hartford, Conn.: L. Stebbins, 1865), 205.

62. "Nomads" from Relyea, "History of the 16th Connecticut Volunteer Infantry," 140. For more on the regiment at Portsmouth, see Lesley J. Gordon, "'Surely They Remember Me': The 16th Connecticut in War, Captivity, and Public Memory," in Paul A. Cimbala and Randall Miller, eds., *Union Soldiers and the Northern Homefront: Wartime Experiences, Postwar Adjustments* (Bronx, N.Y.: Fordham Univ. Press, 2002), 334–36.

63. *Hartford Daily Times*, Sept. 10, 1863. Steele had requested a furlough just days before he penned this letter to the *Times*. See Edgar E. Strong to John B. Clapp, Sept. 1, 1863, in Horace B. Steele Papers, CSL. It does seem significant too that Horace's brother Nathan, a thirty-five-year-old married gunsmith, deserted the regiment in early March 1863. See *Adjutant-General Record of Service*, 630.

64. *Hartford Daily Courant*, Sept. 25, 1863.

65. *Hartford Daily Times*, Oct. 7, 1863.

66. The *Times* refused to publish any more on this subject, stating: "In justice to the soldier who writes this, and much desires us to print it, we give it place, but we prefer not to continue this unpleasant controversy in these columns." See *Hartford Daily Times*, Oct. 7, 1863. Historians have already recorded changes in definitions and reactions to desertion among southern soldiers, although less so among northern men. Drew Gilpin Faust has explored the issue of Confederate desertion and how it played against southern familial obligations and Confederate nationalism in *Mothers of Invention: Women of the Slaveholding South in the American Civil War* (Chapel Hill: Univ. of North Carolina Press, 1996). Brian Holden Reid and John White contend that the widespread desertion in both armies was mainly an issue of inconsistent military discipline clashing with Civil War volunteers' natural propensity for self-autonomy. They dismiss the "cases of overt cowardice in the face of the enemy" as rare and seemingly inconsequential. See Reid and White, "'A Mob of Stragglers and Cowards,'" 64, 75.

67. Leland O. Barlow to Jane C. Barlow, Apr. 11, 1864, Leland O. Barlow Papers, CSL.

68. George N. Champlin Diary, Mar. 24, 1864, CSL.

69. Austin D. Thompson to Electra Churchill, Aug. 17, 1863, CHS.

70. Leander Chapin to Gilbert Chapin, Mar. 19, 1864, MS 82945, CHS.

71. John H. Burnham to Sarah B. Burnham, Jan. 18, 1864, John H. Burnham Papers, CSL.

72. John H. Burnham to Sarah B. Burnham, Mar. 10, [1864], John H. Burnham Papers, CSL.

73. Kellogg, *Life and Death in Rebel Prisons*, 29. A slightly different account of this event is included in Relyea's "History of the 16th Connecticut Volunteer Infantry," 172.

74. Samuel Grosvenor Dairy, Apr. 20, 1864, CHS. When the fighting started on Apr. 17, Company H escorted women and other civilians from Plymouth to Roanoke Island. They would

continue in active service as the 16th Connecticut, even though they numbered only about 100 men. For more on the 16th Connecticut and the siege of Plymouth, see Gordon, "'Surely They Remember Me,'" 339–41.

75. Kellogg, *Life and Death in Rebel Prisons*, 33.

76. Oliver Gates Diary, [May 1864], CHS.

77. *Hartford Evening Press*, Apr. 26, 1864.

78. Robert H. Kellogg to Father, Apr. 20, 1864, MS 68013, CHS; also Kellogg, *Life and Death in Rebel Prisons*, 37.

79. Not all members of the captured 16th Connecticut arrived at Andersonville at the same time, and commissioned officers were sent to Macon instead and were soon exchanged, including Col. Beach and Lt. Col. Burnham. Numbers vary regarding prisoners and deaths. Kellogg estimates 300 men from the regiment were imprisoned at Andersonville, of which nearly one-third died. Other accounts give higher estimates. See for example, *Dedication of the Monument at Andersonville, Georgia, October 23, 1907. In Memory of the Men of Connecticut Who Suffered in Southern Military Prisons 1861–1865* (Hartford: State of Connecticut, 1908), 32; and Kellogg, *Life and Death in Rebel Prisons*, 61. The best studies of the prison include William Marvel, *Andersonville: The Last Depot* (Chapel Hill: Univ. of North Carolina Press, 1994); and Ovid L. Futch, *History of Andersonville Prison* (Gainesville: Univ. of Florida Press, 1968).

80. George N. Champlin Diary, Nov. 7, 1864, CSL.

81. Ira Forbes Diary, May 6, 1864, Civil War Manuscripts Collection, Manuscripts and Archives, Sterling Memorial Library, Yale University, New Haven, Conn.

82. Nearly all the diaries consulted for this essay mention deaths within the regiment. See for example, Ira Forbes, Yale; George N. Champlin Diary, CSL; Robert Kellogg Diary, CHS, Oliver Gates Diary, CHS; Samuel Grosvenor Diary, CHS; and Paul C. Helmreich, ed., "The Diary of Charles G. Lee in the Andersonville and Florence Prison Camps, 1864," *Connecticut Historical Society Bulletin* 41 (Jan. 1976): 19–24.

83. Kellogg, *Life and Death in Rebel Prisons*, 67–68.

84. Helmreich, ed., "Diary of Charles G. Lee," 20.

85. Oliver Gates Diary, Aug. 10, 1864, CHS.

86. All three of these men testified for the defense at the Henry Wirz trial. See N. P. Chipman, *The Tragedy of Andersonville: Trial of Captain Henry Wirz, the Prison Keeper* (Sacramento, Calif.: privately published, 1911), 173–74, 224–25, 251–52, 327–28. Robert Kellogg testified for the prosecution.

87. Robert Kellogg Diary, May 23, 1864, CHS; George N. Champlin Diary, June 27, 1864, CSL.

88. Gates accepted the parole after the transfer to Florence. See Oliver Gates Diary, June 22, 1864, CHS; "an Explanation" is written on the final pages of Diary III.

89. John H. Burnham to Sarah B. Burnham, Jan. 10, 1865, John H. Burnham Papers, CSL.

90. Jacob Bauer Diary, Feb. 17, Mar. 6, 18, 23, May 11, 1865, USMHI.

91. John B. Cuzner to Ellen Van Dorn, Feb. 9, 1865, CHS.

92. *Hartford Daily Courant*, June 30, 1865.

93. "Invocation" by Rev. Charles Dixon, in *Souvenir of Excursion to Antietam and Dedication of Monuments of the 8th, 11th, 14th and 16th Regiments of Connecticut Volunteers Oct. 1894* (Hartford, 1894), 54. For more on the regiment's memory of Antietam, see Gordon, "'All Who Went Into That Battle Were Heroes.'"

94. *Dedication of the Monument at Andersonville*, 23.

95. Qtd. in *Dedication of the Monument at Andersonville*, 71.

96. David F. Ransom, "Connecticut's Monumental Epoch: A Survey of Civil War Memorials," *Connecticut Historical Society Bulletin* 58 (1993): 231. It is Ransom who claims that Kellogg was the model for the statue, although no other evidence has surfaced to support this.

97. Kellogg's address in *Dedication to the Monument at Andersonville*, 34–37. A duplicate of the statue was also placed in Hartford near the state capitol building. For more on the 16th Connecticut and the Andersonville commemoration, see Gordon, "'Surely They Remember Me,'" 356–60.

98. See for example *Hartford Courant*, Sept. 17, 1907; *Hartford Times*, Aug. 1, 1908; *Hartford Post*, Aug. 29, 1912; and Relyea, *16th Connecticut Volunteer Infantry*, xiv. Relyea does complain of cowardice at Antietam, actually listing the names of deserters (172–73).

Confederate Bastille

Jefferson Davis and Civil Liberties

❧ Without Mark E. Neely Jr., there may never have been a Klement Lecture series. Since receiving his Ph.D. from Yale University in 1973, Neely had been director of the Lincoln Museum at Fort Wayne, Indiana. A specialist on Abraham Lincoln and on the art of the Civil War, he published *The Abraham Lincoln Encyclopedia* (1982) and, with coeditors Gabor S. Boritt and Harold Holzer, *The Lincoln Image: Abraham Lincoln and the Popular Print* (1984), and *The Confederate Image: Prints of the Lost Cause* (1991). In his capacity as director of the R. Gerald McMurtry Lecture, at the 1993 Organization of American Historians meeting, he had offered useful advice to the then-director of the Klement Lecture about how to run a lecture series. A month or so later, when funding rather suddenly became available, he was invited to deliver the first Klement Lecture later that year. This was fitting, since he had just published a book that explored the same terrain—although in a very different way—as the work of Frank Klement: *The Fate of Liberty: Abraham Lincoln and Civil Liberties* (1991). Coincidentally, the invitation was delivered on the morning of the announcement that *The Fate of Liberty* had won the Pulitzer Prize. Neely graciously took the phone call, despite, as his assistant reported, his suddenly crowded schedule, and accepted the invitation.

Neely's Klement lecture continued his examination of Civil War–era civil liberties, but this time in the Confederacy, where he discovered that Jefferson Davis, like Abraham Lincoln, "waged war on the home front . . . more with an eye to solving practical problems than to obeying scruples of constitutional conscience." Prior to the lecture, Neely and Klement had met once or twice and corresponded a time or two; on occasion, Neely had criticized "the Klement Thesis." But Klement was touched by Neely's appearance at Marquette and, in his own eyes, was vindicated by the wide acceptance of Neely's argument that the Lincoln administration had, indeed, been lax in its protection of civil liberties.

Neely had already become John Francis Bannon Professor of American Studies and History at Saint Louis University by the time he delivered the inaugural Klement Lecture. In 1998 he went to Pennsylvania State University as McCabe Greer Professor in the American Civil War Era. The research from which his Klement Lecture was drawn appeared as *Southern Rights: Political Prisoners and the Myth of Confederate Constitutionalism* (1999). Since his lecture, he has also published *The Union Divided: Party Conflict in the Civil War* (2002) and *The Boundaries of American Political Culture in the Civil War Era* (2005). In 2004 his *Civil War History* article, "Was the Civil War a Total War?" was chosen as one of the three most influential articles published in the fifty years. ✒

IN 1869 AN OBSCURE MARYLANDER named John A. Marshall published a book called *American Bastile: A History of Illegal Arrests and Imprisonment of American Citizens during the Late Civil War*. Marshall had been chosen as author by the Association of State Prisoners, and the book he wrote can best be described as a *Book of Martyrs* to the tyranny of the Lincoln administration. It sold by subscription only, but it seems to have sold well and steadily—about 1,500 copies a year until 1882 and in the next three years over 2,500 copies per year. Some 27,000 copies were in print by 1885.[1]

The chapters of the first edition of the book told the stories of the arrests of innocent civilians by military authorities. They culminated in the final chapter's discussion of the great Democratic martyr, Clement Vallandigham of Ohio, arrested by the army in 1863, tried by a military court, and banished by President Abraham Lincoln to the Confederacy. *American Bastile* was the political heir of the *Democratic Almanac*, an annual publication full of information useful to Democrats at election time. The *Almanac* for 1867, published by the aggressively white supremacist Van Evrie and Horton in

1866, contained the first list printed after the war of names of political prisoners under the Lincoln administration.[2] Throughout the century Democrats kept alive the bitter memories of civilians arrested by military authorities under the orders of a Republican president in the North during the Civil War, because they liked to depict their political opponents as tyrants.

There is no counterpart of *American Bastile* for the Confederacy. Although Jefferson Davis endured sharp criticism on the habeas corpus issue from many articulate and well-placed opponents, like Confederate Vice President Alexander H. Stephens, this particular part of the anti-Davis tradition shriveled quickly and vanished so completely by the late nineteenth century that the sympathetic twentieth-century editor of Jefferson Davis's papers could unblushingly describe his subject in the subtitle as a "Constitutionalist."[3]

Stephens himself included in the appendix to *A Constitutional View of the Late War Between the States*, published in 1870, the text of his letter condemning the arrest of a Georgia civilian by the Confederate military authorities along with a protest of the suspension of the writ of habeas corpus that had been introduced in the Georgia legislature in 1864 by his brother Linton. He did not otherwise in this famous book of brittle constitutional arguments exert much effort denouncing this aspect of Jefferson Davis's tyranny. And Davis himself did not mention the subject at all in *The Rise and Fall of the Confederate Government*, published in 1881.[4]

Of course, Davis was not likely to bring up the subject, but even someone as likely to dwell on what obviously embarrassed Davis as Richmond newspaper editor and Davis-hater Edward A. Pollard did not bring up the subject either. In 1869, the same year *American Bastile* appeared, Pollard offered a lengthy *Life of Jefferson, with a Secret History of the Southern Confederacy*, but the book contained no secrets of the Confederate bastille. Pollard joined to his loathing of Davis a lofty contempt for the frail patriotism of the Confederate masses (he complained, for example, that the interior decoration of the building in which the Confederate Congress met was "excessively democratic, dingy, and dirty," and he depicted the people's representatives who worked in this hall as "uncultivated" and "common" brawlers).

The Richmond editor regarded the writ of habeas corpus not as the sacred "writ of liberty," as most Americans described it at the time, but as a devious way to avoid military service. "Certainly the claim of patriotic devotion of the South," he wrote, "cannot be maintained in the face of the facts, that only the utmost rigor of conscription forced a majority of its troops in the field; that half of these were disposed to desert on the first opportunities; and that the demands for military services were cheated in a way and to an extent unexampled in the case of any brave and honorable nation engaged in a war for its own existence. We have the remarkable fact that in one year the Confederate States Attorney in Richmond tried *eighteen hundred* cases in that city on writs of habeas corpus for relief from conscription!" Pollard followed this startling revelation with a still more astonishing statement, the like of which appears nowhere else in America in the vast literature of controversy over the writ of habeas corpus in the war:

> This honored writ . . . became the vilest instrument of the most undeserving men; and there is attached to it a record of shame for the South that we would willingly spare. Mr. Humphrey Marshall, a member of the Confederate Congress . . . , added to his pay as a legislator the fees of an attorney to get men out of the army; he became the famous advocate in Richmond in cases of habeas corpus; and he is reported to have boasted that this practice yielded him an average of two thousand dollars a day![5]

Even Abraham Lincoln, who suspended the writ of habeas corpus early and often, affirmed his devotion to the writ in the abstract, and in peaceful times spoke of it always as among the most important liberties of Americans, like "the right of public discussion, the liberty of speech and press, the law of evidence, [and] trial by jury."[6]

Jefferson Davis has had many critics to this day, but no one in modern times criticizes him for crushing dissent and diminishing civil liberties. His own martyrdom as a political prisoner after the Civil War did much—as even the dyspeptic Pollard had to admit—to rescue his reputation. Davis was imprisoned by Union authorities at Fortress Monroe for two years. Pollard set the agenda for the anti-Davis literature to come, and that proved important on the score of civil liberties. Davis's modern critics followed Pollard in focusing on other issues.[7]

To this day, one cannot find in the text of any of the works on habeas corpus in the Confederacy the name of a single individual civilian actually arrested by military authority during the war.[8] Just as there is no *Confederate Bastille*, there is likewise no equivalent for the Confederacy of Frank L. Klement's book, *The Limits of Dissent: Clement L. Vallandigham and the Civil War*, for there is no similarly famous "martyr" to Confederate tyranny. Most of the southerners arrested were obscure men, but there were some genuine candidates for martyr status: William G. "Parson" Brownlow, of Tennessee, and John Minor Botts, of Virginia. Brownlow even enjoyed a brief career as a celebrity, after Jefferson Davis allowed him to cross the lines into Union-controlled Nashville, lecturing all over the North and finding his image reproduced in popular prints, sheet music, and carte-de-visite photographs.[9] Both Botts and Brownlow later wrote books, and Brownlow's sold well—100,000 copies in the summer of 1862 alone. But in the end, neither Brownlow nor Botts gained memorable martyr status. The Tennessee parson's name does not appear in the index to the standard modern survey of Confederate history, Emory M. Thomas's *The Confederate Nation: 1861–1865*, and neither man is ever mentioned in works examining Lincoln's record on habeas corpus by way of suggesting that the Confederate president used the same methods that the Union president did.[10]

In fact, if one looks closely there were some astonishing wrongful arrests in the Confederacy, which in different circumstances might have dogged Jefferson Davis's reputation forever. The postmaster general, John Reagan, was wrongfully arrested. The attorney general of the Confederacy, George Davis, was wrongfully arrested. And the famed jurist George W. Paschal of Texas was wrongfully arrested. Yet such incidents are not staples in histories of the Confederacy.[11]

The absence of any book on the Confederate Bastille can be explained in only one of two ways: either there was no Bastille in the Confederacy to write about, or powerful forces led to the suppression of the memory of it.

The first explanation will no longer work. When examined, the record of the Confederacy and Jefferson Davis on civil liberties resembles that of the North and Lincoln more than it differs from it. Here are five similarities, of varying importance, that I have found to date.

First, the number of civilians arrested by military authority in the Confederacy, when adjusted for population differences, appears to be about the same as the number arrested in the North. The absolute number in the Confederacy was much smaller, but then the Confederate population was much smaller. And the number that can be verified today is much smaller yet because the records appear to be even more incomplete than those kept in the North. One should keep in mind as well that the Confederacy never occupied much Union territory, and the names of civilian residents of conquered southern territory sent north to Union military prisons often swelled the number of civilian arrestees there.[12]

I have found to date—in the Virginia Historical Society, the National Archives, and in various published sources—records of 2,672 civilians arrested by Confederate military authorities.[13] The records are very incomplete, and one can compare the northern and southern records only at rare historical moments in which both offer good series of records. If one does that for the first ten months of the war, the Confederacy arrested almost the same number of civilians as the North did.[14] Another viable moment for comparison comes in March 1863, when the North had on hand about 2.47 times as many civilian prisoners as the Confederacy.[15] But the North had about 2.3 times as much population as the Confederacy. So the numbers are roughly proportionate to population. Moreover, there seems to be no difference in the arrest rate in those periods when the Confederate Congress refused to authorize suspension of the writ of habeas corpus and those periods when suspension was authorized. A stream of civilian prisoners trickled into Confederate military prisons whether the writ of habeas corpus was suspended or not. The appropriate standard for measuring the security of civil liberties remains unclear, but most authorities, from 1863 on, have dwelled on the sheer instances of arrest rather than on the procedures followed by the president in suspending the writ of habeas corpus.

Second, the geographical pattern of distribution of arrests was similar in the North and in the South. In both cases they tended to be concentrated near the borders with the enemy. Both the Union and the Confederacy harbored pockets of disloyalty that caused high concentrations of military arrests of civilians in certain areas. In other words, if Lincoln had his Missouri, Jefferson Davis had his Tennessee. Some troublesome areas lay close to each belligerent's capital, so both governments were embarrassed by having military prisons with many civilian prisoners in them right in their own backyards. If Lincoln had his Old Capitol Prison in Washington, Jefferson Davis had his Castle Thunder in Richmond. One can say there literally was a Confederate Bastille, and it was in Richmond, and its name was Castle Thunder Military Prison.

Third, each president suffered potential martyrs to escape to make trouble. If Lincoln banished Ohio's Clement L. Vallandigham to the Confederacy, Jefferson Davis let Tennessee's "Parson" Brownlow be banished to the Union. Both presidents tended to be personally lenient about prisoners, whatever the zeal of their subordinates in the field. And both had their overzealous lieutenants. The Confederate secretary of war, Judah P. Benjamin, recently moved over from the attorney general's office, ordered accused bridge burners in East Tennessee to be "tried summarily by drum-head court martial and if found guilty executed on the spot by hanging. It would be well," he added, "to leave their bodies hanging in the vicinity of the burned bridges."[16] The U.S.

secretary of state, William H. Seward, who oversaw internal security in the North in 1861, was also notoriously unsympathetic to dissenters and once told a friend: "Let us save the country and then cast ourselves upon the judgment of the people, if we have in any case, acted without legal authority."[17]

Fourth, both presidents experienced serious trouble with fractious judges willing to issue writs of habeas corpus that amounted to judicial nullification of conscription. If Jefferson Davis had to deal with the recalcitrant judiciary of uncooperative North Carolina, Lincoln had serious conflicts with Democratic judges, both state and federal, in Pennsylvania. Lincoln's difficulties are less well-known than Davis's in this instance, but it is clear that Lincoln in 1863 became so infuriated by Pennsylvania judges who frustrated conscription and mobilization with their writs of habeas corpus, that he considered using troops against any efforts the judges might organize to enforce their judicial writs. When the problem was discussed in a special cabinet meeting in September 1863, Secretary of the Navy Gideon Welles, sympathizing with the president's position, said that the navy had been "suffering constant annoyance—vessels were delayed on the eve of sailing, by interference of State judges who assumed jurisdiction and authority to discharge enlisted men . . . on habeas corpus." A "factious and evil-minded judge—and we have many such holding state appointments—could . . . stop armies on the march."[18] Welles's statement bears comparison with Jefferson Davis's remarks to a secret session of the Confederate Congress in February 1864: "In one instance a general on the eve of an important movement, when every man was needed, was embarrassed by the command of a judge even then 200 miles distant to bring, if in his custody, or send if in custody of another, before him on habeas corpus, some deserters who had been arrested and returned to his command."[19]

Surprisingly, President Lincoln may have come closer to unleashing internal civil war over this question than Davis did. President Lincoln, as angry as some cabinet members had ever seen him, threatened to send the judges after Vallandigham and wrote an order instructing military officials to resist with any available force attempts by the judges to enforce their writs after having been answered that the prisoners were held on the president's authority. The debate grew rather heated in the Confederacy as well. Confederate secretary of war James Seddon informed North Carolina governor Zebulon Vance, "It cannot be presumed that any judge will be guilty of the judicial usurpation . . . and attempt to enforce the writ. Should such an assumption be practiced, collision would only result from the wanton, unauthorized attempt by violence to take from the Confederate officer the person of the petitioner, or to take the officer himself for punishment."[20]

Fifth, and finally, if Jefferson Davis had his Humphrey Marshall making an industry of gaining writs to get recruits out of military service, Lincoln had his William F. Howe, an unscrupulous New York lawyer who became known as "Habeas Corpus Howe." In 1862 Howe had joined a New York cavalry regiment, but he was out again by early 1863, and soon he put his experience to work for others. He grew famous for taking soldiers to court and proving to the judge that they had been recruited while drunk or in some other unlawful way and gaining their release from service on a writ of habeas corpus.[21]

The Confederate citizen was not any freer than the Union citizen—and perhaps no less likely to be arrested by military authorities. In fact, the Confederate citizen may have been in some ways less free than his northern counterpart.

For example, freedom to travel within the Confederate states was severely limited by a domestic passport system. When the Confederate House of Representatives inquired about this irritating system in February 1864, J. B. Jones, the famous Richmond diarist and War Department clerk, testified that "the origin of the passport office consisted merely in a verbal order from the first Secretary of War, and subsequently, I . . . was requested to take charge of the office . . . in August, 1861." Jones held the post until martial law was declared in Richmond, when he continued to operate under the orders of the military governor, the much hated General John H. Winder. No one could explain how the system had spread to other Confederate cities, though it seemed likely that it was an outgrowth of local and temporary impositions of martial law.

Here is how it worked. No one could leave Richmond by rail or any other conveyance without a pass, and Jones issued an average of 1,350 passes a day. His office stayed open late, sometimes until after one A.M., but some latecomers were disappointed nevertheless, and often the crowds and consequent delays were so great that the people waiting in line missed their trains. The Confederate government provided separate offices to issue passports for men and women, but despite all their attempts to satisfy the public, the system remained, by the admission of the Richmond provost marshal, "obnoxious." It "trenches odiously upon personal liberty," Maj. E. Griswold added; it was "attended with vexatious delays, and sometimes with questionings and interviews, wounding to the self-respect of worthy and good citizens." Senator Williamson S. Oldham of Texas objected to a system in which he, though a "free citizen, was not allowed to go from [Richmond] ... to North Carolina without going to the Provost Marshal's office and getting a pass like a free negro." And Vice President Alexander H. Stephens denounced "the whole system of passports and provost-marshals" as being "utterly wrong and without authority of law."[22]

Yet the Davis administration was not about to abandon the passport system. It had long since been tied to the conscription system, and, as Major Griswold put it, "Only a few days in this office will convince any one that without passports, deserters from our armies would increase to such an extent as to be truly disastrous. Nothing could prevent the soldier, who desired to do so, from putting on citizens' dress and returning to his home or going where he choose [sic]. Now a passport must be obtained, every person whose age subjects him to military service must give an account of himself, must produce his discharge or evidence of substitution &c." About its effect on conscription, Major Griswold may well have been correct, and the Confederacy's strict regulation of travel helps account for their enjoying a lower desertion rate than the Union army until the autumn of 1864. As Jones pointed out proudly, "Cases are daily occurring where deserters and persons with fraudulent papers are ... arrested." But a modern observer, more concerned about civil liberties, might add: and heaven knows how many innocent civilians wrongfully arrested.[23]

Foreign residents of the Confederate states lived even more restricted and perilous lives. After the imposition of conscription in March 1862, from which foreigners were exempt, residents claiming the exemption were required to register with the local provost marshal. The ledgers for Richmond survive in the National Archives, and they reveal that in 1862 and 1863 alone, 1,078 resident foreigners registered. The ledgers contain a physical description of the individual, his signature, and the name of the consul whose protection he claimed.[24]

Foreigners went from feeling unwelcome to feeling downright insecure when, in October 1863, partly because they were said to be interfering with conscription (but mostly because of deteriorating foreign relations), the Davis administration expelled British consuls from southern ports. With no official representatives left in the Confederacy, there was no longer a place for English residents in the South to obtain their "protection papers" that would prove their exemption from conscription.[25]

This also eliminated an important check on the strong arm of the Confederate government. In the North the Crown's representatives toured military prisons looking for British subjects wrongfully arrested, and British representatives frequently received letters from Irish, Canadian, and other British subjects alleging that they had been wrongfully arrested. Britain loomed large in the foreign policy of both North and South, and when her representatives demanded investigation, the State Department complied. In fact, British inquiries led to the discovery of the use of torture—the "cold-water treatment"—to extract confessions from civilian prisoners suspected of being deserters in the North.[26]

There was both literally and figuratively a Confederate Bastille. Why has no one written about it until today?

There are several reasons, of which one of the most important was the absence of a two-party political system in the South. Contrary to ideas now fashionable in academic circles, this absence worked often to the advantage of the Confederacy and always to the advantage of the reputation of the Confederacy after the war was over.[27]

To the absence of a two-party system can be attributed the surprisingly secure freedom of the press under the thin-skinned and often beleaguered Jefferson Davis.[28] This was a way in which the Confederacy was freer than the North. To be sure, the southern press was accustomed to censorship and had long since compromised its ability to criticize society. State legislation enacted in the 1830s had essentially outlawed criticism of slavery, and the press had lived with that system for a generation.[29] The Confederate press had an established tradition of self-censorship, and Confederate authorities relied on it to insulate the government from criticism and to keep state secrets.[30] More important, the absence of a two-party system aided press freedom in this way: in the North, where dozens of papers were suppressed by the government or the army, the rigid partisan identification of the newspapers kept Republican editors from closing ranks to criticize interference with Democratic papers. In the Confederacy, newspapers could identify their common interests as an information industry in opposition to government well enough to form, in 1863, the Press Association of the Confederate States of America, in which dozens of newspapers banded together to negotiate with government and military officials to guarantee reporters' access to war news.[31]

This relative freedom of the Confederate press meant that after the war there were fewer disgruntled journalists around to write books criticizing Davis's record on civil liberties. One of Lincoln's worst nemeses in this regard was Dennis O. Mahony, a newspaper editor from Dubuque, Iowa, who was arrested in 1862 and thrown into Old Capitol Prison. He wrote a damaging book called *The Prisoner of State*, which was published in 1863, and, most important, he founded the Association of State Prisoners, the organization that sponsored publication of *American Bastile*.[32] By contrast, the most famous disgruntled Confederate journalist, E. A. Pollard, implicitly criticized Davis for doing too little to halt abuse of the writ of habeas corpus by slackers.

An even more important effect of the absence of a two-party system for Confederate reputation came after the war in the circumstance that there was no great organization with a stake in reminding people of Jefferson Davis's transgressions on civil liberties in the Confederacy. Even Alexander Stephens put little emphasis on the subject after the war, though he had been shrill in criticism during the war. Instead, he turned his constitutional skills to arguing that the North had tyrannized over the South and that Lincoln was a tyrant.

Another crucial reason history forgot Davis's record was the absence of a Confederate Supreme Court. The Confederate president was spared the sort of harsh judgment dealt Lincoln by the United States Supreme Court in *ex parte Milligan*, which in 1866 declared that military trials of civilians, like the one for Clement Vallandigham, were illegal where the ordinary courts were functioning. It is important to note also that Davis would likely have been spared such a judgment even if there had been a Confederate supreme court to render it because the Confederate Congress allowed almost no trials by military commission to occur. The North conducted at least 4,271 trials of civilians by military commissions; the South, none, after a brief experiment in Texas in 1862.[33] This was yet another way in which the Confederacy was freer than the North.

Finally, as the example of Pollard shows, even those who criticized Jefferson Davis, and the anti-Davis tradition certainly stayed alive and well to this very day, sometimes criticized him for making too few arrests of disloyal citizens rather than too many.[34] In other words, the presumed absence of a Confederate Bastille could be used both to attack and to defend Davis. Whether the Confederate president was depicted in history as a true defender of the states' rights faith or as a man who failed to lead the South vigorously enough to achieve victory, an assumed absence of political prisoners in the Confederacy fit either portrait.

This essay fits neither Jefferson Davis tradition. It neither makes apology for him nor criticizes him. Instead, in a development that may displease some historians and biographers in both the North and the South, it depicts Jefferson Davis as much more like Abraham Lincoln than most historians have hitherto suggested. Certainly Davis waged war on the home front the same way Lincoln did—more with an eye to solving practical problems than to obeying scruples of constitutional conscience.

NOTES

Mark E. Neely Jr. delivered his Klement Lecture in 1992.

1. John A. Marshall, *American Bastile: A History of Illegal Arrests and Imprisonment of American Citizens during the Late Civil War* (Philadelphia: Thomas W. Hartley, 1869); copies of the 1882 edition were advertised as "the nineteenth thousand." The revised edition was John A. Marshall, *American Bastile: A History of the Arbitrary Arrests and Imprisonment of American Citizens in the Northern and Border States, on Account of Their Political Opinions, during the Late Civil War, together with a Full Report of the Illegal Trial and Execution of Mrs. Mary E. Surratt. . . .* (Philadelphia: Thomas W. Hartley, 1883 [twenty-fifth thousand]); copies of the 1885 edition were advertised as the twenty-seventh thousand. I have not found any later editions, nor have I found all thirty-four printings claimed by the publishers.

2. *Democratic Almanac for 1867* (New York: Van Evrie, Horton & Co., 1866).

3. Dunbar Rowland, ed., *Jefferson Davis, Constitutionalist: His Letters, Papers, and Speeches*, 10 vols. (Jackson: Mississippi Department of Archives and History, 1923).

4. Alexander H, Stephens, *A Constitutional View of the Late War Between the States*, 2 vols. (Philadelphia: National Publishing Co., 1868–70), 2:788ff; Jefferson Davis, *The Rise and Fall of the Confederate Government*, 2 vols. (New York: Appleton, 1881). The president's wife, Varina Howell Davis, quotes without comment a proclamation by her husband suspending the writ of habeas corpus in *Jefferson Davis, Ex-President of the Confederate States of America: A Memoir*, 2 vols. (New York: Belford Co., 1890), 2:184.

5. Edward A. Pollard, *Life of Jefferson Davis, with a Secret History of the Southern Confederacy* . . . (Philadelphia: National Publishing Co., 1869), 310, 327.

6. Roy P. Basler, et al., *The Collected Works of Abraham Lincoln*, 9 vols. (New Brunswick, N.J.: Rutgers Univ. Press, 1953–55), 6:262, 267.

7. Pollard, *Life of Jefferson Davis*, 525–28.

8. See William M. Robinson, *Justice in Grey: A History of the Judicial System of the Confederate States of America* (Cambridge: Harvard Univ. Press, 1941); John B. Robbins, "The Confederacy and the Writ of Habeas Corpus," *Georgia Historical Quarterly* 60 (Spring 1971): 83–101; and Frank Lawrence Owsley, *State Rights in the Confederacy* (Chicago: Univ. of Chicago Press, 1925). Owsley mentions the names of four obscure soldiers arrested (194, 195, 197).

9. See E. Merton Coulter, *William G. Brownlow: Fighting Parson of the Southern Highlands* (Chapel Hill: Univ. of North Carolina Press, 1937), 235ff.

10. W. G. Brownlow, *Sketches of the Rise, Progress, and Decline of Secession: With a Narrative of Personal Adventures among the Rebels* (Philadelphia: George W. Childs, 1862); John Minor Botts, *The Great Rebellion: Its Secret History, Rise, Progress, and Disastrous Failure* (New York: Harper & Brothers, 1866); Emory M. Thomas, *The Confederate Nation: 1861–1865* (New York: Harper & Row, 1979).

11. J. B. Jones, *A Rebel War Clerk's Diary at the Confederate States Capital*, 2 vols. (Philadelphia: Lippincott, 1866), 2:296; James Marten, *Texas Divided: Loyalty and Dissent in the Lone Star State, 1856–1874* (Lexington: Univ. Press of Kentucky, 1990), 73.

12. See Mark E. Neely Jr., *The Fate of Liberty: Abraham Lincoln and Civil Liberties* (New York: Oxford Univ. Press, 1991).

13. Confederate States of America, Department of Henrico Papers, Virginia Historical Society, Richmond; Robert E. Lee Papers, Virginia Historical Society; Prisoners Received at Castle Thunder, Feb. 25, 1863–June 14, 1864, RG 109, ch. 9, vol. 100, National Archives, Washington, D.C.; Record of Political Prisoners, Department of East Tennessee, 1862, RG 109, ch. 9, vol. 219 ½, National Archives; Prisoners Brought before Vowles and Sands, 1864, RG 109, ch. 9, vol. 229, National Archives; *War of the Rebellion: Official Records of the Union and Confederate Armies*, 128 vols., ser. 2, 1:1361–557 (hereafter *OR*); *Message of the President . . . covering a list of all the civilians now in custody, under authority of the War Department, in the city of Richmond . . . , February 16, 1863* (Richmond, 1863); *Message of the President . . . covering a list of the civilian prisoners now in custody at the military prison at Salisbury, North Carolina . . . February 27, 1863* (Richmond, 1863).

14. Neely, *Fate of Liberty*, 23–27.

15. *OR*, ser. 2, 8:989.

16. Ibid., 1:848.

17. Neely, *Fate of Liberty*, 23.

18. Ibid., 68–74.

19. *OR*, ser. 4, 3:68.

20. Ibid., 198.

21. Richard H. Rovere, *Howe & Hummel: Their True and Scandalous History* (London: Michael Joseph, 1948), 43–44. My thanks to James Hitchcock, professor of history at St. Louis University, for this amusing reference.

22. *Communication of the Secretary of War . . . Jan. 27, 1864 [relative to the "domestic passport system"]* (Richmond, 1864); Thomas B. Alexander and Richard E. Beringer, *The Anatomy of the Confederate Congress: A Study of the Influences of Member Characteristics on Legislative Voting Behavior, 1861–1865* (Nashville, Tenn.: Vanderbilt Univ. Press, 1972), 170; *OR*, ser. 4, 3:280.

23. Ella Lonn, *Desertion during the Civil War* (New York: Century, 1928); James M. McPherson, *Ordeal by Fire: The Civil War and Reconstruction* (New York: Knopf, 1982), 468.

24. RG 109, ch. 2, vol. 244, National Archives.

25. Frank E. Vandiver, *Their Tattered Flags: The Epic of the Confederacy* (New York: Harper's Magazine Press, 1970), 228, 230.

26. Neely, *Fate of Liberty*, 109–12.

27. The idea was developed at length by Eric L. McKitrick in "Party Politics and the Union and Confederate War Efforts," in William Nisbet Chambers and Walter Dean Burnham, eds., *The American Party Systems: Stages of Political Development* (New York: Oxford Univ. Press, 1967), 117–51.

28. Robert Neil Mathis, "Freedom of the Press in the Confederacy: A Reality," *The Historian* 37 (Aug. 1975): 633–48.

29. Clement Eaton, *The Freedom-of-Thought Struggle in the Old South*, rev. ed. (New York: Harper & Row, 1964).

30. Pollard recalled in *Life of Jefferson Davis*, "The newspapers could not use remonstrance; and how narrow was the field for critical discussion, may be understood from the fact that they were enjoined to make no reference that could possibly be construed as revealing any weakness in the Confederacy, so as 'to give information to the enemy.' This absurd rule was practiced on the press sometimes to the point of puerility; and once, it is known, that Secretary Benjamin prepared an

order to suppress the *Richmond Examiner*, because its criticisms of public affairs gave information to the enemy. Mr. Davis prudently declined to sign the order, and Mr. Benjamin, or his successors, never dared to repeat the experiment on a free and virile press" (165).

31. Mathis, "Freedom of the Press in the Confederacy," 641–42.

32. Neely, *Fate of Liberty*, 58.

33. Alwyn Barr, ed., "Records of the Confederate Military Commission in San Antonio, July 2–October 10, 1862," *Southwestern Historical Quarterly* 70 (July 1966): 93–109; (Oct. 1966): 289–313; 71 (Apr. 1967): 623–44; 71 (Oct. 1967): 247–77; 73 (July 1969): 83–104; 73 (Oct. 1969): 243–274; Neely, *Fate of Liberty*, 167–75.

34. Owsley, *State Rights in the Confederacy*, 202.

Why Didn't the North Hang Some Rebels?

The Postwar Debate
Over Punishment for Treason

✣ William Blair has become one of the preeminent historians of the Civil War home front since entering the field in the mid-1990s. After working for a number of years as a journalist and editor, Bill changed careers in the late 1980s to study with Gary Gallagher at Penn State University. His dissertation won the Allan Nevins Prize for Best Dissertation in American History from the Society of American Historians and was published by the Oxford University Press in 1998 as *Virginia's Private War: Feeding Body and Soul in the Confederacy, 1861–1865*. Blair argued that the hardships experienced by Virginians during the war, rather than breeding resentment against the Confederate government, actually caused hard-pressed civilians to identify with their new nation—at least as long as the government responded to their pleas and demands for help.

After a three-year teaching stint at the University of North Carolina at Greensboro, he returned to Penn State to head up the Richards Civil War Era Center. In 2000 he added the editorship of *Civil War History* to his portfolio. Like Gallagher, Blair has become a leader among Civil War historians who bridge the gap between academic and public history. Under Blair's direction, the Richards Center at Penn State brings scholars, teachers, undergraduate and graduate students, and the general public together via workshops, battlefield tours, the Brose

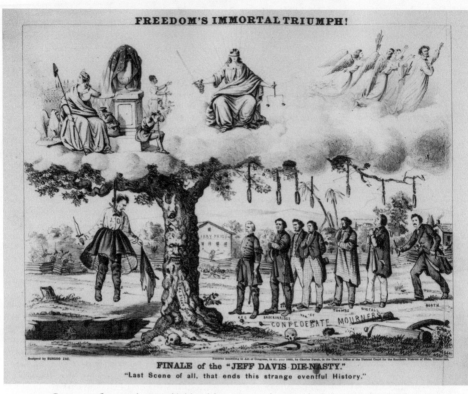

Cartoon reflecting the North's bloodthirsty attitude toward rebels immediately after the war. Library of Congress Prints and Photographs Division.

Distinguished Lecture Series, and teachers' institutes. It also participates in a project sponsored by the United Nations Educational, Scientific, and Cultural Organization called "Breaking the Silence," which partners academics with public school teachers to increase competency in teaching about slavery, race, abolition, and reconciliation.

Despite his administrative responsibilities, Blair's scholarship has continued to flourish. His *Cities of the Dead: Contesting the Memory of the Civil War in the South, 1865–1914* (2004) took him into the realm of memory studies and earned him promotion to full professor in 2005.

The research for his third major book, from which his Klement Lecture was drawn, led him to yet another distinct field: the debate over what exactly to do with the leaders of what northerners called the "rebellion." Although there was a great deal of emotional support for a fairly severe policy, as Blair's colleague at

Penn State and fellow Klement Lecturer, Mark E. Neely Jr., has shown, questions of loyalty and dissent during the Civil War and Reconstruction were never simple. Blair argues that the political and constitutional contexts of treason, as they were understood by mid-nineteenth-century Americans, narrowed the options for the punishment of former rebels by their northern conquerors. ✑

THE CIVIL WAR RESULTED IN THE most gruesome body count in our history, with an estimated 625,000 northerners and southerners dead. Most people know that former Confederates did their best to cope with defeat even as they remained determined to regain the political and economic authority that the war had cost. What people may not realize is that the fighting and losses left northerners bitter—and thirsting for vengeance. Beyond the grim costs of war that affected many families, atrocities were committed during the conflict, especially on black soldiers at Fort Pillow and the Crater. As the conflict wound to a close, northern people learned of the maltreatment of prisoners of war in the Confederacy, which in their view added crimes against humanity to the list of transgressions committed by officials of the rebellion. Then an assassin killed the president of the United States and another slashed at the secretary of state as he lay in bed. Northerners were told by authorities that Confederate leaders had encouraged the conspirators. The conditions seemed ripe for executions. With the least provocation, the North might have conducted its own version of the twentieth century's Nuremburg trials—or, perhaps more relevant for the nineteenth century, reprisals such as those mounted in the French Revolution.

Yet bloody retribution never came. One man, the commandant of Andersonville Prison, was hanged, and four conspirators in the Lincoln assassination met a similar fate. But mass executions did not occur, nor were there trials of high officials to establish the price for secession. Most of the Confederate leaders went home and picked up the pieces of their lives as best they could. Robert E. Lee moved to the Shenandoah Valley of Virginia and became a college president. Nathan Bedford Forrest—the subject of a congressional investigation during the war for the massacre of black soldiers at Fort Pillow—faced neither punishment nor trial. Jefferson Davis, the president of the Confederate experiment, remained in prison for two years while the nation debated his fate. Even he was let go, with his indictment for treason dismissed in 1869, long after the North had realized that Davis bore no complicity in the assassination of Lincoln. When considering the question of postwar punishment, it is striking how few capital crimes were prosecuted given the opportunity, the existing precedents, and the desire of many northerners.

Why didn't the North hang some of the rebels? How can we reconcile the seeming contradiction between the sectional hatred that existed and the soft hand shown by the conqueror? To twist a phrase from Lincoln's First Inaugural, what prevented the awakening of the darker angels of the country's nature?

Answers to these questions at first may seem relatively easy. The simplest might be that northerners had experienced enough death over four years and hoped to move toward more peaceful times in a restored nation. Additionally, most northerners supported the war to maintain the Union and the legitimacy of republican government, so they were inclined to make peace with their fallen brethren and welcome them back into the fold. Or we might say that Lincoln himself stopped the hangings by the lenient example expressed in his proclamation of Amnesty and Reconstruction of December 1863. Finally, we could lay the race card on the table, saying that racism trumped all other concerns, preordaining that white people on both sides would shake hands across the bloody chasm. These conclusions—although each a part of the reason behind leniency—do not capture the complete story. The courts and the Congress at many times in our past have chosen to go a different path from a president, as has the electorate. The record also makes it clear that the precedent of Lincoln's Proclamation of Amnesty was less influential than the paroles that he and Ulysses S. Grant established at Appomattox. Plus, Lincoln had become a martyr to the cause of Union and the public easily could have pushed aside his example of leniency in favor of retribution.

One additional factor proved instrumental in blocking attempts to try and execute former Confederates for treason. Although a significant portion of northerners believed that secession was wrong and ran against the intentions of the Founders, they did not think that the case was solid enough to guarantee the successful prosecution of Confederates in civil courts. Northerners understood that the war had been fought as if between two belligerents or de facto nations, no matter how Congress, the president, or legal authorities split hairs over whether the Union had put down a rebellion or fought a civil war. As the public and Congressional debate over treason and loyalty unfolded, many northerners realized that the secession loophole had not been closed before the war, and that the southern argument perhaps had a foundation, no matter how slim. Even if they refused to go this far, they recognized that the United States was complicit in treating the conflict as a public war between nations through constructing a prisoner exchange system, instituting a blockade, and conducting talks to secure an end to the fighting. Once accepting the notion of a war between nations, northerners faced a true dilemma in how they might draw the line between who faced prosecution and who should not, between who should live and who should die. If the leaders were guilty of treason, then weren't the followers equally culpable? Where would the executions stop? Even those who were not perturbed by these considerations feared that the trial of arch traitors could backfire by leading to acquittal—an outcome many expected if prosecutors strictly and dispassionately followed the rule of law.

TREASON SHOULD BE MADE ODIOUS

Before traveling down this complicated road, we ought to ensure that the questions raised here are valid ones—that they are truly historical. Are we asking something that was not part of the discussion in the nineteenth century? Did a movement exist to hang the traitors to the United States?

There is little doubt that many in the country were angry enough to urge the government to execute the leaders of the rebellion. As historian James G. Randall showed many years ago in his study of constitutional problems during the war, treason indictments surged in 1865 and 1866 as Confederates came under northern control and finally could be prosecuted. It helps to remember that, in a world raised on the notion of state sovereignty, nonfederal activity, particularly in state courts, was an important part of the equation. East Tennessee was particularly active, with more than 1,900 cases on the docket for treason and giving aid to the enemy. Missouri had another four cases for treason and 142 for conspiracy. Maryland had twenty-five indictments, yet there could have been many more. Military authorities there wanted to prosecute everyone who left Maryland to join the rebel army. More than 4,000 names were submitted to a grand jury but it quickly became apparent that the public supported trying only the more prominent Confederates. By the summer of 1865, a number of civilian leaders of the rebellion faced indictment for treason by federal authorities, including Davis, much of his wartime cabinet, the vice president of the Confederacy, and a host of people associated with guerrilla action in Canada that had resulted in a raid on banks in

St. Albans, Vermont. Among the list of military officers indicted were Lee, Joseph Johnston, and James Longstreet.[1] Also in prison were a number of former Confederate officials, especially former governors, who were held without charges or indictment until Union authorities were reassured that hostilities had truly ended.[2]

Considerable public sentiment undergirded the effort to punish traitors. Especially with the capture of Jefferson Davis in May, letters flowed to President Andrew Johnson from most corners of the North demanding that the rebel leaders pay the ultimate price for their actions. Now in the National Archives, the letters contain understandable cries for vengeance from people who had suffered personal loss of loved ones during the war. Levi Alger, a carpenter from Wisconsin, had lost a brother in the conflict. He offered to build the gallows for Jefferson Davis and provided a sketch for the device. Thirty women from Northampton, Massachusetts, sent a petition stating: "We the undersigned are very anxious that Jeff Davis—that traitor who has already lived too long—should be hung up by the neck. Do you not think our wishes just and right? Let him be hung! Is the cry of the daughters of the Bay State."[3] Soldiers threw their lot in with civilians. A petition from six people in Lancaster County, Pennsylvania, identified the signers as men who had served in the army for three years "and met the conscripts of Jefferson Davis, on many a bloody field." They wanted Davis to be hanged so high that from henceforth people would say criminals should be "hung as high as Jeff Davis the great American Traitor."[4]

Mixed with the very serious, often poignant, expressions of personal loss and a quest for vengeance were some rather creative suggestions. Elisha Farnham may have spoken for many when he wrote that if Davis were not going to hang, the government ought to "take him in his crinoline and Boots and cage him up and travel through the whole Country and exhibit as a Show for fifty cents a head (I as poor as I am would give five Dollars to see him so that I could say that I had seen a would be President in my life) and in this way the National Debt could be paid and orphans in our Country and in this way would a great deal of good be done." The crinoline referred to Davis's capture in a shawl from his wife. It was a mark of derision by northerners that he had tried to escape by hiding in women's clothing. In a letter on a different topic, S. P. Hubbard provided another sentence for Davis. He went so far as to say that the former president should be hanged with the same rope that was used to execute John Brown.[5]

These earliest letters held Davis culpable for the losses on the battlefield and the poor care that cost Union prisoners their lives. They considered him to be representative of the men who were trying to destroy the government. Many of the letters referred to Davis as the "Arch Traitor" or "Arch Rebel," clearly considering him guilty of treason against the United States. To them, he was responsible for inaugurating the war and had allowed the inhumane treatment of prisoners. They wanted him and other Rebel leaders tried for war crimes and for disloyalty to the nation. Time and time again they reminded Johnson of his famous comment about making treason odious, begging him to live up to his statement so that punishment of the traitors not only would provide justice for their transgressions but also serve as a warning to those who might consider the same course of action against the United States.

Surprisingly, the intentions expressed in this correspondence were not always indiscriminately bloodthirsty, despite being written in the heat of a real crisis when scarce information suggested the worst kind of complicity among Confederate leaders in the assassination of the president and the maltreatment of Union prisoners. Although exceptions existed, most of the letters did not accuse Davis of the assassination of Lincoln, and they often made distinctions between those southerners who should be tried and those who should be left alone. The attorney general for Michigan was genuinely outraged by Lincoln's death, yet he did not cry for blanket prosecutions: "The honest masses, including the deceived misled, South as well as North, may, no doubt, be safely trusted; but perjured souls, steeped in treason, acting a *leading* part, never. . . . Hang the very worst of them, expatriate many more, and disfranchise a still larger class than the second, thereby teaching that Treason is a crime that must and will receive . . . punishment."[6]

Newspapers supported the efforts for punishment, and portions of the Congress, the cabinet, and President Johnson followed suit in advocating stern measures against the Rebels. As expected, the press split along partisan lines. Democratic organs generally opposed trials for treason, while Republican newspapers, with the notable exception of Horace Greeley's New York Tribune, favored the execution of Confederate leaders. Especially vociferous for the stern punishment of rebels was the Chicago Tribune. The New York Times began in favor of executions but modified its position during the summer of 1865. For a while, in the summer of 1865, Johnson seemed eager to move toward a trial for key Rebels, with executions as a distinct possibility for those who were convicted. The cabinet appeared to be in line with the president. When Johnson asked them for their advice at a meeting on July 21, 1865, he found that most of them agreed that Davis should be tried for treason, although two of them considered it appropriate that a military commission handle the case while the rest thought that the matter belonged in civil courts. Most people crying for vengeance and prosecution of the traitors would have considered themselves in sync with their president and understood that the government would move ahead with the prosecutions. After all, Johnson had held firm on the execution of the conspirators to assassinate Lincoln, refusing to consider a pardon for the first woman sentenced to hang for a public crime in the United States, Mary Surratt.[7]

Even in retrospect, Johnson's intentions and motivations are difficult to pinpoint. He rarely put his deepest thoughts into writing and did not describe specifically his terms for the punishment of rebels. From his actions and from the opinions expressed by observers who met with him, it appears that he was serious about prosecuting Davis and other leaders of the rebellion. In April 1865, Charles Sumner was pleased about Johnson's position on this and other issues—so pleased that the senator believed Providence had elevated the new president, a person who was more inclined to dealing tough with traitors than Lincoln. Sumner indicated that he and Johnson felt that the country should avoid mass executions but exile a number of people to teach them a lesson. The senator targeted R. M. T. Hunter, a former U.S. senator from Virginia, as his first choice for banishment and added that the government should do the same with 100 to 500 others to make an example.[8] Johnson apparently wanted to handle most of the cases without the death sentence, but he was committed to capital punishment for extreme cases that involved the leaders of the rebellion. Through the middle of the summer of 1865, Johnson was further out in front on this issue than all but the most die-hard Radical Republicans.

He certainly was more committed to moving ahead with punishment than his own general-in-chief. Ulysses S. Grant became upset with his commander-in-chief because high military officers—including Lee, Longstreet, and Johnston—were included in the indictments for treason issued by a District Court in Norfolk. The president himself had pushed for the indictments when he perceived that the case against Davis and other leaders had bogged down in debate. But the terms for sending Confederate soldiers home from Appomattox had become the standard for the surrenders of the other southern armies, making prosecution for treason problematic. The prisoners were allowed to go home "not to be disturbed by U.S. authority so long as they observe their paroles and the laws in force where they may reside." The impression conveyed was of complete amnesty—as long as a former soldier obeyed the laws and remained home, he was beyond reach of prosecution.[9]

Grant adhered to the surrender terms that he had helped construct. He was upset that Lee was mentioned in an indictment for treason that came down from Judge John Underwood in Virginia on June 7. He expressly wrote the War Department on Lee's behalf, claiming, "In my opinion the officers and men paroled at Appomattox C. H. and since upon the same terms as given to Lee, can not be tried for treason so long as they observe the terms of their parole." He added: "Bad faith on the part of the Governm't or a construction of that convention subjecting officers to trial for treason, would produce a feeling of insecurity in the minds of all the paroled men. If so disposed they might even regard such an infraction of terms, by the Government as an entire release from all obligation on their part." At one point, he threatened to resign if prosecutors pushed forward the cases of the generals, forcing the government to let Lee and other Confederate military figures remain undisturbed until Jefferson Davis's fate became known.[10]

Grant did not oppose hard measures against traitors, but he reserved military arrests and imprisonment for civilian leaders and guerrilla fighters, rather than officers of conventional forces. Partisan rangers such as John S. Mosby, who had conducted guerrilla warfare, were also fair game. In his case, Grant suggested a bounty of $5,000. He also took a hard line against political leaders. As the war wound down after Appomattox, he pushed Maj. Gen. Henry Wager Halleck to have the military arrest key Confederate politicians in Virginia, including former senator R. M. T. Hunter, former governor John Letcher, "and all the other particularly obnoxious political leaders in the State." Soldiers arrested Hunter and placed him in prison in Richmond, where he remained without charges for a little more than two months. Similarly, Letcher was arrested and imprisoned in Washington from May 20 into July. Orders also went out on May 8 for the arrest of Zebulon Vance, wartime governor of North Carolina, who spent forty-seven days in prison without charges or trial. Days later the military was closing in on the rebel governor of South Carolina.[11]

Clearly, Grant was not squeamish about military arrests, and his reasons for supporting them also supported his position on lenience. He wanted the war to end without provoking guerrilla action, renewed fighting, or alliances with the French in Mexico. The situation south of the border was an especially sore spot with the United States; many officials were concerned that harsh treatment of former Confederates might chase them into the arms of the French and Mexican monarchists who conducted war with the liberals under Benito Juárez.

We know the end of the story: that no further fighting against the United States occurred. Instead of resisting the government on the field of battle, former Confederates channeled their efforts into reestablishing their authority over the South. Northerners could not see into the future, however, and worried for months after Appomattox about the military pacification of the South. The governments had not signed a treaty. The conflict ended through the surrenders of Confederate armies in the field. The sentiments of the southern civilian population for continued resistance were anyone's guess.

Grant paroled Lee and other officers partly to show to the remaining forces in the field that the government intended no harsh treatment of those who accepted the surrender and tried to live peacefully under the law of the United States. At Appomattox, he even asked Lee to use his influence to encourage the rest of the Confederate armies to stand down and the people to accept surrender. Although Lee refused to cooperate, Grant hoped that his treatment of the Army of Northern Virginia—and particularly its leader— made an impression on the rest of the South. "All the people except a few political leaders South will accept what ever he does as right," Grant wrote, "and will be guided to a great extent by his example." He ordered the arrests of public officials and guerrilla leaders like Mosby to head off further resistance. To Grant, the war finally seemed over not with the surrender of Lee but closer to May 9, when he finally took a deep breath and noted, "What a collapse! But a short thirty-five days ago we had a defiant enemy holding the South; to-day we are telegraphing, through their own operators, and over the wires which they controlled so short a time since, regarding dispositions for the capture of their pretended President and Cabinet. Management is all that is now wanted to secure complete peace."[12]

THE LEGAL PROBLEMS OF TREASON TRIALS

By late July and into August, Johnson found other problems impeding the prosecution of traitors. Two legal issues in particular complicated matters. The first was whether the government should prosecute traitors under the auspices of military commissions or if they should transfer the cases to civil courts. The second issue concerned the jurisdiction of civil courts that would have to choose jurors in formerly Confederate areas. These were meaty issues worth considering very carefully because they affected the legality of the proceedings and the chances of bringing in a conviction.

For those wishing to prosecute traitors through military tribunals, the trial of Lincoln's assassins and key capital cases around the country had made this venue distasteful to many northerners. It is no surprise that Democrats—with their suspicions of concentrated power and fears of government encroachment on liberties—had qualms about military commissions, especially when they were conducted by Republicans. Former attorney general Edward Bates followed the proceedings of the Lincoln conspirators and wondered "how the govert [sic] fell into the blunder of insisting upon trying the conspirators, by a military court." Bates, a conservative Republican, stewed on this issue for days and supplied what he saw as the central problem with military trials: "It denies the great, fundamental principle, that ours is a government of Law, and that the law is strong enough to rule the people wisely and well; and if the offenders be done to death by that tribunal, however truly guilty, they will pass for martyrs with half the world."[13] A Cincinnati man wrote the president that he should not put Davis before a military commission: "They are a wide departure from the old, familiar ways in which we have been educated and to which we are attached. Trial by jury is esteemed to be a strong bulwark of liberty and life, and Military Commissions are associated with tyranny and despotism. Our people do not wish to get accustomed to them. On the contrary, they want them put away."[14]

This concern was felt across party lines. At least several Republican papers—the *Philadelphia Public Ledger*, *New York Evening Post*, and *New York Tribune*—echoed these sentiments, as did Republicans across the country. Chief Justice Salmon P. Chase wrote in a private letter in July, "I sincerely hope we have seen the last of Military Commissions." Back in Massachusetts, future attorney John C. Ropes wrote his friend in the judge advocate's office in South Carolina that the trial of the Lincoln conspirators was "outrageous." He added, "Had the prisoners been tried before a respectable Court-Martial I might have judged the Government more leniently. But to try them before [Maj. Gen. David] Hunter and those other weak and prejudiced men is monstrous. The great offence however is trying them at all before a Military tribunal." He also mentioned that Governor John Andrew of Massachusetts, a stalwart Republican during the war, said he would fight the prosecution were he not holding public office.[15] Even more striking was John C. Gray's position. Gray served in the judge advocate's office at Hilton Head and thus was an extension of the administration. He was mortified by the trial of the conspirators. "I am not entirely sure that the trial of the assassins by a military commission is absolutely illegal," he noted, adding, "but it is on the very extreme verge of the law, and of course ought never to have been adopted and the secrecy of the proceedings was a burning shame." He hoped that Jefferson Davis would hang but held great skepticism that it would ever come about. "Judge Holt [the judge advocate general who tried the Lincoln conspirators] has certainly done more to shake the foundations of the law than any one lawyer in the country." For all his dislike of Greeley, Gray appreciated the editor's stubborn protests against violations of a free press or of fair trails.[16]

There were advocates for the use of military trials. First and foremost was Judge Holt, who had used these military courts to try a number of cases, including the Lincoln conspirators. He told Edwin Stanton, secretary of war, that the commissions were good for "bringing to justice . . . a large class of malefactors in the service or interest of the rebellion, who otherwise would have altogether escaped punishment." Military commissions, he added, were "unencumbered by the technicalities and inevitable embarrassments attending to the administration of justice before civil tribunals."[17] Stanton had few scruples against this course for trying traitors, and he vigorously defended this course throughout Davis's imprisonment. Secretary of State William H. Seward was hopeful for a conviction by whatever means, including through military courts, although overall he favored leniency with Confederates. Benjamin Butler—general, lawyer, and politician from Massachusetts—was called in to provide Johnson with a consultation on the way to handle the Davis trial. Butler recommended a commission of senior major generals (not surprisingly he nominated himself) to hear the case and find the ex-president guilty. Once a decision had been rendered, Butler said the president could suggest that the Supreme Court rule on the proceedings to give them the stamp of legality.[18] Congress also had its supporters, although it would be more accurate to think of these men as advocating the best course for a conviction, wherever that might be. These included Senators Jacob M. Howard and Zachariah Chandler of Michigan and Representative George W. Julian of Indiana, to name a few. In the House, Thaddeus Stevens spoke out in favor of a military tribunal for Davis, adding that he would have included all members of the cabinet in the prosecution.[19]

Proponents of military commissions were decidedly in the minority and their position became increasingly untenable, both because public opinion refused to countenance continued military trials and a landmark ruling by the Supreme Court in *ex parte Milligan* made it nearly impossible to move forward with any civilian case in military courts. Lambdin P. Milligan was one of three men from Indiana found guilty of opposing the war and planning to free Confederate prisoners in the Midwest. The cases were heard by a military commission in 1864, which found Milligan guilty. The crimes carried the death penalty. Lincoln delayed the execution, which had been scheduled for May 1865. After the president's assassination, Andrew Johnson approved the sentence and execution would have proceeded had the case not been appealed. When the decision came down in 1866, the Supreme Court ruled that the convictions were illegal. Military commissions, according to the majority opinion, held no jurisdiction as long as the courts were open and functioning.

Issued in the spring of 1866, although not made public until December, *ex parte Milligan* had more to do with civil liberties during Reconstruction than during the Civil War. The ruling held large ramifications for the political battles ahead. The majority opinion issued by Justice David Davis threatened the power of Congress to establish martial law with any practical force behind it—a problem for lawmakers who in 1867 adopted military occupation of the South as a means of carrying out Radical Reconstruction. The ruling supported by five Democratic justices sent Chief Justice Chase and three other colleagues scurrying to their pens to issue a dissenting opinion even though they agreed with the basic reasoning and were no fans of military commissions. They felt compelled to uphold the right of Congress to establish martial law and military rule in times of national emergency—all necessary if the North was going to occupy the South once again or use arms to enforce civil rights. The dissent, however, was completely compatible with the portions of the majority decision that indicated that military courts were inappropriate when civil courts functioned.[20]

The proponents of execution faced a true dilemma when deprived of military tribunals. It was a problem that revealed the sentiments held by many white northerners. Even public officials who wanted treason to be punished—such as Radical politicians like Senator Charles Sumner—considered it likely that a civil court would not result in a conviction. Judge Holt's comment above reveals the concern about moving these cases to civil courts, preferring as he put it a location that would be "unencumbered" by legal technicalities and the inevitable embarrassments of the law. There were two issues involved here. One was the problem of jurisdiction, and the other was the realization that the government stood to lose more than it gained if a conviction failed to come. To us it may seem hardly worth arguing about.

Secession did not work, and the war decided the issue in the negative and reinforced the supremacy of the federal Union. Yet there was no such thing as a sure bet with such complicated constitutional terrain as treason and secession, even after four years of bloody argument. For a good portion of American society, the argument that dissolution of the Union constituted treason was not persuasive.

A consensus concerning jurisdiction emerged in early 1866 that if Davis were to be tried in a civil court, the case would have to be heard in the District Court of Virginia over which Chase presided. The ruling came from Attorney General James Speed in answer to a Senate resolution that demanded the government move forward with the prosecution of Jefferson Davis. Speed was adamant that the case belonged in civil court and that Virginia constituted the scene of the crime. In part, the attorney general was trying to head off attempts to hold trials just about everywhere, for a strong case could be made that the impact of the former president's treason was felt wherever the Confederate army had appeared. One claim had been made for hearing the case in Washington, where a grand jury had handed down an indictment of Davis in 1865, charging him specifically with the Confederate skirmish at the capital in June 1864. But plenty of other offers came in from around the country from jurists and public officials in various states who were more than happy to provide the location of a trial for the Arch Traitor. Speed undercut these efforts by declaring that the Constitution specified that trials for treason must be held in the state or district "wherein the crimes shall have been committed." He denied an interpretation called "constructive presence" that argued Davis had been present everywhere his insurgents conducted raids upon the northern and southern borders of loyal states. Speed was not persuaded by this logic and maintained that it was impractical to follow the doctrine of constructive presence because it meant that anyone at all who had been connected with the rebel armies was liable for trial in any state the military had traveled. He maintained the need to try accused traitors in the state or districts where they were actually present at the time of the crime.[21]

Although Speed's verdict on these matters cleared up one large issue— whether military or civil trials should hear the Davis case—it also created new legal and political dilemmas that resulted in further delay. Practical matters dictated against holding a trial any time soon in Virginia. Legal authority was still tentative and civil order was still being restored. District Courts had not been sitting in the former Confederate states and did not appear to be ready to begin in the near future. Even if they did resume fairly quickly, officials understood that it would be well nigh impossible to put together a jury of twelve individuals who returned a guilty verdict. As in murder trials, the jury in treason cases had to reach a unanimous decision, allowing Davis to go free if only one person dissented.

Speed's decision angered northerners who wanted prompt punishment of rebel leaders. The most consistent man who carried the torch for prosecution of Davis and others in Congress was Senator Jacob M. Howard of Michigan. Howard was a former Whig who became an attorney in the 1830s and served a term in the U.S. Congress. After serving as attorney general of his state, he entered the Senate in 1861 and found a snug home among the most radical of the Radical Republicans. It was Howard who crafted the resolution sent to President Johnson in December 1865 that produced the decision by Speed. He could not help noticing that Speed's jurisdictional decision hampered the ability to mete out justice. He found the logic full of holes as well as the precedent a disastrous one.

Howard attacked the ruling in a long speech to the Senate on February 1, 1866, as he pushed either for trial by military commission or a broader interpretation of the venue for civil action. He believed Speed's assessment was far too narrow. Taken literally, it gave traitors the ability to go overseas to aid foreign enemies in an act against the United States and then escape prosecution. "He will not so construe the instrument as to give to every American citizen an open license to join the enemies of his country in foreign lands or on the high seas under which he can escape the doom of traitors. This would be such a narrow, strict construction as would bring upon us the derision of all other nations."[22] Howard knew better: the Constitution protected against such an eventuality by giving the Congress the power to decide on jurisdiction if the crimes were not committed within any state. He cited the appropriate clauses but tried to use them to convince his colleagues to establish a venue for the trial outside of Virginia. He realized that there was no hope of gaining a conviction from jurors, especially when African Americans did not have the ability to sit on juries.

In the course of this debate, Howard revealed why he remained such a consistent agitator for punishing traitors: he believed that the rebels had not accepted the terms of defeat. "It is true the war has ceased to drench the earth with blood; the rebels have laid down their arms; they are conquered, but with a supercilious sneer at their conquerors, kindly and condescendingly assure them that they 'accept the situation,' that southern independence is a failure, and that they are willing and ready again to be represented in Congress; but we all know that at heart they hate and detest the Government they betrayed four years ago, and which now holds them in the iron grip of conquest." He was only warming to the task: "They hate it, and hate the loyal people who uphold it, for the same reason that any criminal who has sought the life of an innocent man hates the man who has brought him to justice. They hate it because their failure to shake off its authority had deeply stung their pride and brought a total eclipse upon their vainglory and their vanity; because, seeing among themselves the desolation of war, and the poverty, starvation, and beggary it has brought to their own doors, they recognize in these the lasting, the unanswerable evidence of their own folly, weakness, and madness."[23]

Howard's impassioned appeal, and his efforts elsewhere, demonstrate that a serious effort existed in the Congress to push for execution of former Confederates. He led the debate in the Senate and, even more importantly, served as a main inquisitor on the Joint Committee on Reconstruction. Howard examined virtually every person who appeared before the committee on the nature of loyalty in the South. He especially wanted to know whether the administration's leniency with pardons had encouraged resistance of the government and allowed the spirit of the rebellion to continue. Invariably, Unionists or friends of the government told him what he wanted to hear: that disloyalty reared its head because of Johnson's policies; that leniency only begat greater confidence to the traitorous element and resulted in persecution of loyal citizens. It is clear from a reading of the report of the Joint Committee on Reconstruction that Howard used this forum to ferret out why ex-Confederates deserved punishment, including disenfranchisement and, where applicable, execution. For the moment he could not secure all that he wanted. However, he did what he could to punish rebels and the men escaping treason trials through legislation that protected civil rights and created military rule in the South, especially through the disabling clause of the Fourteenth Amendment.

Not even all Radical Republicans were completely behind Howard. Men who presumably should have been sympathetic to him because they shared partisan loyalties and suppositions about the war and emancipation did not support treason trials. The postwar debate over the punishment of Rebels featured a split within the Radicals that few scholars have defined: between men like Senators Howard and Zachariah Chandler of Michigan who pushed for capital punishment and their colleagues in the cabinet, Congress, and the judiciary, who mounted both open and clandestine campaigns against the prosecution of Jefferson Davis. None other than the chief justice of the United States deployed legal technicalities to delay the trial of the Confederate president until the public finally had lost interest. Gerrit Smith, one of the Secret Six who funded John Brown's expedition to Harpers Ferry, not only pushed for clemency but also paid a portion of Davis's bail. Massachusetts senator Charles Sumner talked tough privately but did almost nothing publicly to push for the prosecution of Confederates. Even Pennsylvania congressman Thaddeus Stevens backed away from capital punishment because of moral scruples against killing and a desire to mobilize the Congress to redistribute rebel property to African Americans. Other than Stevens's particular ethics, the motivations behind this drive for Radical lenience involved practical political considerations of nation building and maintaining the Republican Party, partisan ruptures between a president and Congress over Reconstruction policies that drained the momentum for execution, and beliefs about the nature of representative government that professed commitment to the rule of law rather than military coercion.

Chief Justice Chase used legal technicalities to block the progress of the Davis trial. In explaining his position, even in private letters, the chief justice never admitted to foot-dragging but claimed that he only tried to follow the law scrupulously. He refused any attempt to put Davis on trial until civil authority had been restored in the former Confederate states. As long as the military ruled and the rebellion was not declared officially over, the chief justice said the Supreme Court could not function. Chase wanted more than a mere proclamation of peace, which Johnson had issued already. "I am not willing," he wrote his former law partner in May 1866, "as a member of the Supreme Court to hold Circuit Courts where martial law has not been abrogated or the habeas corpus restored. Some think that these things are accomplished by the proclamation of peace; but the fact that military commissions are still held & other like facts bring this conclusion into doubt."[24] He thus shifted the blame for any delays in the prosecution of traitors to the executive and legislative branches.

Despite this posture, it did not take too observant an individual to conclude that Chase wanted nothing to do with the prosecution of Davis. His behavior alone announced this. A few weeks after taking office, Johnson invited the chief justice to the White House to confer about the South. Chase had just returned from a trip that included the Sea Islands of South Carolina. Johnson wanted advice on the Jefferson Davis case, but the justice

refused to discuss the matter because "this did not seem to me a proper subject of conference between the President & Chief Justice & so I respectfully
told him."[25] Late summer 1865, the president tried again to discuss the issue
but, according to Secretary of the Navy Welles, "Chase [put] himself on his
judicial reserve." The cabinet member added that Chase "little understands
the character of President Johnson if he supposes that gentleman will ever
again introduce that subject [to him]." Welles concluded, "I have seen no
indications of a desire on the part of the Chief Justice to preside at the trial
of Davis."[26]

History may forgive a jurist for upholding the integrity of the judicial process, especially in a case so politically sensitive, but Chase was using the high
legal ground to shield his true sentiments from the public. When Johnson
finally proclaimed martial law ended in the South, the chief justice refused
to do anything to move the trial along and threw up two more obstacles to
prosecution. First, Congress had reduced the size of the Supreme Court
from ten to seven but, Chase said, had not set the jurisdictional boundaries for the Circuit Courts. So he delayed again, holding off any movement
on the case until the Congress reestablished the judicial boundaries and
clarified who presided over which District. Second, he claimed scheduling
problems. His calendar was full with Supreme Court business, preventing
him from traveling to Richmond at times convenient to government prosecutors. All told, the excuses he supplied effectively put the matter off at
least into 1867.[27]

Johnson and his supporters in the cabinet were not pleased with these
tactics and viewed them as an attempt to embarrass the executive branch,
especially before the elections. Chase caught some public criticism for his
positions, but Republicans overall found it much easier to blame a Democratic president than the chief justice. Johnson apparently understood the
devilish situation he was in. If he pardoned Davis, he risked incurring political damage that might have tipped power more quickly to the Radicals.
Yet the chief judge of the land refused to move forward with the treason
case. So Davis sat in limbo while the criticism fell on Johnson.

During the 1866 campaign season, Johnson tried once more to provoke
some progress on the case. The new attorney general, Henry Stanbery, attempted to force the issue by surrendering Davis to federal marshals, even
if it meant keeping him in Fort Monroe, the place of his original incarceration. Stanbery hoped to transfer the case from military authorities and then
make the decision public in order to put pressure on Chase. As reported
by interior secretary Orville Hickman Browning, Stanbery claimed, "it be-

ing charged that the administration was obstructing the trial of Davis, and shielding him from punishment the attorney Genl wanted the case placed in its true light, and the courts and the Country informed that Mr. Davis was held subject to the order of the Court whenever it chose to call for him." This time Stanton vigorously blocked the effort, because he claimed Davis was a traitor who had forfeited all rights and awaited the pleasure of the government.[28]

It is small wonder, although hardly forgivable, that the president snapped when he was confronted by hecklers on this issue during his "Swing around the Circle" in 1866. The story is well-known. As he toured the country making stump speeches to win support for Democratic candidates for Congress, someone in the crowd yelled out to him, "Hang Jefferson Davis." The president sputtered back, "Why don't you hang him?" and added, "Why don't Judge Chase. . . . Why don't he try him?" He told the crowd that he was neither the chief justice nor the prosecuting attorney and stated: "Why not hang Thaddeus Stevens and Wendell Phillips?"[29] These last two men were the congressman from Pennsylvania and the famed abolitionist, both Radical Republicans. Johnson's battles with such men dwarfed his concern over the hanging of traitors, but the case obviously created an additional friction with him and an additional target for those wishing to attack the president during his stumping.

Critics such as Gideon Welles viewed Chase as an obstructionist acting for political gain, and analysis supports his contention that partisanship played a role in thwarting the trial of Davis and others indicted for treason. Chase entertained presidential ambitions and flirted with the idea of doing so as a Democrat.[30] He gained more than he lost by refusing to act on the Davis trial. If it moved to civil court, the controversy fell squarely on him and could then benefit the president. Should the case be botched by the government, the chief justice might lose stature. And even if a conviction came, the president retained the power to pardon Davis. Johnson then could have the best of both worlds, appearing magnanimous while allowing the government to establish the legal precedent against secession.

THE DILEMMA OF A WAR BETWEEN NATIONS

It would be too limiting, however, to see the fate of treason trials as derailed only by politics. Radicals who strayed from what seems to have been a more likely position in favor of punishment of the rebels did so partly from humanitarian concerns and partly from ideological beliefs about the role of government and the rule of law. The most prominent people from the Radical camp to advocate clemency for the rebels, including Jefferson Davis, were Horace Greeley and Gerrit Smith. Both men exchanged correspondence with the chief justice, urging him against a conviction for Davis on treason. At first, Greeley had been in favor of a treason trial in order to clarify the issue of state sovereignty and secession. He then shifted his position because, in the words of his biographer, the trials "would martyr their victims, produce unnecessary bitterness, and hinder national reconciliation." Greeley has been portrayed as an idealist and a reformer who often took stands on principle. It is no stretch to consider that sympathy for an oppressed or downtrodden group might draw a person to both abolition and clemency for rebels.[31]

Gerrit Smith's exchange with the chief justice is even more interesting because he held beliefs that enjoyed wide currency especially outside of the old-line abolitionists and Radicals. Smith was a well-known, influential abolitionist and philanthropist who had funded the expedition of John Brown to Harpers Ferry. One might expect a man so dedicated to the cause of antislavery to relish punishing the rebels, not only for bringing on the war but also for perpetuating a sin that had stained the country for centuries. Yet he believed that the United States had no right to charge even the leaders of the Confederacy with treason and spent a good deal of energy and ink after the conflict arguing to that effect. His logic is interesting. In an address at the Cooper Institute in New York during the height of the conspiracy trials in June 1865, Smith admitted that the South had committed treason. He claimed, however, that the North condoned the act by entering a reluctant compact with the Confederate states. In essence,

> we agreed that she should not be [tried]. We came, in effect, into this agreement by consenting, reluctantly it is true, to have our War with her conducted according to the law of war—by which I mean the law of international war. That we consented to have our war so conducted is indisputable. We followed other nations, and recognized in the South the rights of a belligerent. The Supreme Court of the United States were unanimous in recognizing them. We entered upon, and continued in, an exchange of prisoners with her. Innumerable have been our truces with her: and, formally as well as informally, we have negotiated with her for Peace.

To Smith the war was governed by the same rules as if it were conducted between the United States and Mexico.[32]

Smith echoed his comments nearly a year later in a public letter to Salmon P. Chase that dealt more specifically with the Jefferson Davis trial. Written in May 1866, the letter contended that the Supreme Court did not have the right to try Davis. He insisted that the South needed to be treated as a conquered nation. Again, he did not completely exonerate the South of treason; he did not want to condone the act of secession. But he made the United States complicit because its leaders accepted, through allowing certain practices, a tacit compact that allowed the war to proceed as if between two belligerents, subject to international law. As a conquered people, Confederate southerners could not be bound by the laws of treason, nor were pardons by the president necessary or appropriate. "Pardons to Southern men," he observed, "are no more in place than would be pardons to Englishmen had we conquered England." Again arguing about the practicalities of the situation, Smith did not know how under the circumstances the courts could stop with one conviction. "If we punish Davis and [Vice President Alexander] Stephens, consistency requires us to punish thousands; and, if we let the thousands go unpunished, consistency requires us to let Davis and Stephens go unpunished." There had been enough suffering in the Civil War, especially for the defeated party. They had already paid the price for their actions. There was no need to salt the wounds after the bleeding had stopped.[33]

Smith entered more dangerous ground with comments toward the end of his letter to Chase. Here he raised a doubt more common than we might expect about states' rights ideology and whether the war had settled the issue of secession. "I have admitted the plainness of the Constitution at one point [concerning treason]," he observed, adding, "its lack of plainness at another and most vital point is of itself a sufficient reason why the South should not be held for treason. It was not slavery alone, but slavery combined with the doctrine of State sovereignty, that brought on the War." He said that no small number of statesmen in the North and South, dating back to Thomas Jefferson and James Madison, believed that they found the doctrine of states' rights in the Constitution: "Perhaps, the streams of blood shed in this horrid War have not washed away, entirely and forever, this pernicious doctrine. Then, let it be provided for, if not in a Constitutional Amendment, at least in the terms of 'Reconstruction,' that it shall no more return to curse us." Smith claimed that no one should be punished until the doctrine of states' rights was indisputably determined to be wrong, according to the laws of the land.[34]

Smith hoped that the public understood that the best way to preserve the republic and prevent further civil wars was through mercy rather than bloodshed. Here he took a similar position to Grant but went a step further by claiming that leniency in the case of the American Civil War had a better chance than violence of maintaining peace in the future. He had a ready example south of the border of the United States. During our Civil War, the French made incursions into Mexico, accepting the overtures of monarchists to set up a government. They were opposed by liberals under Benito Juárez, and soon the French troops found themselves in open warfare with Mexicans. Facing considerable pressure from the liberal opposition, and also from the United States, the French withdrew their forces in 1866. Emperor Maximilian attempted to remain. He was captured and later executed by firing squad, along with a couple of his top generals. To observers like Smith, this unsavory episode demonstrated that executions were out of step with republican values. He explained that

> one of my long-cherished doctrines is that the sufferings of the conquered party in every civil war are quite enough without super-adding punishments at the close of it. A sad mistake is it in the present conquering party in Mexico to hold the contrary of this doctrine. It is argued that such punishments will warn and intimidate; and thus serve to prevent wars. But a sounder philosophy teaches that they will exasperate and brutalize, and thus tend to multiply wars. The following of the present Mexican War with bloodshed will help to keep Mexico a land of frequent and almost incessant wars.

Later he added, "There is but one legitimate, and indeed but one peaceful, way to prevent civil wars—and that is justice on the part of Government. Had our Government been just . . . this horrid War would not have been."[35]

One might dismiss Smith's opinions as lying far from the Republican mainstream—or even the sentiments of War Democrats—except that other members of the party entertained similar doubts about a treason trial in civil court. Chase did not agree with his abolitionist friend that southerners were exempt from trials for treason or that a universal law of war existed that overrode the Constitution. But after seeing the explanation for Smith's posting of Davis's bail, he admitted to reading it "with great pleasure" and distributed it both to a former staff officer of Stonewall Jackson and to a law associate.[36] Another person who raised concerns about the impact of a trial was Edwin D. Morgan, a prominent Republican who had served as governor of New York during the war and was the state's current U.S. senator. "Grave doubts exist," he wrote the president in May 1865, "whether this

[Davis's trial] can be accomplished by a trial for treason at Common Law, and whether such a trial, with the able counsel that will be employed, and their revival of the Doctrine of State Sovereignty as a Constitutional defense of Davis, would not tend to demoralize the public mind and weaken our position." He claimed that a New York newspaper, as well as some English periodicals, insisted that treason was committed by the State of Mississippi, not Davis, "that is by obeying the orders of that state he obeyed his sovereign &, that having recognized him as a Belligerent the United States, cannot now charge him with treason." Morgan thought the case was stronger to charge Davis with atrocities during the war, such as the massacre of black soldiers at Fort Pillow and the starvation of prisoners.[37]

Even private letters to the president talked about the problem of states' rights and secession. It has been a commonplace in books on the Civil War to state with assurance that the war resolved the issue of secession. Yet people at the time were not convinced that arms had been the best way to arbitrate such an important national position. As mentioned in the case of Horace Greeley, some hoped for a trial of traitors so that the issue of secession could be decided once and for all with a legal precedent. Along these lines, A. R. Brown—an attorney from Lowell, Massachusetts, who wrote President Johnson—hoped that Davis could be used as an example to clarify this ambiguity in the Constitution. According to Brown, Davis and the other rebels needed to be tried before the highest civil tribunal, not a military court, so that an authoritative judgment could be rendered on two key questions: whether states could secede and whether a state could command allegiance over that owed to a central government. "These points no doubt would be adjudicated rightly, & if so it would settle American law and liberty for all future times & be a more potent bind of Union than thousands of armed men." Brown continued, "These questions have now been settled by brute force only. They would then be settled by reason." As an example, he cited the state trials after the English Civil War, which he claimed settled important questions of law, liberty, and sovereignty.[38]

Other observers, including hard-line Republicans who favored treason trials for former Confederates, harbored doubts about the likelihood of bringing forth convictions. Although generally in favor of exiling political leaders of the rebellion, Charles Sumner did hope for the trial and execution of Davis. Yet as early as 1862 he predicted that no one would hang for treason. By the end of August 1865, nothing had changed his mind. He wrote John Bright in England that great uncertainty existed with regard to the prosecution of Davis, especially for his complicity in the assassination of Lincoln and for his treatment of prisoners of war. "There is little doubt of his guilt under both these heads," he noted, adding, "but I do not know if it can be proved in a court of justice." Sumner did not share why he believed this and wrote little more on the issue. Significantly, he did not take the lead in the debate and rarely spoke up in the Senate. He possibly believed that the trials of the leaders of the rebellion either did not contain evidence of treason or lacked sufficient public support for a jury to bring in a conviction. More than once he expressed his wish for a different solution: that Jefferson Davis had been shot during his capture, like John Wilkes Booth.[39]

These issues found a public airing during Senate debates in the 39th Congress. In fact, speculation on the loyalty and disloyalty of the rebel South pervaded much of the discussion on many issues facing the chamber, from mundane discussions of postal privileges to the debate about the meaning of citizenship in the Civil Rights Act. The concerns of Gerrit Smith and Edwin Morgan were repeated by Senator Edgar Cowan of Pennsylvania, one of the more conservative Republicans in the chamber. On January 30, 1866, as the Senate discussed the Civil Rights Act and who should be considered a citizen with full political rights, Cowan defended the mass of southerners as blameless for treason. He listed three reasons for leniency. First, they had already paid the price—the destruction of war was a penalty for their crime. Second, they had submitted to the government by laying down arms and accepting rule by the United States. And third, not every southerner was complicit in secession. Many in the South had no chance to assent to ordinances of secession and, Cowan reasoned, once the state declared itself out of the Union, its citizens had to follow out of their own self-interest. "We know the people, and we know their weakness," Cowan said. "We know how readily they are led away by their leaders; we know how subject they are to have their passions excited, and we know how quickly the flame of war may be kindled among them without the wicked, treasonable intent which is necessary to constitute the offence of treason." Upon questioning from Howard, Cowan admitted that treason was still possible for leaders, but he was adamant that the mass of southerners should not be denied citizenship because they allegedly committed treason against the United States.[40]

This discussion reveals the powerful hold that state sovereignty retained over many Americans. Cowan excused most of the white South from treason because they had no ability to resist their state government. Flawed human nature explained some of this weakness, and the powerful pull of the states explained the rest. Individuals scarcely could resist such an entity. It was natural to him that people went over to the Confederacy, even if they were not totally willing in the beginning. He may have realized that he overstated the helplessness of the citizens in the South, but he wanted to believe they had a forgivable offense so that the country could move on and achieve its greater glory as a new United States. "I like to believe it, because it enables me to think that we can restore the Union again; it enables me to think that we can have the greatest republic, and not only the greatest republic, but ... the greatest empire, the world has ever seen." Treason trials jeopardized this march toward a great republican empire.[41]

The Last Gasp and the Fourteenth Amendment

Those beyond the Republican circle held even stronger opinions about leniency for the South based on both ideological and practical reasoning. Jefferson Davis's defense counsel planned to capitalize on the position that Davis had acted constitutionally when he left the Union. They intended to argue that the United States had acknowledged the existence of a public war through various actions such as the exchange of prisoners. The entire defense team came from the North, led by chief counsel Charles O'Conor, a New York attorney, Democrat, and proponent of states' rights. The approach had been anticipated by Ben Butler when he advised the president on how best to proceed with the Davis trial. Butler's counsel reveals how powerful the logic was and why it was essential to have a military tribunal handle the case if the country wanted to guarantee a conviction. He expected the defense to argue for the legal existence of the Confederate government and the right of states to secede. He answered this line of attack by refusing to allow any debate whatsoever. The reply of the presiding military officers to such contentions should be, "All of us sitting here have fought four years to decide those questions in the negative, and therefore it would be useless to argue them here." He obviously saw that the government had little chance for success in arguing the legalities of the matter, which had to rest on a decision arrived at by force.[42]

Beyond the legal issue, practical matters stymied the momentum for treason trials. As already mentioned, no one was sure exactly where to stop once trials and executions had begun. Southerners argued that Davis had been merely a representative of the people, and if he hanged so must every former Confederate. Some northerners offered a murky distinction between the culpability of leaders and the innocence of the led, as evidenced by the debate between Howard and Cowan. No one, however, provided a precise definition for who was eligible for execution. Then there was the concern about what might happen if executions occurred. Some feared, as Grant did, creating desperate men who would resort to further armed resistance, perhaps by heading to Mexico. This might set back pacification of the South, while creating more bloodshed and vexation for federal authorities. Still others raised the specter of creating martyrs out of these men. A newspaper editor in Springfield, Massachusetts, put it this way: "Do we wish to finish the rebellion, to turn out its very ashes? Then make no martyrs. The wounds inflicted in cold blood are what keep animosities alive." The view was seconded by the *Catholic Telegraph*: "If the advocates of 'hang him,' will devote a few days to the history of other countries they will find that martyr-making is a dangerous and unprofitable business."[43]

The government finally came to the conclusion that no trial was better than one that led to a tacit endorsement of secession and state sovereignty. Richard H. Dana Jr., prominent Boston attorney, from time to time advised his friend, Attorney General William Evarts. In 1868 Evarts read a letter from Dana to the cabinet that stated, "by pursuing the trial, the Government can get only a re-affirmation by a Circuit Court ... of a rule of public law settled for this country in every way in which such a matter can be settled [i.e., by war], on giving to a jury drawn from the region of the rebellion a chance to disregard the law when announced." Dana reminded Evarts that it took only one juror to set aside a conviction: "The risks of such absurd and discreditable issues of a great state trial are assumed for the sake of a verdict which, if obtained, will settle nothing in law or national practice not now settled, and nothing in fact not now history, while no judgment rendered thereon do we think will be ever executed."[44] Hugh McCulloch, secretary of the treasury under Johnson, remembered that the attorney general found that treason was not appropriate because the war had been "a revolution which had been attempted by the Southern States." McCulloch repeated that belligerent rights had been accorded to the Confederacy, adding, "They could not, therefore, be charged with treason, nor could one of their number be singled out and legally convicted of the crime."[45]

Jefferson Davis, of course, was never convicted. By May 1867, support had grown to transfer the case to civil authorities. His counsel immediately filed for bail that was posted by a number of northerners, including Horace

Greeley, Gerrit Smith, and Cornelius Vanderbilt. Davis soon went to Canada with his family, with the promise to return for further hearings the following year. Some movement occurred on the case in November 1868, but for many technical reasons nothing happened. With a sweeping proclamation on Christmas Day, President Johnson effectively granted a complete amnesty to all participants in the rebellion, including its former president.

The case against Davis, however, still needed to be dismissed officially, with the last actions on these proceedings revealing another dimension to the Fourteenth Amendment. Most historical attention to this cornerstone of civil rights has focused appropriately on how it changed the meaning of citizenship. The third section, however, had been controversial and featured one of the last gasps of the would-be executioners to exact at least some punishment for treason. This particular section disqualified a specified range of former Confederates from holding a range of public offices. The ban existed indefinitely but could be lifted by a two-thirds vote of both houses of Congress. Yet it had begun as a far more sweeping clause that denied the right to vote to all former rebels until 1870. Thaddeus Stevens had spoken in favor of this disfranchisement clause in debates before the House. "My only objection to it is that it is too lenient," he told the chamber. "I know that there is a moribund sensibility, sometimes called mercy, which affects a few of all classes from the priest to the clown, which has more sympathy for the murderer on the gallows than for his victim." He morally opposed capital punishment. "But I never dreamed that all punishment could be dispensed with in human society. . . . Here is the mildest of all punishments ever inflicted on traitors." Later, he noted that the House was fairly unanimous on all but the third section. He pleaded, "Give us the third section or give us nothing. Do not balk with the pretence of an amendment which throws the Union into the hands of the enemy before it becomes consolidated."[46]

Contrary to the intentions of people such as Stevens, the third section of the Fourteenth Amendment ironically became Chief Justice Chase's legal escape from punishing Jefferson Davis and other leaders of the rebellion. On February 15, 1869, the government entered a *nolle prosequi*, or no prosecution, allowing Chase to dismiss the case. But during the complicated maneuvering that led up to the decision, Chase had let it slip that he believed the Fourteenth Amendment prohibited further proceedings. According to Chase, Davis's disqualification from public office had been a punishment for his crime, and no one was allowed to be punished twice for the same offence. [47]

Ultimately, trying rebels as traitors in civil court proved far more dangerous than letting the criminals go unpunished. Once Davis's prosecution fell apart, no other case had a chance of moving forward. Besides, by this point the country was wrestling with new demons in implementing Reconstruction governments and enduring the impeachment of a president. The situation as a whole resulted in a Constitution that to this day remains ambiguous concerning secession. The legal precedent that warns against disunion cannot be found in the document of the national state and resides only in the constitutions enacted by the former Confederate states upon readmission to the Union. In those documents, former rebels had to declare that secession was null and void in order to regain their political rights.

The short answer to the question of why the North did not hang some rebels is that not enough northerners believed that treason had occurred or that it could be proved in a court of law. Reunion was a driving political force behind the war and Reconstruction—a desire that cannot be underestimated in this equation. Yet one can imagine many other choices that could have been made even when trying to repair the country. The military tribunals could have taken over the matter, as Ben Butler recommended. Davis could have been tried, convicted, and then pardoned to establish the case against secession while underscoring the mercy of the government. The trial could have been set for Washington or Ohio or Pennsylvania instead of Virginia. Or, as Judge Underwood of the U.S. District Court in Richmond suggested, the jury could have been packed to secure a favorable outcome even in the former Confederacy. Legal formalism and stated ideals of how a representative government should function prevented such maneuvering. Yet the irony of this situation remains that a people so concerned about the rule of law ultimately were forced to rely on the rule of blood and military force as the deciding precedent for the health of their national body.

Notes

William Blair delivered his Klement Lecture in 2004.

The author gratefully acknowledges the research assistance of Matthew Isham and Daniel James Flook, who supplied invaluable evidence and served as sounding boards for this paper. He also appreciates the editing eye of colleague Meredith H. Lair.

1. James G. Randall, *Constitutional Problems Under Lincoln* (1951; repr., Gloucester, Mass.: Peter Smith, 1963), 97 [indictments], 103n20 [persons indicted].

2. Ellis Paxson Oberholtzer, *A History of the United States Since the Civil War*, 2 vols. (New York: MacMillan, 1936), 1:11–4.

3. Levi Alger to Andrew Johnson, June 3, 1865, and Petition to "His Excellency Andrew Johnson," both in Amnesty Papers, Adjutant General's Office, 1780s–1917, Record Group 94, box 250, National Archives, Washington, D.C. (hereafter AGO Papers).

4. F. W. Eshelman and others to President Andrew Johnson, May 18, 1865, AGO Papers.

5. Elisha Farnham to Andrew Johnson, May 17, 1865; S. P. Hubbard to Andrew Johnson, May 15, 1865, both in AGO Papers. See also Lilla C. Shelby to President Johnson, May 23, 1865, AGO Papers.

6. Albert Williams to Andrew Johnson, Apr. 21, 1865, qtd. in Leroy P. Graf, ed., *The Papers of Andrew Johnson*, vol. 7: *1864–1865* (Knoxville: Univ. of Tennessee Press, 1986), 609.

7. Howard K. Beale, ed., *The Diary of Gideon Welles* (New York: Norton, 1960), 2:337–39, 335.

8. David Herbert Donald, *Charles Sumner and the Rights of Man* (New York: Knopf, 1970), 220–21; Beverly Wilson Palmer, ed., *The Selected Letters of Charles Sumner, Volume Two* (Boston: Northeastern Univ. Press, 1990), 303.

9. Qtd. in Randall, *Constitutional Problems*, 101.

10. John Y. Simon, ed., *The Papers of Ulysses S. Grant*, vol. 15: *May 1–December 31, 1865* (Carbondale: Southern Illinois Univ. Press, 1988), 149. See also Randall, *Constitutional Problems*, 101–2.

11. Simon, ed., *Papers of Ulysses S. Grant*, 15:6–8, 10.

12. Ibid., 15:11, 30.

13. Howard K. Beale, ed., *The Diary of Edward Bates* (Washington, D.C.: Government Printing Office, 1933), 481, 483.

14. William S. Groesbeck to Andrew Johnson, Nov. 9, 1865, in Leroy P. Graf, ed, *The Papers of Andrew Johnson*, vol. 9 (Knoxville: Univ. of Tennessee Press, 1991), 362

15. Salmon P. Chase to James S. Pike, July 8, 1865, Salmon P. Chase Papers, microfilm, reel 35, Library of Congress, Washington, D.C.; John C. Ropes to John Grey Jr., May 29, 1865, in Worthington Chauncey Ford, ed., *War Letters, 1862–1865, of John Chipman Gray and John Codman Ropes* (Boston: Houghton Mifflin, 1927), 496–97.

16. John C. Gray to John Codman Ropes, May 24, 1865, Ford, ed., *War Letters*, 493–94.

17. Qtd. in Elizabeth Leonard, *Lincoln's Avengers: Justice, Revenge, and Reunion after the Civil War* (New York: W. W. Norton, 2004), 166.

18. Benjamin F. Butler, *Butler's Book: A Review of His Legal, Political, and Military Career* (Boston: Thayer, 1892), 915–18.

19. Beverly Wilson Palmer and Holly Byers Ochoa, eds., *The Selected Papers of Thaddeus Stevens*, vol. 2: *April 1865–August 1868* (Pittsburgh: Univ. of Pittsburgh Press, 1998), 317–18.

20. Frederick J. Blue, *Salmon P. Chase: A Life in Politics* (Kent, Ohio: Kent State Univ. Press, 1987), 268–69.

21. Message of the President of the United States, Senate Executive Documents No. 7, 39th Cong., 1st sess., 1–4.

22. *Congressional Globe,* 39th Cong., 1st sess., 568.

23. Ibid., 569.

24. John Niven et al., eds., *The Salmon P. Chase Papers,* 5 vols. (Kent, Ohio: Kent State Univ. Press, 1993–1998), 5:94.

25. Ibid., 5:64.

26. Beale, ed., *Diary of Gideon Welles,* 2:367–68.

27. Blue, *Salmon P. Chase,* 263–64.

28. Beale, ed., *Diary of Gideon Welles,* 2:614; Theodore Calvin Pease and James G. Randall, eds., *The Diary of Orville Hickman Browning,* 2 vols. (Springfield: Illinois State Historical Library, 1925, 1933), 2:98–99.

29. Hans L. Trefousse, *Andrew Johnson: A Biography* (New York: W. W. Norton, 1989), 263–64; Foner, *Reconstruction,* 265; Blue, *Salmon P. Chase,* 264.

30. William J. Cooper Jr., *Jefferson Davis, American* (New York: Knopf, 2000), 560; John Niven, *Salmon P. Chase: A Biography,* (New York: Oxford Univ. Press, 1999), 409–10.

31. Glyndon G. Van Deusen, *Horace Greeley: Nineteenth-Century Crusader* (Philadelphia: Univ. of Pennsylvania Press, 1953), 353.

32. Gerrit Smith, *No Treason in Civil War* (New York: American News Co.,1865), 4, in Gerrit Smith Broadside and Pamphlet Collection, Call no. Smith 533, Syracuse University Library, http://libwww.syr.edu/digital/collections/g/GerritSmith.htm.

33. Letter to Chief Justice Chase, Peterboro, May 28, 1866, Chase Papers, reel 36, frames 490–91, LC.

34. Letter to Chief Justice Chase, Peterboro, May 28, 1866, Chase Papers, reel 36, frame 491, LC.

35. Gerrit Smith on the Bailing of Jefferson Davis, Gerrit Smith Broadside and Pamphlet Collection, Call no. Smith 540, 2.

36. Niven, ed., *Chase Papers,* 5:161–62.

37. Edwin D. Morgan to Andrew Johnson, May 29, 1865, in Paul Bergeron et al., eds., *Papers of Andrew Johnson,* vol. 8: *May–August 1865* (Knoxville: Univ. of Tennessee Press, 1989), 134–35.

38. A. R. Brown to President Johnson, Dec. 10, 1865, AGO Papers.

39. Palmer, ed., *Selected Letters of Charles Sumner,* 2:321.

40. *Congressional Globe,* 39th Cong., 1st sess., pt. 1:501–2.

41. Ibid., 502.

42. Cooper, *Jefferson Davis,* 560; Butler, *Butler's Book,* 917.

43. *Springfield Republican,* qtd. in *Pittsburgh Post-Gazette,* May 26, 1865; *Catholic Telegraph,* qtd. in *Pittsburgh Post-Gazette,* May 22, 1865.

44. Qtd. in Roy F. Nichols, "United States vs. Jefferson Davis, 1865–1869," *American Historical Review* 31 (Jan. 1926): 281.

45. Hugh McCulloch, *Men and Measures of Half a Century* (New York: Scribner's, 1888), 408–9.

46. Palmer and Ochoa, eds., *Selected Papers of Thaddeus Stevens,* 2:136, 137.

47. Nichols, "United States vs. Jefferson Davis," 282.

🖎 JOAN WAUGH 🖎

Personal Memoirs of U. S. Grant

A History of the Union Cause

🖎 Joan Waugh's first book, *Unsentimental Reformer: The Life of Josephine Shaw Lowell* (1997), interpreted the life of a woman whose main contributions to society came long after the Civil War. But Waugh's transition into a historian of the Civil War is less strange than it might seem, for the war cast a very long shadow over Lowell's life. She was the brother of Robert Gould Shaw, who was killed leading the 54th Massachusetts at Fort Wagner, and widow of Charles Lowell, another New Englander killed at Cedar Creek in 1864. And Lowell performed her first charitable work for the United States Sanitary Commission during the Civil War. More importantly, as Waugh illustrates, the war instilled in Lowell the importance of sacrifice and of the willingness of Americans to assume public responsibility for the moral health of the nation. These qualities led her to become one of the best-known reformers on behalf of poor families and children in the late nineteenth century.

So, it is not surprising that Waugh has sought out other projects to help us understand the ways in which Americans came to understand the Civil War. She turned next to the memorialization of Ulysses S. Grant after his death, which provides a key reference point for attitudes about nationalism and the Union in Victorian America. Her Klement Lecture provided a sample of that forthcoming book.

U. S. Grant writing his memoirs on the porch of the Mt. McGregor cottage.
Library of Congress Prints and Photographs Division.

Hero and president, drunkard and butcher—there are many words that have been used to describe Ulysses S. Grant. But "historian" is not normally one of them. That changed in Waugh's 2003 lecture. She was the third lecturer in a row to take on the sometimes ticklish subject of memory. But unlike David Blight, who focused on race and memory, and Matt Gallman, who examined literary manifestations of memory, Waugh explored memory through the words of perhaps the most famous hero of the war. Her analysis of Grant's *Personal Memoirs* as more than a reminiscence, as a *history* whose author intended it to serve as a counterpoint to the cult of the Lost

Cause that had caught the imagination of southerners and northerners alike by the time the *Memoirs* was published in 1885, reveals a side of an iconographic American that most have never considered.

Waugh, an associate professor at UCLA whose multimedia course on the Civil War draws hundreds of students, continued to explore these themes after her Klement Lecture. Her anthology of essays, *The Memory of the Civil War in American Culture*, edited with Alice Fahs, appeared in 2004. She continues to work on her book about Grant and on another project related to the war's meaning: the political culture of Civil War soldiers. 〰

HIS TROUBLES BEGAN ON A FESTIVE holiday. Christmas Eve in the year of 1883 was cold and rainy, and by late evening the sidewalk was frozen in front of Ulysses S. Grant's house on 3 East 66th Street in New York City, not far from Central Park. Stepping out of a rented carriage, Grant slipped on the ice and sustained a painful injury. As the formerly robust general struggled to regain his health, another blow struck. In May of 1884, he learned that Grant and Ward, an investment firm that held his fortune, had failed. Aged sixty-two, Grant was penniless.

Friends and supporters rallied around Ulysses and his wife, Julia. He was able to keep his residence, but little else. In desperation, he agreed to write an account of the battle of Shiloh for the *Century Magazine*. He did it for the money at first but found that he liked the task. He decided to write more articles. One thing led to another, and before he knew it he had signed a book contract. A brief period of happiness ensued, but fate once again intervened. In the summer of 1884 Grant bit into a peach and was immediately seized with a terrible pain in his throat. A few months later, his doctors confirmed the worst: he had a fatal throat cancer. Most men might have abandoned an ambitious writing project at such a time. Not Grant. Famed for his quiet determination on the battlefield, he decided to finish the manuscript before he died.

Through many months of indescribable agony Grant painstakingly recorded his role in the history of the great conflict. His family's financial future depended upon the successful completion of the book, and he would not let them down. But the writing also took on a special urgency; he felt an obligation to tell what he knew to be true about himself, about the war, about the United States. "I would like to see truthful history written," declared Grant, "such history will do full credit to the courage, endurance, and ability of the American citizen soldier, no matter what section he hailed from, or in what rank."[1]

U. S. Grant wrote those words just a week or two into July of 1885. In mid-June he traveled by train from the city to a wealthy supporter's summer cottage atop Mount McGregor, a beautiful resort in the Adirondacks, near Saratoga Springs. When he felt well enough, he liked to sit on the large and comfortable porch to read the newspapers and to enjoy the cool air. Grant reserved what little energy he had left for his memoirs. He fretted over the page proofs for the first volume, revising and pointing out errors that should be corrected. He continued working on the second volume, still in manuscript, adding pages, even chapters, and providing detailed commentaries.

A poignant photograph showed Grant writing intently while seated in a wicker chair on the porch at Mount McGregor. Swathed in scarves and shawls, with a woolen cap perched on his head, and propped up by a pillow, he was simply unrecognizable as the strong Union general who led the federal armies to victory. But a sharp observer of the image will note the resolution in his frail, ravaged countenance. Even as he faced death, Grant openly relished his role as a writer of history. As Bruce Catton described, U. S. Grant had become a "man of letters."[2] "I pray God," Grant wrote to his wife, "that [my life] may be spared to complete the necessary work upon my book."[3] His unfinished work kept him alive beyond the time his doctors had predicted. Grant died two days after writing his last words on July 23, 1885.[4]

The posthumous publication in December of the two-volume *Personal Memoirs of U. S. Grant* (1,231 pages in total) proved a spectacular popular and critical success. The publisher, New York's Charles L. Webster and Company, eventually sold more than 300,000 sets. Within the first two years, royalties totaled over $450,000, bringing financial security to his widow and four children. With the publication of Grant's memoirs, "historian" could be added to his list of accomplishments.

My essay explores the interpretative significance of the *Personal Memoirs*. It does not present a detailed review or analysis of the narrative; rather, it offers an elucidation of the process that led to the massive work. In other words, I am concerned about the battle over the meaning of the American Civil War and Grant's role in that battle as an historian. I am defining historian broadly, as someone who is "a writer or student of history."[5] I argue that Grant's account of the war, above all, conveyed what he himself called "truthful history." It can be simply put. According to Grant, the northern cause (based upon the sacredness of unionism and opposition to slavery before and during the war) was the morally superior one. Grant challenged the idea, just beginning to take hold in the 1880s, that the northern and southern causes were equivalent. He reminded the country's citizens that "the cause of the great War of the Rebellion against the United States will have to be attributed to slavery."[6]

Thus, the *Memoirs* were written both to advance a larger truth, that of Union moral superiority, and to remind Americans of Grant's contribution to the victory that remade America into "a nation of great power and intelligence."[7] In Grant's mind the two were linked. If the northern war's aims were union and freedom, then his reputation was forever secured. Few expressed Grant's thoughts better than his supporter Frederick Douglass: "May we not justly say, will it not be the unquestioned sentiment of history that the liberty Mr. Lincoln declared with his pen General Grant made effectual with his sword—by his skill in leading the Union armies to final victory?"[8]

Grant's importance as a symbol of Unionism for his generation was undisputed. As lieutenant general, as general-in-chief, as a twice-elected president, as an international figure, as private citizen, and as a dying hero, Grant sought actively to influence and to shape the historical memory of the "rebellion." That he identified himself with the Union Cause made it even more imperative to control the memory of the war. Grant was a historian of the war and the Union Cause. Broke and discouraged in 1884, Grant turned the *Century* articles into the basis of his hefty memoirs. When he did that, he was emphatically not, as is sometimes portrayed, starting from scratch. Importantly, the volumes were the last stage of a process that began during the war and continued, gathering steam, in the decades of his postwar career. An exploration of these antecedents will form an important part of the essay. Grant explained his literary credentials in the following way:

I have to say that for the last twenty-four years I have been very much employed in writing. As a soldier I wrote my own orders, plans of battle, instructions and reports. They were not edited, nor was assistance rendered. As president, I wrote every official document, I believe, usual for presidents to write, bearing my name. All these have been published and widely circulated. The public has become accustomed to my style of writing. They know that it is not even an attempt to imitate either a literary or classical style; that it is just what it is and nothing else. If I succeed in telling my story so that others can see as I do what I attempt to show, I will be satisfied. The reader must also be satisfied, for he knows from the beginning just what to expect.[9]

Grant's late-blooming literary masterpiece therefore represented a culmination, by one of the major figures in the conflict, of twenty-four years of thinking, writing, and talking about the meaning of the war for the United States. Finally, Grant's interpretation of the war was interwoven with and reactive to controversies and events—such as the development of the "Lost Cause" ideology and the publication of the *Official Records*—that shaped the "writing of the civil war."[10]

The Personal Memoirs: A Background

A brief background on the reception and reputation of *The Personal Memoirs of U. S. Grant* is necessary. In the decade of the 1880s, there was an explosion of publications about the Civil War. Indeed, the amount of literature pouring forth from the presses seemed unstoppable: books, newspaper and magazine serials, and the publication of the conflict's official documents. Much of it was military in nature—descriptive accounts of battles, fictional portraits of soldiers coming to grips with the war, biographies and memoirs of soldiers, unit histories—and it fed an insatiable appetite on the part of the public. Grant facilitated, and benefited from, this publishing phenomenon. For example, even before Grant's death, 60,000 sets of *The Personal Memoirs* had been ordered by subscription, much to the astonishment of the ailing general. "General Grant," wrote an Ohio veteran, now an agent selling subscriptions for the books, "the people are moving en masse upon your memoirs."[11]

The reviews were effusive, and many compared *The Personal Memoirs* favorably with Caesar's *Commentaries*. Grant's great friend and publisher, Mark Twain, pronounced, "General Grant's book is a great unique and unapproachable literary masterpiece."[12] *The Personal Memoirs* elicited praise from intellectuals such as Henry Adams, Henry James, and Matthew Arnold. Military comrades, such as former Union general William T. Sherman and former Confederate general Simon B. Buckner, who both served as pallbearers at Grant's funeral, were also delighted with *The Personal Memoirs*. Grant the historian was almost universally praised for his direct, simple, honest, and fair-minded portrayal of the Civil War, and for his modesty in downplaying his own considerable role in bringing about northern victory. Many readers observed that Grant's memoirs, above all other accounts of the war, told the "truth" about the nation's greatest conflict. People were impressed by his ability to write a compelling narrative of the war's battles. His narrative seemed calm, measured, objective, and buttressed by solid documentation.[13] The Personal Memoirs sold briskly into the first decade of the twentieth century before falling into obscurity by the late 1920s and 1930s. It was no coincidence that Grant's reputation reached a nadir in those particular decades, as the popular culture celebrated the romantic image of the Confederacy epitomized in Margaret Mitchell's Gone With the Wind and immortalized in the movie of the same title.[14]

When interest revived in Grant's life and career, it sparked a reappraisal of his military and political record. Although The Personal Memoirs never again achieved its late-nineteenth-century "best-seller" status, modern scholars and critics turned to them to help explain the man and the war. Edmund Wilson's famous assessment of the volumes as "a unique expression of national character" included a forceful argument for considering Grant as a writer who deserved to be included in the American literary canon. The editor of The Papers of U. S. Grant, John Y. Simon, asserted that The Personal Memoirs offered "candor, scrupulous fairness, and grace of expression."[15] Bruce Catton called them "a first-rate book—well written with a literary quality that keeps it fresh." Recent scholars William McFeely, James McPherson, and Brooks D. Simpson have singled out Grant's memoirs as a historical and literary tour de force, and all have written introductions to new editions.[16] In short, a strong consensus has emerged. The Personal Memoirs offers a literate, accurate, and indispensable resource for understanding the military and political history of the war that neither the professional historian nor the amateur can afford to ignore. But they offer much more than that. For the modern reader, The Personal Memoirs can also explain two interrelated questions: why the North won and why they fought. Not surprisingly, Grant's own experiences in the war laid the foundation for his later writing efforts; his pen first captured those experiences in battlefield reports.

BATTLEFIELD REPORTS

The history of the Civil War and of individual battles of that war began as soon as the muskets and cannons fell quiet on the battlefield. The old saying "the pen is mightier than the sword" is applicable to the official reports that had to be written by the leading participants in a particular battle in which the winners and losers of both sides had to justify their successes or failures to their military and political superiors. Grant's major (and minor, as well) battles and campaigns from Fort Donelson to Shiloh to Vicksburg to Chattanooga to Cold Harbor had to be analyzed, explained, and defended, with blame cast and praise awarded to the major officers.

The eminent editor of the *Century* series on the Civil War, Robert Underwood Johnson, was a close reader of many conflicting accounts of numerous battles. In frustration, he turned to humor to explain the process. He observed that every battle has at least four points of view: that of the man who gets credit for the victory; that of the man who thought he should get the credit; that of the man who is blamed for the defeat; that of the man who is blamed by the man who is blamed for the defeat. Out of such confusing elements, Johnson mused, history is written.[17] During the war, however, many reputations were advanced or damaged by the official reports, and if a high-ranking general was perceived as committing a serious blunder on the battlefield, he knew that his actions would be written up immediately and he could expect a rebuke at best or, at worst, to be fired or court-martialed.

General Grant was no different than any other officer in the Civil War in this respect. Like other generals, he suffered from negative reports and evaluations, as well as vicious attacks in the press. Like other generals, he cultivated certain politicians and reporters who would support him through thick and thin and to whom he would explain and justify controversial actions. Grant's great supporter in Congress during the war was Illinois Republican Elihu B. Washburne.[18] Washburne made sure that Grant's accomplishments were brought to the attention of President Lincoln. By August of 1863, with Vicksburg secured, Grant had emerged as Lincoln's favorite general. In that month Grant sent a crisp letter to the president informing Lincoln of his plans regarding the enrollment of black soldiers in the Union Army. He added, "I have given the subject of arming the Negro my hearty support. This, with the emancipation of the negro, is the heaviest blow yet given to the Confederacy." Those are exactly the words that Lincoln had been waiting to hear. Grant's wartime correspondence shows that he approached the ending of slavery as a practical problem to be dealt with as dictated by military necessities. Grant also judged the South harshly for slavery and often commented on the virtues of the free labor system. Grant's enthusiastic support, with both words and action, of Lincoln's emancipation policy endeared him to his commander-in-chief almost as much as his winning record on the field.[19]

Grant became a master of writing clear and forceful battle reports, presenting his views so successfully that his superiors—President Lincoln, Secretary of War Edwin Stanton, and Lincoln's chief military adviser, Henry Halleck—rarely disputed them. An aide observed Grant at his desk during the war: "His work was performed swiftly and uninterruptedly. . . . His thoughts flowed as freely from his mind as the ink from his pen."[20]

The same clarity of thought that marked his official reports was also present in his instructions to his subordinates in written orders, telegrams, and letters. A member of Gen. George Meade's staff remarked, "There is one striking feature of Grant's orders; no matter how hurriedly he may write them on the field, no one ever has the slightest doubt as to their meaning, or even has to read them over a second time to understand them." Examples of his superior prose—clear, incisive, and terse—abound.[21] During the Chattanooga campaign, Grant sent a brigadier general the following message: "Act upon the instructions you have, and your own discretion, and if you can do any thing to relieve Burnside, do it. It is not expected you will try to sacrifice your command, but that you will take the proper risks." Grant sent an urgent telegram to General Sheridan after the battle of Cedar Creek: "If it is possible to follow up your great victory until you reach the Central road and Canal do it even if you have to live on half rations." In the midst of the bloody battle known as Spotsylvania, Grant dashed off a communiqué to Stanton that contained a line subsequently famous because it demonstrated his resolve to fight to the end: "We have now entered the sixth day of very hard fighting. The result to this time is much in our favor. Our losses have been heavy as well as those of the enemy. . . . I propose to fight it out on this line if it takes all summer."[22] Grant's farewell message to Union soldiers issued on June 2, 1865, was written with heartfelt precision: "By your patriotic devotion to your country in the hour of danger and alarm . . . you have maintained the supremacy of the Union and the Constitution, overthrown all armed opposition to the enforcement of the Law, and of the Proclamations forever Abolishing Slavery, the cause and pretext of the Rebellion, and opened the way to the Rightful Authorities to restore Order and inaugerate [sic] Peace on a permanent and enduring basis on every foot of American soil."[23]

The constant stream of reports, orders, and letters issuing from Grant's headquarters sharpened his perceptions of the larger issues of the conflict—

loyalty, unionism, freedom, political democracy—as well as demonstrated his mastery of military strategy, thus uniting what Gen. Horace Porter called Grant's "singular mental powers and his rare military qualities."[24] By the end of the war, Grant had accumulated a treasure trove of materials from his headquarters' records to draw upon when he presented his 1866 "Report to Congress."

"Report to Congress"

In his report, Grant laid out for the nation's review the winning strategy of the war and how it was implemented for 1864–65. Firstly, "I ... determined ... to use the greatest number of troops practicable against the armed force of the enemy." Secondly, he determined "to hammer continuously against the armed force of the enemy, and his resources, until by *mere attrition*, if in no other way, there should be nothing left to him but an equal submission with the loyal section of our common country to the constitution and laws of the land."[25] Was the phrase "mere attrition" Grant's admission that the North won by sheer numbers and brute force? Did Grant diminish his own generalship? Hardly. He immediately pointed out the fact that no northern military leader (except himself) had been able to use the numerical superiority in the most effective way to achieve total victory.

Moreover, Grant argued that the South, in fact, enjoyed significant advantages: a vast territory, a largely united and supportive population, and long lines of river and railroad commerce. The North, Grant remembered, had huge disadvantages: a fractured, disaffected population politically represented by the Democratic Party. The Democrats, he observed, had an excellent chance to win the 1864 presidential election and perhaps end the war on terms unfavorable to the Union. In addition, enlistments were up, and too many experienced soldiers were honorably discharged and lost to the army when they were needed the most. However, enrollments were down. The people, he wrote, were sick and tired of the war. "It was a question," Grant reminded his readers, "whether our numerical strength and resources were not more than balanced by these disadvantages and the enemy's superior position."[26]

Presaging his later criticisms of the "marble man," Grant disparaged the generalship of his southern counterpart, Gen. Robert E. Lee, the commander of the Army of Northern Virginia. Grant praised Lee's dignity at

Appomattox Court House, the place where he accepted Lee's surrender on April 9, 1865. During the Overland campaign, however, Grant felt that Lee's defensive strategy had unnecessarily and tragically prolonged the war. Instead of meeting him face-to-face in battle, Grant said, "He acted purely on the defensive, behind breastworks, or feebly on the offensive immediately in front of them, and where, in case of repulse, he could easily retire behind them."[27] Grant wished the world to know that he and he alone of all the northern generals was fearless in the presence of Robert E. Lee.

The top northern general also made clear his low opinion of the Confederate nation: "In the South, a reign of military despotism prevailed, which made every man and boy capable of bearing arms a soldier; and those who could not bear arms in the field acted as provosts for collecting deserters and returning them. This enabled the enemy to bring almost his entire strength into the field."[28] Grant concluded the report with a tribute to the armies he commanded, a call for reconciliation, and stated, "Let them [Union soldiers] hope for perpetual peace and harmony with that enemy, whose manhood, however mistaken the cause, drew forth such herculean deeds of valor."[29]

Grant's 1866 "Report to Congress" provided the basic interpretation or "larger truth" of the war that for him no new information or factual evidence would ever change: The Union had justice on its side; the cause of the war was slavery; Confederates had advantages that offset Union superiority in both numbers and resources; northern soldiers fought just as well as southern soldiers, under more difficult conditions; and Robert E. Lee's generalship was deeply flawed. Later, Grant would say of Lee, "I never could see in his achievements what justifies his reputation. The illusion that nothing but heavy odds beat him will not stand the ultimate light of history."[30] How wrong he was in this assessment.

INFLUENCING THE HISTORY

U. S. Grant continued in public service, first as general-in-chief of the U.S. Army (1865–68) and then as president until 1877. While Grant could not devote time to writing the history of the war during these years, he did expend much energy to advance what he considered to be the "truth" of the war for public edification. There were three ways that he influenced the historical memory of the war during his presidency. First was the obvious symbolic nature of his position as the chief executive who was also the military savior of the Union; second was Grant's constant attention to veterans' needs and affairs; and third, his enthusiastic sponsorship of military histories that reflected his point of view.

Scholars and students of Grant's career often pose the question: Why did the deliberately apolitical commander-in-chief accept the 1868 nomination for the presidency? Did he want to be president for the power, or the glory? Many have argued that Grant was unprepared and naive, and, moreover, he could not have chosen a path more likely to destroy his cherished reputation.

According to Brooks D. Simpson, a highly respected Grant scholar and biographer, the answer is simple and straightforward, like the man. Grant agreed to be president during this incredibly difficult time because he did not wish to leave the legacy of the war in the hands of politicians. Grant explained his motives for accepting the nomination to his friend William T. Sherman: "I could not back down without, as it seems to me, leaving the contest for power for the next four years between mere trading politicians, the elevation of whom, no matter which party won, would lose to us, largely, the results of the costly war which we have gone through."[31] Simpson argues that Grant, throughout his presidency, remained steadfast in the belief that the goals of the war should be preserved in the policies of a firm Reconstruction that focused on establishing and protecting black economic and political rights. "My efforts in the future will be directed to the restoration of good feeling between the different sections of our common country," declared Grant in his second inaugural address. Those efforts, Grant made clear, included cementing the gains that had been made for African Americans: "The effects of the late civil strife have been to free the slave and make him a citizen. Yet he is not possessed of the civil rights which citizenship should carry with it."[32] Grant desired sectional harmony, but always in the service of remolding the South in the northern, and thus national mold. Grant later wrote to Elihu Washburn, "All that I want is that the government rule should remain in the hands of those who saved the Union until all the questions growing out of the war are forever settled."[33]

The Union Cause versus the Lost Cause

By the time Grant left the presidency in 1877 his views seemed increasingly out of date. The American people were tired of Reconstruction. Northerners, whether they were Democrats or Republicans, were now more willing to trust southern whites to protect black freedom, if not their right to vote, and to rule at home. The 1870s also witnessed the rise of a strictly southern history of the Civil War that disparaged Grant's generalship.

The North's, and Grant's, interpretation of the righteousness of the Union Cause was challenged in the decades after the war by an ideology about the Confederate nation called the "Lost Cause." The elements that define the Lost Cause are well-known: The cause of the war was not slavery but states rights; southern armies were never defeated but rather overwhelmed by numbers; the southern soldier was brave and true, echoing the perfection of the patron saint of the Lost Cause, the courtly Virginia gentleman of impeccable lineage Gen. Robert E. Lee. In the pages of the influential journal the *Southern Historical Society Papers* and in numerous speeches to southern veterans groups, ex-Confederate general Jubal A. Early and his supporters actively and successfully promoted their own version of "truthful history." There was a milder variation of the Lost Cause that was appealing to northerners as well.

For the unreconstructed, however, it was not enough to idolize Robert E. Lee; Ulysses S. Grant's reputation had to be destroyed.[34] From the 1870s onward, the "myths" of Lee and Grant assumed distinctly different trajectories. Taking his cue from the content of Lee's 1865 farewell address ("The Army of Northern Virginia has been compelled to yield to overwhelming numbers and resources"), Early claimed that Grant was a bloody butcher who was not even remotely equal to Lee as a military strategist or tactician. Moreover, he used an impressive array of facts and figures gathered for the purpose of putting before the public the Confederate side of the story.[35]

The negative portrayal of Grant that emerged not only tarnished Grant's national and international military stature but also increased Lee's, which was the goal. Referring in part to the pro-Confederate histories that were critical of him, Grant said, "The cry was in the air that the North only won by brute force; that the generalship and valor were with the South. This has gone into history, with so many other illusions that are historical."[36] This seemingly unstoppable, and to Grant, grotesque, adulation of Lee was neatly summed up by the English writer Matthew Arnold, who explained that in his view Grant "is not to the English imagination the hero of the American Civil War; the hero is Lee."[37] Just as Lee was presented as a flawless icon, so the Confederate cause was whitewashed. States' rights was elevated to be the southern cause worth living and dying for, not slavery. Reflecting the sectional divide during the war, two sharply differing interpretations of the conflict emerged in full force only a decade after Appomattox.[38]

Grant was aware that Lee's reputation was in some ways overshadowing his own. The growing influence of the Lost Cause owed much to the power of the criticisms hurled against Grant's hated Reconstruction policy in the South. From the pages of Early's *Southern Historical Society Papers* came a decidedly hostile evaluation of Grant's presidency: "In reviewing the history of this century it will be impossible to find a rule so barren of statesmanship . . . as Grant's has been. . . . It is uncharitable and of little profit to speculate upon the remnant of his life left to him. But we may well believe 'his [remaining] days will be few and evil.'"[39] White southerners connected Grant's brutal generalship with his so-called imposition of Republican rule on the defeated region.

However, Grant connected the goals of the war—reunion and freedom— with an attempt, very imperfect, to make the South a place where black and white, Republican and Democrat could live together. He failed. "There has never been a moment since Lee surrendered," Grant said ruefully, "that I would not have gone more than halfway to meet the southern people in a spirit of conciliation. But they have never responded to it. They have not forgotten the war."[40]

Ironically, in the next century, understanding or appreciation of the Union Cause steadily declined against the appeal of southern nobility and romanticism. Although the Lost Cause ideology has been thoroughly discredited in the university, it retains a powerful grip on popular imagination, albeit in a less racist form than during the last decades of the nineteenth century. The myth of Robert E. Lee is still immensely appealing to large numbers of Americans, and not just southern Americans. Lee's brilliant generalship, his stainless character, supposed old-fashioned, gentlemanly style of war, and noble acceptance of defeat commends him to us.[41] In contrast, the warfare conducted by U. S. Grant—butcher, drunk, and above all lucky—is repellent because it has been deemed modern. "Grant was a preview of the dead-eyed murderers one meets in fictional and factual twentieth-century texts," declared Andrew Delbanco.[42] This statement from a highly regarded historian reflects the standard Lost Cause mythology, although he would undoubtedly distance himself from that worldview. Often, the revolutionary, progressive impact of the Union's victory is downplayed, brushed aside, or ignored, especially in light of the failures of Reconstruction. Perhaps that stance is appropriate for skeptical times. Grant and the generation of Americans who lived through the Civil War did not, as a rule, embrace either skepticism or moral relativism. That is what made the stakes so high and so meaningful in controlling the historical memory of the war for future generations.

Grant enjoyed a special relationship, during and after his presidency, with the Union veterans. A powerful interest group whose influence extended widely and deeply into the country's political, social, and economic sectors, the veterans who joined organizations like the Grand Army of the Republic were the bulwark of the Republican Party for many years.[43] A review of President Grant's calendar and correspondence for just one year, 1873, provides compelling evidence of the enormous investment of time, energy, and passion on his part to keep the "Union Cause," before the citizenry and before the judgment of history.[44] Although he accepted many fewer invitations than he received, Grant made frequent appearances at veterans' reunions and other commemorative occasions, striking a balance between the Union's eastern and western wings. On February 6, "the Great Commander" attended a meeting in Wilmington, Delaware; May 15 found him at an Army of the Potomac reunion in New Haven, Connecticut; on September 17 the veterans of the Army of the Cumberland enjoyed their former top general's presence at an event in Pittsburgh; while on October 15–16 Grant joined the two-day reunion of the Army of the Tennessee in Toledo, Ohio. He enjoyed being with "his old comrades in arms," declaring the meetings as being "attended . . . with a revival of old associations and sympathies, formed in such trying times."[45]

The president supported a new holiday commemorating the deaths of Union soldiers. On May 21, 1873, Grant issued an order closing the government "in order to enable the employees of the Government to participate, in connection with the Grand Army of the Republic, in the decoration of the graves of the soldiers who fell during the rebellion." Grant did more than attend celebrations and support Decoration Day. He also answered innumerable letters from veterans asking for government pensions for injuries or losses. Grant also reviewed manuscripts on the war and weighed in on some of the numerous controversies about the war.[46]

During his years as president, Grant rarely responded personally to criticism of his military leadership. He did defend his reputation indirectly, and by doing so, influenced the writing of Civil War history. As one historian commented wryly, "Grant's apparent indifference to what was said about him masked reality."[47] He lent his prestige, his oral recollections, and his collection of wartime materials to reporters and partisans who wrote important defenses of his generalship. The first significant volume to appear was that of Adam Badeau in 1868. Badeau, Grant's military secretary during the last year of the war, was in part responding to William Swinton's *Campaigns of the Army of the Potomac* (published) in 1866. Swinton, a northern journalist banned by Grant during the war, argued that Lee in the 1864 Overland campaign, although vastly outnumbered by the Union army, managed to outgeneral the blundering Grant. Then, instead of a certain and relatively painless victory, Lee forced the Union commander to settle for a costly siege at Petersburg. Not surprisingly, Swinton's work was highly praised by the southern press and condemned in many northern circles.

Badeau's book (eventually the three-volume *Military History of Ulysses S. Grant, 1868–1882*) was respectfully received by some and bitterly denounced by southern partisans, who were particularly outraged by Badeau's claim (which was Grant's) that the pro-Confederate historians inflated Union troop numbers while minimizing their own. Badeau's first volume in particular was the object of controversy in northern newspapers allied with the Democratic Party, always hostile to Grant. One such attack claimed, "It is in everything but name the carefully prepared memoir of Grant, by himself." Calling the memoirs a "Panegyric and special pleading," the reviewer said, "For his own good name and fame it is to be lamented that he did not put the task in more competent hands."[48] This unfriendly review provided evidence that Grant was almost as controversial within some parts of northern society as he appeared to be in the South. Nevertheless, he was most definitely the guiding force behind Badeau's history, and he expressed satisfaction that Badeau had rebutted effectively Swinton and especially the circle led by Jubal Early.

Other Grant partisans who wrote admiring accounts of his wartime achievements were Horace Porter and John Russell Young, a reporter for the *New York Herald*. Young accompanied the ex-president and his wife Julia on their two-year (1877–79) world journey as they visited the European continent and many other countries. Grant gave Young a series of remarkable interviews in which he offered candid and controversial reflections on the art of war, on Union and Confederate generals, other Civil War leaders, and important battles, particularly Shiloh. Young's recounting of the general's "conversations," published in the *Herald* (and later in a book, *Around the World with General Grant*), were reviewed carefully by Grant.

Many of Grant's pronouncements caused controversy and discussion back home, including his thoughts about Robert E. Lee's generalship. Grant's analysis printed in Young's interviews formed the basis for his evaluation of Lee found in *The Personal Memoirs*.[49] His assessment of Lee was harsh: "Lee was a good man, a fair commander, who had everything in his favor. He was a man who needed sunshine. He was supported by the unanimous voice of the South; he was supported by a large party in the North, he had the support and sympathy of the outside world ... [and he] was treated like a demi-god."[50] Moreover, Grant rejected the Lost Cause claim that the two sides fought for equally honorable causes. Although Grant lauded the courage of the Rebel soldier, he attacked the idea that only southern soldiers were brave: "When I look for brave, noble characters in the war, men whom death has surrounded with romance, I see them in characters like McPherson, and not alone in southern armies." He was also distressed by recent attacks on his character and military abilities and, by extension, on the typical northern citizen soldiers. "While I would do nothing to revive unhappy memories in the South," Grant declared, "I do not like to see our soldiers apologize for the war."[51]

Quite obviously, there was sharp contention over which version of history was "truthful." For Grant, as for others who wrote about the war in the two and a half decades immediately following 1865, there were "facts," verifiable, quantifiable, recoverable, objective, rational. As this essay demonstrates, he sought the most accurate and up-to-date factual information with which to make his case. These facts could be retrieved from memory, from conversations, from written reports, letters, maps, telegrams, and diaries. Facts were supposedly objective and formed the narrative of history. There was also a "truth." Truth was derived from facts, but not dependent upon them. Truth was subjective and morally based. The truth had a higher meaning. Truth was based in the facts but ultimately not answerable to them. Today, professional historians call truth, interpretation.[52]

That Grant read, digested, and was displeased with so many of the newly published accounts of the war was evident in his comment that they "only show how often history is warped and mischief made." Such writers "study out dispatches, and reach conclusions which appear sound ... but which are unsound in this, that they know only the dispatches, and nothing of the conversation and other incidents that might have a material effect upon the truth." Grant concluded, "Wars produce many stories of fiction, some of which are told until they are believed to be true."[53]

OFFICIAL RECORDS OF THE WAR OF THE REBELLION

Grant's comment was made at a time when more and more material with which to evaluate the war was being published. A monumental decision in favor of making the history of the war permanently accessible was handed down by the federal government in 1864. The goal was to publish the complete records (battle reports, telegraph messages, and so on) of the Federal and Confederate armies of the Civil War. The story of the funding, the debates over the location of the records, and the intense editorial politics of the publication of the 128 volumes of the *Official Records of the War of the Rebellion* (OR) is almost as fascinating as the war itself. The editors of the *OR* selected materials to be published if deemed "significant, official, and produced during the war."[54]

There was a vast amount of paperwork collected. The Civil War was the first conflict during which so many records were written and were required to be copied, recopied, and stored. Veterans and their organizations—who, along with military historians, were considered to be the buying public for the *Official Records*—supported the project with enthusiasm. By 1877 forty-seven volumes were completed, with the first one published in 1881. Needless to say, veterans were not the only ones to have benefited from the *OR*, as generations of professional historians have used it as an indispensable source.

Equally momentous was the decision by the War Records Office to make this project as nonpartisan and as nonpolitical as possible. This dedication was present even before the project was officially launched. Gen. Henry Halleck ordered Confederate records retrieved from the burning ruins of Richmond, declaring them to be important to the history of the conflict. Grant lent his strong support to the effort in an 1865 letter to Edwin Stanton: "If it is desirable to have all rebel documents Captured in Richmond and elsewhere in the South examined and notes made of their contents for convenient reference I would respectfully recommend Brig. Gn. Alvord . . . for the duty."[55] Throughout the 1870s and 1880s, over fifty tons of materials was stored in various buildings in the D.C. area.

From the beginning, then, the *OR* set a high professional standard of even-handedness in the portrayal of the war. Every effort was made to locate and include Confederate military records and publish them alongside the more voluminous Union records. The War Records Office hired former Union and Confederate officers as editors. Government officials formed a liaison with ex-Confederate brigadier general Marcus J. Wright, who scoured the South for hidden treasure troves. This liaison led to an agreement between the *Southern Historical Society Papers* (*SHSP*) and the War Record Office for "reciprocal free access" to each other's Confederate documents. Generally, the volumes of the *OR* were praised in the pages of the *SHSP*.[56]

The influential publishing project's emphasis on fairness to both sides was echoed in the larger society's desire for reconciliation. As the extreme bitterness of the war years receded, another interpretation, or "truth," about the Civil War emerged. It took the least controversial elements from both sides—North (the Union Cause) and South (the Lost Cause)—in an effort to bolster an official national ideology upon which a majority of citizens could agree. This interpretation, rising in popularity by the 1880s, can be described as promoting "sectional harmony." Increasingly, the idea that slavery caused the war and that the Union Army became a revolutionary instrument in bringing freedom to millions of slaves became an embarrassment, an impediment, to reconciliation. As such, the African American presence before, during, and after the war was de-emphasized.[57]

This denatured ideology encouraged a professional and nonpartisan style of writing the history of the war. The emphasis on reconciliation was supported by important elements of the northern and southern press and public, and to a more limited extent by veterans, especially in the blue and gray reunions that were regularly held on the anniversary of important battles, like Gettysburg. The less divisive explanation of the great conflict portrayed the two sides as equally honorable. Both sides fought for noble causes, and happily, for white harmony's sake, the still controversial issues of slavery and emancipation were rarely mentioned.

THE CENTURY SERIES

The popular press both inspired and reflected reconciliation sentiment. Scribner's profited greatly with their well-received volumes of *Campaigns of the Civil War*. Then, in 1884, the first issue of the famous *Century Magazine*'s serial "Battles and Leaders of the Civil War" appeared. The leading officers of the war published their accounts of important battles in the series. Conceived in the early 1880s, editors Robert Underwood Johnson and Clarence Buel explicitly demanded neutral contributions from their authors. Johnson later described the series thusly: "On the whole 'Battle and Leaders of the Civil War' is a monument to American bravery, persistence and resourcefulness, and has the additional distinction of having struck the keynote of national unity through tolerance and the promotion of good will. We rightly judged that articles celebrating the skill and valor of both sides would hasten the elimination of sectional prejudices and contribute toward reuniting the country by the cultivation of mutual respect."[58]

Although not every contributor hewed to the stated guidelines, most did, and the series was a smashing success, if judged by the quality of the contributions and the extraordinary rise in subscriptions for the magazine. The publication of the series, fortunately, from the editors' point of view, coincided with U. S. Grant's need to earn money for his family. A famous collaboration was born as Grant agreed to write four articles for the series, which ensured prestige and profits for the magazine.

U. S. GRANT, HISTORIAN

Grant had actually refused the editors' entreaties to be a participant, but early in the summer of 1884, broke from the failure of his last business enterprise, he agreed to write four accounts of major battles for $500 (later raised to $1,000). His first submission, "The Battle of Shiloh," was stilted and formal. Johnson disliked it immensely and begged Grant to adopt a more casual, entertaining style. Grant quickly rewrote the article to everyone's satisfaction. Its immediate success brought forth an offer from Johnson and the Century Publishing Company for an exclusive book from the general. But by this time there were several publishing firms bidding for Grant's complete memoirs.

The same day, October 22, 1884, that Grant learned he was ill with cancer, he verbally accepted the *Century* contract that provided him with 10 percent royalties on an expected subscription sale of 25,000 sets. Mark Twain and his nephew and business partner, Charles Webster, counteroffered in December with a $50,000 advance and, to sweeten the deal, 70 percent of the profits. U. S. Grant could not refuse those terms, and he signed their contract on February 27, 1885, just five months before his death. Well before the contract was signed, however, Grant was working hard on his manuscript, which was going to be divided into two volumes (volume 1: birth to Vicksburg; volume 2: Chattanooga campaign to Appomattox).

Grant's work methods are well documented. With pen in hand, and later through dictation, Grant provided the narrative structure of the book. Elsie Porter, daughter of Horace Porter, recorded that her father and Adam

Badeau met with Grant daily in the summer of 1884. She vividly recalled Grant writing with his pencil "racing over his pad."[59] He usually worked from a table—in the kitchen or on the pleasant piazza overlooking the sea at his summer home in Long Branch, New Jersey, where he wrote the *Century* articles. Later, in the Grants' New York City brownstone, his writing table was set in a small room at the head of the stairs.

In Grant's final days in the cottage at Mount McGregor, when he was too weak to sit at a proper desk, a specially constructed lap table was made available. In all of these places, Grant's surrounding "office" space was crammed with his maps, his primary materials, and his books. A friend and former Union general, James Grant Wilson, noted the obsessive nature of Grant's writing: "His mind was absorbed with the one subject of his military autobiography and a desire to be accurate in the most minute particulars. . . . In all matters aside from his book Grant took but a slight and passing interest."[60]

Grant's written or transcribed draft would then be passed along to his "staff." Grant had a small group of researchers and assistants to help him revise, edit, check facts and dates, and procure other needed papers. "What part are you reading up and verifying?" he asked his son, Frederick Dent Grant, who was his principal, although not only, assistant.[61] Other staff at various times included Adam Badeau; Horace Porter; Fred's wife Ida Grant; his two other sons, Ulysses Jr. and Jesse Grant; Harrison Tyrell, his personal valet; Nathan E. Dawson, his stenographer; and his two principal doctors, John H. Douglas and Henry M. Shrady. Mark Twain also played an important role in facilitating the publication of both volumes. In mid-March Twain checked the manuscript's progress almost daily, and by mid-April he was correcting the galley proofs for grammatical and other errors.[62]

Chronology is critical in understanding the evolution of *The Personal Memoirs*. From September 1884 to March 1885, Grant was able to work in a fairly productive and calm manner. The first volume was almost entirely handwritten by Grant before the worst of his illness set in and is generally considered to be superior to the second volume, which was largely dictated, or written when he lost his voice and was suffering from intense pain. The period from late March to his death in July was punctuated with constant medical crises, during which he was temporarily incapacitated. Indeed, the dosages of cocaine, and later morphine, given by Grant's doctors often prevented him from working with a clear head. Drs. Douglas and Shrady demonstrated a great sensitivity toward Grant's desire to finish his work. They both expressed amazement at his dedication. Douglas recalled a typical consultation where they "found the General engaged in writing. As we entered he raised his hand and said, 'I shall reach a period in a moment.' . . . After the consultation, he resumed his literary work, and I learned, at my evening visit, that he had worked in all four or five hours."[63] The two doctors, along with the members of his family (especially Fred and his valet, Harrison), are to be credited with providing the controlled and supportive environment which allowed the desperately ill general to complete his memoirs.[64]

During this time Grant wrote, or directed Fred to write, letters to pertinent individuals seeking information about precise dates, movements, and details of various battles. He wrote to the War Department as well, asking for specific maps or documents, which the department was only too happy to send to him. Clearly, writing his memoirs had become the major and only pleasurable activity during his illness, and as William McFeely observed, "The book was now his life."[65]

In April of 1885 Grant headed off a potentially disastrous threat to the sales and reception of his history. Adam Badeau, his military biographer and current hired assistant, became unhappy at his increasingly marginalized status within the Grant household. Badeau was a professional writer who rightly considered himself the expert on U. S. Grant's military career. He was contemptuous of the idea of Grant writing his memoirs and was bitterly at odds with Fred Grant, who replaced Badeau as his father's chief assistant. Badeau was worried that the publication of Grant's book would cut into his own books' profitability. Badeau told Grant that publication would damage "my reputation as your historian."[66] He demanded a renegotiation of his contract, which Grant refused. His unhappiness found its way into a newspaper article in the Democratic newspaper the *New York World* that implied strongly that Badeau, not Grant, was the author of the forthcoming memoirs. Hurt and angry, Grant immediately wrote a rejoinder in which he unequivocally stated that "the Composition is entirely my own."[67] Badeau was fired from the project, and bitter feelings between him and the Grant heirs continued for many years. For Grant, however, the painful issue was resolved with satisfaction, and with continued support and perseverance, he was able to complete his memoirs.

THE PERSONAL MEMOIRS OF U. S. GRANT: AN EVALUATION

The Personal Memoirs can be said to offer many things to many people. Grant's volumes are a history of the Civil War, an unmatched military narrative of the conflict, a carefully constructed autobiography of a man, a commentary on American character and institutions, and an exegesis of the Union Cause. They provide a comprehensive and uniquely rich story of the war between the United States and the Confederate States of America. Grant's memoirs are far superior to those published by other leading military officials of the Civil War, including the books written by the two other top Union generals, William T. Sherman and Philip Sheridan. The volumes follow the war chronologically, providing analysis and background on specific battles, overall military strategy, portraits of people, and description of events.[68]

U. S. Grant portrayed himself as a representative character of the northern nation, the victorious nation. In doing so, he consciously, or unconsciously, invited the reader to appreciate the good, solid if unspectacular virtues of the typical northerner living in a free labor society. Grant took pains to point out his many "flaws": his simple and rustic background, his trusting nature, and his unmilitary-like bearing. His personal simplicity endeared him to his soldiers and retained the northern veterans' loyalty to his death. The same simplicity is present in his writing style and is similarly endearing. Grant continued his own story by remarking that he did not do well at West Point and was uncertain if he would continue in the professional army at all. Although he distinguished himself in the Mexican War of 1846–48, he did not support that effort, declaring the war "one of the most unjust ever waged by a stronger against a weaker nation." Grant's hero in that war was not the tall, aristocratic Winfield Scott, which raised a deliberate contrast between himself and Lee, who admired Scott. Although Grant made clear that he did admire Scott's abilities, his true model was the plain, simple soldier, later president, Zachary Taylor, who eschewed fancy dress uniforms and spit and polish for a commonsensical approach to battle and to life.[69]

Slavery is addressed throughout the memoirs, interwoven with Grant's discussions of the causes and consequences of the Civil War. In one such discussion Grant traced the war with Mexico to the southern states' desire to expand its slaveholding territory: "The Southern rebellion was largely the outgrowth of the Mexican war. Nations, like individuals, are punished for their transgressions. We got our punishment in the most sanguinary and expensive war of modern times."[70] Grant presented an articulate overview of the events that led to the outbreak of war in 1861. His position reflected exactly the antislavery position of the 1850s Republican Party. The South had to control the national government in order to protect slavery, the foundation of its prosperity. The North was compelled to prevent the extension of slavery in order to protect free labor. Secession and the rebellion that followed were treasonous and had to be stopped. The subsequent detailed unfolding of Grant's wartime career provided his firsthand view of the inexorable march toward the end of the system of slavery, first as a military and political necessity, and then as moral imperative.[71]

There were other issues to contend with in *The Personal Memoirs*. As the leading Union general, Grant's portrayal (both facts and truth) of the war and separate battles was influential, but by no means was it universally accepted either by northerners or southerners. During and after the war, his actions sparked controversy, and there were criticisms of Grant's generalship that appeared in newspapers, articles, and books, particularly surrounding the Battle of Shiloh in April of 1862 and the Overland campaign in the spring of 1864.[72] Indeed, Shiloh is a good example of facts/truth as played out in *The Personal Memoirs*. There were two controversies on the northern side of Shiloh. First, Grant was unprepared for the Confederate attack on the morning of April 6, 1862. Second, his failure to prepare the ground defensively resulted in a devastating defeat that was only staved off by the timely arrival of General Buell's division, and thus the credit for the victory should have gone to Buell, not Grant.

Grant wrote a strong rebuttal based on his evidence: he was not surprised by the attack; he himself was all over the field deploying "green" troops and staving off disaster; Buell's men, while very welcome, did not "save" the battle, because the Confederates clearly were going to be defeated the next day anyway. Facts were disputed bitterly in histories of the battle, and oppositional points of view remained entrenched.[73]

Grant mitigated his criticism of another general, Lew Wallace, when new information on Wallace's role at Shiloh came to light.[74] Grant never, however, wavered in his larger truth of Shiloh. First, Shiloh was the making of the western armies. Second, Shiloh convinced him that the South would not give up, even after suffering a string of terrible defeats: "Up to the battle of Shiloh, I, as well as thousands of other citizens, believed that the rebellion against the Government would collapse suddenly and soon, if a decisive victory could be gained over any of its armies.... [After Shiloh] I gave up all idea of saving the Union except by complete conquest."[75] This interpretation was very important to Grant in advancing his larger argument within the memoirs about Union motives and strategy throughout the rest of the war. The "hard hand of war," Grant argued, was brought about by southern intransigence: "The Northern troops were never more cruel than the necessities of war required."[76]

Understandably, Grant explained and defended his actions (as he could not during the war itself) against newspaper charges and coverage that he considered shoddy, inaccurate, and defeatist. Indeed Grant's sensitivity to reporters and the impact of the press demonstrated a keen appreciation for the political nature of the Civil War. He constantly drew attention to the "big picture," never allowing the reader to forget that battlefield fortunes were linked to the home front. His explanation of Vicksburg was typical: "The campaign of Vicksburg was suggested and developed by circumstances. The elections of 1862 had gone against the prosecution of the war. Voluntary enlistments had nearly ceased and the draft had been resorted to; this was resisted, and a defeat or backward movement would have made its execution impossible. A forward movement to a decisive victory was necessary." Commenting on Lincoln's chances of reelection in 1864, he stated that Sherman and Sheridan's "two campaigns probably had more effect in settling the election of the following November then all the speeches, all the bonfires and all the parading with banners and bars of music in the North."[77]

There is an obvious connection in *The Personal Memoirs* between Grant's personal memories, the era's social or historical memory (the memory of millions in a generation who shared war experiences), his ability to turn those experiences into meaningful narratives, and history (written accounts purporting to be objective).[78] A caveat: what ostensibly was an "autobiography" was not in any way like current autobiographies, that is, a form of intimate personal revelation. Many embarrassments were left out. One can search in vain, for example, for any reference to his struggle with alcohol or his famous General Order No. 11 (December 1862) barring Jews from his command. *The Personal Memoirs* also fails to provide an evenhanded history, as much more attention is given to the western theater of the war than the eastern theater. This flaw is corrected after Grant moves east in 1864! No time is spent on his two troubled terms as president, although his observations on the effect of Lincoln's assassination were trenchant and timely. Grant also did not leave any record as to his thoughts on Reconstruction policy, although a hint came in the last chapter: "The story of the legislation enacted during the reconstruction period . . . is too fresh in the minds of the people to be told now."[79]

CONCLUSION

The Personal Memoirs of U. S. Grant presented the moral, as well as the political, economic, and social, argument for waging war against the rebellious
states and touted the benefits of the destruction of slavery for the southern
people. Yet, more often than not, Grant's memoirs are also celebrated for the
theme of reconciliation. In an oft-quoted passage Grant wrote, "I feel that
we are on the eve of a new era, when there is to be great harmony between
the Federal and the Confederate. I cannot stay to be a living witness to the
correctness of this prophecy; but I feel it within me that it is to be so."[80]
Embedded within the style and substance of Grant's *Personal Memoirs* is
a contradiction that was also played out in his public actions. On the one
hand, Grant was the magnanimous victor of Appomattox who said, "The
war is over. The rebels are our countrymen again." The thrust of the war was
reunion with the "rebellious" states. On the other hand, Grant also was the
head of the Union Army, responsible after 1863 for smashing the institution of slavery and bringing a revolution in race relations. There is no doubt
that Grant deeply hoped for a permanent and genuine restoration of "great
harmony" between North and South. But what exactly did he mean by expressing that desire? Did he mean that sectional peace (which all agreed was
a good thing) should deliberately elide a still widely accepted belief among
northerners in 1885 that it was the Union, and not the Confederate cause,
that was noble? Do Grant's memoirs reflect this sentiment?

In his memoirs, Grant sought to bring back what he perceived was the
reality of those causes, even as he promoted reconciliation—but on northern terms. True enough, *The Personal Memoirs*, which is "dedicated to the
American soldier and sailor," has much about Civil War battles. It notice-
ably highlights the courage and valor of the soldiers on both sides. But by
describing what happened on those battlefields, Grant tellingly emphasized
that citizens can learn about the history of a nation, a nation that was forged
anew at Appomattox with Union victory.

Thus, readers of *The Personal Memoirs of U. S. Grant* will note Grant's
contempt for the southern cause of slavery, and for the general so associated
with that cause, Robert E. Lee. He explained why the "complete conquest"
was necessary to destroy slavery, save the Union, and restore harmony. The
victor, not the vanquished, Grant claimed, should dictate the terms to end
the war and should define the conditions for the reestablishment of peace
and harmony within the Union. Grant's memoirs offer readers a stark and

ugly depiction of a southern society mired in backwardness and deeply tainted by slavery. The thrust of his history emphasized the best qualities of northern free democratic society, avoiding serious criticism of America. He concluded that the modern war waged by the United States benefited, and would continue to benefit, the former Confederate Nation: "The war begot a spirit of independence and enterprise."[81] Indeed through his frequent tributes to northern character and civilization Grant was not only highlighting the superiority of wartime Union strength and resources but also asserting the ideological superiority of northern free labor over southern slave labor.

The essence of Grant's memoirs goes beyond a definition of autobiography: "the writing of one's own history."[82] The eminent military scholar John Keegan commented that Grant had provided "an enthralling history of one man's generalship, perhaps the most revelatory autobiography of high command to exist in any language." Grant's volumes were a deliberately triumphal narrative of the Civil War written from the viewpoint of the man most closely identified with bringing about northern victory. But the individual is merged with the event and the era, leading Keegan to conclude rightly, "If there is a single contemporary document which explains 'why the North won the Civil War,' it is *The Personal Memoirs of U. S. Grant.*"[83]

NOTES

Joan Waugh delivered her Klement Lecture in 2003.

1. Ulysses S. Grant, *The Personal Memoirs of U. S. Grant*, 2 vols., eds. Mary Drake McFeely and William S. McFeely (New York: Library of America, 1984), 1:169 (hereafter *PMUSG*).

2. Bruce Catton, "U. S. Grant: Man of Letters," *American Heritage* 19 (June 1968).

3. U. S. Grant to Julia Dent Grant, July 8, 1885, the Papers of Ulysses S. Grant, Series 10, box 2, Manuscript Division, Library of Congress (LC), Washington, D.C.

4. This account of Grant writing his memoirs is based partly on the following: Adam Badeau, *Grant in Peace: From Appomattox to Mount McGregor, a Personal Memoir* (Hartford, Conn., 1887), and "The Last Days of General Grant," *Century Magazine* 30 (Oct. 1885). Richard Goldhurst, *Many Are the Hearts: The Agony and Triumph of Ulysses S. Grant* (New York: Thomas Y. Crowell Co., 1975); William S. McFeely, *Grant: A Biography* (New York: W. W. Norton, 1982); *PMUSG*, 2:1162–70; and Thomas Pitkin, *The Captain Departs: Ulysses S. Grant's Last Campaign* (Carbondale: Southern Illinois Univ. Press, 1973).

5. *The American Heritage Dictionary of the English Language*, ed. William Morris (Boston: Houghton Mifflin, 1969). Autobiography as a genre is considered in the following: Joyce Appleby, *Inheriting the Revolution* (Cambridge, Mass.: Harvard Univ. Press, 2000); Robert Folkenflick, ed., *The Culture of Autobiography: Constructions of Self-Representation* (Stanford Univ. Press, 1993); Jacquelyn Dowd

Hall, "'You Must Remember This': Autobiography as Social Critique," *The Journal of American History* 85 (Sept. 1998): 439–65; and Charles Taylor, *Sources of the Self: The Making of Modern Identity* (Cambridge, Mass.: Harvard Univ. Press, 1989).

6. *PMUSG*, 2:773.

7. Ibid., 779.

8. Frederick Douglass, "U. S. Grant and the Colored People: His Wise, Just, Practical and Effective Friendship," speech given on July 17, 1872, in Washington, D.C., Special Collections, UCLA, Westwood, Calif.

9. Qtd. in Catton, "U. S. Grant: Man of Letters," 98.

10. Daniel Aaron, *The Unwritten War: American Writers and the Civil War* (Madison: Univ. of Wisconsin Press, 1987); James M. McPherson and William J. Cooper Jr., eds., *Writing the Civil War* (Columbia: Univ. of South Carolina Press, 1998).

11. Edward E. Henry, Fremont, Ohio, 23rd Regiment Ohio Volunteers, to U. S. Grant, June 22, 1885, in U. S. Grant Family Correspondence, box 15, Grant Papers, LC.

12. Mark Twain, "Rejoinder," in Matthew Arnold, *General Grant*, ed. and intro. by John Y. Simon (Kent, Ohio: Kent State Univ. Press), 57. Twain (also known as Samuel Clemens) was not only an admirer of Grant but was an investor in Webster and Co. and profited from the sales of *The Personal Memoirs*.

13. There were dissenters. Perhaps a few ex-Confederates bought *The Personal Memoirs* as a gesture to the magnanimous victor at Appomattox. More probably agreed with the dismissive review given by the influential organ of the ex-Confederate officers, *The Southern Historical Society Papers*. That review described *The Personal Memoirs* as "a book full of blunders and flat contradictions of the official reports (both Federal and Confederate), and the future historian who attempts to follow it will be led very far astray from the real truth." *SHSP* 14 (1886): 574–76.

14. Bruce Chadwick, *The Reel Civil War: Mythmaking in American Film* (New York: Knopf, 2001), and Jim Cullen, *The Civil War in Popular Culture: A Reusable Past*, are two of the best books that include discussions of the impact of *Gone With the Wind* and the Lost Cause on American culture.

15. John Y. Simon, *Ulysses S. Grant: One Hundred Years Later* (Springfield: Illinois State Historical Society, 1986), 245–56.

16. *The Personal Memoirs* have never gone out of print. For discussion of the work's importance, see Edmund Wilson, *Patriotic Gore* (New York: Oxford Univ. Press, 1962), 133; Bruce Catton, "Two Porches, Two Parades," *American Heritage* 19 (June 1968): 99; John Keegan, *The Mask of Command* (London: Jonathan Cape, 1987); and McFeely, *Grant: A Biography*. Three recent editions of *The Personal Memoirs* include *PMUSG*, eds. Mary Drake McFeely and William S. McFeely; *Personal Memoirs*, intro. and notes by James M. McPherson (New York: Penguin, 1999); and *Personal Memoirs of U. S. Grant*, intro. Brooks D. Simpson (Lincoln: Univ. of Nebraska Press, 1996).

17. Robert Underwood Johnson, *Remembered Yesterdays* (Boston: Little Brown, 1923), 193.

18. This noteworthy relationship is chronicled in the Elihu Washburne Papers, Manuscript Division, LC. Grant's relationship with journalists is the topic of Harry J. Maihafer, *The General and the Journalists* (New York: Brassey's Inc., 1998); and Sylvanus Cadwallader, *Three Years with Grant*, ed. Benjamin P. Thomas (Lincoln: Univ. of Nebraska Press, 1996).

19. *The Papers of Ulysses S. Grant*, ed. John Y. Simon et al. 28 vols. (Carbondale: Southern Illinois Univ. Press, 1967–), 9:196 (hereafter *PUSG*). For insightful discussions of Grant's relationship with Lincoln, see Gabor S. Boritt, ed., *Lincoln's Generals* (New York: Oxford Univ. Press, 1994); and Joseph T. Glatthaar, *Partners in Command: The Relationships Between Leaders in the Civil War* (New York: Free Press, 1994). Grant's stance on black soldiers is explored in Brooks D. Simpson, "Quandries of Command: Ulysses Grant and Black Soldiers," in David W. Bight and Brooks D. Simpson, eds., *Union and Emancipation* (Kent, Ohio: Kent State Univ. Press, 1997), 123–50.

20. Horace Porter, *Campaigning with Grant* (New York: Century Co., 1897), 7.

21. Qtd. in Keegan, "Grant and Unheroic Leadership," *The Mask of Command*, 200. See also James M. McPherson, "Grant's Final Victory," in *Drawn with the Sword: Reflections on the American Civil War* (New York: Oxford Univ. Press, 1996), 159–73, for a superb discussion of Grant's writing style from his battlefield reports to his memoirs.

22. *PUSG*, 9:436–37, 12:334, 10:422.

23. Ulysses S. Grant, General Orders No. 108, Ibid., 15:120–21.

24. Porter, *Campaigning with Grant*, 514.

25. Ulysses S. Grant, "Report of Lieutenant-General U. S. Grant, of the United States Armies—1864–65," *PMUSG*, 2:781–848; Brooks D. Simpson, "Continuous Hammering and Mere Attrition: Lost Cause Critics and the Military Reputation of Ulysses S. Grant," in Gary W. Gallagher and Alan T. Nolan, eds., *The Myth of the Lost Cause and Civil War History* (Bloomington: Indiana Univ. Press, 2000): 147–69.

26. *PMUSG*, 2:781.

27. Ibid., 794.

28. Ibid., 783.

29. Ibid., 847–48.

30. Qtd. in John Russell Young, *Around the World with General Grant: A Narrative of the Visit of General U. S. Grant, Ex-President of the United States, to Various Countries in Europe, Asia, and Africa, in 1877, 1878, 1879*, 2 vols. (New York: American News Co., 1897), 2:459.

31. *PUSG*, 18:292.

32. Ibid., 24:61–62.

33. As qtd. in Brooks D. Simpson, *Let Us Have Peace: Ulysses S. Grant and the Politics of War and Reconstruction, 1861–1868* (Chapel Hill: Univ. of North Carolina Press, 1991). Two outstanding biographies on Grant have been published recently: Brooks D. Simpson, *Ulysses S. Grant: Triumph Over Adversity, 1822–1865* (Boston: Houghton Mifflin, 2000), and Jean Edward Smith, *Grant* (New York: Simon & Schuster, 2001).

34. An excellent discussion of the controversy over Grant's generalship can be found in William A. Blair, "Grant's Second Civil War: The Battle for Historical Memory," in Gary W. Gallagher, ed., *The Spotsylvania Campaign* (Chapel Hill: Univ. of North Carolina Press, 1998), 223–53.

35. Lee, as qtd. in Emory M. Thomas, *Robert E. Lee: A Biography* (New York: W. W. Norton, 1995), 367.

36. Young, *Around the World with General Grant*, 2:459.

37. Arnold, *General Grant*, 11–12. Books on the Lost Cause include Thomas Connelly, *The Marble Man: Robert E. Lee and His Image in American Society* (New York: Knopf, 1977); and Gaines M. Foster, *Ghosts of the Confederacy: Defeat, the Lost Cause, and the Emergence of the New South* (New York: Oxford Univ. Press, 1987).

38. Gary W. Gallagher, "Jubal A. Early, the Lost Cause, and Civil War History: A Persistent Legacy," in Gallagher and Nolan, eds., *The Myth of the Lost Cause*, 35–59.

39. Gen. Dabney H. Maury, *Southern Historical Society Papers*, vols. 5–6, (May 1878).

40. As qtd. in Young, *Around the World with General Grant*, 1:360.

41. For an effective rebuttal to the common assumptions about Lee, see Gary W. Gallagher, "An Old-Fashioned Soldier in a Modern War? Robert E. Lee as a Confederate General," *Civil War History* 45 (Dec. 1999): 295–312.

42. Andrew Delbanco, *The Death of Satan: How Americans Have Lost the Sense of Evil* (New York: Farrar, Straus and Giroux, 1995): 139. Good studies of the powerful hold of the Lost Cause on American culture include Tony Horwitz, *Confederates in the Attic: Dispatches from the Unfinished Civil War* (New York : Vintage, 1999); Carol Reardon, *Pickett's Charge in History and Memory* (Chapel Hill: Univ. of North Carolina Press, 1997); and Kirk Savage, *Standing Soldiers, Kneeling Slaves* (Princeton: Princeton Univ. Press, 1999).

43. Stuart McConnell, *Glorious Contentment: The Grand Army of the Republic, 1865–1900* (Chapel Hill: Univ. of North Carolina Press, 1992); and Mary R. Dearing, *Veterans in Politics: The Story of the GAR* (Baton Rouge: Louisiana State Univ. Press, 1952), are the two classic works on northern veterans.

44. The meetings are recorded in the calendar of *PUSG*, 24:xxi–xxii.

45. Ibid., 23:289.

46. For example, Grant read a portion of Adam Badeau's second volume of *Grant's Campaigns*. *PUSG*, 24:166–70; see also correspondence regarding the war actions of Gen. David Hunter, ibid., 221.

47. Simon, *Ulysses S. Grant: One Hundred Years Later*, 253; see also James G. Barber and John Y. Simon, *U. S. Grant: The Man and the Image* (Washington, D.C.: National Portrait Gallery, Smithsonian; and Carbondale: Southern Illinois Univ. Press, 1985).

48. "HFK," *Philadelphia Times*, Aug. 5, 1881. Early histories of the war provoking controversy include Adam Badeau, *Military Memoirs of Ulysses S. Grant*, 3 vols. (New York: D. Appleton 1868–1882); and William Swinton, *Campaigns of the Army of the Potomac: A Critical History of Operations in Virginia, Maryland, and Pennsylvania from the Commencement to the Close of the War, 1861–65* (1866; repr., New York: Univ. Publishing Co., 1871). Grant discussed Swinton in *PMUSG*, 2:486–88.

49. Young, *Around the World with General Grant*. See also a fine new abridged edition edited by Michael Fellman (Baltimore: Johns Hopkins Univ. Press, 2002). Adam Badeau, *Military Memoirs of U. S. Grant*, 3 vols. (New York: D. Appleton, 1868–82).

50. Young, *Around the World with General Grant*, 2:459.

51. Ibid., 2:445.

52. See Joyce Appleby, Lynn Hunt, and Margaret Jacob, *Telling the Truth About History* (New York: W. W. Norton, 1994), for a thoughtful discussion of the modern historical profession.

53. Young, *Around the World with General Grant*, 2:293; and *PMUSG*, 2:732.

54. Alan C. and Barbara A. Aimone, *A User's Guide to the Official Records of the American Civil War* (Shippensburg, Pa.: White Mane, 1993), 8.

55. Ulysses S. Grant to Edwin Stanton, May 29, 1865, *PUSG*, 16:106.

56. One reviewer noted approvingly that *OR* volumes are "fair in the treatment of Confederate as well as Federal reports and documents." However, he advised the government to drop the hated word "Rebellion" from the title. *SHSP* 11, no. 11 (Nov. 1883): 575–76.

57. See David W. Blight, *Race and Reunion: The Civil War in American Memory* (Cambridge, Mass.: Harvard Univ. Press, 2001), for explication of the "whitewashing" of Civil War memory, commemoration, and history.

58. Johnson, *Remembered Yesterdays*, 208. See also Stephen Davis, "'A Matter of Sensational Interest': The Century 'Battles and Leaders' Series," *Civil War History* 27 (Dec. 1981): 4:338–49.

59. Elsie Porter Mende and Henry Greenleaf Pearson, *An American Soldier and Diplomat: Horace Porter* (New York: Frederick A. Stokes Co., 1927), 141.

60. James Grant Wilson, *General Grant* (New York: D. Appleton and Co., 1897), 354.

61. Ulysses S. Grant to Frederick Dent Grant, undated in an envelope marked "Small messages written by U. S. Grant Gen'l and president to his son F. D. Grant, during last illness, July 1885," U. S. Grant Family Correspondence, box 1, Grant Papers, LC. Many letters in this collection document fully Grant's work in writing his memoirs.

62. Albert Bigelow Paine, *Mark Twain, A Biography: The Personal and Literary Life of Samuel Langhorne Clemens*, 3 vols. (New York, 1912), remains the best source for documenting their professional and personal relationship.

63. John Douglas, June 3, 1885, "Journal," John H. Douglas Collection, Library of Congress, Washington, D.C.; Horace Green, "General Grant's Last Stand," *Harper's Magazine* 170 (Apr. 1935); George T. Shrady, *General Grant's Last Days* (New York: DeVinne Press, 1908).

64. For an excellent discussion of the impact of U. S. Grant's bout with cancer on American society, see James T. Patterson, *The Dread Disease: Cancer and Modern American Culture* (Cambridge, Mass.: Harvard Univ. Press, 1987), 1–11.

65. McFeely, *Grant*, 515.

66. Bruce Catton, "U. S. Grant: Man of Letters," 98.

67. Ibid.

68. In addition to the works already cited, three scholars have helped me in understanding the full impact of Grant's writing: Henry M. W. Russell, "The Memoirs of Ulysses S. Grant: The Rhetoric of Judgment," *The Virginia Quarterly Review* 66 (Spring 1990): 209; Elizabeth D. Samet, "'Adding to My Book and to My Coffin': The Unconditional Memoirs of Ulysses S. Grant," paper in author's possession; and Michael W. Schaefer, *Just What War Is: The Civil War Writings of De Forest and Bierce* (Knoxville: Univ. of Tennessee Press, 1997).

69. *PMUSG*, 1:41. Grant compared the styles of the two generals in ibid., 94–95.

70. Ibid., 42

71. Ibid., 142–51. Grant's conclusion also offers a lengthy explication of slavery as a cause of the war.

72. Controversies in the Overland campaign are well covered most recently by William A. Blair, "Grant's Second Civil War: The Battle for Historical Memory"; and Brooks D. Simpson, "Continuous Hammering and Mere Attrition: Lost Cause Critics and the Military Reputation of Ulysses S. Grant." For information on Grant and the Battle of Shiloh, see Simpson, *Ulysses S. Grant: Triumph Over Adversity*, 119–46.

73. Ulysses S. Grant, "The Battle of Shiloh," in *Battles and Leaders of the Civil War* (New York: Century Co., 1884–87), 1:465–87. An excellent overview of the battle and the controversies can be found in Jay Luvaas, Stephen Bownman, and Leonard Fullenkamp, *Guide to the Battle of Shiloh* (Lawrence: Univ. Press of Kansas, 1996).

74. *PMUSG*, 1:236. There are many examples of Grant reconsidering his stance when new information came to light. For one, see *General Ulysses S. Grant's Unpublished Correspondence in the Case of Fitz-John Porter* (New York: Martin B. Brown, 1884).

75. *PMUSG*, 1:246.

76. Young, *Around the World with General Grant*, 2:307; Kevin Donovan, "The Court-Martial of Fitz-John Porter," *Columbiad* 2 (Winter 1999): 73–97.

77. *PMUSG*, 1:386, 2:652.

78. See Earl J. Hess, *The Union Soldier in Battle: Enduring the Ordeal of Combat* (Lawrence: Univ. Press of Kansas, 1997), for a useful discussion of this literature. Outstanding examples of books that examine the memory of the war are Blight, *Race and Reunion*; Gary W. Gallagher, *Lee and His Generals in War and Memory* (Baton Rouge: Louisiana State Univ. Press, 1998); and McConnell, *Glorious Contentment*.

79. *PMUSG*, 2:761.

80. Ibid., 2:779.

81. Ibid.

82. *The Compact Edition of the Oxford English Dictionary*, vol. 1 (New York: Oxford Univ. Press, 1971).

83. Keegan, *The Mask of Command*, 202, 459.

"Touched with Fire?"

Two Philadelphia Novelists Remember
the Civil War

🦅 After writing well-received books on a number of Civil War–era topics, in the spring of 2006 J. Matthew Gallman completed a project that had been near and dear to his heart for some time. As only a close and trusted friend could, in *America's Joan of Arc: The Life of Anna Elizabeth Dickinson*, Gallman faithfully interpreted the life of this remarkable and important nineteenth-century woman for an audience who may have never heard of her. Through her life and his retelling of it, Gallman demonstrates his facility with a variety of historical topics, including ideas of social construction, gender, race, and political culture. The book is not only a biography of an important woman but a window into the Victorian era, where one remarkable woman's life could serve as both an example of the possibilities for women in public life and as a warning of the potential costs of such fame in a world dominated by men and male culture.

The son of the noted economic historian Robert E. Gallman, J. Matthew Gallman grew up in Chapel Hill, North Carolina, and studied at Princeton University and Brandeis University, where he completed his Ph.D. in 1986. He taught at Loyola College in Baltimore for twelve years before moving on to Gettysburg College as Henry R. Luce Professor of the Civil War Era and director of the program in Civil War era studies. Since delivering his Klement Lecture he became

Anna E. Dickenson. Library of Congress Prints and Photographs Division.

professor of history at the University of Florida. He is the author of numerous books and articles, all of which highlight his multiple interests. In addition to *America's Joan of Arc*, Gallman has written *Mastering Wartime: A Social History of Philadelphia During the Civil War* (1990), *The North Fights the Civil War: The Home Front* (1994), and *Receiving Erin's Children: Philadelphia, Liverpool, and the Irish Famine Migration, 1845–1855* (2000). Gallman was also the general editor of *The Civil War Chronicle* (2003), which utilized newspaper accounts, memoirs, battle dispatches, and letters to create a day-to-day documentary account of life during the Civil War.

Gallman showcased his expertise on Anna Elizabeth Dickinson and the northern home front in his 2002 Klement Lecture. In this piece, focusing on two Philadelphia writers—Dickinson and Dr. Silas Weir Mitchell, a neurologist who worked in one of Philadelphia's military hospitals and for a local branch of the Sanitary Commission—he looks closely at the ways that civilians remembered the Civil War. While many scholars have argued that the Civil War deeply affected the values and attitudes of soldiers—in the well-loved words of the veteran and Supreme Court justice Oliver Wendell Holmes Jr., their "hearts were touched with fire"—Gallman questions whether Americans on the home front shared that transforming fire. 🖎

Introduction: Oliver Wendell Holmes Jr. Recalls the Civil War

"Through our great good fortune, in our youth our hearts were touched with fire." Oliver Wendell Homes Jr. made this bold declaration on Memorial Day 1884 at a gathering of the Grand Army of the Republic. Before this audience of fellow veterans, Holmes recalled fallen comrades and declared that "the generation that carried on the war has been set apart by its experience." The following Memorial Day the famed jurist took up similar themes when he spoke before Harvard University's graduating class. But to the civilian audience Holmes's 1885 address had a bit more bite. Not only had the war made his generation better men for having endured the traumas of combat, but twenty years of peace had produced a nation that failed to recognize the value of true heroism and sacrifice. Captains of industry and selfish business tycoons had replaced true heroes in the nation's affections now that war was "out of fashion." And the nation was worse for it. Perhaps to startle his young listeners out of their complacency, the orator declared that "I rejoice at every dangerous sport that I see pursued," including fencing and polo. "If once in a while in our rough riding a neck is broken, I regard it, not as a waste, but as a price well paid for the breeding of a race fit for headship and command."[1]

For the historian, such words invite various interpretations. It is at once a strong statement about postwar politics and power and clear evidence of how participants remembered the war a generation after Appomattox. I find the latter theme particularly compelling in light of recent scholarship examining how postwar Americans constructed a usable memory of the Civil War, sometimes at the expense of the conflict's true dimensions and meaning. That rich scholarship has followed various paths. In his award-winning book *Race and Reunion*, David Blight explored how the forces of postwar regional reconciliation often constructed a narrative that muted the significance of racial tension in the sectional conflict. Other scholars have examined the emergence of the myth of the "Lost Cause" in southern historiography. Still others have asked how veterans' organizations, battlefield commemorations, and monument building both reflected and shaped our national memory.[2]

Holmes and a generation of veterans were intent on reminding Americans of the patriotic sacrifices they made on the battlefield, while often stressing that heroism—and even patriotism—knew no particular uniform or ideology. But in addition to celebrating heroic memory and attacking contemporary sloth, Holmes was saying something very important about change, and how change happens. Civil War soldiers were "touched with fire," and in the furnace of warfare, new and stronger characters were forged. This is certainly not a unique observation. Many an author has explained—and often celebrated— the ways in which military experiences transform boys into men.[3] As a historian who has spent much of his career considering the northern home front, I have asked similar questions of different Civil War participants and come to quite different conclusions. I have argued that the crisis of war did not really transform the North so much as the North "adjusted" to the conflict's substantial challenges within the context of long-established experiences and practices.[4] In a sense these findings confirm Holmes's point. The Civil War soldier had the "great good fortune" to be "touched with fire," whereas those who stayed behind—like the men of the postwar generation—were robbed of the war's true transformative effects.

Still, I have always been a bit dissatisfied with these findings, at least insofar as they are applied to individuals on the home front. After all, my previous work emphasized how individuals and institutions *behaved* during the war years, but I readily acknowledged that my research was not likely to uncover the sort of character developments on the home front that Holmes celebrated in his various addresses. That is partially because behavior and character are not the same, and it is not always possible to glean the latter by observing the former. Moreover, there is an important reflective component in the postwar declaration. True, the passage of time distorts memories of the past and historical actors are prone to construct their memories to serve their present. However, we do not always fully comprehend important changes as we experience them, and thus the diarist or correspondent might not fully grasp—or record—her own personal transformations as they are occurring.

With that in mind, I approached the scene of my earlier scholarship—the northern urban home front, and particularly the City of Brotherly Love—from a new perspective. Rather than asking how those noncombatant participants experienced the war, I wish to explore how they made sense of the experience after the fact. Thus, I am paying my only modest homage to the burgeoning field of Civil War memory. But I remain interested in this notion of the war as an instrument of change. How did Philadelphians who participated on the home front recall the war years? Did they claim to have survived their own fiery furnaces, leaving them with stronger characters and souls? Even if I, as a modern historian, waded through their diaries, letters, newspapers, and annual reports and found strong continuities with an antebellum past, what about those people who actually worked in those military hospitals, received those letters, attended those parades, and woke up one day to black-bordered newspaper reports of a president's assassination? How much did they later feel that the war had left them permanently altered?

Like so many interesting historical questions, this one is hard to answer. One strategy would be to consider the postwar memoir. As the nineteenth century came to a close, hundreds—perhaps thousands—of military veterans published their recollections, providing valuable, albeit deeply biased, sources for the military historian. Perhaps partially in response to this flood of military recollection, quite a few veterans of wartime activism and voluntarism told their own tales.[5] But these texts generally have other goals in mind, and they do not strike me as the best place to look for reflections on the war's role in personal character transformation. Instead, I have decided to turn to postwar fiction for some tentative answers.

I am drawn to fiction for various reasons. First, the scholarship on Civil War–era popular literature—like the recent work on memory—is a particularly exciting field these days, so this lecture becomes sort of a double scholarly homage, honoring both historiographic trends.[6] Moreover, if I am interested in how postwar Americans *understood* the war's transformative effects, I am on perfectly sturdy ground working with novels, which offer a window into how the author remembered—or wished to remember—the war years. The novelist (or at least these nineteenth-century novelists) generally creates characters who then navigate various events and circumstances. With the Civil War providing the factual backdrop, the opportunities for dramatic character development are almost irresistible. Or so we might assume.

I wish today to focus on two postwar novels: Anna Elizabeth Dickinson's *What Answer?* which was published in 1868, and Silas Weir Mitchell's *In War Time*, which appeared in book form in 1884, the same year that Holmes delivered his Memorial Day address.[7] Both Dickinson and Mitchell were Philadelphians. The former was born in 1842, the latter in 1829. Dickinson had been a celebrated orator during the war, speaking out for abolitionism and women's rights but earning particular fame as a charismatic and biting Republican stump speaker. In January 1864, while still only twenty-one, Dickinson spoke in the halls of the House of Representatives before an illustrious audience that included President and Mrs. Lincoln and most of the party's congressmen and senators. At the time she was one of the nation's most famous women. *What Answer?* written three years after the war, was Dickinson's first book and only novel.[8] *In War Time* was also Mitchell's first novel. A well-known neurologist, Dr. Mitchell worked as a contract physician in one of Philadelphia's military hospitals during the war and also played a substantial role in the local branch of the Sanitary Commission. In later life he managed to maintain a highly successful dual career, publishing numerous novels and several highly respected medical tracts. His fame was so great that in the late 1880s the economist and author Charlotte Perkins Gilman went to see Mitchell about her growing depression. Mitchell's draconian "rest cure," and Gilman's disgust with that treatment, became the centerpiece of her famous book *The Yellow Wallpaper.*[9]

In War Time and *What Answer?* are certainly very different sorts of books, but they are knit together by several common traits beyond the crucial fact that both take place in the North during the Civil War. Both books are the first novels of authors who had achieved substantial professional success in another arena and who lived in Philadelphia during the war years. That shared Philadelphia background is potentially significant. Unlike many Confederate cities, the City of Brotherly Love never faced an invading army, and its citizens did not endure terrible economic hardships. But Philadelphia was close enough to the seat of war that Union soldiers were a familiar sight on its streets, and after each major eastern battle the city's hospitals filled with wounded.[10]

The plots also share common traits. Each story is set in the urban North-east, specifically in New York and in the Philadelphia area. Both are packed with characters and subplots, but each has a central love story at its core. And in each love story the lovers transgress conventional lines: *In War Time* pairs a southern woman and a northern man, and *What Answer?*—more dramatically—features the love between a white man and a black woman. Although neither book is a superb piece of writing (I am personally most partial to *What Answer?*), each provided the author with a forum for re-calling what it was like to live in the Northeast during the Civil War, and each book suggests some set of answers to my central concerns about the importance of the war in transforming individuals on the home front.

How might the historian evaluate these home front novels? Dickinson and Mitchell were both enthusiastic readers, but not professional writers. I would argue that it was quite natural for them to set their first literary efforts during the tumultuous war years. After all, the scenes and events of the war provided an ideal—and familiar—narrative backdrop for an inexperienced novelist, while also suggesting all sorts of possibilities for excitement, tragedy, heroism, and of course character development. The question then is: How did each novelist choose to use the war in shaping his or her plot? Did the Civil War *change* the men and women in the novel, or did it really only provide a context for the story? What sorts of home front scenes did the author elect to portray? Are the main characters regularly engaged in supporting the war effort? In discussing military and political events? Or do they live in a calm and peaceful world largely insulated from the battlefield's tumult?

Of course the point is not to apply a particular analytic template to each book. I have no checklist of anticipated traits that one might expect from a Civil War novel. But by setting their books in the Civil War home front, Weir Mitchell and Anna Dickinson gave themselves the opportunity to present a version of the war years as they understood them, stressing what they wished, omitting what they chose. Let us consider the two books sepa-rately, starting with S. Weir Mitchell's *In War Time*.

In War Time

In War Time opens in July of 1863, just days after the Battle of Gettysburg. Some of the wounded who are strong enough to be transported have been taken to the bustling military hospital on Filbert Street in Philadelphia. It is, Mitchell explains in the novel's first paragraph, one of those scenes that "has been lost, in the healing changes with which civilizing progress, no less quickly than forgiving nature, is apt to cover the traces of war."[11] With these words Mitchell promises a recovered wartime memory, but perhaps without the hint of bitterness that surrounded Holmes's address.

Right away we meet four of the novel's central characters. Dr. Ezra Wendell and his sister Ann are transplanted New Englanders from Cape Cod. Ann is an earnest, slightly stiff Yankee who is utterly devoted to her brother's happiness and comfort. Ezra is a contract surgeon, working in the hospital while also maintaining a small private practice. Later we will learn that Dr. Wendell had had a brief stint in the military that ended abruptly by mutual consent. Much later still, we discover that he had been dismissed for cowardice after abandoning two fellow doctors and a group of wounded men in the face of the enemy. But for the moment all we know is that the young doctor is kind and competent but also rather weak and self-absorbed and distinctly not military in his bearing. His flaws are illustrated on that very first day, when a patient under his care dies and Dr. Wendell suspects that his poor advice was partially to blame. This realization leaves him remorseful but also annoyed and distracted. On his journey home he loses himself in a soothing smoke, but his reverie is broken when he drops his favorite pipe, which shatters on the ground. For a moment Wendell stares in horror as if he had lost a good friend. To his credit, the young doctor recoils in horror when he recognizes that he is mourning his broken meerschaum every bit as much as the deceased patient.

At this stage the cynical reader—particularly one who is familiar with the sentimental popular fiction of the nineteenth century—would be forgiven for sighing out loud. Here we have a character who is torn between his weaker nature and his better self, with two years of warfare and roughly 400 pages to come to a happy resolution. Moreover, the character is clearly the author's alter ego: a contract surgeon in a military hospital. The only dramatic tension, it would seem, concerns exactly what crisis will Dr. Mitchell construct to lead Dr. Wendell to become a better, more courageous, and less self-absorbed man. But as the book unfolds, we will discover such cynicism is unfounded.

The other two crucial characters who appear in that first chapter are among the hospital's many patients. Both Major Morton, a distinguished man from nearby Germantown, and Captain Gray, a Confederate officer from South Carolina, were wounded on the third day at Gettysburg near the famed copse of trees. In fact, Captain Gray eventually comes to suspect that he was wounded by Major Morton's own pistol. The two old soldiers swiftly bond, in a symbolic display of sectional reconciliation. As the captain's health declines, he sends for his fifteen-year-old daughter, Hester, who has been in school in New Jersey since her mother passed away four years earlier. The captain dies soon after Hester's arrival, but not before securing a promise from Mrs. Morton that she would protect his daughter's well-being.

The scene then shifts to Germantown, a manufacturing village north of downtown Philadelphia. The slowly recuperating Major Morton (who has been promoted to colonel) has enlisted Dr. Wendell as his private physician, necessitating almost daily visits. Meanwhile, the Wendells have agreed to take in Hester Gray as their ward, assisted by a $10,000 trust fund sent to her by a distant cousin from the South. Three more important characters enter the mix. Alice Westerly is a lively, quick-witted widow who immediately takes an interest in Dr. Wendell. The Mortons have two sons, both of whom find Hester particularly fascinating. Arty, the youngest, is nearly eighteen and itching to follow his father into military service. Ned, the eldest, is an athletic outdoorsman by nature, but a fall from a horse has left him with a mysterious debilitating illness that is slowly robbing him of his ability to walk and will probably kill him before long.

The central love story proceeds roughly as one might expect. Hester is sent off to school and returns transformed, both mentally and physically, into a terribly attractive young woman. (Mitchell comments on this maturation so often and so effusively that the reader almost blushes for Hester.) Arty goes to Europe with his parents, leaving Ned behind to be treated by Dr. Wendell and bond with the lovely Hester. When Arty returns he promptly enlists and soon joins the siege around Petersburg. While his brother is away, Ned comes to realize that it is not his lot in life to win the love of the fair Hester, and so he does his best to suffer in silence. As he grows progressively frail, Ned exhibits more "womanly" virtues (thus Mitchell exhibits the sort of gender assumptions which would drive Charlotte Perkins Gilman to acts of literary vengeance). Soon the war ends and Arty returns home as an officer, having received a minor wound in his arm but otherwise no worse for wear. Much as Hester had clearly matured, many observers marvel at Arty's physical transformation, repeatedly commenting on how bronzed he has become during his time in uniform.

Soon the young couple acknowledge their love for each other and agree to marry, but of course there are various obstacles to be overcome. Mrs. Morton is not happy that her son wants to marry at such a young age and beneath his social class; Hester's southern uncle appears and resists the idea that his relative should marry a Union soldier; and the ever-conscientious Ann Wendell insists that the couple should be told that Arty's father was perhaps the one who killed Hester's father. But when Colonel Morton telegraphs his consent from Europe (where he has stayed behind, having apparently having taken an Italian mistress), the various barriers dissolve and the couple is eventually united.

Ezra Wendell's romantic life follows a rockier course. Although Dr. Wendell is almost distressingly drawn to long nature walks with his young ward, Hester, he clearly also reciprocates Alice Westerly's more mature and appropriate attractions. The problem for the ever-brooding doctor is that he is mired in financial difficulties and potential embarrassments. When his love of expensive scientific equipment outstripped his meager income, Wendell had dipped into Hester's trust fund, initially rationalizing that he was only spending the profits from wise investments that he had made, and not the principle. But his investments did poorly, and soon he was digging deeper into that fund. These secret developments cause Wendell to question his interest in Alice Westerly: was he only after her money, he wonders. In the meantime, Alice has secretly learned of Wendell's cowardly military past, but still she resolves to stick with him and help him to a brighter future.

This resolve cannot survive Wendell's final great sin. Here Mitchell turns to a complex, and somewhat murky, plot twist. The sickly Ned, who had already lent his friend Ezra quite a bit of money, agrees to give the doctor an additional $5,000 to cover all his outstanding debts, thus freeing Wendell to marry Alice Westerly without guilt. But before this money can change hands, Wendell makes a terrible mistake involving two medicine vials. In a characteristically distracted moment, Wendell gives Arty the wrong vial to administer to his brother, and as a result Ned receives a poisonous dose of "tincture of aconite," killing him almost instantly. A distraught Arty assumes that he had made the error, but Dr. Wendell—quickly recognizing his own mistake—assures everyone that Arty had administered the correct medication and that Ned had merely died of his illness. Mrs. Morton and Alice both assume that Dr. Wendell is graciously protecting the young boy, even at the expense of his professional oath, when in fact he is lying to cover up his own error while also allowing his intended bride to believe him something of a hero.

Before he died, Ned had told his mother of his intended gift to Dr. Wendell, and she honored her son's last wishes by sending Ezra a check for $5,000.

Alice is sure that the doctor will decline the gift under the circumstances, since it would appear to be a payment for protecting Arty. When Ezra accepts the money, an astonished Alice refuses to marry him, explaining that she could never wed a man she did not respect. At this point the morally obtuse doctor reveals that he was really responsible for Ned's death, and insisted that he had kept it a secret for fear of losing her. Needless to say, this news is the final straw for poor Alice Westerly. She immediately flees to Europe and is not heard from again. Ezra and Ann Wendell return to New England, but not before collecting an additional $10,000 from Ned's will, which of course makes Ezra feel even more guilty. The story ends with a brief epilogue. A year or so after these events Ann Wendell sends Mrs. Morton a note explaining the true circumstances of Ned's death and returning the $10,000. Her brother, she explains, was thoroughly broken in health and spirit.

In War Time is in many senses a typical popular novel for its day, and certainly not a bad effort for a first-time author.[12] How did S. Weir Mitchell incorporate the Civil War into this tale that he consciously set "in war time"? The war is certainly present in all sorts of ways: the main characters initially meet at a military hospital; both Arty and Hester are the children of soldiers, and Arty himself goes off to war; a few other minor characters are soldiers; all the women volunteer at the local branch of the Sanitary Commission and various scenes occur in those offices. But although the war is present throughout the narrative, it is hardly a powerful agent for change.

Consider the experiences of Dr. Ezra Wendell, the novel's central character. Here we have a man who experienced the war both as an army doctor in the field and as a contract surgeon in a military hospital. Yet the character flaws that failed him months before the novel opened and continued to mar his behavior in the book's first scenes remained essentially unchanged two years later. He was, to the bitter end, weak, self-absorbed, and fundamentally clueless about what it meant to behave honorably. Although he witnessed the impact of war around him, Ezra Wendell, unlike Oliver Wendell Holmes, seems never to have been properly touched with fire.

What of Arty Morton, who proudly served his country for the final year and a half of war before returning home to marry his sweetheart? Arty certainly saw combat; he even took a bullet in the arm and was nearly captured by Rebel troops. But he never said anything, either in person or in his letters from camp, to indicate that the profound experiences of warfare had left him a different man. Instead, Arty came home somewhat older and nicely tanned but fundamentally unmarked by the experience. In one particularly revealing letter, Arty acknowledged that he did not really enjoy combat but he did find "something of a wild joy about" the "mad rushes at death" he had survived.[13] It was Ned, Arty insisted, who really belonged in uniform, demonstrating his valor and patriotism and athleticism. Of course elder brother Ned, despite his love of the active life, had been robbed of his chance to serve by an injury totally unrelated to the war. How ironic that fate would have treated him so. Under other circumstances Ned would have followed his father into military service and—so we are led to believe—might well have won the hand of the lovely Hester.

It is certainly significant that S. Weir Mitchell constructed his plot this way. Ned is the only character who truly evolves in the course of the war, and those changes are not driven by the war itself. As his body declines, he becomes increasingly sensitive to the needs of those around him while growing reconciled to his own sad fate. The younger Hester and Arty certainly mature over the two years, but their evolutions seem to owe less to the traumas of the war and more to natural biological processes. How different *In War Time* would have been had Ned's decline and death been caused by a wound or injury suffered while in uniform, thus meaning that the Civil War was the root cause of the novel's great tragedy. And Mitchell could have created all sorts of plot devices so that the two lovers somehow matured because of the war. Hester might have volunteered in the hospital and come away from the experience transformed; Arty could have left for war as a frivolous young man who came home with newfound wisdom born of heroism. But the author declined all opportunities to cast the conflict as a force for good or ill.

WHAT ANSWER?

Anna Dickinson's *What Answer?* had its own ironies and ambiguities, but there is no doubting that the novel's central tragedy was caused by the Civil War, and it is equally clear that the nation's great conflict had unleashed enormous potential for future change. Contemporary reviewers praised the novel for its powerful scenes drawn directly from the war's history and for the courage of the central love story, but some critiqued Dickinson for her overly complex narrative with its multitude of characters and occasionally awkward plot devices. My summary will try to shave off a few of those rough edges, sacrificing some of the intricacies along the way.

262 / J. MATTHEW GALLMAN

The novel opens in New York City in the fall of 1860, as a handsome young man gazes out a window onto a bustling 5th Avenue. The young man is Willie Surrey, the bright, charming, privileged son of a wealthy foundry owner. As he watches the crowd below, Willie catches a glimpse of a beautiful woman and is immediately smitten. He will meet her soon enough, but first we meet another key character: Abram Franklin. Abe is a young African American man who works as a clerk for Willie's father. Lame from birth, Abe must limp the long walk home each day because the city streetcars are segregated. Much worse, the predominantly Irish factory workers have come to Mr. Surrey threatening to go out on strike unless he fires their black coworker. Willie and Abe are boyhood friends, and in fact Willie had helped Abe get his first position in the foundry. Now, however, our hero is powerless to stop the racist tide and can only do his best to find Abe another position.

The following day, Willie, still stewing over racial injustice, attends a school recital with his best friend, Tom Russell. There he witnesses the woman from 5th Avenue—Miss Francesca Ercildoune—read an impassioned poem attacking slavery. The two quickly begin a courtship and are clearly on their way to falling in love, until Willie tells her the tale of Abe's firing (while foolishly omitting the fact that he had found his friend another appointment). Francesca disappears without explanation, leaving Willie distraught and confused. As luck would have it, at this moment national events intercede as New York becomes overwhelmed with war fever following the firing on Fort Sumter. Willie enlists in the 7th New York Volunteers and leaves for the seat of war without hearing from his beloved Francesca.

Slowly the reader learns Francesca's secret. Although she looks white and attends a prestigious New York school alongside young white women, Francesca's father is half black, the son of a Virginia slaveholder and an enslaved woman.[14] At a young age her father had been sent to England, where he had married Francesca's mother, an English woman who was long since deceased. Mr. Ercildoune had eventually brought his family home to the United States, intent on joining the battle against slavery, and quickly discovered that northern society was also thick with prejudice and injustice. Francesca now lives in Philadelphia with her father and her brother, Robert, both of whom are much darker skinned. Dedicated to racial justice, and disgusted by the fact that her fair skin enables her to move freely in white society, Francesca has mistakenly concluded that Willie is in his marrow no different from the rest.

For two years the couple is apart. Willie's letters to Francesca are returned unopened. Meanwhile, Dickinson packs the narrative with smaller episodes, several of which demonstrate Willie's true commitment to racial justice. At Chancellorsville in 1863, Willie loses his arm and is sent home on furlough. While riding a Philadelphia streetcar he witnesses an ugly row over efforts to force a one-legged black soldier off the segregated car. Willie intercedes on the soldier's behalf just as we discover that Francesca is also a passenger on the car. Francesca is impressed and agrees to let Willie call on her, and it is just a matter of time before their various misunderstandings are resolved and the two are once again deeply in love. As in *In War Time*, the real challenge is to win the support of family and friends. Francesca's brother and father are initially skeptical but soon accept that Willie's intentions are honorable and that he fully realizes the rocky road ahead. Willie's family and friends are less understanding. Although they had earlier embraced Francesca, when the Surreys learn her true racial identity and the couple's plans to marry, the family summarily disinherits the young war hero and heir. The two lovers marry and move into a home along the Hudson River, largely isolated from white society.

Their bliss does not last long. Now firmly committed to racial equality, Willie agrees to go into New York City to help raise a brigade of free blacks. It is now mid-July 1863. In New York some old friends come up to shake Willie's hand, but more refuse to acknowledge him on the streets, illustrating the limits of progress in the wartime North. Willie takes a break from recruiting to go visit his sickly old friend Abe Franklin, who is confined to his bed. While he is visiting the Franklins, the infamous New York City draft riots rip through the city. Dickinson devotes two powerful chapters to the riots, leveling strong criticisms on the predominantly Irish rioters and the city's disloyal local press and politicians. The rioters, targeting African American homes and institutions, break into the Franklins' house, knock Willie out, and drag poor Abe from his bed. Relying heavily on actual events, Dickinson describes Abe's horrible death at the hands of the mob.[15] Unable to spare Abe from torture and execution, Willie does his best to protect Mrs. Franklin and sets off to warn Francesca. But the mob sets upon the young officer, beating him to death. (This, too, was based on actual events that the reader would have recognized.[16]) Francesca learns of the killing and rushes to her dying husband's side, only to be brought down by a stray bullet. In a touch of heavy-handed irony, the two star-crossed lovers die on the street immediately in front of the Surreys' home.

Dickinson juxtaposes this tragedy on the home front with equally powerful, but far more uplifting, events on the battlefield. Only days after the
draft riots, the black soldiers of the 54th Massachusetts Volunteers led the
charge on Fort Wagner, near Charleston, South Carolina.[17] This charge
failed in its military objective but succeeded in elevating the status of black
troops in many white eyes. Once again, Dickinson places her characters
within actual events, casting Robert Ercildoune as the brave soldier who
picked up the 54th's fallen colors and returned them to safety despite receiving several wounds. The charge earned the applause of white soldiers on
the scene and was also the subject of admiring discussion among the men
from Willie's old regiment, including Jim Given, the ex-foreman from Mr.
Surrey's factory. After the attack, the injured Robert is carried to a hospital
ship for the journey home. On board, the other wounded men, both white
and black, cheer the hero of Fort Wagner, and Jim Given—who had been
wounded in a different engagement—generously gives the black soldier his
own lower berth.

Dickinson devotes the novel's final chapters to tying up a wealth of
loose ends involving various characters. Jim Givens, the ex-factory foreman
and wounded veteran, comes home to marry Sallie, a seamstress who had
fallen on hard times and gone to work for the Ercildounes. The wealthy Ercildounes pay for Sallie's dress and even give the couple a small home as a
wedding present. Meanwhile, Tom Russell—Willie's oldest friend—returns
home from the war, having been rescued from Confederate troops with the
assistance of two runaway slaves. In the aftermath of the deaths of Francesca
and Willie, Tom Russell and Robert Ercildoune come together in their grief
and become fast friends, discovering they share the same "gentle blood" and
have "tastes and interests in common."[18] The novel closes on Election Day
1865. Tom and Robert ride a carriage to the polling place. Despite Robert's
warnings, a naïve Tom believes that his black comrade will be able to exercise
the franchise. But when they arrive a mob is there to greet them. "Challenge
the vote!" they cry, "No niggers here!" A melancholy Robert turns to Tom
and asks, "1860 or 1865?—is the war ended?" This then, is the question that
the book's title challenged the reader to answer. Writing three years after the
war, and in the midst of debates over the Fifteenth Amendment—legalizing
black male suffrage—Dickinson clearly felt that the black vote was an important step toward permanent change.

The characters in *What Answer?* were "touched with fire" both at home
and on the battlefield. How were they transformed by these experiences?

Clearly Anna Dickinson wrote with a powerful political agenda, challenging her readers to examine the state of race relations in the North. The individuals navigate the war years with racial dilemmas as a constant backdrop. Unlike Mitchell's conflicted Ezra Wendell or morose Ned Morton, Dickinson's main characters generally lack such nuance, leaving her main themes more transparent.

At the outset, the racially mixed Francesca is suspicious of the kindness of whites who do not know her true identity. With time, she comes to believe that in Willie Surrey she has found a man who sees beyond race. Willie's heart is in the right place in the book's initial chapters as he recoils at the unjust treatment of Abe Franklin. But it is not until he returns from war that he becomes a man of action, supporting the wounded black soldier on the streetcar and risking his life for Mrs. Franklin during the draft riots. Of course the solutions here are not so clear as they might seem. The man of action was a martyr to the rioters, and the reader is uncertain how any sort of action could have saved Abe's job in the face of 272 angry white employees. Thus, Dickinson appears to be suggesting on the one hand that Willie became more committed to racial justice through the course of the war, but on the other hand perhaps no individual man's efforts could have saved Abe's job in 1860 or his life in 1863.

If the two main characters were fundamentally good and strong from the beginning of the novel, various other characters illustrate the sort of social transformation that Dickinson envisioned. Jim Givens, Tom Russell, and various other white soldiers witness the heroism of black men—both the soldiers of the 54th Massachusetts and several escaped slaves they encounter in South Carolina—and return from the war with a new respect for African Americans. At home, Sallie bonds with Francesca and becomes a loyal servant, in a fascinating reversal of more familiar class and race relations. And of course the novel ends with a celebration of the close interracial bonds between Tom Russell and Robert Ercildoune.

Other characters who remained at home throughout the war are less transformed by the conflict. Willie's family and friends reject the interracial couple, despite the larger national context of emancipation and social change. The passengers on the streetcar divide over how to treat the crippled black soldier, but before Willie intercedes the emerging consensus seems—tellingly—to lean toward enforcing the segregationist law despite their moral qualms. Most powerfully, the rioters kill Abe, Willie, and Francesca in a rage that Dickinson portrays as explicitly racist. The message is clear. The war unleashed forces that had the potential to transform both soldiers and civilians, but such positive changes were certainly not preordained, and in fact these events had within them the seeds of disaster. The social chasm between the races could be bridged, but only with the sort of close personal contacts that brought blacks and whites together as equals. Such transitions occurred most readily in the heat of battle, but folks at home could—she implied—overcome their prejudices. Still, as of 1868 the chances of such larger transformations remained distinctly problematic.

CONCLUSIONS

Is it possible to squeeze these two home front novels into a single narrative about the Civil War and memory? There are certainly differences to contend with. Anna Dickinson was only twenty-six when she wrote *What Answer?* Sixteen years later Mitchell was in his midfifties when he published *In War Time.* Age and gender, as well as year of publication, certainly helped shape these two distinctive tales. Moreover, Dickinson had dedicated her public life to reform, and she intended her first novel to exhort as well as entertain.[19] Only three years after the war, America was struggling with its racial future in the North as well as in the Reconstruction South when she published *What Answer?* Silas Weir Mitchell wrote from a much more centrist position nearly two decades after the war, reflecting both the times and his own politically moderate inclinations.

Therefore, one way to read these two novels is as books with distinctly different agendas, where in each case the goal was to shape memory to suit contemporary needs. Writing in 1868, Dickinson described an imagined recent past in which the Civil War forced white Americans to rethink their racial prejudices. But true to the actual events, Dickinson also portrayed a parallel history in which those northern whites who were furthest from the battlefield and who had the most limited contact with African Americans resisted racial change, sometimes to the point of violence. If *In War Time* had a larger political agenda, it was certainly not about Civil Rights. No African Americans appear in the novel, and the characters barely mention race or emancipation. The only exception is when Hester's cousin Henry describes a long lost—and happily forgotten—relative who had freed his slaves and moved to the North where he had reportedly been involved in recruiting a black regiment. But this intriguing narrative thread is quickly, and perhaps significantly, forgotten.

According to his biographer, Mitchell shifted his allegiances from the Democratic to the Republican Party in the course of the war but was never particularly engaged in partisan politics. As a northerner with southern family ties (his father was a Virginian), Mitchell clearly supported harmonious national reconciliation.[20] From the outset we see Captain Gray and Major Morton as two old soldiers and not as political or ideological adversaries. When Mitchell does address the sectional conflict, the recurring theme is that the crisis was created by politicians and not the men on the battlefield. After Lincoln's assassination, one northerner worries that the action will reflect badly on other southerners, and Colonel Fox, a crusty old Quaker, tells Alice Westerly that he hopes that the politicians will behave as temperately as the soldiers, adding that the most belligerent northerners are the editors and not the military men. Even Hester's cousin's hostility to his niece marrying a Union officer rapidly dissolves once he meets the charming Arty.

The marriage between Arty and Hester clearly symbolizes the prospect of sectional reconciliation, much as the pairing of Francesca and Willie illustrates the potential for racial harmony.[21] Interestingly, each author seems to devalue the point in the telling. Hester Gray is a southerner but without the regional loyalty or passion of the prototypical southern white woman. Having lived for years in New Jersey, and then in Germantown with the Wendells, Hester's links to the Confederacy are abstract and easily set aside. Similarly, Francesca Ercildoune certainly sees herself as a woman of color, but she looks white and moves freely within white society. Although Willie remained loyal to his love when he learned Francesca's true racial heritage, the reader cannot forget that he fell in love thinking that she was a white woman. Thus, both of these crucial marriages were technically transgressive and thus politically important, but in fact in each case the bride's unclear identity undercuts the symbolic power of the match. Moreover, both young women had long since lost their mothers and had been living apart from their fathers while in school, thus making it that much easier to imagine that they might abandon their pasts to marry across racial or regional lines.

These larger political and symbolic concerns have lured me away from my initial question. Did these two authors portray a Civil War that truly transformed women and men on the home front, or did the four years of conflict leave no mark at home comparable to the "fire" that Oliver Wendell Holmes Jr. recalled from the battlefield? Clearly the answer is a resounding "no." No character in either novel appears to have grown or evolved because of their own war work; none are left emotionally scarred or fundamentally recast by the war's terrible military tragedies. The death of Captain Gray left Hester an orphan, but Mitchell makes no effort to explore the psychological effects of the loss. Instead, the novel's crucial tragedy is the accidental death of poor Ned Morton, who never had the opportunity to show his valor on the battlefield. Dickinson's main characters are victims of wartime violence, but the draft riots are portrayed more as an extension of antebellum race rioting rather than as a domestic front of the Civil War. The men who go off to fight in both novels almost always return with some sort of wound or lost limb, but none seem emotionally scarred by the experience and their loved ones seem able to carry on without any ill effects.

I am particularly interested in how the Civil War affected northern women. How did four years of conflict recast gender roles? Tens of thousands of women threw themselves into war work, but what was the evolving legacy of these efforts, both for those individuals and for the larger society? In her wartime career Dickinson bent all sorts of gender norms, speaking on abolitionism, women's rights, and politics to enthusiastic audiences across the country. She even did a small stint as a hospital volunteer, providing fodder for one of her popular lectures. But gender themes are completely absent from *What Answer?* Dickinson had disappointed many friends and admirers in the women's movement by siding with those male reformers who prioritized the black male vote over woman's suffrage. Her novel, written in the midst of debates that would eventually yield the Fifteenth Amendment granting black male suffrage, underscored her commitment to those priorities.

In War Time is in fact much more attentive to gender issues. Mitchell peppered his text with comments about the fundamental natures of different sorts of women, and he set several scenes in women's voluntary societies. During the war the Germantown women all gathered periodically at the Sanitary Commission offices to engage in unspecified war work; after Appomattox the same women organized to assist war orphans. But the novelist is clearly most concerned with creating scenes where various conversations and conflicts can occur, rather than in exploring the war's impact on women. We learn nothing about how these women had assisted the war effort, and there is no indication that their experiences had transformed them politically or ideologically. In fact, the conversations are invariably personal gossip unrelated to national political or military themes. Of course Mitchell's portrayal of women's organizations tells us nothing about what really went on in those meetings, but it does tell us a bit about how the author chose to remember that crucial moment in the history of women. The Sanitary Commission's volunteers ranged from the highly organized and well-read to the empty-headed and silly. The most progressive woman is the articulate, level-headed Miss Clemson, who repeatedly steers the conversation away from destructive gossip toward more elevated topics. Mitchell clearly wants the reader to admire Miss Clemson as a highly educated and morally sound individual. Although she takes part in the Sanitary Commission's work, Miss Clemson neither rises to a position of prominence in the committee nor speaks about the war or any larger political issues in these conversations. Instead, she impresses by demonstrating a knowledge of modern science, quoting the latest medical theories on malaria and vaccination. Perhaps Mitchell had no larger purpose than to have a character be a mouthpiece for some of his favorite medical theories, but it is telling that the woman who seems most "modern" is intellectually engaged in the world of science rather than in the swirl of contemporary events or the pull of woman's rights.

Sherlock Holmes used to tell Dr. Watson to be attentive to the dog that does not bark. Sometimes the best clues are in those silences. It is always easiest for the historian to examine that which is said and written, rather than to try to make sense of the absence of evidence. These two books are too few to support a comprehensive argument, but it is interesting to consider what Anna Dickinson and Silas Weir Mitchell had to say in their first novels, and also to consider the dogs that don't bark. Like many inexperienced writers, they both selected locations that they knew well, and of course the Civil War years provided an ideal backdrop for compelling narratives. Somehow their imaginations and their memories did not lead either Philadelphian to create wartime characters who were truly transformed by their home front experiences.

NOTES

J. Matthew Gallman delivered his Klement Lecture in 2002.

1. Oliver Wendell Holmes Jr., "In Our Youth Our Hearts Were Touched with Fire," May 30, 1884, address, and Holmes, "The Soldier's Faith," May 30, 1885, address. Both speeches are available at http://harvardregiment.org/holmes.html. This site acknowledges Richard Posner, *The Essential Holmes: Selections from the Letters, Speeches, Judicial Opinions, and Other Writings of Oliver Wendell Holmes, Jr.* (Chicago: Univ. of Chicago Press, 1992), as its original source.

2. See David Blight, *Race and Reunion: The Civil War in American Memory* (Cambridge, Mass.: Harvard Univ. Press, 2001); Alice Fahs and Joan Waugh, eds., *The Civil War and Memory* (Chapel Hill: Univ. of North Carolina Press, 2003); Lesley Gordon, *General George E. Pickett in Life and Legend* (Chapel Hill: Univ. of North Carolina Press, 1998); Carol Reardon, *Pickett's Charge in History and Memory* (Chapel Hill: Univ. of North Carolina Press, 1997); Jim Cullen, *The Civil War in Popular Culture: A Reusable Past* (Washington, D.C.: Smithsonian Institution Press, 1995); and Stuart McConnell, *Glorious Contentment: The Grant Army of the Republic, 1865–1900* (Chapel Hill: Univ. of North Carolina Press, 1992).

3. Various scholars have examined the attitudes and experiences of the Civil War soldier. For a survey of this literature, see Reid Mitchell, "'Not the General but the Soldier': The Study of Civil War Soldiers," in James M. McPherson and William J. Cooper Jr., eds., *Writing the Civil War: The Quest to Understand* (Columbia: Univ. of South Carolina Press, 1998), 81–95. For a study of the World War II soldier, see Gerald Linderman, *The World Within War: America's Combat Experience in World War II* (New York: Free Press, 1997). The soldier's experience has always been a popular subject for the novelist as well. Three of the most celebrated novels are Stephen Crane, *The Red Badge of Courage* (1895); Norman Mailer, *The Naked and the Dead* (1948); and Tim O'Brien, *Going After Cacciatto* (1978). O'Brien, a veteran of the war in Vietnam, has written several powerful works of fiction and nonfiction examining the soldier's experience.

4. J. Matthew Gallman, *Mastering Wartime: A Social History of Philadelphia during the Civil War* (New York: Cambridge Univ. Press, 1990) and *The North Fights the Civil War: The Home Front* (Chicago: Ivan R. Dee, 1994).

5. Perhaps the most famous of these memoirs is Mary Livermore, *My Story of the War* (Hartford, Conn.: A. D. Worthington, 1887; repr. New York: Perseus, 1995).

6. See Alice Fahs, *The Imagined Civil War: Popular Literature of the North and South, 1861–1865* (Chapel Hill: Univ. of North Carolina Press, 2001); Lyde Cullen Sizer, *The Political Work of Northern Women Writers and the Civil War, 1850–1872* (Chapel Hill: Univ. of North Carolina Press, 2000); and Elizabeth Young, *Disarming the Nation: Women's Writing and the Civil War* (Chicago: Univ. of Chicago Press, 1995).

7. Anna Elizabeth Dickinson, *What Answer?* (1868); and Silas Weir Mitchell, *In War Time* (1884). Mitchell's novel was initially serialized in the *Atlantic* in 1884. *What Answer?* was reissued by Humanity Press in Jan. 2003.

8. This portion of this essay is part of a much longer project on Dickinson's life.

9. Ernest Earnest, *S. Weir Mitchell: Novelist and Physician* (Philadelphia: Univ. of Pennsylvania Press, 1950); Lynne Sharon Schwartz, introduction to Charlotte Perkins Gilman, *The Yellow Wallpaper and Other Writings* (New York: Bantam, 1989).

10. Gallman, *Mastering Wartime.*

11. Mitchell, *In War Time*, 1.

12. Mitchell had earlier begun another wartime novel that was not published. Earnest, *S. Weir Mitchell*, 95.

13. Mitchell, *In War Time*, 226.

14. Dickinson clearly modeled Francesca and her family on the family of Robert Purvis, one of the most prominent black abolitionists in Philadelphia. Dickinson and her family were quite friendly with the Purvises, and Dickinson and Hattie Purvis were particularly close. (In a note at the end of the novel, Dickinson refers to, but does not name, the family.) See Gallman, introduction, to Dickinson, *What Answer?* (New York: Prometheus, 2003).

15. An African American man named Abraham Franklin was lynched during the riots in a manner quite similar to the grisly murder of Dickinson's fictional Abe Franklin. Adrian Cook, *The Armies of the Streets: The New York City Draft Riots of 1863* (Lexington: Univ. Press of Kentucky, 1974), 143.

16. In her "Note" Dickinson explains that Willie Surrey's death is modeled on the murder of Colonel O'Brien, a Union soldier killed by the rioters. On Colonel O'Brien's death see Cook, *Armies of the Streets*, 118–19.

17. The attack on Fort Wagner happened shortly after the draft riots, but Dickinson describes the attack immediately before portraying the riots. In her "Note" Dickinson explains that she modeled Robert Ercildoune's actions on the heroics of W. H. Carney. (This is the charge that was featured in the movie *Glory*.)

18. Dickinson, *What Answer?* 294.

19. Lyde Cullen Sizer makes a similar point about Dickinson's novel in *The Political Work of Northern Women Writers*, 236–44.

20. Earnest, *S. Weir Mitchell*, 46–48.

21. For a fascinating discussion of intersectional romance in postwar novels of reconciliation, see Nina Silber, *The Romance of Reunion: Northerners and the South, 1865–1900* (Chapel Hill: Univ. of North Carolina Press, 1993).

Gary W. Gallagher

Jubal A. Early, the Lost Cause, and Civil War History

A Persistent Legacy

In the quarter century since receiving his Ph.D. from the University of Texas at Austin, Gary W. Gallagher has been a tireless missionary for the study of the Civil War era. He has encouraged the expansion of the conflict's historiography beyond drums and bugles history; helped organize and lead the Society of Civil War Historians, the professional organization to which most historians of the era belong; given countless talks to Civil War Round Tables and other organizations; conducted battlefield tours for dozens of groups; and served as president of the Association for the Preservation of Civil War Sites. Along the way he has written, edited, or introduced scores of books for audiences of all kinds, including *Stephen Dodson Ramseur: Lee's Gallant General* (1985), *Fighting for the Confederacy: The Personal Recollections of General Edward Porter Alexander* (1989), *The Confederate War* (1997), and *Lee and His Army in Confederate History* (2001).

In addition to his own writings, Gallagher has contributed to the outpouring of Civil War scholarship by editing several book series and a number of essay collections. He has solicited junior and senior scholars alike to contribute to his anthologies on major campaigns and has helped the list of Civil War–era books published by the University of North Carolina Press to expand not only in quantity but, more importantly, in quality through the Civil War America Series (he has acquired and made detailed suggestions on more than fifty titles in that series alone) and the forthcoming, sixteen-volume Littlefield History of the Civil War Era, also at the UNC Press. Many of the authors of the essays in this anthology have participated in at least one of Gallagher's projects.

Gallagher has been associated with the topic of his lecture for many years. Although the Lost Cause is hardly a new idea, his assertion that the postwar campaign to memorialize the Confederacy and her heroes led by Jubal Early and others still shapes the approaches of novelists, filmmakers, and even historians has been perhaps his major contribution to our understanding of the war. Although he has none of the personal quirks or political attitudes of the hard-edged and profane Confederate who Lee purportedly called his "bad old man," Gallagher does share the Virginian's passion for telling the story of the Civil War, and for making that story a part of the consciousness of the general population.

Since delivering his lecture in 1995, when he was a professor at Pennsylvania State University, he has become John Nau Professor of History at the University of Virginia. He was the George W. Littlefield Lecturer at the University of Texas at Austin in 1995–1996 and the Robert Fortenbaugh Memorial Lecturer at Gettysburg College in 2005. ❧

JUBAL ANDERSON EARLY UNDERSTOOD the power of the printed word to influence perceptions of historical events. A former Confederate general who had fought under Robert E. Lee during the Civil War, he sought to create a written record celebrating the Confederacy's military resistance. Early hoped future generations would rely on this record, the essence of which can be distilled into a few sentences. Lee was a heroic soldier who led an outnumbered army of Confederate patriots against a powerful enemy. With "Stonewall" Jackson initially at his side, he faced northern generals of minimal talent who later lied in print to explain their failures. Against these men and later against Ulysses S. Grant, a clumsy butcher who understood only that vast northern resources of men and matériel must be expended freely, the Confederate commander worked his magic across a Virginia landscape that functioned as the cockpit of the war. Lee and his Army of Northern Virginia set a standard of valor and accomplishment equal to anything in the military history of the western world until finally, worn out but never defeated, they laid down their weapons at Appomattox. If the youth of the white South and succeeding generations of Americans and foreign readers accepted his version of the war, believed Early, ex-Confederates would have salvaged their honor from the wreck of seemingly all-encompassing defeat.

These ideas constitute part of what has come to be called "the Myth of the Lost Cause," an explanation for secession and Confederate defeat propagated in the years following the Civil War. Early's role as a leading Lost Cause warrior has been explored by several talented historians, all of whom portray him as so violently antinorthern that he eventually isolated himself from the southern white mainstream. Resolutely unreconstructed, goes the common argument, Early watched disapprovingly as proponents of the New South gained increasing power and ultimately rendered him a crabby anachronism long before his death in 1894.[1] This interpretation neglects Early's long-term impact on the ways in which Americans have understood the Civil War. Clear-eyed in his determination to sway future generations, Early used his own writings and his influence with other ex-Confederates to foster a heroic image of Robert E. Lee and the southern war effort. Many of the ideas these men articulated became orthodoxy in the postwar South, eventually made their way into the broader national perception of the war, and remain vigorous today. To put this phenomenon within the context of current historical work, Early understood almost immediately after Appomattox that there would be a struggle to control the public memory of the war, worked hard to help shape that memory, and ultimately enjoyed more success than he probably imagined possible.[2]

Before examining Early's largely persuasive efforts in this regard, it is worth noting that many of his other ideas found little favor in the postwar South. A conservative Whig who venerated property and rule by the slaveholding class during the antebellum period, he had resisted changes to the existing order. When Virginians debated a new constitution that would broaden the franchise in 1850, for example, Early warned that mob rule, with its attendant menace to property, might follow adoption of the document. He insisted that "every innovation is not reform—every change not improvement" and spoke of "unmistakable signs of an approaching conflict, between the conservative principles of all true government on the one hand, and the turbulent and disecrating [sic] spirit of innovation on the other."[3] After Appomattox, Early remained a self-styled conservative Whig who never relinquished his elitist conception of how society should be organized. He continued to praise the institution of slavery, adamantly opposed the South's embracing any northern notions about industrial progress, and attacked southern politicians who catered to the mass of white voters (and occasionally threatened to fuse portions of the white and black electorates). Early praised antebellum southern society as a model to be emulated in the former Confederate states. Gaines M. Foster has shown that most southerners displayed little inclination to embrace Early's elitist and nostalgic views. They preferred instead to follow John Brown Gordon and others whose vision of the New South permitted them to acknowledge that the war had altered their world while still honoring the leaders of the Confederacy and the motives that had brought secession.[4]

"I have been in a minority all my life," Early stated during Virginia's secession debate in reference to his being a Whig, and he quite readily accepted a comparable position regarding his politics after the war. While other southern whites trimmed their ideological sails to suit changed times, he clung tenaciously to every element of his antebellum worldview. "A very small portion of the civilized world is guiltless in regard to the wrongs done our people," he observed in a typical statement shortly after the end of the war, "and I want to see all the nations punished for their folly & wicked intermeddling in regard to the institution of slavery, about the propriety, advantages and justice of which my opinion grows daily stronger." Early castigated Republican politicians for trampling on the South's constitutional rights and sneered at any southern Democrat who sought accommodation with the North. This posture often rendered him precisely the type of cranky outsider described by several historians, but it was a status he accepted as a consequence of his maintaining ideological purity. Gaines Foster likens Early and his cohorts to the Native American ghost dancers of the late nineteenth century: "They appeared captivated by a dream of victory, a dream of a return to an undefeated Confederacy. This aspect of their historical vision does not appear very different from another revitalization movement of the late nineteenth century, the Ghost Dance among the Plains Indians. . . . They clung to the past, defended old values, and dreamed of a world untouched by defeat." In the end, adds Foster, very few white southerners "joined the ghost dance."[5]

Because of Early's passionate interest in how the future would judge the Confederacy, however, it is a mistake to see him as looking only to the past. His opinions about Confederate military history, which he hoped would have force among subsequent generations, earned a very receptive hearing across the postwar South. Before any other principal Civil War commander, he began work on memoirs of his wartime service. But first he left the United States. A much maligned figure in the Confederacy after his army suffered utter defeat against Philip H. Sheridan's forces in the Shenandoah Valley during the fall and winter of 1864–65, Early was relieved of command in March 1865 and missed the surrender of the Army of Northern Virginia at Appomattox. Upon hearing of Lee's capitulation, he traveled westward with the hope of joining Confederates in the trans-Mississippi theater. After learning en route that they also had surrendered, he then decided, as he put it, to leave the United States "to get out from the rule of the infernal Yankees." "I appreciate the motives and conduct of those who have determined to submit to the result & remain in the country," he explained to General Lee, "but my temperament is such that I cannot follow their example. I cannot live under the same government with our enemies. I go therefore [sic] a voluntary exile from the home and graves of my ancestors to seek my fortunes anew in the world." Traveling first to Havana, then to Mexico, and eventually settling in Canada, Early spent four years abroad before returning to Virginia in 1869. From Canada he followed events in the United States with mounting bitterness, declaring at one point, "I have got to that condition, that I think I could scalp a Yankee woman and child without winking my eyes."[6]

While in Mexico during the winter of 1865–66, Early crossed pens with his old foe Sheridan in a newspaper exchange that anticipated in tone and focus his later writings about the war. At dispute were the strengths and casualties of the forces in the Shenandoah campaign. Sheridan asserted that Early had lost nearly 27,000 men killed, wounded, and captured; Early countered that his force had consisted of fewer than 14,000 men and could not have suffered the losses claimed by Sheridan. Early's numbers were more accurate, but winning this argument constituted only a means to the larger end of compiling a written record aimed at both contemporaries and future readers. By insisting that he had commanded far fewer men than Sheridan, Early cast his own performance in a better light and sustained the honor of hopelessly outnumbered Confederates. "Sheridan's letter has furnished another evidence of the propriety of my caution to all fair minded men of other nations," insisted Early, "to withhold their judgments upon the reports of our enemies until the truth can be placed before them."[7]

Robert E. Lee figured prominently in Early's crusade to establish the Confederate side of the war's military history. Early exhibited unbounded admiration for Lee even before the Civil War, agreeing with other Virginians (including Winfield Scott, the ranking officer in the U.S. Army) that Lee's record during the war with Mexico marked him as a brilliant soldier. In the spring of 1862, a witness noted that Early, who habitually criticized

Confederate civilian and military leaders, never spoke negatively about Lee. "For Lee he seemed to have a regard and esteem and high opinion felt by him for no one else," remarked this man, who pronounced Early's attitude especially significant because Lee had yet to achieve any success in the field. Although Lee "had but recently been called to the command of the army," Early "predicted his great future with unerring judgment." During the war, Lee appreciated Early's talents as a soldier and displayed personal fondness for his cantankerous and profane lieutenant, calling him affectionately "my bad old man." Only Stonewall Jackson among Lee's corps commanders received more difficult assignments from Lee, a certain indication of the commanding general's high regard.[8]

Lee ensured his subordinate's utter devotion with a gentle handling of Early's removal from command in the spring of 1865. He expressed regret at having to replace Early but noted that defeats in the Shenandoah Valley had alienated that vital region's citizens and raised doubts among Early's soldiers. "While my own confidence in your ability, zeal, and devotion to the cause is unimpaired," stated Lee, "I have nevertheless felt that I could not oppose what seems to be the current of opinion, without injustice to your reputation and injury to the service." Lee closed with thanks for "the fidelity and energy with which you have always supported my efforts, and for the courage and devotion you have ever manifested in the service of the country."[9]

In late November 1865, a letter arrived from Lee that likely inspired Early to begin work on his memoirs. Lee intended to write a history of the Army of Northern Virginia, but the loss of official papers during the chaotic retreat from Richmond to Appomattox left him without sufficient information about the period 1864–65. Would Early send whatever materials he had relating to that last phase of the conflict? Seven and a half months earlier Lee had spoken of the Union's "overwhelming resources and numbers" in his farewell order to the Army of Northern Virginia. Now he specifically asked Early for information about Confederate strengths at the principal battles from May 1864 through April 1865. "My only object," concluded Lee in language Early would echo many times in his own writings, "is to transmit, if possible, the truth to posterity, and do justice to our brave Soldiers."[10]

Lee sent Early another request in March 1866 for "reports of the operations of your Commands, in the Campaign from the Wilderness to Richmond, at Lynchburg, in the Valley, Maryland, &c." Lee wanted all "statistics as regards numbers, destruction of private property by the Federal troops, &c." because he intended to demonstrate the discrepancy in strength between the two armies and believed it would "be difficult to get the world to understand the odds against which we fought." "The accusations against myself," Lee wrote in reference to various newspaper accounts, "I have not thought proper to notice, or even to correct misrepresentations of my words & acts. We shall have to be patient, & suffer for awhile at least.... At present the public mind is not prepared to receive the truth."[11]

Three months after he received Lee's letter, Early had completed a draft of his wartime memoirs. He published the last section of this manuscript— the first book-length reminiscence by any major Civil War commander—in Canada in late 1866 as *A Memoir of the Last Year of the War for Independence, in the Confederate States of America*. Lee's letter of March 1866 can be read as an outline for Early's book, which covered precisely the period the letter defined, strongly emphasized the North's advantage in numbers, and detailed Federal depredations in the Shenandoah Valley. A desire to satisfy Lee's request for information about the conflict's final year may have prompted Early to hurry this portion of his larger narrative into print. The fact that he never published the whole memoir suggests that he contemplated revisions and printed only the chapters that would serve Lee's most immediate needs (as well as place his own controversial activities in the Shenandoah Valley in the best possible light). Early subsequently sent Lee drafts of chapters from his manuscript dealing with the 1862 Maryland campaign and other operations.[12]

Early also may have read Lee's letter of March 1866 as an unintentional summons to champion Lee against all detractors. Distressed by the mention of attacks on Lee, Early may have decided to persuade the public to "receive the truth" about his old commander—to spell out in vigorous detail, and with an attention to evidence befitting Early's years of experience as a lawyer, a case for the greatness of both Lee and his army.

Early discussed the need to tell the Confederate side of the war in a letter to Lee in late November 1868. Decrying the proliferation of errors (which he did not identify) in everything he had read about the conflict, Early urged Lee not to "abandon your purpose of writing a history of the operations of the Army of Northern Virginia." He enclosed documents relating to the Chancellorsville campaign and promised to help with other materials if possible. In one passage Early got to the heart of his concern about the published record: "The most that is left to us is the history of our struggle, and I think that ought to be accurately written. We lost nearly everything but honor, and that should be religiously guarded." Former Confederates could expect no fair reckoning from the North, which presently persecuted the white South "with even more vindictive hatred than during the war, when we had arms in our hands." Lee had comported himself with a sense of dignity that "commanded admiration in all quarters." Early praised this behavior and suggested that all former Confederates delighted in seeing their old hero "pursue a course worthy of the cause."[13]

Apart from his concern about future perceptions of Lee and his army, Early sought to guard his own long-term reputation. A series of schoolbooks sponsored by the University of Virginia afforded an opportunity to express his thoughts on this point and the larger question of creating a suitable record of Confederate military activities. "I thought the University Series was gotten up because of the mischief likely to be done by northern school books," Early wrote to Charles Venable, a former officer on Lee's staff and member of the university's faculty. "According to my view, the most important books of all are those put into the hands of the rising generation." One of the new schoolbooks implied that Early should have captured Washington during his raid across the Potomac in the summer of 1864. "It is by no means a pleasant reflection that I am to be held up in that light before not only the rising generation of this day," groused Early, "but all those to come hereafter." He warned Venable that they must try to get the correct version of the war into print immediately because "we all know how hard it is to eradicate early impressions."[14]

In lectures, writings, and personal correspondence over the last twenty-five years of his life, Early sought to get his impressions of the war on record. He took an active role in publishing the *Southern Historical Society Papers*, wherein former Confederates reexamined old battles and assessed both comrades and enemies. Thomas L. Connelly, Gaines M. Foster, William Garrett Piston, and other historians have explored this aspect of Early's postwar career in detail. Although some of their conclusions are open to debate, the focus of this essay must remain elsewhere. It is enough to note that Early achieved a position in the South as a leading arbiter of questions relating to Confederate military history. He orchestrated the effort to isolate James Longstreet—Lee's senior subordinate throughout the war—as a pariah because he had dared to criticize Lee in print. Other former Confederates took notice. If Early could savage a soldier of Longstreet's wartime accomplishments and reputation, scarcely anyone could be safe criticizing Lee. At Early's death, the Virginia legislature passed a resolution honoring him as "one who since 1865 has lived in the memories of that great struggle and has devoted himself to the truth of its history and the exposure of falsehood and pretenders." Robert Stiles, a former Confederate artillerist who wrote a much-quoted volume of recollections, also commented about Early's concern for how the Confederacy was portrayed: "After the war, its memories were Early's religion; his mission, to vindicate the truth of history with regard to it." As for Early's influence among ex-Confederates who wrote about the war, Stiles observed that as long as "the old hero" lived, "no man ever took up his pen to write a line about the great conflict without the fear of Jubal Early before his eyes."[15] Early interpreted key military events and personalities in a series of publications between 1866 and 1872. His major points can be summarized quickly: 1) Robert E. Lee was the best and most admirable general of the war; 2) Confederate armies faced overwhelming odds and mounted a gallant resistance; 3) Ulysses S. Grant paled in comparison to Lee as a soldier; 4) Stonewall Jackson deserved a place immediately behind Lee in the Confederate pantheon; and 5) Virginia was the most important arena of combat.

Lee towers above all other Civil War figures in Early's writings. The preface to *A Memoir of the Last Year of the War* unabashedly announced Early's "profound love and veneration" for Lee. In an address at Washington and Lee University in 1872, which was widely distributed as a pamphlet and stands as a classic Lost Cause tract, Early hoped to help the audience form "a really correct estimate of [Lee's] marvellous ability and boldness as a military commander." Defending his subject at every turn, Early explained Gettysburg as an instance where Lee's subordinates (especially James Longstreet) failed to execute a sound plan of battle. The public misunderstood the campaign only because Lee's magnanimity had prevented his revealing the true causes of that defeat. "This campaign did not accomplish all that we desired," Early conceded, but it "left General Lee in possession of his legitimate line of defence, with the enemy's plans thwarted for that year." Had the Confederate fortress at Vicksburg not fallen at the same time, "the public would not have taken as gloomy a view of the results of the campaign as it did." Early explained the fall of Richmond in April 1865 and the surrender of Lee's army as "consequences of events in the West and Southwest, and not directly of the operations in Virginia." In rendering this judgment that failures elsewhere had undone Lee, Early professed to shun invidious comparisons between his hero and Confederate leaders in other theaters. He meant only to note "an apparent and indisputable historic fact, that ought not to be overlooked in a review of General Lee's military record." It was vain to seek any parallel to Lee, averred Early: "Our beloved Chief stands, like some lofty column which rears its head among the highest, in grandeur simple, pure and sublime, needing no borrowed lustre; and he is all our own."[16]

Northern numbers rendered Lee's successes all the more remarkable to Early. He repeatedly stressed the unequal pools of Confederate and Federal manpower, heaping scorn on northern officers who overestimated Lee's strength. "When the future student of history comes to examine the documents which our enemies have prepared for the purpose of misleading him, and sees that nearly everywhere the Confederate Government, with a population of only 5,000,000 of whites to draw from, could almost always put into the field overwhelming numbers, against the Government at Washington, which had a population of about 22,000,000 to draw from," wrote Early in his best sarcastic tone, "he must come to the conclusion that the Southern people were nearly all men, and the Northerners nearly all women, or that their men were of a very inferior order of non-combatants." Northern attempts to play down Grant's advantage in manpower over Lee elicited an especially strident reaction. When Adam Badeau, Grant's military secretary during 1864–65, placed Union and Confederate numbers in early May 1864 at 98,000 and 72,000 respectively, Early characterized the article as part of "a persistent and systematic effort to falsify the truth." Addressing his reply to the editor of the *London Standard*, he placed the numbers at 141,000 and 50,000 (Grant actually outnumbered Lee by about 2–1). Again with an eye on history's verdict, Early pointed out that a people "overpowered and crushed in a struggle for their rights" had but one resource upon which to rely for vindication—an appeal to "foreign nations and to the next age."[17]

Early found only honor in the Confederate performance against daunting odds. In his scenario, a band of noble Confederates led by the peerless Lee held off a mechanistic North blessed with inexhaustible reserves of men and matériel for nearly three years. Exploiting an array of scientific breakthroughs applicable to military use and relentlessly piling in men, the Federals "finally produced that exhaustion of our army and resources, and that accumulation of numbers on the other side, which wrought the final disaster." The Army of Northern Virginia "had been gradually worn down by the combined agencies of numbers, steam-power, railroads, mechanism, and all the resources of physical science." Early repeatedly juxtaposed steadfast Confederates against craven northern soldiers who manipulated numbers to rationalize their defeats at the hands of Lee's smaller army. A passage from an address to the South Carolina Survivors' Association in late 1871 typifies Early's tendency to question the virility of Federal officers and their men. "I might multiply the instances of the attempts of our enemies to falsify the truth of history," he said after discussing George B. McClellan's habit of grossly inflating Lee's strength "in order to excuse their manifold failures, and to conceal the inferiority of their troops in all the elements of manhood, but I would become too tedious."[18]

Early cast Ulysses S. Grant as the principal agent of northern power, a butcher who relentlessly threw his hapless soldiers against Lee's veterans. His analysis contained no hint of Grant as a master of maneuver whose willingness to take breathtaking risks and ability to rebound from reverses brought victory at Vicksburg, Chattanooga, and elsewhere. "When Grant took command of all the armies," suggested Early, "he determined ... to have the odds on his side, so that he might destroy us by the mere attrition of numbers." In the ensuing Overland campaign from the Wilderness through Cold Harbor, Lee brilliantly parried his clumsy but powerful enemy in a performance "unsurpassed in the annals of warfare." Grant had three men to send against every Confederate defender (Early also was adept at manipulating numbers when he chose to do so), and he battled his way to the James River at the cost of 50,000 northern casualties, pinned Lee's army in the trenches at Richmond and Petersburg, and eventually forced the evacuation of Richmond. Grant's decisive triumph came over a mere shadow of the legendary army that had frustrated his efforts for nearly a year: "Finally, from mere exhaustion, less than eight thousand men, with arms in their hands, of the noblest army that had ever fought ... were surrendered at Appomattox to an army of one hundred and fifty thousand men," wrote Early. "The sword of Robert E. Lee, without a blemish on it, was sheathed forever."[19]

Unwilling to concede anything to Grant, Early insisted that he "had none of the requisites of a great captain, but merely possessed the most ordinary brute courage, and had the control of unlimited numbers and means." Were Grant to publish a work on strategy, the appropriate title would be "The Lincoln-Grant or Pegging-Hammer Art of War." "Shall I compare General Lee to his successful antagonist?" asked Early toward the end of his address at Washington and Lee. "As well compare the great pyramid which rears its majestic proportions in the valley of the Nile, to a pigmy perched on Mount Atlas."[20]

Stonewall Jackson rather than Grant received Early's nod as the second superior military leader of the war. Lee was the unsurpassed chief, Jackson the peerless subordinate who "always appreciated, and sympathized with the bold conceptions of the commanding General, and entered upon their execution with the most cheerful alacrity and zeal." Jackson's unquestioning determination to execute Lee's plans had helped bring victory on more than one difficult field. Had Longstreet exhibited a similar attitude at Gettysburg, the Confederacy could have converted that battle into another triumph. "Contending against such odds as we did," asserted Early, "it was necessary, always, that there should be the utmost dispatch, energy and undoubting confidence in carrying out the plans of the commanding General." Early often linked Lee with Jackson, urging fellow white southerners to "be thankful that our cause had two such champions, and that, in their characters, we can furnish the world at large with the best assurance of the rightfulness of the principles for which they and we fought." Always conscious of the need to influence future generations, Early counted on this team to garner sympathy for the Confederacy: "When asked for our vindication, we can triumphantly point to the graves of Lee and Jackson and look the world square in the face." The pious Lee and sternly Calvinist Jackson easily lent themselves to religious imagery, which Early employed in calling on Virginians "to remain true to the memory of your venerated leaders. . . . Let the holy memories connected with our glorious struggle, afford stronger incentives to renewed efforts to do our duty."[21]

With Lee and Jackson so important to his vision of the Confederate experience, Early inevitably defined the war as predominantly a Virginia phenomenon. He only occasionally mentioned events west of the Appalachians and usually avoided overt criticism of the Confederacy's western leaders and their armies. Yet his writings consistently identified Richmond as the ultimate target of northern military planning and credited Lee and his soldiers with extending the war through their dogged defense of the Confederate capital. Because of failures in every other theater by the spring of 1865, he argued, "the Confederacy had been practically reduced to Richmond city, the remnant of the Army of Northern Virginia, and the very narrow slips of country bordering on the three railroads and the canal running out of that city into the Valley, Southwestern Virginia and North Carolina."[22]

The Southern Historical Society Papers, whose contents Early influenced to a greater degree than anyone else, were published in Richmond and leaned very heavily toward topics associated with Lee and the Eastern Theater. This bias prompted some ex-Confederates who had fought elsewhere to find other forums for their writings about the war. The *Southern Bivouac* and the *Confederate Veteran*, begun respectively in Louisville and Nashville in 1882 and 1893, paid far more attention to campaigns and leaders outside

Virginia but never approached the *Southern Historical Society Papers* in terms of influencing historians. James Power Smith, secretary of the society and a former member of Stonewall Jackson's staff, noted with obvious pride in 1914 that the *Papers* had been placed "on the shelves of the great public and university libraries throughout this continent and in other lands. Each passing year adds testimony to the value and importance of the publications of the Society." To support his claim, Smith quoted statements from foreign and northern sources, including *The New England Historical and Genealogical Register*'s comment that "no library, public or private, which pretends to historical fullness, can afford to be without these volumes."[23]

At a convention of the Southern Historical Society held in August 1873, Early explained the organization's goals. "The history of our war has not been written," he said in the keynote address, "and it devolves upon the survivors of those who participated in that war, to furnish the authentic materials for that history." A flyer subsequently circulated by the society announced that "generations of the disinterested must succeed the generations of the prejudiced before history, properly termed such, can be written. This, precisely, is the work we now attempt, to construct the archives in which shall be collected . . . memoirs to serve for future history." Ever since the society first described its purpose, legions of historians and other writers have mined the fifty-two volumes of its *Papers* for material on the Confederate war effort.[24]

Disseminated by Early and other former Confederates through publications including the society's *Papers*, Lost Cause interpretations of the war gained wide currency in the nineteenth century and remain remarkably persistent today. The longevity of these ideas can be attributed, at least in part, to their being grounded to varying degrees in fact. Robert E. Lee was a gifted soldier who inspired his army to accomplish prodigious feats on the battlefield. The Army of Northern Virginia and other Confederate forces consistently fought at a disadvantage in numbers and often of matériel. A number of northern newspapers as well as some soldiers in the Army of the Potomac joined Confederates in complaining about Grant's "hammering" tactics in 1864. Stonewall Jackson won his reputation honestly and served Lee as a superb lieutenant. Many people at the time—northern, southern, and European—looked to Virginia as the crucial arena of the war, as have a number of historians since. The distortion came when Early and other proponents of the Lost Cause denied that Lee had faults or lost any battles, focused on northern numbers and material superiority while ignoring Confederate advantages, denied Grant any virtues or greatness, and noticed the Confederacy outside the Eastern Theater only when convenient to explain southern failures in Virginia. With these thoughts in mind, a brief review of recent scholarly and popular literature, fiction, documentaries and films, and the thriving market in Civil War art reveals trends that almost certainly would bring a smile to Jubal Early's lips.

A striking irony of the Civil War is that the rebel Lee rather than the Union's protector Grant has joined Lincoln in the popular mind as one of the conflict's two great figures.[25] Frederick Douglass complained of friendly treatments of Lee in the North as early as the aftermath of the general's death in October 1870. "Is it not about time that this bombastic laudation of the rebel chief should cease?" asked the nation's most famous black leader. "We can scarcely take up a newspaper ... that is not filled with nauseating flatteries of the late Robert E. Lee." Douglass surely would lament the fact that the U.S. government, whose sovereignty Lee nearly compromised, has honored the Confederate leader with five postage stamps and made his antebellum home at Arlington a national memorial. Douglas Southall Freeman's Pulitzer Prize–winning *R. E. Lee: A Biography* was issued to a chorus of praise in the mid-1930s and cemented in American letters an interpretation of Lee very close to Early's utterly heroic figure. In the annotated bibliography for *R. E. Lee*, Freeman acknowledged his debt to the *Southern Historical Society Papers* by stating that they contain "more valuable, unused data than any other unofficial repository of source material on the War Between the States."[26]

Anyone writing about Lee since the mid-1930s has contended with Douglas Southall Freeman's immense shadow. Historians such as Thomas L. Connelly and Alan T. Nolan have discovered that challenging the heroic Lee triggers a response reminiscent of Early's attacks on James Longstreet. Nolan's *Lee Considered: General Robert E. Lee and Civil War History*, which appeared in 1991, followed a trail blazed in 1977 by Connelly's starkly revisionist *The Marble Man: Robert E. Lee and His Image in American Society*. Questioning several elements of what he labeled "the Lee tradition," Nolan argues that Lee's famous victories came at so high a cost in manpower that they probably shortened the life of the Confederacy. Many academic reviewers welcomed Nolan's study, but the book took a severe beating from Lee's admirers. One historian called it an "anti-Lee" book that used "always-perfect hindsight" to reach flawed conclusions. A prominent student of the Army of Northern Virginia termed Nolan "a bootless revisionist" with "a total lack of perspective of historical time and sense." Writing in the popular journal

Blue & Gray Magazine, a third reviewer observed that "Prosecutor Nolan epitomizes the lawyer's trade through selective evidence" (Nolan practiced law in Indiana). Even more to Jubal Early's taste would have been the plea mailed to Civil War scholars from a retired military officer: "I call upon every true student of the Civil War, every son and daughter of the veterans of that war both North and South, and every organization formed to study, research, reenact, perserve [sic] and remember our Civil War heritage not to purchase Nolan's book. . . . If you have it already, burn it as it is not worth recycling."[27]

Those who prefer Lee as Early's icon have found much to applaud in recent literature. A pair of works published within the past three years that have reached wide audiences through book clubs and paperback editions typify this phenomenon. Paul D. Casdorph's *Lee and Jackson: Confederate Chieftains* bluntly claims that Lee forged "the foremost military career in the American saga." Describing Grant as "the Yankee Goliath" who outnumbered Lee 2–1 in the spring of 1864, Casdorph judges Lee "nothing short of brilliant in the campaign of attrition that followed." At Lee's side through most of Casdorph's book is Stonewall Jackson, whose "eagerness to undertake independent orders had insured Lee's great successes throughout the battles of 1862; at Chancellorsville, he had been the supreme isolated commander." In his study of the Chancellorsville campaign, Ernest B. Furgurson invokes superlatives in describing Lee and Jackson. "American history offers no other pair of generals with such perfect rapport, such sublime confidence in each other," he claims (overlooking the obvious tandem of Grant and William Tecumseh Sherman). "There was a synergism in their mutual confidence. It inspired them to dare things together that they would not have tried with anyone else." Furgurson sees Chancellorsville as the "climax of two great military careers, each made greater by the other."[28]

Winston Groom's *Shrouds of Glory: From Atlanta to Nashville, the Last Campaign of the Civil War* illustrates that Lost Cause arguments remain current in 1995. Although Groom treats a campaign far removed from the Eastern Theater, his narrative includes numerous references to Lee and Jackson and to Grant's inability, despite superior manpower, to subdue his wily opponent. Grant had introduced "a new kind of war, a grinding nightmare of armed embrace in which the victorious dog never turns loose of his victim, but pursues him relentlessly, attacking whenever he can." Lee countered this new threat effectively, "a cunning commander who picked and chose his battlefields shrewdly, making Grant pay for every inch of his new strategy." Earlier in Virginia, Confederates had learned that their "esprit tended to offset federal superiority in numbers and manufacturing." They sought to isolate and strike segments of the enemy's larger armies, causing confusion that opened the way to victory. "Stonewall Jackson wrote the book on this technique," states Groom. "Northern armies, on the other hand, had come to rely on their overwhelming numbers to wreck the Confederates' logistics system, then simply grind their armies down by attrition." Grant's strategy against Lee in 1864 earned him "a reputation in certain quarters on both sides as a 'butcher' or 'murderer' rather than a general. . . . Deserved or undeserved as such sobriquets might have been, the fact was that the North was becoming war wearier by the day." Greeted by generally favorable reviews, selected by book clubs, awarded a prize within weeks of its publication, and beneficiary of its author's wide name recognition because of his success with the novel *Forrest Gump*, *Shrouds of Glory* seemed destined to reinforce Lost Cause images among thousands of readers.[29]

The wide availability of hundreds of reprinted older titles also keeps Early's Lost Cause arguments current. New paperback editions of books by Clifford Dowdey illustrate this point. A gifted writer who inherited Douglas Southall Freeman's mantle as the principal chronicler of the Army of Northern Virginia, Dowdey published between 1958 and 1964 a biography of Lee and studies of the Seven Days, Gettysburg, and Overland campaigns. "Out of the crucible of the Seven Days," Dowdey writes of Lee, "he molded an army that would be man for man the greatest fighting force ever on the continent." By the time Lee perfected his organization of the Army of Northern Virginia, however, he faced an impossible task: "He would no longer be fighting off only another army, or even other armies. Lee's Army of Northern Virginia," concludes Dowdey in language reminiscent of Early's address at Washington and Lee University, "was a personally designed, hand-wrought sword fending off machine-tooled weapons that kept coming in immeasurable, illimitable numbers." Elsewhere Dowdey describes Lee and Traveller as "a symbol of indestructibility" to Confederate soldiers, "a reassuring quality that existed outside the mutations of time and circumstance." The most important fact about Lee's image, argues Dowdey, "is that the legendary aspects were always present. There was no later building of the legend, no collections of sayings or anecdotes; the Lee of the legend emerged full-scale, larger than life, during his command of the army."[30] Here Dowdey reinforces

Early's interpretation of Lee—while at the same time ignoring the postwar efforts by Early and many other Lost Cause writers to burnish Lee's image and defend it against any assailants.

During the 1860s and 1870s, Jubal Early exhibited special interest in how successive generations of young people and foreign readers would view the Confederate struggle. Lost Cause writings have carried great weight with both audiences in the twentieth century. Books on the Civil War for young readers in the 1950s and 1960s emphasized Lee and his campaigns within an interpretive framework substantially attuned to the writings of Early and Freeman. The roster of ninety titles in Random House's Landmark Books on American history included four relating to the military side of the Civil War—all of which featured Lee as a major actor. Hodding Carter's *Robert E. Lee and the Road of Honor* affirmed that Lee should be admired "so long as men respect and remember courage and high purpose and a sense of duty and honor." Visitors entered Lee's burial crypt at Lexington, Virginia, "as if it were a hallowed place," wrote Carter, and "that is as it should be." Jonathan Daniels's *Stonewall Jackson* lauded the virtues of Lee and his lieutenant as soldiers and men, and MacKinlay Kantor's *Gettysburg* praised Lee and described units of the Army of Northern Virginia "as the most capable troops ever to go into action." The Landmark Books include neither a biography of Grant (or of Sherman or any other Union general) nor a narrative of any of his victories in the Western Theater. Only MacKinlay Kantor's *Lee and Grant at Appomattox* devotes appreciable attention to Grant, and it follows conventions far more favorable to Lee than Grant. Kantor's Grant is a "silent, shabby, stubborn" man who liked animals more than people: "Maybe it is necessary to be like that, if one is to squander a thousand lives through some mistake of judgment during a battle." For Lee, who had a "grave magnificence," Kantor chooses knightly and religious allusions: "You could imagine him in the wars of long ago, in polished armor. You could imagine him in the wars of Biblical times, proud in his chariot, facing the Philistines."[31]

Houghton Mifflin's North Star Books for children also ignored Grant but offered Jonathan Daniels's appreciative *Robert E. Lee.* Daniels's penultimate sentence could have been written by Jubal Early. "He went almost as though he rode into eternity," writes Daniels of Lee's death, "again at the head of a column—a long gray line, ragged and barefoot, lean and hungry, but on its certain way to glory of which no power on earth could deprive it."[32]

No foreign nation has manifested more interest in the Civil War than Great Britain, whose authors generally have followed Lost Cause interpretive contours. Field Marshal Viscount Garnot Wolseley, Arthur James Lyon Fremantle, and Francis C. Lawley, all of whom spent time with Lee as observers or reporters, wrote very favorably about the Confederate leader and his soldiers between 1863 and 1890.[33] George Francis Robert Henderson's *Stonewall Jackson and the American Civil War*, first published in England in 1898 and reprinted there and in the United States numerous times in the twentieth century, marked a milestone of laudatory British writing about the Confederacy. Douglas Southall Freeman remarked in 1939 that no author before or after Henderson "succeeded so well in capturing in print the spirit of the Army of Northern Virginia. . . . The reception of Stonewall Jackson by old Confederates was, needless to say, enraptured." In 1933, Maj. Gen. J. F. C. Fuller departed from these earlier British historians in *Grant and Lee: A Study in Personality and Generalship*, wherein he dismisses Henderson's biography of Jackson as "almost as romantic as Xenophon's Cyropaedia." Fuller also questions Lee's strategic grasp and accuses him of too often taking the tactical offensive. "In several respects," states Fuller, Lee "was one of the most incapable Generals-in-Chief in history."[34]

The most renowned British author to write seriously about the Civil War was Winston S. Churchill, whose assessments echoed Henderson rather than Fuller. In the late 1950s, Churchill told readers that Lee's "noble presence and gentle, kindly manner were sustained by religious faith and exalted character." Lee and Jackson formed a brilliant partnership that faced awful odds: "Against Lee and his great lieutenant, united for a year of intense action in a comradeship which recalls that of Marlborough and Eugene, were now to be marshalled the overwhelming forces of the Union." Churchill's Grant also filled a typical Lost Cause role. Mentioning "Grant's tactics of unflinching butchery" during the Overland campaign, Churchill observed that "more is expected of the high command than determination in thrusting men to their doom." Grant's tactics and strategy at Petersburg and Richmond "eventually gained their purpose," but "must be regarded as the negation of generalship." The former prime minister also touched on the theme of honor so important to Early and other Lost Cause advocates. "By the end of 1863 all illusions had vanished," claimed Churchill. "The South knew they had lost the war, and would be conquered and flattened. It is one of the enduring glories of the American nation that this made no difference to the Confederate resistance."[35]

Two imperfect but highly suggestive measures of Lee's triumph over Grant as a popular figure can be found in Civil War fiction and art over the past few years. Lee and his army are central to a number of successful novels. Harry Turtledove's *The Guns of the South* (1992) presents Lee with the tantalizing prospect of overcoming northern numbers and superior military hardware by acquiring modern automatic weapons from time-traveling South Africans (who hope to gain a twentieth-century ally by helping the Confederacy win its independence). Douglas Savage's *The Court Martial of Robert E. Lee* (1993) posits a scenario wherein Lee faces charges from his own government for the defeat at Gettysburg, while Richard Adams's *Traveller* (1988) follows the Confederate commander from the perspective of his favorite horse. Lee's victory at Second Manassas serves as the backdrop for Tom Wicker's sprawling *Unto This Hour* (1984), Bernard Cornwell's *Battle Flag* (1995), and a significant portion of Thomas Keneally's *Confederates* (1979)—all of which include long sections devoted to Stonewall Jackson. Jackson predictably looms large in another novel titled *A Bullet for Stonewall* (1990), the literary merits of which could be exhausted in a brief sentence.[36]

What of Grant? He appears along with Lee in Richard Slotkin's *The Crater* (1980), a masterful evocation of the botched Federal attempt to breach the Confederate lines at Petersburg in July 1864. He is also the protagonist in Robert Skimin's *Ulysses: A Biographical Novel of U. S. Grant*. Offered to a largely indifferent reading public in 1994, *Ulysses* gives a mixed reading of Grant as a man and a general. In the opening two sentences, however, Skimin adopts a tone entirely absent from novels that sketch Lee: "As he looked blearily into the cracked mirror, Grant tried to recall his foray, but only glimpses returned. His hands shook, his eyes were blood red, and his filthy uniform reeked of whiskey and vomitus."[37] No successful novels have been built around Grant, his campaigns, or the armies he led. The fact that the Confederate commander's horse has gotten as much recent novelistic attention as the general-in-chief of the United States armies delineates the chasm separating Lee and Grant in fiction (the notion that someone might write a novel about Cincinnati, Grant's favorite horse, is beyond imagining). Novelists admittedly portray Lee in different ways; some sketch military limitations and others fall closer to Jubal Early on the interpretive scale. Interpretations aside, however, Lee's presence dwarfs that of Grant in novels published during the last twenty-five years.[38]

The same pattern holds true in Civil War art. The past decade has witnessed a proliferation of artists who cater to the Civil War market. Their advertisements adorn the pages of leading popular magazines devoted to the subject, a perusal of which leaves no doubt that Jubal Early's heroes have dominated the war on canvas and in clay to a degree they never achieved against the Union armies. Lee and Jackson far outstrip Grant as subjects for prints, sculptures, and other items. During 1983–95 *Blue & Gray Magazine* ran advertisements for more than twenty-five works with Lee as the primary subject, more than fifteen featuring Jackson, and more than a dozen of the two men together. No ads for works highlighting Grant appeared during these years. During the same dozen years in *Civil War: The Magazine of the Civil War Society*, the totals were thirty ads for Lee, seventeen for Jackson, three for the pair together, and two for Grant. The magazine with the largest circulation in the field is *Civil War Times Illustrated*. Its first issue for 1995 contained advertisements for a print of Lee, a framed carte de visite of Lee, a bust of Lee, a Lee commemorative china plate, a "Robert E. Lee Limited Edition 1851 Navy Colt Revolver," rubbings from the gravestones of Lee and Jackson, a print of Lee and Jackson at Chancellorsville, and a print of Jackson and his wife Mary Anna. Prospective buyers could find only two opportunities to acquire something featuring Grant—a Civil War chess set that also included Lee and Jackson as Confederate king and bishop respectively, and a catalog of autographs with Lee and Lincoln sharing space with Grant as the highlighted subjects.[39]

A recent flyer announced publication of *Jackson and Lee: Legends in Gray*, a coffee-table book featuring seventy-five paintings by Mort Künstler and a narrative by Civil War historian James I. Robertson Jr. Many parts of the accompanying brochure echo Jubal Early's language. "In the pantheon of American soldiers, none stands taller than Confederate generals Thomas J. 'Stonewall' Jackson and Robert E. Lee," reads one passage. Another affirms that "these two Southern generals forged the greatest partnership in command in American history." Although they fought for a cause that would have dismembered the United States, Lee and Jackson are described as men who "epitomized the virtues of duty, valor and honor that patriotic Americans hold so dear."[40] Grant has been the subject of no such book—for the apparent reason that despite his sense of duty, unquestioned valor, and unmatched contributions to Union victory, there is no comparable market among Civil War enthusiasts for works of art devoted to him. What explains this situation more than 130 years after he extended generous and honorable terms of surrender to Lee at Appomattox? Part of the answer probably lies in the often repeated stories about Grant as a drunkard and prewar failure that contrast so dramatically with descriptions of Lee as a devout Christian who made self-denial and self-control cardinal elements of his personal philosophy. Another major factor must be Grant's enduring image—carefully nurtured by Jubal Early and other Lost Cause writers—as an unimaginative officer who bludgeoned the Army of Northern Virginia into submission.

In 1987 Mark E. Neely, Harold Holzer, and Gabor S. Boritt published *The Confederate Image: Prints of the Lost Cause*, a superb analysis of nineteenth-century prints depicting Lost Cause themes. They concluded that by the end of the century, "Throughout the South, and particularly in the iconography of the Lost Cause, Robert E. Lee had emerged as first in war, first in peace, and first in the hearts of his countrymen." Stonewall Jackson also inspired a number of nineteenth-century prints, and "one of the most enduring" of all Lost Cause images was an engraving of E. B. D. Julio's "The Last Meeting of Lee and Jackson"—a subject that has been painted repeatedly by modern artists.[41] Current Civil War art demonstrates that, if anything, Lee and Jackson are more dominant than in the heyday of the original Lost Cause writers.

Apart from their penchant for depicting Lee and Jackson, modern artists select topics using other criteria that conform to Early's framework for understanding the war. For example, Confederate topics outnumber Union ones by 2 or 3–1 (and according to price sheets for prints and sculpture typically appreciate more rapidly). Subjects associated with the Eastern Theater are painted four or five times as often as those relating to all other theaters combined. If prints depicting Nathan Bedford Forrest—a great favorite of many artists—were deducted from the total of those on non-eastern topics, the imbalance would be even more striking. Modern artists and the Civil War public to which they cater clearly join Early in considering the arena of Lee's activities the most important of the conflict.[42]

Elements of Jubal Early's arguments also run through Ken Burns's *The Civil War*, the eleven-hour documentary that reached an unprecedented public television audience in 1990. An estimated 14 million viewers tuned in for the first episode, and more than twice that number saw some portion of Burns's sweeping treatment. In a cover story on the series, *Newsweek* reported that "a substantial minority of northern scholars, especially blacks," believed "sympathy for the colorful rascals and noble, long-suffering patricians of the Confederacy—the 'Lee cult' in other words"—undermined the series.[43] Burns did opt for a very conventional Lee who never earned a demerit at West Point, opposed slavery, habitually called the Federals "those people" (all distortions of the truth), and won magnificent victories on eastern battlefields (which he of course did). If the filmmaker was aware of Thomas L. Connelly's work on Lee, he chose to ignore it in crafting a comfortable profile well attuned to Lost Cause images. To his credit, Burns gave Grant and Sherman full and evenhanded attention.[44]

Apart from his handling of Lee, Burns evokes Lost Cause writers in two major elements of his military coverage. His first episode examines manpower and resources and concludes that "the odds against a southern victory were long." The northern advantage in these categories was undeniably large, but Burns completely ignores other factors that favored the Confederacy and evened the odds. For example, the sheer size of the Confederacy, with 750,000 square miles of territory and 3,500 miles of coastline, posed a formidable obstacle to northern armies. Federal forces would have to seize huge pieces of this vast area if it were to compel the seceded states to return to the Union, whereas the Confederacy had the easier task of defending itself or winning by default if the North chose not to press the issue of reunion. Confederates at the outset of the war realized they were not in a hopeless contest. George Wythe Randolph, a Virginian who served as the Confederacy's third secretary of war, spoke for many fellow southerners in the summer of 1861: "They may overrun our frontier States and plunder our coast but, as for conquering us, the thing is impossible. There is no instance in history of a people as numerous as we are inhabiting a country so extensive as ours being subjected if true to themselves."[45]

Burns's discussion of resources creates a mood of doomed Confederate resistance that elevates the performance of Lee and his men and certainly would have delighted Jubal Early. The documentary heightens this feeling by overstating the odds against the Confederates in some specific battles. The third episode affords a good example when Burns labels Lee's army outside Richmond in June 1862 "a tiny force" facing George B. McClellan's massive Army of the Potomac. The Seven Days' battles thus take on the character of a Confederate David overcoming a Union Goliath. Readily available scholarship should have showed Burns that Lee commanded at least 90,000 men (the largest army the Confederacy ever put into the field) against McClellan's 100,000–105,000. Contrary to Burns's assessment, the Seven Days witnessed a pair of evenly matched opponents fighting on ground that should have favored the defending Confederates.[46]

Early also would endorse Burns's emphasis on military campaigns in the Eastern Theater. Historians have argued the relative importance of events in the East and West, with different scholars marshaling evidence to support the primacy of each. Burns seems totally unaware of this debate and willing—as was Jubal Early—to accept as a given that Lee's theater was the more strategic. The coverage of Vicksburg and Gettysburg reveals this one-sidedness. Burns allocates more than forty-five minutes to Lee's movement into Pennsylvania but just eleven to the complex maneuvering and fighting between December 1862 and July 1863 that enabled Grant to capture an entire Confederate army at Vicksburg. Other examples abound. Twin Confederate offensives swept into loyal border states in the autumn of 1862. Lee's march into Maryland consumes twenty-five minutes of Burns's attention; Braxton Bragg's and Edmund Kirby Smith's strike into Kentucky about one minute. The largest battles fought during the winter of 1862–63 break down similar-ly—twelve minutes for Lee's defensive victory at Fredericksburg and less than a minute for William S. Rosecrans's Union success at Stones River, Tennessee (the bloodier of the two battles). For most viewers of Burns's documentary, the swath of territory bounded by the Atlantic Coast on the east, the Appa-lachians on the west, North Carolina on the south, and Gettysburg on the north probably defines the strategic heartland of the Civil War.[47]

The four-hour epic film *Gettysburg*, based closely on Michael Shaara's Pulitzer Prize–winning novel *The Killer Angels*, would by turns delight and upset Lost Cause adherents. The primacy of the Eastern Theater shines through both the screenplay and the novel, which understandably define Gettysburg as the decisive moment of the conflict. "I think if we lose this fight," remarks Union colonel Joshua Lawrence Chamberlain at one point, "the war will be over." Early and other Lost Cause writers also treated Get-tysburg as the most important battle, repeatedly reexamining it in the *Southern Historical Society Papers* and other publications. If only Longstreet had obeyed Lee's orders more expeditiously, they insisted, Gettysburg would have been a great victory and Confederate independence a reality. So Early would have approved of a sprawling film devoted to Gettysburg and appreciated as well Shaara's tribute to an Army of Northern Virginia that maintained a jaunty confidence despite being outnumbered and outgunned: "The barefoot, sunburned, thin and grinning army, joyful, unbeatable, already immortal." Shaara's portrayal of Lee as an aging and ill lion, blindly insistent on attack-ing despite James Longstreet's sagacious advice to the contrary, would have riled Lee's nineteenth-century champions, however, and Early would have seethed at Shaara's description of his own conduct at Gettysburg as timid and motivated by concern for reputation and position.[48]

On October 30, 1865, Early composed his last letter to Robert E. Lee before leaving the country for self-imposed exile. "I have brought away with me feelings of the highest admiration and respect for yourself," wrote Early, "and I am satisfied history will accord to you the merit of retiring from the struggle with far more true glory than those who, by overwhelming numbers and resources, were enabled to thwart all your efforts in defence of the liberties and independence of our unfortunate country." Almost precisely five years later, Early struggled to come to terms with news of Lee's death. "The loss is a public one," he remarked to former Confederate artillerist William Nelson Pendleton, "and there are millions of hearts now torn with anguish at the news that has been flashed over the wires to all quarters of the civilized world." Early wanted to honor Lee and asked Pendleton what he considered a "suitable mode by which the officers who served under General Lee can give expression to their sentiments, and manifest to the world their appreciation of his talents, his virtues, and his services."[49] Deciding that Lee's memory could be served best through attention to the written record of the war, Early worked tirelessly in the vineyards of Lost Cause advocacy. He proved himself a devoted lieutenant of Lee to the end of his life—and together with other Lost Cause authors helped demonstrate that the victors do not always control how historical events are remembered.

As much as anyone, then, Jubal Early constructed the image of the Civil War that many Americans north and south still find congenial. To explain why they do so would require another essay far longer than this. It would have to address the degree to which Lost Cause warriors wrote accurately about their war against the Union, what subsequent generations of Americans really wanted when they called for state rights, how conservatism and race fit into the equation, and why the ultimate goals of Union and freedom for which more than a third of a million northern soldiers perished often have figured only marginally in the popular understanding of the conflict.

NOTES

Gary W. Gallagher delivered his Klement Lecture in 1995.

1. The most influential interpretations of Early as a Lost Cause figure have been Thomas L. Connelly, *The Marble Man: Robert E. Lee and His Image in American Society* (New York: Knopf, 1977); and Gaines M. Foster, *Ghosts of the Confederacy: Defeat, the Lost Cause, and the Emergence of the New South* (New York: Oxford Univ. Press, 1987). Also useful is William Garrett Piston, *Lee's Tarnished Lieutenant: James Longstreet and His Place in Southern History* (Athens: Univ. of Georgia Press, 1987); and Thomas L. Connelly and Barbara L. Bellows, *God and General Longstreet: The Lost Cause and the Southern Mind* (Baton Rouge: Louisiana State Univ. Press, 1982). Each of these books depicts Early as a soldier of limited talent who worked out his personal and professional frustrations after the war by championing Robert E. Lee—an interpretation open to revision but beyond the scope of this essay to examine.

2. A useful introduction to the subject of historical memory is David Thelen, ed., *Memory and American History* (Bloomington: Indiana Univ. Press, 1990). See also Michael Kammen's *Mystic Chords of Memory: The Transformation of Tradition in American Culture* (New York: Knopf, 1991), esp. pt. 2.

3. Jubal A. Early, "To the Voters of Franklin, Henry & Patrick Counties," July 20, 1850, Scrapbook, Jubal A. Early Papers, Library of Congress (LC), Washington, D.C.

4. For an example of Early's describing himself as a Whig after the war, see Jubal A. Early to J. Randolph Tucker, Aug. 8, 1884, Tucker Family Papers, Southern Historical Collection, Wilson Library, University of North Carolina, Chapel Hill (hereafter SHC). Early's obituary in the Mar. 3, 1894, edition of the *Lynchburg News* described him as "a lifelong Whig, of the most conservative type." See Jack P. Maddex Jr., *The Virginia Conservatives, 1867–1879: A Study in Reconstruction Politics* (Chapel Hill: Univ. of North Carolina Press, 1970); and James Tice Moore, *Two Paths to the New South: The Virginia Debt Controversy, 1870–1883* (Lexington: Univ. Press of Kentucky, 1974), for some of the postwar debates that revealed Early's conservatism. Foster's analysis is in chapter 4 of *Ghosts of the Confederacy*.

5. George H. Reese, ed., *Proceedings of the Virginia Secession Convention of 1861*, 4 vols. (Richmond: Virginia State Library, 1965), 1:428; Jubal A. Early to John C. Breckinridge, Mar. 27, 1867, collection of William C. Davis (who kindly granted permission to quote from the document); Foster, *Ghosts of the Confederacy*, 60–61.

6. Jubal A. Early to John Goode, June 8, 1866, Early Papers, LC; Jubal A. Early to R. E. Lee, Oct. 30, 1865, Mss 3 L515a, Virginia Historical Society, Richmond (hereafter VHS); Jubal A. Early to John C. Breckinridge, Mar. 27, 1867, collection of William C. Davis.

7. Philip H. Sheridan to Editors, *New Orleans Daily Crescent*, Jan. 8, 1866, and Jubal A. Early to Editor, *New York News*, Feb. 5, 1866, newspaper clippings in Scrapbook, Early Papers, LC.

8. John S. Wise, *The End of an Era* (Boston: Houghton Mifflin, 1899), 228. For a wartime reference to Lee's calling Early his "bad old man," see the *Mobile Advertiser*, Sept. 15, 1864.

9. R. E. Lee to Jubal A. Early, Mar. 30, 1865, reproduced in Jubal A. Early, *Lieutenant General Jubal Anderson Early, C.S.A.: Autobiographical Sketch and Narrative of the War Between the States* (Philadelphia: J. B. Lippincott, 1912), 468–69.

10. R. E. Lee to Jubal A. Early, Nov. 22, 1865, George H. and Katherine Davis Collection, Howard-Tilton Memorial Library, Tulane University, New Orleans (hereafter HTML); R. E. Lee, General Order No. 9, Apr. 10, 1865, in R. E. Lee, *The Wartime Papers of R. E. Lee*, ed. Clifford Dowdey and Louis H. Manarin (Boston: Little, Brown, 1961), 934.

11. R. E. Lee to Jubal A. Early, Mar. 15, 1866, George H. and Katherine M. Davis Collection, HTML.

12. Jubal A. Early to John Goode, June 8, 1866, Early Papers, LC. The first edition of *A Memoir of the Last Year of the War* was printed in Toronto by Lovell & Gibson. Subsequent editions, each slightly revised, were published in 1867 in New Orleans, Lynchburg, Virginia, and Augusta, Georgia. Early's full memoir, edited by his niece Ruth H. Early, was published eighteen years after his death under the title *Lieutenant General Jubal Anderson Early, C.S.A.* For Early's sending Lee portions of his manuscript devoted to campaigns prior to May 1864, see R. E. Lee to Jubal A. Early, Oct. 15, 1866, George H. and Katherine M. Davis Collection; and Jubal A. Early to R. E. Lee, Nov. 20, 1868, box 25, folder titled "Introductory Chapter (Notes & Pages of a Rough Draft) I," John Warwick Daniel Papers, Alderman Library (hereafter AL), University of Virginia, Charlottesville.

13. Jubal A. Early to R. E. Lee, Nov. 20, 1868, Daniel Papers, AL.

14. Jubal A. Early to Charles Venable, June 9, 1871, Charles Scott Venable Papers, SHC.

15. Virginia General Assembly joint resolution, quoted in the *Lynchburg News*, Mar. 4, 1894; Robert Stiles, *Four Years Under Marse Robert* (New York: Neale Publishing Co., 1903), 190–91.

16. Early, *A Memoir of the Last Year of the War*, vii; Jubal A. Early, *The Campaigns of Gen. Robert E. Lee. An Address by Lieut. General Jubal A. Early, before Washington and Lee University, January 19th, 1872* (Baltimore: John Murphy & Co., 1872), 3–4, 29–33, 40–41, 45. The acrimonious controversy surrounding Longstreet's role at Gettysburg produced a mind-numbingly large and contentious literature, the best introduction to which is in Piston, *Lee's Tarnished Lieutenant*, chaps. 7–9.

17. Jubal A. Early, "Address of General Jubal A. Early," in *Proceedings of the Third Annual Meeting of the Survivors' Association, of the State of South Carolina; and the Annual Address by Jubal A. Early, Delivered before the Association, November 10, 1871* (Charleston: Walker, Evans & Cogswell, 1872), 20–21; Jubal A. Early, *The Relative Strength of the Armies of Genl's Lee and Grant. Reply of Gen. Early to the Letter of Gen. Badeau to the London Standard* (1870), 1–2, 5.

18. Early, *Campaigns of Lee*, 40; Early, *Address to S.C. Survivors' Association*, 31–32. Walter H. Taylor of Lee's staff spent more time than any other ex-Confederate attempting to show that the Federals vastly outnumbered Lee. See his *Four Years with General Lee* (1877; repr., Bloomington: Indiana Univ. Press, 1962).

19. Early, *Address to S.C. Survivors' Association*, 33; Early, *Campaigns of Lee*, 39.

20. Early, *A Memoir of the Last Year of the War*, 34–35; Early, *Campaigns of Lee*, 44.

21. Early, *Campaigns of Lee*, 27, 31, 44, 47.

22. Ibid., 39.

23. Gaines M. Foster correctly notes that the *Veteran* enjoyed a far wider circulation than the *Papers* but does not address the question of which publication wielded greater influence on the writing of Confederate military history. Foster, *Ghosts of the Confederacy*, 106. Smith's statements appear in J. William Jones and others, eds., *Southern Historical Society Papers*, 52 vols. (1876–1959; repr. with 3-vol. index, Wilmington, N.C.: Broadfoot Publishing Co., 1990–92), 39:214–15.

24. *The Proceedings of the Southern Historical Convention, Which Assembled at the Montgomery White Sulphur Springs, Va., on the 14th of Aug., 1873; and of the Southern Historical Society, as Reorganised, with the Address by Gen. Jubal A. Early, Delivered before the Convention on the First Day of Its Session* (Baltimore: Turnbull Brothers, [1873]), 37–38; Southern Historical Society, *Official Circular* ([Richmond]: [Southern Historical Society, 1876]), 3.

25. The best examination of the process by which Lee became a national hero is Connelly's *The Marble Man*, chaps. 4 and 6. Readers should approach this work, which combines insights and distortions in almost equal measure, with an understanding that Connelly grossly underestimated Lee's stature as the preeminent hero in the Confederacy from early 1863 through the close of the war.

26. David W. Blight, *Frederick Douglass' Civil War: Keeping Faith in Jubilee* (Baton Rouge: Louisiana State Univ. Press, 1989), 229; and Douglas Southall Freeman, *R. E. Lee: A Biography*, 4 vols. (New York: Charles Scribner's Sons, 1934–35), 4:558. Freeman summed up his interpretation of Lee as a man and a soldier in chaps. 11 and 28 of vol. 4. The five stamps appeared in 1937 (Lee and Stonewall Jackson with Stratford Hall in the background), 1949 (Lee and George Washington with Washington and Lee Univ. in the background), 1955 (a bust of Lee), 1970 (Lee with Jackson and Jefferson Davis on the Confederate memorial at Stone Mountain, Georgia), and 1995 (a three-quarter-length portrait of Lee). Pictures of the first four stamps are in U.S. Postal Service, *The Postal Service Guide to Stamps*, 20th edition (Crawfordsville, Ind.: R. R. Donnelley & Sons, 1994), 107, 123, 131, 164.

27. Reviews of *Lee Considered* by James I. Robertson Jr., in the *Richmond News Leader*, May 29, 1991; Robert K. Krick in the *Fredericksburg (Va.) Free Lance-Star*, July 20, 1991; and Dennis E. Frye in *Blue & Gray Magazine* 9 (Feb. 1992): 26; Brig. Gen. (Ret.) M. H. Morris to "Dear Civil War Scholar," Apr. 28, 1992 (copy in author's files). For a positive reaction by an academic historian, see Drew Gilpin Faust's review on the front page of *The New York Times Book Review*, July 7, 1991.

28. Paul D. Casdorph, *Lee and Jackson: Confederate Chieftains* (New York: Paragon House, 1992), 403, 401, 400, 194; Ernest B. Furgurson, *Chancellorsville 1863: The Souls of the Brave* (New York: Knopf, 1992), 146.

29. Winston Groom, *Shrouds of Glory: From Atlanta to Nashville, the Last Great Campaign of the Civil War* (New York: Atlantic Monthly Press, 1995), 8–9, 11. On the reception of Groom's book, see "'95 Kirkland Book Award Goes to Winston Groom," *The Civil War News*, Aug. 1995, 24. For a dissenting view, see my review in *The New York Times Book Review*, Apr. 16, 1995, 23.

30. Clifford Dowdey, *The Seven Days: The Emergence of Lee* (1964; repr., Lincoln: Univ. of Nebraska Press, 1993), 358; Clifford Dowdey, *Lee's Last Campaign: The Story of Lee & His Men Against Grant—1864* (1960; repr., Lincoln: Univ. of Nebraska Press, 1993), 5–6.

31. Hodding Carter, *Robert E. Lee and the Road of Honor* (New York: Random House, 1955), 174, 176; MacKinlay Kantor, *Gettysburg* (New York: Random House, 1952), 19; and MacKinlay Kantor, *Lee and Grant at Appomattox* (New York: Random House, 1950), 26–27, 32–33. Each of these titles went through many printings in the 1950s and 1960s. The Landmark Books also included two titles on Abraham Lincoln.

32. Jonathan Daniels, *Robert E. Lee* (Boston: Houghton Mifflin, 1960), 180.

33. See Garnot Wolseley, *The American Civil War: An English View*, ed. James A. Rawley (Charlottesville: Univ. Press of Virginia, 1964), which collects Wolseley's writings about the Civil War; A. J. L. Fremantle, *Three Months in the Southern States: April–June 1863* (Edinburgh: W. Blackwood and Sons, 1863; repr. in New York and Mobile, Ala., 1864); and Francis C. Lawley, "General Lee," *Blackwood's Edinburgh Magazine* 101 (Jan. 1872): 348–63.

34. Douglas Southall Freeman, *The South to Posterity: An Introduction to the Writing of Confederate History* (New York: Charles Scribner's Sons, 1939), 165; and J. F. C. Fuller, *Grant and Lee: A Study in Personality and Generalship* (1933; repr., Bloomington: Indiana Univ. Press, 1957), 8. Longman's, Green and Co. of London published the first edition of Henderson's *Jackson* in 1898.

35. Winston Churchill, *The American Civil War* (New York: Dodd, Mead, 1961), 39, 41, 123, 119. This book is a reprint of the chapters on the Civil War from vol. 4 of Churchill's *A History of the English Speaking Peoples: The Great Democracies* (New York: Dodd, Mead, 1958).

36. Harry Turtledove, *The Guns of the South: A Novel of the Civil War* (New York: Ballantine Books, 1992); Douglas Savage, *The Court Martial of Robert E. Lee: A Historical Novel* (Conshohocken, Pa.: Combined Books, 1993); Richard Adams, *Traveller* (New York: Knopf, 1988); Tom Wicker, *Unto This Hour* (New York: Viking Press, 1984); Bernard Cornwell, *Battle Flag* (New

York: HarperCollins, 1995); Thomas Keneally, *Confederates* (New York: Harper & Row, 1979); and Benjamin King, *A Bullet for Stonewall* (Gretna, La.: Pelican Publishing Co., 1990).

37. Richard Slotkin, *The Crater* (New York: Atheneum, 1980); and Robert Skimin, *Ulysses: A Biographical Novel of U. S. Grant* (New York: St. Martin's Press, 1984), xi. Like Harry Turtledove, Slotkin is a professional historian.

38. Douglas Savage, for example, credits the writings of Douglas Southall Freeman, Thomas L. Connelly, and Alan T. Nolan for influencing his portrait of Lee. One advertisement for the book included a blurb from William Garrett Piston calling it "a remarkable accomplishment."

39. *Civil War Times Illustrated* 33 (Jan.–Feb. 1995), ads on pp. 4, 5, 13, 14–15, 21, 64, 66, 73, 75.

40. The flyer was produced by the Easton Press of Norwalk, Connecticut. Künstler also published a book titled *Gettysburg: The Paintings of Mort Künstler,* with text by James M. McPherson (Atlanta: Turner Publishing, 1993). Issued in conjunction with the release of the film *Gettysburg,* this book includes eight depictions of Lee at Gettysburg.

41. Mark E. Neely Jr., Harold Holzer, and Gabor S. Boritt, eds., *The Confederate Image: Prints of the Lost Cause* (Chapel Hill: Univ. of North Carolina Press, 1987), 168, plate 11. On Lee and Jackson, see especially chaps. 6, 10, and 11.

42. These comparative figures were compiled from advertisements in *Civil War Times Illustrated, Civil War: The Magazine of the Civil War Society,* and *Blue & Gray Magazine.* The data on prices come from sheets listing out-of-print works by Don Troiani, Dale Gallon, Mort Künstler, Don Stivers, and other leading Civil War artists.

43. "Revisiting the Civil War," *Newsweek* 116 (Oct. 8, 1990), 61–62.

44. See Episodes I, V, and VI of *The Civil War* for sections devoted to Lee.

45. George W. Randolph to Molly Randolph, Oct. 10, 1861, qtd. in Herman Hattaway and Archer Jones, *How the North Won: A Military History of the Civil War* (Urbana: Univ. of Illinois Press, 1983), 18. For summaries of the relative strengths and weaknesses of the two sides going into the war, see chap. 1 of *How the North Won* and chap. 10 of James M. McPherson, *Battle Cry of Freedom: The Civil War Era* (New York: Oxford Univ. Press, 1988).

46. The standard work on the topic, Thomas L. Livermore's *Numbers and Losses in the Civil War in America: 1861–65* (1900; repr., Bloomington: Indiana Univ. Press, 1957), 86, puts Lee's engaged strength during the Seven Days at 95,481.

47. For a discussion of the relative importance of the eastern and western theaters, see Gary W. Gallagher, "'Upon Their Success Hang Momentous Issues': Generalship," in Gabor S. Boritt, ed., *Why the Confederacy Lost* (New York: Oxford Univ. Press, 1992), 90–107.

48. The quotations are from Michael Shaara, *The Killer Angels* (New York: David McKay Co., 1974), 33, 85. Almost all of the film's dialogue comes directly from the novel. Like Jubal Early, Joshua Chamberlain understood the power of the printed word. His publications rank among the most evocative by any veteran and have impressed generations of historians and other writers. Shaara's fascination with Chamberlain prompted him to make the Maine soldier a key character in *The Killer Angels,* which in turn helped convince the public that Chamberlain was perhaps the best regimental commander on the field at Gettysburg. Visitation at the site on Little Round Top where Chamberlain and his 20th Maine fought at Gettysburg increased dramatically following publication of *The Killer Angels* and again after the release of the film *Gettysburg.* Telephone conversation between Kathy Georg Harrison (historian at Gettysburg National Military Park) and the author, Aug. 11, 1995.

49. Jubal A. Early to R. E. Lee, Oct. 30, 1865, Mss 3 L515a, VHS; Jubal A. Early to William Nelson Pendleton, Oct. 13, 1870, William Nelson Pendleton Papers, Southern Historical Collection, University of North Carolina, Chapel Hill.

Suggested Readings

Home Front and Society

Ash, Stephen V. *When the Yankees Came: Conflict and Chaos in the Occupied South, 1861–1865.* Chapel Hill: University of North Carolina Press, 1995.

Ball, Edward. *Slaves in the Family.* New York: Farrar, Straus & Giroux, 1998.

Blair, William. *Virginia's Private War: Feeding Body and Soul in the Confederacy, 1861–1865.* New York: Oxford University Press, 1998.

Cashin, Joan E., ed. *The War Was You and Me: Civilians in the American Civil War.* Princeton, N.J.: Princeton University Press, 2002.

Cimbala, Paul A., and Randall M. Miller, eds. *An Uncommon Time: The Civil War and the Northern Home Front.* New York: Fordham University Press, 2002.

Clinton, Catherine. *Civil War Stories.* Athens: University of Georgia Press, 1998.

———. *The Plantation Mistress: Women's World in the Old South.* Pantheon Books, 1982.

———, ed. *Southern Families at War: Loyalty and Conflict in the Civil War South.* New York: Oxford University Press, 2000.

———, and Nina Silber, eds. *Divided Houses: Gender and the Civil War.* New York: Oxford University Press, 1992.

Cohen, Patricia Cline. *The Murder of Helen Jewett: The Life and Death of a Prostitute in Nineteenth-Century New York.* New York: Knopf, 1998.

Crawford, Martin. *Ashe County's Civil War: Community and Society in the Appalachian South.* Charlottesville, Va.: University Press of Virginia, 2001.

Durrill, Wayne K. *War of Another Kind: A Southern Community in the Great Rebellion.* New York: Oxford University Press, 1990.

Faust, Drew Gilpin. *Mothers of Invention.* Chapel Hill: University of North Carolina Press, 1996.

Forbes, Ella. *African American Women during the Civil War.* New York: Garland Press, 1998.

Frankel, Noralee. *Freedom's Women: Black Women and Families in Civil War Era Mississippi.* Bloomington: Indiana University Press, 1999.

Gallman, J. Matthew. *America's Joan of Arc: The Life of Anna Elizabeth Dickinson*. New York: Oxford University Press, 2006.

———. *Mastering Wartime: A Social History of Philadelphia during the Civil War*. New York: Cambridge University Press, 1990.

———. *The North Fights the Civil War: The Home Front*. Chicago: Ivan R. Dee, 1994.

Genovese, Eugene D. *The Slaveholders Dilemma: Freedom and Progress in Southern Conservative Thought, 1820–1860*. Columbia: University of South Carolina Press, 1992.

Hill, Marilyn Wood. *Their Sisters' Keepers: Prostitution in New York City, 1830–1870*. Berkeley: University of California Press, 1993.

Hodes, Martha. *White Women, Black Men*. New Haven, Conn.: Yale University Press, 1997.

Iobst, Richard W. *Civil War Macon: The History of a Confederate City*. Macon, GA: Mercer University Press, 1999.

Marten, James. *The Children's Civil War*. Chapel Hill: University of North Carolina Press, 1997.

Quarles, Benjamin. *Lincoln and the Negro*. New York: Oxford University Press, 1962.

Rable, George. *Civil Wars: Women and the Crisis of Southern Nationalism*. Urbana: University of Illinois Press, 1991.

Silber, Nina. *Daughters of the Union: Northern Women Fight the Civil War*. Cambridge, Mass.: Harvard University Press, 2005.

Sutherland, Daniel E. *Seasons of War: The Ordeal of a Confederate Community, 1861–1865*. New York: Free Press, 1995.

Taylor, Amy Murrell. *The Divided Family in Civil War America*. Chapel Hill: University of North Carolina Press, 2005.

Vinovskis, Maris A., ed. *Toward a Social History of the American Civil War: Exploratory Essays*. New York: Cambridge University Press, 1990.

Memory and Meaning

Aaron, Daniel. *The Unwritten War: American Writers and the Civil War*. Madison: University of Wisconsin Press, 1975, 1987.

Ayers, Edward L. *The Promise of the New South: Life after Reconstruction*. New York: Oxford University Press, 1993.

Blair, William. *Cities of the Dead: Contesting the Memory of the Civil War in the South, 1865–1914*. Chapel Hill: University of North Carolina Press, 2003.

Blight, David W. *Frederick Douglass' Civil War: Keeping Faith in Jubilee*. Baton Rouge: Louisiana State University Press, 1989.

————. *Race and Reunion: The Civil War in American Memory.* Cambridge, Mass., Harvard University Press, 2001.

Clinton, Catherine. *Tara Revisited: Women, War, and the Plantation Legend.* New York: Abbeville Press, 1995.

Edwards, Laura F. *Scarlett Doesn't Live Here Anymore: Southern Women in the Civil War Era.* Urbana: University of Illinois Press, 2000.

Fahs, Alice, and Joan Waugh, eds. *The Civil War and Memory.* Chapel Hill: University of North Carolina Press, 2003.

Foster, Gaines M. *Ghosts of the Confederacy: Defeat, the Lost Cause, and the Emergence of the New South.* New York: Oxford University Press, 1987.

Fredrickson, George M. *The Inner Civil War: Northern Intellectuals and the Crisis of the Union.* New York: Harper and Row, 1965; Urbana: University of Illinois Press, 1993

Gallagher, Gary W. *Lee and His Generals in War and Memory.* Baton Rouge: Louisiana State University Press, 1998.

————, and Alan T. Nolan, eds. *The Myth of the Lost Cause and Civil War History.* Bloomington: Indiana University Press, 2000.

Leonard, Elizabeth. *Lincoln's Avengers: Justice, Revenge, and Reunion after the Civil War.* New York: W. W. Norton, 2004.

McConnell, Stuart. *Glorious Contentment: The Grand Army of the Republic, 1865–1900.* Chapel Hill: University of North Carolina Press, 1992.

McPherson, James M. *Drawn with the Sword: Reflections on the American Civil War.* New York: Oxford University Press, 1996.

————, and William J. Cooper Jr., eds. *Writing the Civil War: The Quest to Understand.* Columbia: University of South Carolina Press, 1998.

Peterson, Merrill D. *Lincoln in American Memory.* New York: Oxford University Press, 1994.

Pressly, Thomas J. *Americans Interpret Their Civil War.* Princeton, N.J.: Princeton University Press, 1954.

Reardon, Carol. *Pickett's Charge in History and Memory.* Chapel Hill: University of North Carolina Press, 1998.

Savage, Kirk. *Standing Soldiers, Kneeling Slaves: Race, War, and Monument in Nineteenth-Century America.* Princeton, N.J.: Princeton University Press, 1997.

Schwartz, Barry. *Abraham Lincoln and the Forge of National Memory.* Chicago: University of Chicago Press, 2000.

Waugh, Joan. *Unsentimental Reformer: The Life of Josephine Shaw Lowell.* Cambridge, Mass.: Harvard University Press, 1998.

Whites, LeeAnn. *Gender Matters: Civil War, Reconstruction, and the Making of the New South.* New York: Palgrave Macmillan, 2005.

Wills, Garry. *Lincoln at Gettysburg: The Words That Remade America.* New York: Simon & Schuster, 1992.

Wilson, Edmund. *Patriotic Gore: Studies in the Literature of the American Civil War*. New York: Oxford University Press, 1962.

Young, Elizabeth. *Disarming the Nation: Women's Writing and the Civil War*. Chicago: University of Chicago Press, 1999.

POLITICAL AND MILITARY ISSUES

Ambrose, Stephen E. *Halleck: Lincoln's Chief of Staff*. Baton Rouge: Louisiana State University Press, 1962.

Ayers, Edward. *In the Presence of Mine Enemies: War in the Heart of America, 1859–1863*. New York: W. W. Norton, 2003.

———. *What Caused the Civil War?: Reflections on the South and Southern History*. New York: W. W. Norton, 2005.

Blight, David W., and Brooks D. Simpson, eds. *Union and Emancipation*. Kent, Ohio: Kent State University Press, 1997.

Blue, Frederick J. *Salmon P. Chase: A Life in Politics*. Kent, Ohio: Kent State University Press, 1987.

Carmichael, Peter S. *The Last Generation: Young Virginians in Peace, War, and Reunion*. Chapel Hill: University of North Carolina Press, 2005.

Coffman, Edward M. *The Old Army: A Portrait of the American Army in Peacetime, 1784–1898*. New York: Oxford University Press, 1986.

Davis, William C. *Jefferson Davis: The Man and His Hour*. New York: HarperCollins, 1991.

Faust, Drew Gilpin. *The Creation of Confederate Nationalism: Ideology and Identity in the Civil War South*. Baton Rouge: Louisiana State University Press, 1989.

Freehling, William W. *The Road to Disunion: The Secessionists at Bay*. New York: Oxford University Press, 1990.

———. *The South vs. the South: How Anti-Confederate Southerners Shaped the Course of the Civil War*. New York: Oxford University Press, 2001.

Gallagher, Gary W. *The Confederate War*. Cambridge, Mass.: Harvard University Press, 1997.

Grimsley, Mark. *The Hard Hand of War: Union Military Policy Toward Southern Civilians, 1861–1865*. New York: Cambridge University Press, 1995.

Goldhurst, Richard. *Many Are the Hearts: The Agony and Triumph of Ulysses S. Grant*. New York: Thomas Y. Crowell Company, 1975.

Gordon, Lesley. *General George E. Pickett in Life and Legend*. Chapel Hill: University of North Carolina Press, 1998.

Hummel, Jeffrey Rogers. *Emancipating Slaves, Enslaving Free Men: A History of the American Civil War*. Chicago: Open Court, 1996.

Johannsen, Robert W. *Lincoln, the South, and Slavery: The Political Dimension*. Baton Rouge: Louisiana State University Press, reprint edition, 1993.

————. *Stephen A. Douglas.* Urbana: University of Illinois Press, 1997.

Klement, Frank L. *The Copperheads in the Middle West.* Chicago: University of Chicago Press, 1960.

————. *Dark Lanterns: Secret Political Societies, Conspiracies, and Treason Trials in the Civil War.* Baton Rouge: Louisiana State University Press, 1984.

McFeely, William S. *Grant: A Biography.* New York: W. W. Norton, 1982.

McPherson, James M. *The Battle Cry of Freedom: The Civil War Era.* New York: Oxford University Press, 1988.

————. *For Cause and Comrades: Why Men Fought in the Civil War.* New York: Oxford University Press, 1997.

————. *Ordeal by Fire: The Civil War and Reconstruction.* New York: Knopf, 1982.

Neely, Mark E., Jr. *The Boundaries of American Political Culture in the Civil War Era.* Chapel Hill: University of North Carolina Press, 2006.

————. *The Fate of Liberty: Abraham Lincoln and Civil Liberties.* New York: Oxford University Press, 1991.

Paludan, Philip Shaw. *"A People's Contest": The Union and Civil War, 1861–1865,* 2nd ed. Lawrence: University Press of Kansas, 1996.

Rable, George. *The Confederate Republic: A Revolution Against Politics.* Chapel Hill: University of North Carolina Press, 1994.

————. *Fredricksburg! Fredricksburg!* Chapel Hill: University of North Carolina Press, 2001.

Robertson, James I. *Soldiers Blue and Gray.* Columbia: University of South Carolina Press, 1988.

Royster, Charles. *The Destructive War: William Tecumseh Sherman, Stonewall Jackson, and the Americans.* New York: Knopf, 1991.

Simpson, Brooks D. *Ulysses S. Grant: Triumph over Adversity, 1822–1865.* Boston: Houghton Mifflin, 2000.

Smith, Jean Edward. *Grant.* New York: Simon & Schuster, 2001.

Stout, Harry S. *Upon the Altar of the Nation: A Moral History of the American Civil War.* New York: Viking, 2006.

Thomas, Emory M. *The Confederate Nation: 1861–1865.* New York: Harper & Row, 1979.

————. *Robert E. Lee: A Biography.* New York: W. W. Norton, 1995.

Wiley, Bell Irvin. *The Life of Billy Yank: The Common Soldier of the Union.* Indianapolis: Bobbs-Merrill, 1952.

Williams, T. Harry. *Lincoln and His Generals.* New York: Knopf, 1952.

————. *Lincoln and the Radicals.* Madison: University of Wisconsin Press, 1941.

Index

More Than a Contest Between Armies.

Cover and interior designed and composed by Darryl ml Crosby

in 11/14 Adobe Jenson Pro with display type in Pall Mall bold & Rockwell regular;

printed on 50# Writers Natural Hi-Bulk stock

by Sheridan Books, Inc., of Ann Arbor, Michigan;

and published by

THE KENT STATE UNIVERSITY PRESS

Kent, Ohio 44242